For Vi
for Independence

For Virginia and for Independence

Twenty-Eight
Revolutionary War Soldiers
from the Old Dominion

HARRY M. WARD

McFarland & Company, Inc., Publishers
Jefferson, North Carolina, and London

LIBRARY OF CONGRESS CATALOGUING-IN-PUBLICATION DATA

Ward, Harry M.
For Virginia and for independence :
twenty-eight Revolutionary War soldiers
from the Old Dominion / Harry M. Ward.
p.   cm.
Includes bibliographical references and index.

ISBN 978-0-7864-6130-1
softcover : 50# alkaline paper ∞

1. Virginia — History — Revolution, 1775–1783 — Biography.
2. Soldiers — Virginia — Biography.   3. Heroes — Virginia — Biography.
4. United States — History — Revolution, 1775–1783 — Biography.
5. Virginia — Biography.   I. Title.
E263.V8W36 2011   975.5'03 — dc23   2011028715

BRITISH LIBRARY CATALOGUING DATA ARE AVAILABLE

Front cover: John Trumbull. *The Capture of the Hessians
at Trenton, 26 December 1776*. 1786–1828 (detail). Oil on canvas.
54 × 79.1 cm. (Yale University Art Gallery/Art Resource, New York)

Manufactured in the United States of America

McFarland & Company, Inc., Publishers
Box 611, Jefferson, North Carolina 28640
www.mcfarlandpub.com

Table of Contents

Continental Artillery

Militia

State Legion

Overmountain Men

Spy

Quartermaster

Commissioner of War

Preface

Here are pen portraits of Virginia Revolutionary soldiers of distinction. Most of the 27 men and one woman have not received proper attention. Of this group about a half dozen are probably familiar but deserve to have their story retold.

Virginia made use of a vast reservoir of manpower — volunteers, draftees, and militia — as soldiers to fight for American Independence. In 1779, at the height of participation in military service, the state had 15 Continental Army regiments plus units of riflemen, artillerists, cavalry, and "additional" troops. During the British southern invasions of 1779–1782, large numbers of state militia were mobilized and sent for short periods of time into the field to oppose the enemy both in Virginia and in the Carolinas and Georgia.

Very few Virginians, under arms won any special recognition from either the public or military authorities, as was also the case for soldiers from other states. Washington, never praised an individual enlisted man in his general orders or in letters, and very seldom praised officers. On the one hand, the commander in chief did not usually learn about individual soldiers' exploits, and he was fearful that singling out the individual praiseworthy conduct of officers might elicit jealousies from members of an always sensitive officer corps.

This book by necessity has to award most of the hero citations to officers rather than to the enlisted men, though it was the latter who were most expected to sacrifice their lives. The reason is that there is very little information on the biographies of the enlisted men. There was also the situation of the aristocratic nature of the armed services at the time, with the public and military authorities having a fair amount of contempt for the common soldier, who, as the war bore on, increasingly came from the deprived strata of society. Furthermore, in the public's eye it was deemed — with some justification — that the common soldier had joined the armed forces not so much out of patriotism but to secure livelihood or because of some escapist factor. In any event, it was the officer who shaped the military character of soldiers and who led them to victory. Still, it is regrettable that the heroism of common soldiers went unmentioned and unrewarded. Thus, of the persons selected for this study, only four are from the enlisted ranks: one strongman who performed superhuman feats during battle; a woman who actually fought as a soldier; a spy; and a militiaman who sounded an alarm.

Criteria for inclusion on the roster of Virginia Revolutionary War heroes are generous. The definition of a war hero is so broad and varied that a person may be so designated simply for competent military service. Thus included are not only those who died or bled or rose in triumph above the furor of the battlefield, but also others who contributed to victory in different ways. Some staff personnel would certainly be honored, including such persons as quartermaster Edward Carrington and William Davies, the dictatorial Virginia commissioner of war. Those engaged in espionage, such as James Armistead Lafayette, would also fit into the category.

All the persons selected performed important service related to the armies. Many shifted back and forth from the Continental Army to militia. Most had infantry experience, but some served with a greater distinction as artillerists or cavalrymen. Here they are classified according to their most essential role.

Some officers demonstrated superb leadership in the command of their troops on and off the battlefield. Several died heroic deaths; others were terribly wounded and died prematurely after the war. Some of the soldiers excelled the most as frontier militiamen. All had a common denominator — distinction in service that contributed to victory.

It may seem unusual that among the selectees is Alexander Dick, who never participated in a major battle, although he fought at Petersburg and came close to engaging Benedict Arnold's expeditionary force as it invaded central Virginia. Dick initially went into the Continental Marines, and he stirred the wrath of John Paul Jones. Resigning his commission, Dick later became a major in the militia. But it is clear that Dick was not only a selfless, devoted patriot, but had excellent abilities as a military leader had he been given the opportunity.

Most of the persons here were tied not to a single event that merits recognition but to military careers of exemplary service. The heroes are not glory hunters, although it must be admitted that members of the 18th century officer fraternity had that as a primary goal. With few exceptions, the heroes functioned best in team work, and were highly regarded by members of the officer corps and the enlisted men.

There are certainly oddities among the Virginia heroes. One general was noted by Thomas Jefferson to be a wife murderer. Cruelty towards the enemy surfaces among the frontier militiamen. One of their leaders, a close friend of George Washington, met death from horrible torture by Indians.

Excluded in this selection of heroes are all the Virginia generals: George Washington; major generals Charles Lee, Horatio Gates, William Woodford, and Adam Stephen; and brigadier generals Andrew Lewis, Hugh Mercer, George Weedon, Charles Scott, Daniel Morgan, and John Peter Muhlenberg. Each of these persons have been well served by at least one substantial biography. Although most excluded significant figures were passed over chiefly for want of sufficient information, there was one omitted on whom much detail exists — Christian "Old Denmark" Febiger. This omission is because Febiger was a citizen of Denmark and had only a short-time affiliation with Virginia. Coming to Boston as a merchant on the eve of the war, Febiger joined a Massachusetts regiment, fought at Bunker Hill, and was captured at Quebec. He performed heroically at Monmouth and Stony Point. Febiger commanded Virginia troops under Lafayette and at the siege of Yorktown.

It is hoped that the short biographies will stimulate further inquiry into the lives of Virginia's Revolutionary War soldiers. The collections of the Library of Virginia, Virginia Historical Society, the Alderman Library of the University of Virginia, and other depositories, contain vast resources for further fleshing out the persona and deeds of these early heroes. The University of Richmond library staff, in particular Betty Tobias and Amita Mongia of the interlibrary loan section, have been of great assistance.

Introduction: "Virtute et Armis"
(*By Valor and Arms*)

"Pity the land that has no heroes," asserts a pupil in Bertolt Brecht's play *The Life of Galileo*, to which the master responds, "Pity the land that needs heroes."[1] One, however, may side with Galileo's pupil. "Scarcely any man is so poor in spirit that he has no heroes," notes a social historian, "that he finds nothing to stir his blood in the memories of his race and nation or the acts of his fellows."[2]

Unlike many other places, in the United States there has been a reluctance to create mythic heroes, who are larger than life and capable of super human deeds. Perhaps George Washington, Daniel Boone, and Abraham Lincoln might be among those who might be viewed in this respect. Heroes can appear one day and be debunked the next. This may explain why Americans would just as well honor celebrities instead of heroes. Indeed, Americans are mindful that persons who appear larger than life can sieze power at the expense of liberty. To be on the safe side, with the help of the media, Americans rally in support of the small hero, the everyman — a fireman rescuing a child from a burning building or pulling an infant out of a mine shaft.

The American public, in its homage to all things military, during time of war has been generous in awarding laurels to military officer-leaders, but has not been so willing to do the same for the common soldier until the 20th century. Now, more so than before, in the United States a person simply taking up arms in defense of his/her country in wartime is automatically regarded, at least in some respect, as a hero. This explains as one factor the public's uncritical support of the wide-embracing military establishment. As one historian writes, the soldier "symbolized strength, courage, responsibility. He was the man who inspired other men to act bravely, who rallied a community and enabled its members to defend their sovereignty."[3]

The true military hero demonstrates extraordinary competence and drive. He or she exhibits courage — willingness to take a risk to win an objective on the battlefield — and makes a great effort to protect the lives and welfare of comrades. The hero is capable of rallying soldiers by leadership and example to press forward in an attack, putting his or her life on the line.

In any event, there would be no military heroes if there were no witnesses to the actions of heroism. Even if the knowledge of such actions is hearsay, it must have come from somewhere. Is unsung heroism any less than that which is reported? Besides reported action might not a military hero simply be one who exudes the capabilities and qualities of valor, including the ability to inspire troops and win the utmost trust from both men and officers.

What are the specific qualities that make a hero? Thomas Carlyle, with Napoleon in mind, said that a hero is one who has an "instinctive ineradicable feeling for reality."[4] Other writers note that the hero "must be greater than the average, but in ways agreeable to the average,"[5] and he/she should have an "absolute independence of mind."[6] Intuition plays an important role: One should have "the ability to arrive at decisions or conclusions without explicit or conscious processes of reasoned thinking"; furthermore, the hero should have the ability to recognize change in a situation.[7] Ralph Waldo Emerson, in his essay on heroism, lists certain essentials: (1) contempt for safety and ease; (2) self-trust; (3) a balanced mind so that nothing can disturb its will; (4) "an obedience to a secret impulse of an individual's character"; and (5) persistence regardless of what others may think. Emerson adds that "the heroic cannot be common, nor the common heroic." Furthermore, "times of heroism are generally times of terror … whoso is heroic, will always find crises to try his edge."[8]

Luck, it seems, has a lot to do with the creation of a hero. One needs to be at the right place at the right time and be involved in special events or crises. As Napoleon said when he was asked about the essential quality of a successful general, he has to be lucky. But heroes as well as generals need to contribute to their own luck, for example by employing correct calculations and using intuition shaped by intelligent assessment.[9]

Like many who achieve success, a hero often has to contend with failure. As Emerson observed, "Defeated all the time and yet to victory born."[10] Emerson had George Washington especially in mind. Thomas Paine had the same view. "I love the man that can smile in trouble," he said, "that can gather strength from distress, and grow brave by reflection," who "will pursue his principles into death."[11]

Does a hero always have to endorse war? Is one who stands up against the majority in order to resist wrongful war any less a hero than one who dutifully answers the call to duty? One of the many examples in our own times is that of First Lieutenant Ehren Watada, who was threatened with a court martial and punishment because he refused to deploy to Iraq. Watada felt the American military engagement in Iraq during the first decade of the 21st century to be illegal and that his continued service would make him a party to war crimes. He finally accepted the government's offer to be discharged "under other than honorable conditions" in lieu of further prosecution.[12]

In America's deep past, individual heroism was rarely publicly recognized by either civilian or military authorities. Washington almost never singled out anyone for bravery during a battle, and when he did, the recipient of modest praise was a general or field officer. Congress and the state legislatures, however, from time to time, bestowed distinction upon officers, usually presenting the honoree with some visible token of appreciation, such as a specially cast medal, a gilded sword, or a caparisoned horse. Nothing came the way of enlisted men until Washington yielded at war's end to authorize the Badge of Military Merit to recognize "instances of unusual gallantry," "extraordinary fidelity," and "essential service." The badge, intended for enlisted men, was a heart-shaped piece of cloth sewn onto the coat of the uniform.[13] The badge was awarded to only three sergeants: David Bissel, Daniel Brown, and Elijah Churchill.[14]

The Badge of Military Merit fell into disuse after the Revolutionary War. It was revived in 1863 as the Medal of Honor, awarded to "such officers, noncommissioned officers, and privates as have most distinguished or who may hereafter most distinguish themselves in action."[15] Over time, many other medals were bestowed for meritorious service; in World War II alone, 1,800,729 medals were issued.[16]

As of September 2009, there have been 3,448 recipients of the Medal of Honor.[17] One can only think of the many service personnel deserving of the Medal of Honor but whose deeds went unrecorded or overlooked. Consider just one of many such occasions: at Iwo Jima, in February to March 1945, 5,931 marines were killed and 20,000 wounded, yet only a very few Medals of Honor went to those who fought there.[18]

The heroes that came out of the Revolutionary War gave Americans symbols that bound them together in a new nationality. Appearing in the top echelon of the nation's Revolutionary War pantheon were George Washington, Nathanael Greene, Marquis de Lafayette, and John Paul Jones. It is interesting, nevertheless, that a number of the highest-ranking officers did not emerge from the war as heroes — for example Virginia generals Charles Lee, Horatio Gates, Adam Stephen, and Charles Scott because of military mistakes or not measuring up to a larger than life image, and Andrew Lewis, Hugh Mercer and John Peter Muhlenberg for want of opportunity to sustain popularity. The exception to this group may be Daniel Morgan, who, along with his riflemen, was a hero in several battles.

Then there is the second tier of Revolutionary War heroes, who have been extolled largely for a single activity, such as Anthony Wayne (Stony Point), Henry Lee (Paulus Hook), Francis Marion and Thomas Sumter (guerrilla warfare), Count Casmir Pulaski (killed at Savannah), Richard Montgomery (killed at Quebec), Hugh Mercer (killed at Princeton), Henry Knox (delivering a train of artillery to the army), Margaret Corbin (battle for Manhattan), and Molly Pitcher (Monmouth). Nathan Hale, who willingly offered up his life through an inglorious death, may be styled "the ideal youthful hero of the Republic."[19]

In the main, it may be said that the real heroes have eluded history. As one modern writer notes:

> In our nation's history military leaders left the job of killing to the enlisted men. They usually "observed the fray" from a removed and elevated position, usually one that guaranteed their survival. Unfortunately, success in battle was credited to the officer(s) in charge, and those individuals who made up the majority of the enlisted ranks were seldom mentioned for their individual heroic deeds.[20]

MARINES

1. Alexander "Sawney" Dick

One of the nation's first marine officers and also a militia defender against British invasions of Virginia, Alexander Dick seemed naturally disposed for military service. Known to his friends as "Sawney" Dick, with the moniker being a British nickname for Alexander,[1] Dick, as a young man, sought out a niche away from his father's mercantile community. Although nothing is known of Alexander Dick's childhood, it can be assumed that like other members of well-placed families of central Virginia he received a solid rudimentary education from tutors. The youngster probably acquired some erudition from simply delving into his father's ample library collection, which emphasized history and geography.

The young Alexander Dick had a promising future. Handsome and popular, he had close ties with the colony's elite. He was appealing to the ladies; one of his courtships involved Polly Ambler, who, unfortunately for Dick, was snatched away for matrimony by a more determined rival, John Marshall, the future chief justice.[2]

Alexander Dick had all the markings that made for a wartime hero. He had courage, intense loyalty to the cause, leadership skills, the ability to stir confidence among comrades, and ambition to contribute to American victory. He had opportunities to gain the laurels of war. The only problem was that among all his admirable traits, he was a born loser. Or, to refer again to Napoleon's view of the chief ingredient for military success, Alexander Dick was unlucky.

When diplomat John Adams met Alexander Dick in France, he commented that the young Virginian was "of good family and a handsome fortune."[3] Indeed, Alexander Dick hailed from one of the Old Dominion's most prominent families. Born in 1753, he was the son of Charles and Mary Roy Dick. His two sisters, Eleanor and Mary, married into leading Virginia families. An uncle, Archibald Dick, was rector of St. Margaret's Parish in Caroline County.[4] Charles Dick had emigrated from England in 1743, and built up a thriving retail business catering to planters along the Rappahannock River. Eventually he had extensive real estate holdings in Caroline and Spotsylvania counties and in Fredericksburg. Six years before the revolution the Dick family moved into a large house in upper Fredericksburg at Princess Anne and Amelia streets. Besides dispensing household furnishings, clothing, hardware, and other commodities from his store, before the revolution Charles Dick also manufactured potash and pearl ash as fertilizers.[5]

The elder Dick was appointed a commissary during the early phase of the French and Indian War for the purpose of forwarding supplies to Virginia troops invading the Ohio frontier.[6] He, along with George Washington, was one of the 40 members of the Ohio Company, which was poised for a giant land grab; it, however, was never realized.[7] Charles Dick and George Washington became close acquaintances. When visiting Fredericksburg to see his sister Betty, wife of Fielding Lewis, a real estate partner of Charles Dick, or to attend Masonic meetings and the horse races, Washington on occasion dined with the Charles Dick family, and during visits at Rising Sun Tavern in Fredericksburg, Washington likely shared convivial moments with Dick over rum punch. Several times Washington and Dick were traveling companions on trips to Williamsburg.[8]

Father and son joined the movement for the boycott of British goods in response to the Coercive Acts of 1774. Charles was a member of the Spotsylvania County Committee of Safety, while Alexander, at age 21, served as clerk for the group. Charles was also one of a six-man committee, which in conjunction with other local committees in the colony, alerted the Virginia Convention to the "Alarming Situation of America."[9] Charles was a leader in persuading the Spotsylvania Committee to cooperate with other Virginia localities in providing economic assistance to the "distressed brethren of Boston," who were suffering from a British blockade for not granting recompense for tea dumped by patriots in the harbor.[10] On October 17, 1775, the committee interdicted all water-borne provisions from the county unless permission was granted by the committee.[11]

The colony veered toward war. The Virginia conventions during spring and summer 1775 established active duty military units. In early May 1775, Patrick Henry, at the head of militia, marched on Williamsburg, compelling the royal governor to make payment for powder seized by royal marines from the Williamsburg magazine. On November 17 at Kemp's Landing and then at Great Bridge on December 9, 1775, fighting ensued between royal troops and militia, thus making war in Virginia a reality.

Charles Dick became one of the leading sustainers of the war effort in Virginia. On September 22, 1775, the Spotsylvania Committee of Safety, acting on a directive from the Virginia Committee, ordered that "a manufactory of arms be erected in or near Fredericksburg," to be run by a five man commission (appointed were Charles Dick, Fielding Lewis, Mann Page, Jr., William Fitzhugh, and Samuel Selden) or any three of them. Charles Dick and Fielding Lewis took on the responsibility of running this state gun manufactory; Dick, however, soon assumed the major responsibility. The gunnery was located on 102 acres just east of Fredericksburg.[12] Charles Dick labored diligently, often investing his own resources until his death in the last year of the war, when Alexander then succeeded to the management.

With the outbreak of the Revolutionary War, Alexander Dick answered the call to naval service. On December 9, 1775, the Fairfax County Committee of Safety requested the Virginia Convention to order construction of ships to be used to counter Governor Lord Dunmore's invasion of his own colony. The convention followed suit and instructed the colony's committee of safety to provide a row galley and a sloop, both well armed, to form the "Potowmack Navy." Soon vessels were also built for defense along the Rappahannock River and coastal areas. The several naval entities were soon combined into a state navy under the direction of a navy board.[13]

On January 1, 1776, the Virginia Convention ordered the recruitment of a state marine corps and, on April 15, 1776, established a committee for the appointment of officers "for the several Companies of Marines to be Employed in the Naval department."[14] Serving aboard the state's armed vessels, the Virginia marines had varied duties, including giving assistance to naval gunners, acting as sharpshooters in naval battle, and serving in shore patrols and landing parties.[15] As a militia captain, Alexander Dick had charge of Virginia marines as early as April 1776; he officially received his commission as captain of marines on June 15, 1776.[16] Two days later Dick and marines were ordered aboard the *Defiance*, a cruiser-sloop commanded by Captain Eleazar Callender.[17] The *Defiance* did duty primarily as a transport, conveying tobacco, flour, and other commodities between Virginia ports and troops, including those from North Carolina, up the Chesapeake on the way to the Continental Army.[18]

In September 1776 Dick was transferred to the galley *Manley*, under Captain Edward Travis. The *Manley* was also used mainly as a transport vessel.[19] Thus far the only military action that Dick had seen was when the little ships that he served on were occasionally pursued by one of Governor Lord Dunmore's ships of war. By the end of 1776 Dick was ready for a larger assignment. On December 4 Governor Patrick Henry (with Dunmore now having abandoned Virginia), directed Dick to collect 25 militiamen and board the brig *Mosquito*. Dick picked his recruits from Captain George Catlett's militia company at Port Royal. Dick's marines then boarded the *Mosquito* at Portsmouth. The *Mosquito*, captained by its owner, John Harris, had been commissioned by Virginia as a privateer to prey on British commerce in the West Indies.[20]

On February 6, 1777, the *Mosquito* sailed out of the Chesapeake for the vicinity of Pointe-à-Pitre and Grande Terre, the two islands that made up French-held Guadeloupe. The Virginia Navy Board made arrangements with several merchants in Martinique to sell any prizes the *Mosquito* would bring in.[21]

In early March 1777, the *Mosquito* captured the scow *John*, which got away during the night, and the next day the *Noble*; both ships were loaded with provisions and clothing for the British troops at Antigua. The *Noble* was brought into Pointe-à-Pitre and sold. Since one of the crew of the *Noble* had smallpox, it was necessary to inoculate the members of the *Mosquito*, which delayed another voyage for several months.[22]

Finally, on June 1, 1777, the *Mosquito* set sail again, and three days later was accosted by HMS *Ariadne*, a ship of 20 guns, and forced to surrender "windward of Barbadoes." On June 7 the *Ariadne* sent 56 seamen of the *Mosquito* ashore at Bridgeton, Barbados, for imprisonment; the officers were kept aboard for transport to England as prisoners of war.[23]

Captured American seamen fared much better in detention in England than the rebel military prisoners held by the British in America, especially those assigned to the makeshift jails of New York City and the prison ships off western Long Island. Forton and Mill prisons in England incarcerated a large number of American seamen.

On August 9, 1777, Alexander Dick and the six other officers of the *Mosquito* were led ashore along with 42 enlisted sailors at Portsmouth. They were then marched up the coast two miles to the village of Portsea, where they were placed in Forton prison.[24] The jail, formerly Queen Anne's Hospital for seamen, had two spacious buildings, one for officers and the other for enlisted personnel. A three-quarter acre yard, which prisoners were let into during daylight hours, separated the two buildings; surrounding the whole complex was an eight-foot-high picket fence. The population at Forton averaged 200 to 250 men during 1777–79 and 350 during 1779–82; from June 13, 1777, to November 6, 1782, some 1200 American prisoners passed through Forton.[25]

Actually Dick and his comrades did not fare too badly at Forton. Rumors that Dick and others were cruelly treated reached the ears of General Washington, who informed General William Howe that unless conditions improved, he would condone retaliation on British prisoners held by the Americans. Howe informed British authorities of Washington's concerns, and that was the end of the issue.[26] The main grievances of Dick and others were the need for "necessaries," and being "threatened with a prosecution for treason."[27]

Several factors alleviated hardship at Forton. Being let out into fresh air daily aided in keeping the prisoners healthy; guards were regularly changed and hence hatred did not build up; schooling and even French lessons were offered, and corporal punishment was virtually non-existent (only one instance was recorded).[28] Still, prison was prison. In the way of punishment, prisoners would have reduced food allowances, and worst of all, might be sentenced to 40 days in the black hole (the maximum if caught escaping).[29] Although rations were sometimes moldy or maggoty, for the most part they were adequate, equal to two-thirds of normal British military rations, and at Forton consisted of beef, bread, cheese, vegetables, and beer.[30]

Alexander Dick and the other prisoners at Forton depended on supplementary aid from persons outside the prison. The most prominent of the abettors was the Reverend Thomas Wren, a Presbyterian minister in Portsmouth. As one prisoner noted, Wren went "round the neighborhood to beg clothes and money for us."[31] Every Monday morning Wren visited the prison, bringing supplies and money to be divided among the prisoners. Wren also brought mail and news. For his aid to the prisoners, in 1783 Wren was awarded a Doctor of Divinity from Princeton.[32] Benjamin Franklin also engaged in relief efforts on behalf of the American prisoners in England. From his diplomatic post in France he applied to authorities and friends in England to look after the welfare and treatment of the prisoners.[33]

During his 13 months in Forton prison, Alexander Dick and other captives were deeply involved in preparing for escapes. Amazingly, the American captives were highly successful in fleeing from their confines: Twenty-seven percent of the prisoners at Forton successfully fled the prison, not to mention those who got out but were captured. Apparently, Dick was not one of those who absconded and were returned to prison to serve time in the black hole. His one try, it seems, was on September 8, 1778. Reasons that escape from Forton was relatively easy were that security was lax, with an insufficient number of guards, and local citizens often abetted the escapes. The locals were offered a £5 reward for apprehending an escapee, a fee which was often shared by the "five pounders" with guards.[34]

Dick escaped in a mass break-out. He and 55 others made it to freedom. The prisoners in on the scheme dug a tunnel 35 feet deep, passing through the black hole and beneath "the public road." Among the escapees were 13 Frenchmen and two Americans who had been thrown into the black hole.[35] Dirt removed from the tunneling wound up in an "old stack of chimneys," fireplaces, and ventilators (located between ceilings and roofs).[36]

A kind of "underground railroad" that terminated with the crossing of the channel to France proved invaluable to the Forton escapees. Thomas Wren had enlisted helpmates in the 75-mile stretch between Forton and London. The first stop was the Unitarian chapel in Portsmouth. Provided with clothes, money, and identification papers, the runaways boarded one of the many stagecoaches headed for London. Once in the capital Dick met up with Thomas Digges, an eccentric Marylander, who had settled in England as a mercantile agent. While awaiting passage across the channel, Dick hid out in Digges' house; Digges conveyed to him a £25 note drawn on Benjamin Franklin.[37]

Most likely Dick crossed the channel in one of the many wherries that dotted the river banks and coasts — these were square-sterned rowboats, each about 14 feet long. On the continent, Dick went ashore probably at Ostend, Belgium or a Dutch port. At any of these locations he found easy contact with an agent working for the American commissioners to France. Benjamin Franklin himself had created a network of agents, mostly among French merchants doing business in America, for the purpose of assisting American escapees from England.[38]

Dick quickly moved on to Nantes, on the northwest coast of France and a leading port for the American trade. There he found comradery with some "southern gentlemen."[39] The young Virginian placed his hope for further assistance primarily on Arthur Lee, a Virginia physician and currently an American commissioner to France residing at Nantes. Dick felt that Benjamin Franklin was too much "in his dotage" and overly influenced by another commissioner, John Adams.[40] Besides, he had already become personally acquainted with Lee back in Virginia.

Now again a free man, Dick thought he had two immediate choices: go home or stay in France and hook up with an American privateer or warship, preferably again taking on command of marines. To go aboard a continental navy ship he would need a commission from Congress. For that matter he could not go back to the Virginia Marines because that corps had been dissolved by early 1777 and its members had been placed in state garrison regiments. For a while Dick considered he had solved his dilemma. He wrote Arthur Lee on December 10, 1778, that "Captain Livingston has given me the command of the Marines on board his ship."[41] Dick undoubtedly was referring to Army Lt. Musco Livingston, a relative of New Jersey's governor, William Livingston. Musco Livingston appears to have been entrusted with conducting a merchant ship or two. Governor Livingston, almost a year later, unsuccessfully tried to get Congress to give Musco preferment (probably a regular navy commission at a captain's rank).[42] At any rate, Dick did not serve in any capacity on a ship commanded by Musco Livingston.

Still, there was hope for reclaiming a command of marines. Dick saw an opportunity to serve with John Paul Jones, who was readying a squadron of three frigates at Lorient, France, to be used in attacking British ships in European waters. Jones personally took charge of the *Bon Homme Richard* and had his hands full in obtaining a crew. Eventually he had on board 380 officers and men, including 137 marines. For officers, Jones retained three members of the Irlandaise Infanterie Regiment de Walsh-Serrant in the French army: Eugene Robert MacCarthy, Edward Stack, and James Gerald O'Kelly. These three Irishmen, upon recommendations from Benjamin Franklin, received lieutenant commissions from Congress. It seems all the officers aboard the *Bon Homme Richard* were English-speaking, in contrast to the seamen, who were of seven national origins.[43]

Dick offered himself to John Paul Jones as captain of marines. Jones was delighted to have Dick as a "volunteer" aboard the *Bon Homme Richard* "under my command." Jones informed Dick that he accepted "the offer with the greatest pleasure."[44] Dick, who spoke French, was expected to serve as a liaison between the officers and seamen. In the future he could expect to receive a Continental Navy commission. Arthur Lee was pleased that his countryman had been re-employed as a marine commander. Lee wrote John Paul Jones regarding Dick and another appointee, Peter Amiel, that he had "no doubt that they will second the gallantry of their commander."[45] The anomaly of Dick's new position was underscored by the fact that his French marines were "dressed in the English Uniform, red and white."[46]

Serving as volunteer captain over French marines instantly proved troublesome. First of all, John Paul Jones was not quite so easy-going around landlocked civilians. John Adams described his impression of John Paul Jones: "Excentricities, and Irregularities are to be expected in his Character, they are in his Eyes."[47] Bad feelings developed between the *Bon Homme Richard*'s motley crew and English-speaking officers, and even some of the officers were incompetent, at least so reported Alexander Dick. As he informed Jones in April 1779:

> It is with the utmost uneasiness I acquaint you that discord is crept into our little society, that ungenerous hatred which some of our illiterate Countrymen bear the French Nation too much influenced our present commanding officers the sailors & volunteers have been in continual broils since your departure ... variety of orders so confused the Men that they can't possibly do their duty, they are sometimes order'd to let no one ashore....[48]

Although they later proved their mettle, the seamen aboard the *Bon Homme Richard* at this stage of their service presented disciplinary problems that verged on mutiny.[49]

Dick's own relationship with Jones became unbearable. The cause of Dick's resentment toward Jones is not known, but evidently Jones treated Dick rather contemptuously. The situation was enough that Dick decided to leave the *Bon Homme Richard*, which he did by the end of April 1779. Dick justified his action to Arthur Lee. "I had left Capt. Jones, by Heavens I would not sail with him for all Europe," said Dick in a letter of May 5.[50] Three weeks later he explained himself more fully:

> I could never brook the insults to which a Marine Officer is exposed: Capt. Jones I believe is a brave and experienced Officer but sometimes Officers in general contract such an insulting manner of behavior that it is impossible for any Gentleman of Spirit to serve under them: I boast myself to be a Virginian & it shall never be held that I let any man insult me with impunity ... hope you will recommend me to the Favour of the Marque Lafayet, in whose suit I would wish to go to America, as by that means I shall have an opportunity of mortifying the *Mons. John Paul Jones Esq: commander of all the American Ships in Europe* (a style he has lately adopted)....[51]

Apparently John Paul Jones wanted to make amends with Alexander Dick, but not vice versa. Again confiding in Arthur Lee, Dick wrote in June:

> I would undergo any hardship rather than go with Capt. Jones. I have too much of our country's—[?] to put up with any Insult, & whenever Gentleman affronts me I make him give me Satisfaction.... Capt. Jones declared he had no intention to affront me and that he should look upon it as an Honour if I should go with him. I am glad he gave me a Specimen of his behavior before I was too far engaged with him. I would be very foolish if I should put it in his power to use me ill a second time.[52]

Selected to replace Dick in command of Jones' marines were two French lieutenant colonels: Paul de Chamillard and Antoine-Felix Wuibert de Mézieres.[53]

Despite his alienation from John Paul Jones, Dick attended "an elegant dinner" given by Jones for his officers, with diplomat John Adams a special guest, at the L'Epee Royal in Lorient on May 13, 1779.[54] Meanwhile Dick looked for passage back to Virginia. Of course, he was not with his marines when the *Bon Homme Richard* sailed out of Lorient on June 17 for a maiden cruise under Jones, returning on July 1.[55]

Away in the service of his country for two years, Dick returned home in the fall of 1779. His capture by the enemy, the long internment in England as a prisoner of war, and the fact that he was not reinstated as a commander of marines abroad did not exactly entitle him to a hero's homecoming.

Before leaving France, Dick applied to Benjamin Franklin for some monetary assistance. Captain Benjamin Chew of Cecil County, Maryland, who had commanded a privateer and was a prisoner of war along with Dick at Forton prison (escaping in July 1779), put in a good word for Dick to Benjamin Franklin. "He is a Gentleman of Considerable fortune in Virginia," wrote Chew. Further contributing to Dick's ability to repay Franklin for a loan, which was forthcoming, was the fact that Dick had substantial military pay coming to him.[56]

Having returned to Fredericksburg, Virginia, Dick whiled away his time for several months during which he probably assisted in his father's gun manufactory. He petitioned successfully to the Virginia legislature both for reimbursement of £2730 expended while in Forton prison and a promotion in rank to major of militia.[57]

Dick accepted the post of aide-de-camp to General Peter Muhlenberg, who came to Virginia in February 1780 to assume command of Continental troops being raised there and activated militia. Dick and Muhlenberg's troops saw a little action in skirmishing in October 1780 with an incursionary force under General Alexander Leslie which established a beachhead in the lower Tidewater region.[58] The British invaders soon departed to join Cornwallis' army in the Carolinas. The American Continentals in Virginia were now to be sent to link up with General Nathanael Greene's Southern Army. Alexander Dick wanted very much to be in on this transition. He entreated the Virginia authorities to use their influence in securing for him a field command in the Southern Army (necessitating a rank of lt. col. or colonel) from the Continental Congress. Dick commented that he saw "no prospect of actual Service" in Virginia.[59]

Dick might well have ended up commanding a Virginia regiment in the Southern Army had not startling events intervened that reversed his priorities: three successive British invasions of Virginia. On December 20, 1780, an expeditionary force of 1,600 men and 27 ships, consisting mostly of the loyalist Queen's Rangers and New York volunteers, commanded by Benedict Arnold, set out from New York for Virginia. Arnold was given instructions to destroy munitions and materiél that could be used by the Southern Army and to establish a strong post at Portsmouth. Arnold's flotilla reached Hampton Roads on December 30, whereupon he gave orders for half his force to sail immediately up the James River. By the evening of January 3, Arnold's troops reached Hood's Point, 14 miles below the mouth of the Appomattox River. Here Lt. Col John Graves Simcoe's Queen's Rangers routed a small militia group. On the morning of January 4, Arnold concluded his force further up the James to the site of Westover Plantation.

At Westover, which, ironically, was presided over by Arnold's cousin-in-law, the widowed Mrs. William Byrd III, a consultation between Arnold and his officers led to the conclusion that the 25-mile march to the new Virginia capital, Richmond, could be accomplished with little risk because it was known that the sizeable number of American troops that could be brought together to oppose the British advance had not yet coalesced in central Virginia. Arnold had been instructed not to take any risks. He was aware that thousands of militia could turn out from an aroused countryside. He also knew that the rebels would go to great lengths to apprehend an arch-traitor. But Arnold was advised by lt. cols. Simoce and Thomas Dundas, the men next in command of the expedition, that they could proceed "with perfect security"; and so it was, "On to Richmond!"[60]

As the British movement up the James and towards Richmond had been so precipitous, Governor Jefferson and other authorities had not been able to set a firm defense in motion. As Arnold moved up the James River, General Steuben, the commander of all Virginia forces, sent 150 Continental troops from Chesterfield Courthouse, all the men of this caliber fit for duty, to Petersburg to protect munitions there. General Thomas Nelson was collecting about 150 militia at Williamsburg. No one had been much concerned for the defense of Richmond. As Arnold paused at Westover, Governor Jefferson and other state officials struggled to save official papers, which turned out not to be very successful and ended in themselves scrambling out of the town. At the last moment Steuben, who had hoped to send a sizeable force to oppose the direct march of the British troops to Richmond, found that he could only assemble about 100 men. Alexander Dick, who had been stationed with Steuben, was ordered to "harrass the Enemy by firing at them from every favorable piece of ground." Steuben would later comment that "these orders were however illy executed."[61] It was not really the fault of the young Virginia militia major that no injury was done to the 800 oncoming British troops.

In the "very dark" night of January 4–5, the British force silently marched toward Richmond. If Dick was hoping to find a Thermopylae where he and 100 farmer militiamen could check a force of British regulars eight times their number, he was disappointed. Just before Dick's troops came up to the invaders there could have been such a chance. A Hessian officer serving with Arnold commented: "We passed the defile of Turkey Island Creek, which cut through two steep heights, over which was a bridge. A half a dozen men could have easily defended this pass at night."[62]

Pausing at Mayo Plantation, not far from where the enemy took a brief respite at Four Mile Creek, Dick "resolved to make the best defense I can." He drew up his men "in a little field secured from the sight of the enemy." When the invaders approached to within 60 yards of Dick's militia, a "smart fire" would ensue from a group of 24 militiamen on each side of the road. Also a sergeant and 12 men were given the task "to cover our retreat or to assist in annoying the Enemy in my rear." As it turned out, none of Dick's men fired on the enemy. The Virginians, however, did manage to destroy the bridge over Bailey's Creek, "but it was rebuilt within a half an hour." As the enemy continued their march toward Richmond, Dick and several of his fellow officers decided to move a little further down the James River to link up with militia under Thomas Nelson, who were expected to mount a rearguard action against Arnold's troops. But not long after he began his march to join Nelson, Dick saw "a large smoke" from Richmond. He therefore thought it "better to be at hand" when the enemy would evacuate Richmond, and then harass their rear and helpfully take a few prisoners of war. Because his men were fatigued and there were "violent" rains during the night of January 6, Dick and his would-be valiant militiamen were always a tad too late to engage in any action.[63]

If Dick and his little band did not win any laurels during Arnold's invasion of central Virginia, at least they came off better than another small group of militiamen in Richmond itself. As Arnold entered Richmond on a road along the riverbank, his Hessian jaegers climbed up Church Hill at the east end of the town where frightened militia fled posthaste. Arnold's force stayed in the town exactly 24 hours, 1 P.M. January 5 to 1 P.M. January 6. During the occupation two memorable events occurred: the burning of most of the edifices in the town and Lt. Col. Simcoe's Queen's Rangers going about six miles up the river, where they demolished the munitions depot at Westham.

Arnold's troops returned to Westover Plantation on January 7, and lingered there for three days. On the 8th Simcoe and 40 of his men routed militia at nearby Charles City Courthouse; the Virginians fled several miles to General Nelson's camp on the Chickahominy River and even some of them and Nelson's men continued in flight until they reached Williamsburg. It can be assumed that Dick and his little band were not among the refugees from the courthouse, but rather, failing to catch up with Arnold's force before it reached Westover, moved directly to form a junction with Nelson's men on the Chickahominy at its junction with the James River.[64]

With Arnold having returned to Portsmouth, General Steuben, in command of all Virginia forces, had to decide on the next tactics versus the invading enemy. Ruling out direct confrontation, Steuben, consulting with Muhlenberg and others, concluded that best objective was to contain the British force at Portsmouth. Dick stayed in the field, being attached to Muhlenberg's immediate command. The bulk of Muhlenberg's troops (800 infantry and Col. Armand's cavalry) were stationed at Cabin Point, on the south side of the James River near Suffolk.[65] Steuben also drew up other militia in the Portsmouth vicinity, namely several hundred militia under Colonel Josiah Parker at Cowper's Mill on the south bank of the James and 800 militia commanded by Brig. Gen. Robert Lawson at McKay's Mill several miles to Parker's rear.[66] Occasionally there was skirmishing on the outer lines.[67]

At long last Dick saw opportunity for glory. He would command a light infantry unit. Other than the leading generals, the heroes of the Revolutionary War were almost all leaders of light infantry or cavalry. At the beginning of February, Steuben ordered Dick to select 200 men from the commands of Gen. Thomas Nelson (stationed in and above Williamsburg) and Muhlenberg. Dick would receive his future orders from Gen. Robert Lawson. Dick and his "150 Musqueteers," and Colonel Sampson Matthews' nearly 350 riflemen, took post 24 miles below Cabin Point.[68] Happy to lead a unit of select light infantry, Dick was emboldened to request an appointment similar to that held by Virginia's young hero of the time, "Light Horse" Harry Lee. In writing to Steuben, Dick complained of not seeing any real action and stated, "I have no greater wish than by some bold action to deserve your Interest to get me a Legion."[69]

Several factors held up militia at the Portsmouth sector from any attack mold. There had not been many militiamen arriving for active service, and those who did were "totally without arms."[70] General Lafayette and 1,200 Continental troops arrived in early March and joined with Muhlenberg's troops for several weeks before going to Baltimore to await further orders from Washington. The Continentals would be in the forefront of any attack on Portsmouth, thereby diminishing opportunity for militia heroism. Even assisted by Lafayette's troops there was not strong enough a force to take battle to the British.[71]

Through early spring Dick retained his command of light infantry, attached to Muhlenberg's command.[72] Still he felt that his position in military service was insecure. On April 10, while posted at Everard's Mill, Dick learned that the three state regiments (militia in regular service) were to be reduced and combined into one regiment and "the oldest [in rank] Officer to take command." Unhesitating, Dick wrote Governor Jefferson, "I am entitled to a Command with said Regiment."[73] This request provoked no immediate action, but several months later Dick began serving in the sole state regiment.

The stage was now set for the coming to Virginia of another British army, which would form a junction with Arnold's troops at Portsmouth. British war planners now recognized the futility of toying unproductively in the Carolinas and Georgia; it was best to strike the trunk of the rebellion in the South — Virginia. At the end of March a 2,000-man force from New York arrived to reinforce Arnold's little army at Portsmouth. General William Phillips, a Royal artillery officer, commanded the new troops and superseded Arnold in the overall command of British forces in Virginia. With the British military presence in Virginia now amounting to nearly 4,000 soldiers, Alexander Dick could expect to see battle action. He still was acting commander of what amounted to a regiment of select light infantry; this explains why soldiers who served with Dick at this time would later, when applying for pensions, refer to Dick as having rank of colonel.

On April 18, 2,300 of the British troops in Virginia, under Phillips, with Arnold second in command, embarked from Portsmouth.[74] The intent of the expedition soon became clear: destroy munitions and matériel in central Virginia that could be sent to the American Southern Army. Not unlike Arnold's winter incursion up the James, Phillips also moved quickly. On Tuesday, April 24, the enemy debarked at City Point, about five miles southwest of Petersburg. Steuben, from his headquarters at Chesterfield Courthouse, ordered Muhlenberg's troops to rendezvous with other militia at Petersburg.[75] Steuben appropriated all the rum in Petersburg to give to the Virginia troops.

Muhlenberg's men formed a defense line one mile east of Petersburg at Blandford Village.

On Tuesday, April 25, the enemy marched toward Petersburg. At 2 P.M. they approached the American position. Captain Lawrence House, at the head of 40 militia, formed the American vanguard. Firing a round at advancing Hessian jagers they retreated until they came to the outer American defense position composed of 300 light infantry under Major Alexander Dick forming the right flank and Lt. Col. Thomas Meriwether's infantry regiment holding the left flank. For a half an hour the troops under Dick and Meriwether kept up "a constant fire," preventing the enemy from "taking the heights." The British attackers, making good use of artillery and greatly outnumbering the defenders, pushed ahead. As Dick and Meriwether's men made an orderly retreat, they formed in groups of 100 men who fired one volley and then retreated, with successive groups of 100 men doing the same. As the militia backed up to the Appomattox River, American cannon on the other side of the river were able to get in play and provided cover as the American troops crossed the Pocahontas Bridge, tearing up the planks of bridge behind them. The battle of Petersburg had lasted two hours.[76] American losses were 150 killed, wounded, or captured; the British casualties totaled about 30.[77]

The courageous stand against the oncoming British army several times their number proved redemption for the Arnold march on Richmond debacle. General Steuben, who had previously only had harsh words for Dick and his compatriots in their yielding too soon before Richmond, now offered generous praise. He thanked "in the most cordial manner the officers and soldiers who so very much distinguished themselves in defending the post of Petersburg." The officers "in general behaved with that spirit and firmness which will always entitle them to his highest approbation." In his report to Congress, Steuben declared that "our troops disputed the ground inch by inch, and executed their manoeuvres with great exactness"; he cited "the gallant conduct of all the officers and the particular good behavior of the men."[78]

Dick went along with the American retreat towards Richmond. Phillips' army, on April 26, entered Petersburg, where they destroyed 400 hogsheads of tobacco and one large and several small naval vessels. Phillips then led part of his force to Chesterfield County Courthouse, where he burned the military barracks and destroyed provisions. Arnold, with the other British troops, went to Osborne's Landing, halfway between Petersburg and Richmond, where amazingly he annihilated the major ships of the Virginia navy. The two sections of the British army reunited, and on April 29 were poised at Manchester, ready to cross the James to Richmond on the opposite shore. The next morning, as Phillips's troops started their crossing, boldly silhouetted against the bright dawn on the city's hills were some 3,000 men — Lafayette's newly arrived Continentals and militia. The British, after burning supplies in Manchester, made their way back to Petersburg.[79]

For the time being Lafayette's Continentals and militia, including Muhlenberg's troops, checkmated the enemy at Petersburg. The arrival of General Cornwallis and his army from North Carolina, forming a junction with the troops under Phillips, who had died a few days before, made for a British army in the field of 6,000 men, too large a number for Lafayette to engage directly. Subsequently, Lafayette chased after Cornwallis as the British general moved in a circuitous route through central Virginia before dropping back to Richmond, Williamsburg, Portsmouth, and ultimately Yorktown. Simcoe's Rangers and Tarleton's Dragoons ranged widely, with impunity. Alexander Dick was not present at two battles, Spencer's Ordinary and Green Spring, near Williamsburg in June-July, which were fought by Cornwallis troops and mainly Lafayette's and Anthony Wayne's Continentals.

To help remedy the continual problem of not enough militia hanging around to fight, Dick came up with an idea, though not entirely original, as James Madison and others had made similar suggestions. In May 1781 he proposed recruitment of slaves. "Likely young negro fellows" could be enrolled, with their owners compensated and also persons drafted could send their slaves as substitutes. Dick also proposed that when the war was over all slaves who had enlisted would be "intitled to all the benefits of Continental Soldiers." He felt that black slaves would "be equal to any."[80]

In early summer Major Dick was transferred to a new state regiment that consolidated three former regiments into one, commanded by Col. Charles Dabney. It seems that Dick did duty mainly at Yorktown. On August 8, 1781, he reported to Governor Nelson that he was ordered to Fredericksburg to collect militia. Dick complained that many recruits at that location were unfit for military duty and would be a disgrace to the state.[81]

Dick may or may not have been with Dabney's regiment at the siege of Yorktown. In early September he was still in Fredericksburg. Dabney's regiment was definitely at the battle of Yorktown, but is not signaled out for having any distinctive role, other than for a while being assigned to General Henry Knox's artillery camp.[82] Certainly, just after the British surrender at Yorktown, Dick had returned to his state regiment. Reporting to the Virginia governor on supply problems, he pointed out that Col. Dabney ordered "the Stockade at York cut down" for use as firewood.[83]

In December the Virginia state regiment was moved to be quartered in Portsmouth. Dabney took leave and Dick served as acting commandant of the regiment. He reported to the state's commissioner of war that 130 of his men were in the hospital for smallpox.[84] On December 23 Dick formed his troops into six companies, including a grenadier and a light infantry company. He hoped that if he could have permission to purchase "infantry caps" and spatterdashes he could greatly increase recruiting. Dick pointed out that his regiment was short on provisions, having gone for days without meat, flour, or rum. The hospital where his militiamen had been confined for smallpox was so much without medicines and "any conveniences for the Sick" that it may be said to be the "Enemies Country." Furthermore, another pressing difficulty was that "Tories and

Refugees," using swamps as their bases, were terrorizing the people of Princess Anne County; for better security Dick recommended he should erect "a Redoubt at the Cape."[85]

Acting upon a proposal by General Muhlenberg, Governor Benjamin Harrison, on January 18, 1782, ordered that the state regiment along with the state company each of cavalry, dismounted dragoons, and artillery be consolidated into a "legionary corps." The state legion was, therefore, formed of three companies, two troops of cavalry, and one artillery company, consisting of 225 men, with Dabney in charge and Dick as second in command. Garrisons for this new unit were established at Yorktown, Hampton, and Richmond.[86] By fall 1782 Dick was stationed at Yorktown, presumably as acting commander of the legion.[87]

With the war at an end and the state's legion now having room for only one field officer (with Colonel Dabney deciding to stay on), Dick had little option than to submit his resignation from his commission. On January 1, 1783, he asked the governor for permission to retire, which was granted.[88] The legion itself was disbanded on April 24, 1783.[89] For his seven years of military service Dick was awarded 5,333 acres of land in the western country.[90]

Unfortunately, only a few days after he left the army in January 1783, Alexander Dick's father, Charles, suddenly died.[91] On January 7, Alexander Dick applied to Governor Harrison for an appointment to succeed his father as the manager of the gun manufactory in Fredericksburg. The governor did not do Dick any great favor in granting permission. Charles Dick had gone into much debt by mixing his own funds with the factory's operation. His partner, Fielding Lewis, had died two years before. Wages were in arrears and all but three of the 30 to 40 workers usually employed were left on the job. Workers had been partly paid by being given room and board, and now there was not enough money to buy food. Work had come to a standstill.[92] One small factor contributed to the decline of the gun manufactory; it lost its special classification as a war industry, and employees could no longer claim exemption from military service.[93]

Thus far in his young life, Alexander Dick had been equally unsuccessful in personal finances as he had been in love and war. Not only did he now assume the obligations of his deceased father but he had come out of the war much indebted himself. For a very short period it looked like he might be able to make something of the idled gun factory. The state finally made good on a debt of 28 hogsheads of tobacco owed his father; a contract to clean nearly 100 rifle barrels also helped some.[94] But with the war over there was not enough demand for arms repair work. Dick in 1783 formed a mercantile partnership with John Lewis, son of his father's associate, Colonel Fielding Lewis, but both men were unable to defray a requisite bond of £3,000.[95] Dick was so impoverished that he had to sell personal property at a loss of 25 percent in order to pay personal expenses.[96]

On February 24, 1783, the Virginia Council of State declared that the Fredericksburg gun factory be closed and "the whole business of repairing arms be accomplished at the arsenal at Point of Fork near Charlottesville. In May 1783 the gun factory closed.[97]

Dick was unable to pay any of his father's debts, which had equaled ten times his assets, and was heavily in debt himself. He had no choice but to place, in February 1784, all his property in the hands of his lawyer brother-in-law, James Mercer, for liquidation.[98] The Dick family home was rented to General George Weedon, who had removed himself from the tavern business.[99] Later, on June 6, 1786, after Dick's death, James Mercer sold most of Dick's real estate property, excluding most of the western lands, which were practically worthless, at public auction.[100]

Alexander Dick contemplated moving to the western country, which would soon be a receptacle for a mass of war veterans, but he really did not have the resources to do even that. The next best thing was to enter into frontier settlement by way of government appointment. In late 1784, hearing that "the Indians were very troublesome" in the Ohio Valley, Dick solicited the Virginia government for appointment as a commander of troops as "a half pay officer." He also pointed out that since he had formed an acquaintance with one of the Indian chiefs when earlier visiting Pittsburgh, he would be ideal to be "empowered" as a peacemaker.[101]

Alexander Dick died suddenly on March 17, 1785. He was only 32 years old. James Mercer served as executor. Dick's will divided what property was unattached among his sister Mary Taliaferro, and Mary's son, Charles C. Taliaferro, and nephew John Fenton Mercer.[102]

During most of his short adult life, Alexander Dick did military duty in the Revolutionary cause — as a marine, prisoner of war, and militia officer in the field against an invading enemy. He had all the earmarks that would normally shape him as a publicly-recognized hero. Had he found himself an officer early in the war in the Continental Army rather than in the more limited situation as a militia officer, he might have been more able to claim the laurels of victory.

COAST GUARD

2. John "Jack" Cropper

John "Jack" Cropper was one of those young Virginians in their 20s who gave their all during the war and almost did not survive. Cropper's main distinction was to lead militia in coastal defense along the eastern shore versus picaroons (shore pirates) of Chesapeake Bay. Born on December 23, 1755, the eldest son of Sebastian and Sabra Corbin Cropper, John Cropper grew up on a plantation called Bowman's Folly, nestled on the shores of Chesapeake Bay along Folly Creek near its mouth at Metompkin Inlet. The plantation was at the southernmost part of the Eastern Shore in Accomac County. The Croppers were one of the few large landholding families in the region; most residents were small farmers or tenants.[1] The isolation of the Eastern Shore and the proximity of British naval vessels during the war guarding the entrance into the bay contributed to a major segment of the local population being Loyalist. Accomac County had somewhat of a diversified economy, with its shipbuilding, shoemaking, and salt production.[2]

In May 1775 the 20-year-old Cropper was elected captain of a minuteman company of militia, and on February 5, 1776, he received a commission from the Virginia Committee of Safety as captain of the first company of the Ninth Virginia Regiment. This appointment brought Cropper into the Continental Army.

Cropper married Margaret "Peggy" Pettit on August 15, 1776; they had four daughters, two of whom died in infancy. Peggy Cropper died on June 3, 1784. Both of Cropper's parents died in 1776. Cropper married Catharine Bayly on September 18, 1790; the union produced five daughters and five sons.[3]

Cropper's military duties through 1775 on to the end of 1776 involved helping to defend coastal waters from intrusions of Governor Lord Dunmore's motley force of British seamen, Loyalists, and slaves.[4] On January 4, 1777, Cropper was named a major in the Seventh Virginia Regiment, in General William Woodford's brigade, and joined Washington's army in New Jersey.[5]

At the Battle of Brandywine, on September 11, 1777, Cropper's regiment, along with that of George Weedon, endured the heaviest fighting of the battle. During the action Cropper was bayoneted in the thigh. As the story goes, General Woodford, seeing Cropper wounded, jumped from his horse and embraced Cropper, shouting, "The Boy we thought lost is found!" The young major made a quick recovery, and three weeks later fought at the battle of Germantown.[6]

On October 26, 1777, Cropper was appointed lieutenant colonel in the Eleventh Virginia Regiment.[7] With Daniel Morgan, the commander of this unit, frequently absent, Cropper had interim charge of the regiment. After being in the cantonment at Valley Forge, Cropper and his regiment were in the detachment led by Daniel Morgan that pursued the retreating British army after the Battle of Monmouth, June 28, 1777.[8] Cropper stayed with Washington's army in New Jersey and New York through September 1778, and then returned home on furlough.[9]

With the war turning southward, Cropper, as did many Virginia officers, did not relish service in the "tropical Climes" of the Carolinas and Georgia. Besides, he knew he was needed to defend his home territory.

While remaining at his plantation during his extended leave from the army, Cropper experienced the first of his three moments of terror with marauding picaroons. His

John Cropper. **By Charles Willson Peale (1792). Courtesy of the Division of Political History, National Museum of History, Smithsonian Institution.**

plantation underwent a devastating attack from the crew of a privateer vessel manned by Loyalist picaroons. These coastal pirates landed at the dock facing the bay at Bowman's Folly on February 12, 1779. The enemy completely surprised everyone on the plantation in the dead of night, using muffled oars for their rowboats. They surrounded the mansion house before they were detected. Creeping into a bedroom, the intruders made Cropper a prisoner. Leaving Cropper in the bedroom guarded by two sentries at the door, the picaroons proceeded to ransack the house for all kinds of valuables and destroyed furniture. Finding ample wine in the cellar, they became drunk. While the malcreants were occupied in looting and drinking, Cropper saw an opportunity to escape. Bolting past his two guards, he ran out into the darkness and through a marsh to reach a neighbor's house. There sounding the alarm, he and several comrades gathered a few firearms and went to the scene of the desolation. Firing repeatedly from cover in the garden and shouting "come on boys we have got them now," and the like, they made the robbers believe that they were besieged by a hearty band of patriots. The intruders hightailed it back to the shore and rowed away.[10]

Shortly after this episode Cropper returned to Washington's army. On March 20,

1779, he was awarded a commission as lieutenant colonel in the Seventh Virginia Regiment. He became increasingly unhappy being on active duty. Writing to John Jay, president of the Congress, on August 16, 1779, Cropper asked to resign, stating five reasons for his decision:

(1) "I have a young & increasing family, whose situation & circumstances require my presence at home, to improve the remaining part of my patrimony for their maintenance."
(2) "My pay is not one tenth part adequate to the necessary expenses in supporting the dignity of my Commission."
(3) "The high [property] taxes in Virginia ... do not yield me one single six pence profit per annum; nor does profit arise from any part of my property in my absence."
(4) The raid of February 12, 1779, "destroyed and carried off great part of my property."
(5) "My Regiment is highly reduced to a Captain's Command ... it will probably soon be incorporated with some other regiment, when great part of its officers become supernumerary."

Congress denied Cropper's request to resign, but because of the high distinction of his military service allowed him to take an unlimited furlough.[11]

The mounting pressure from the British-supported picaroons in the Chesapeake Bay region made it all the more convincing that Cropper should stay at home in order to ward off attacks in his neighborhood — especially since the state of Virginia was negligent in providing for defense on the Eastern Shore.

In May 1781 Cropper became a member of the Accomac County Court, and was appointed county lieutenant, in charge of the local militia.[12] A direct challenge from the picaroons was not long in coming. In September 1781, picaroons from three barges disembarked near Hersey's Point, where they were met by Cropper's militiamen. During the fight the militiamen backed off, stranding Cropper and a slave named George Latchom, both of whom had been in an advanced position. Although they kept on firing, Cropper and Latchom retreated into a marsh, pursued by several of the invaders. Cropper was stuck in waist-deep mud when one of the enemy was about to bayonet him. Latchom managed to shoot and kill the would-be assailant and pulled the 240-pound militia leader from the mud and brought him to safety. Later the grateful Cropper purchased the slave and set him free.[13]

During 1782 enemy picaroons were especially active off the Eastern Shore. Although occasionally they might have a larger vessel, these marauders operated from open boats of various sizes, either propelled by sail or oars, with usually a small cannon and swivel guns fore and aft.[14] The deteriorating situation in the Chesapeake Bay region provided the backdrop to a bloody affair, the last military engagement of the war, occurring on November 30, 1782, the same day as the Anglo-American Preliminary Treaty of Peace was signed in Paris. So devastating had the picaroon raids become that the Maryland government ordered a flotilla of four barges, under the command of Commodore Zedekiah Whaley, to go after the troublemakers. The result of this decision was the Battle of the Barges (or of Cager's Strait).

Moving down the bay, Whaley discerned six barges under the command of Captain John Kidd. Realizing that his force was not sufficient enough to give battle, Whaley, on November 28, sent a dispatch to Colonel John Cropper in Accomac County to give assistance. While anchored in Onancock Creek, Whaley's flagship barge, the *Protector*, welcomed aboard Cropper and 25 Virginia volunteer militiamen. On November 30 the Marylanders and Virginians caught up with Kidd's barges at Cager's Strait, six miles above the Maryland-Virginia border and in Tangier Sound. At 9:30 A.M., the two forces, initially 300 yards apart, began a furious exchange of arms fire. The *Protector* sailed ahead of the other rebel barges, and the picaroons immediately concentrated their efforts on that vessel. Meanwhile, the other American barges, for whatever reason, held back from the fray, and eventually withdrew from the battle altogether and sailed away. Aboard the *Protector*, Cropper and his men faced "one continual shower of musket balls." As Cropper said later, refering to the retreat of the other Maryland barges, "There was never before upon a like occasion, so much cowardice exhibited."

At the Battle of the Barges, the men aboard the *Protector* seemed to be holding their own against the fierce arms fire and the grape and round shot from the surrounding enemy barges. Then, all of a sudden, something horrific occurred: A spark from the firing pin of a small cannon aboard the *Protector* ignited spilled powder, which in turn set off huge explosions first from one ammunition chest and then another. Four of the militia seamen were immediately seared to death; others, with clothes aflame, jumped overboard. Commodore Whaley was shot dead. The enemy saw their advantage and closed in on the *Protector* and boarded. A furious fight of bayonets and swords ensued. Cropper, wielding his sword, rallied his men, but the odds were against him. Cropper felt a cutlass brushing against his head; blood flowed onto his eyes. Then he was hit on the head and thigh with a boarding pike, and an officer's cutlass cut into his shoulder. Cropper surrendered. But this was not all. A crazed enemy seaman, whose jaw had been shot away, struck the Virginian on the head with a cannon rammer, rendering Cropper unconscious. Cropper was sent home on parole to begin a slow recovery.

Thus ended the Battle of the Barges. Captain Kidd gave chase to the fleeing Maryland barges, but abandoned the pursuit after 30 miles on December 3. Cropper was not released from parole until he was exchanged on January 12, 1783.[15]

After the war John Cropper remained a popular figure on Virginia's eastern shore. Although he had run unsuccessfully for a seat in the House of Delegates in 1780, he won annual elections from 1784 to 1792. In the legislature he served variously on the committees of propositions and grievances, claims, and privileges and elections. He was consistently a staunch Federalist, taking stands against the Jefferson and Madison administrations. He helped draft a protest against the Congressional Declaration of War in 1812. The following year Cropper was elected a Virginia senator and served a four-year term until 1817. From 1801 to 1803 Cropper was sheriff of Accomac County.[16]

Like Cincinnatus, John Cropper answered calls to military duty. In May 1793 he became lieutenant colonel of the Second Virginia Regiment. In this capacity he was in the call-out for troops to enforce an embargo, and participated in the taking over of vessels in Assawaman and Metompkin inlets. During the War of 1812, which he opposed, Cropper commanded a militia regiment for protecting the coasts of the Eastern Shore.[17]

Cropper's community service positions included vestryman; president of Margaret Academy (named after his wife), which opened in 1807; and president of the Virginia Society of the Cincinnati, 1816 to 1817. Otherwise, John Cropper lived quietly, looking after his 1,300-acre plantation and his large family. He died on January 15, 1821, and was buried in the family's cemetery.[18]

CONTINENTAL INFANTRY

3. Richard Clough Anderson

Richard Clough Anderson fought bravely in the northern campaigns and at Savannah, was severely wounded twice, served nine months as a prisoner of war, and after the war, supervised the meting out of Virginia military lands in the Ohio Valley. Born on January 12, 1750, he was reared on the Gold Mine plantation on the South Anna River in Hanover County, near Richmond, Virginia. He was the son of Robert Anderson (1712–1792) and Elizabeth Clough (1722–1779), daughter of Richard Clough and Ann Poindexter of New Kent County. Although he gave evidence of solid learning, nothing is known of Anderson's education. Indeed, Anderson's early lessons in life were mainly acquired out-of-doors; he remained an avid hunter throughout his life — according to tradition, while living on the Kentucky frontier as an adult, he and companions bagged 1,500 squirrels in one day.[1]

Contrary to his father's wishes, at age 16, Anderson went to sea as a supercargo on a merchant ship owned by Patrick Coots, who ran a countinghouse in Richmond. For nine years Anderson remained in the employ of Coots, travelling principally to Martinique, Barbados, and England. It is said that the relationship between Anderson and Coots heatedly came to an end in 1775 over arguments involving divided loyalties in taking sides concerning the American rebellion.[2] Back in Hanover County, Anderson was a member of the county's Committee of Safety during 1775 to 1776.[3]

On March 7, 1776, Anderson signed on as a captain of a company in William Peachy's Fifth Virginia Regiment.[4] Colonel Peachy resigned on May 7, 1776, and Charles Scott succeeded him. Until mid–August Anderson and his comrades were positioned along Virginia's Chesapeake shores, preparing to attack Governor Lord Dunmore's shipboard force. When Dunmore evacuated Virginia in August 1776, Anderson, along with Scott's regiment (now taken into the Continental Army), awaited at Hampton and then Portsmouth for orders to move northward to join Washington's army. In September, the Fourth Fifth, and Sixth Regiments of General Adam Stephen's brigade received notice to begin their march. On October 24, at Chester, Pennsylvania, the three regiments were ordered to Trenton to await further orders from Washington. Still the Virginians were held in abeyance. On November 8 they left Trenton and were expected to link up with General Hugh Mercer's "Flying Camp" at Amboy. When they arrived at Amboy, however, the Virginians found that Mercer and his troops had left. Ordered to join General Nathanael Greene at Fort Lee, it was soon discovered that this post had surrendered to the British (on November 18). Finally the Virginians connected with

Washington's army above Princeton as it retreated through New Jersey. Anderson and Stephen's brigade provided the rear guard as the army headed for Trenton and the crossing into Pennsylvania. On December 8, as the last of the American troops to go across the Delaware River, the Fifth Regiment were among those who skirmished with Cornwallis' oncoming troops.[5]

At the re-crossing of the Delaware and the descent upon Trenton for a surprise attack on Hessian troops, Anderson, along with Stephen's Virginians, formed Washington's vanguard. The role of only a few individual attackers at the Battle of Trenton (e.g. Lt. James Monroe helping to spike a cannon and being wounded) are known. Suffice it to say that Richard Clough Anderson was among the victors.

After the Battle of Trenton, Washington's army made two crossings of the Delaware: to Pennsylvania and on December 30 back to the New Jersey shore above Trenton. Thereupon, events led to the second Battle of Trenton on January 2, 1777. Anderson and his comrades of the Fifth Virginia Regiment played a prominent role in this running engagement. As Washington positioned his army on the low-lying hill above Trenton, he sent out a vanguard composed principally of Virginia and Pennsylvania troops to contest an oncoming Hessian brigade spearheading Cornwallis' advancing army. From 8 A.M. to near dusk, the two forces skirmished alongside the Princeton-Trenton road. In continual fighting the Americans eventually retreated back into Trenton and across the Assunpink Bridge to rejoin Washington's army. At some point in the battle Anderson received a Hessian rifle ball in a thigh. Apparently the wound was of only grazed flesh. Anderson's stay in a Philadelphia military hospital was somewhat extended because once there he contracted smallpox. By May 1777 he had recovered sufficiently to return to the army as it prepared to break out of its Morristown encampment to begin a summer campaign.[6]

As a company commander in the Fifth Virginia Regiment under Colonel

Richard Clough Anderson. **By an unknown American artist, late 18th century. The Society of the Cincinnati, gift of Isabel Anderson, 1941. Reproduced by permission of the Society of the Cincinnati, Washington, D.C.**

Josiah Parker, who had succeeded Charles Scott, Captain Anderson fought at the Battle of Brandywine. Assigned to General Muhlenberg's brigade in Nathanael Greene's division, he entered the battle late — as Muhlenberg's troops moved from the center, which was not under attack, to support George Weedon's Virginia brigade as it tried to contain Cornwallis' surprise attack on the American right flank near Birmingham Meetinghouse. After fierce fighting, primarily involving Weedon's troops, in the "Ploughed Field," Washington's army went into full retreat.[7]

Nearly a month later, Anderson had a similar experience at the Battle of Germantown on October 4. In one of the four columns converging on the British encampment, with Muhlenberg's brigade in Greene's division, he arrived after the fighting was well underway. Greene's troops, however, did manage to push the enemy back to the Schuylkill River but then fell back to join in the general American retreat.

While he was stationed at the Valley Forge encampment of December 1777 to June 1778, Anderson, like so many of his comrade officers, may have spent a good part of this time on extended furlough in Virginia. On February 10, 1778, he was promoted to major and transferred to the Sixth Virginia Regiment, commanded by Colonel John Gibson. Anderson was in Muhlenberg's brigade with Lafayette at the Battle of Monmouth, but was kept in the reserve and not in the detachment that Lafayette brought into the battle.[8] Anderson's luck would change, and he would in a year's time find himself in a military theater of red-hot action.

Anderson was among the first Virginia troops ordered by Congress to join the Southern Army to make the transfer from Washington's army in late 1778. Now in the First Virginia Regiment, he would soon be serving under General Benjamin Lincoln, who assumed command of the Southern Army in early October. Posted 40 miles above Augusta, Anderson and his comrades assisted in protecting the Georgia-lower-South-Carolina backcountry. On September 16, 1779, Lincoln's army began the siege of British-held Savannah. Lincoln's 1500 Continentals, accompanied by Count Pulaski's 300-man cavalry and soon joined by 5800 men of a French naval flotilla commanded by Admiral d'Estaing, expected to carry a siege of Savannah, which was defended by nearly 5,000 British, German, and Loyalist troops. Cannon bombardment for five days (October 4 through 9) did little damage to the enemy's bastions and, therefore, a grand assault was put into effect on the 9th.

Given the town's protection by surrounding swamps, woods, ditches, and abbatis, about the only way to penetrate Savannah's defenses was to aim at the as yet uncompleted Spring Hill Redoubt. American and French troops bravely scaled a bluff, but became entangled in the abbatis and found the parapet too tall to easily reach the top. The attackers met a blistering arms fire. Pulaski's cavalrymen were especially easy targets of the enemy. Anderson found himself near Pulaski when the Polish leader was fatally wounded; according to tradition Anderson administered to Pulaski before he was removed from the field of battle. Anderson almost met the same fate as Pulaski. As

British troops came down to charge the attackers, Anderson found himself in mortal hand-to-hand combat with Captain Thomas Tawse. Reaching the top of the parapet, Anderson was bayoneted in the shoulder by Tawse and knocked into a ditch. In the fall, Anderson received a rupture so severe that he never recovered from it, and was lame the rest of his life.[9]

Anderson was sent to the military hospital at Fort Moultrie (formerly Fort Sullivan), located 100 yards out in the Charleston, South Carolina, harbor. Fort Moultrie and its 200-man garrison surrendered to the British without a fight on May 7, 1780, with Charleston and the whole of Lincoln's army surrendering five days later.[10] Anderson was transferred to the internment site for the prisoner-officers on Haddrell's Point, a barren stretch of land on the north bank of the harbor, five miles from Charleston. Because of the severity of his wounds, he was allowed to return to his home on parole ahead of the release of the other officers. Exchanged in February 1781, Anderson immediately retired from the Continental Army as lieutenant colonel in the Third Virginia Regiment.[11]

Although out of the Continental Army, Anderson served in the Virginia State Line from April to October 1781 at the rank of lieutenant colonel. His primary duty was acting as General Lafayette's adjutant general while the Frenchman commanded troops in Virginia opposing Cornwallis' invasion on the state. He served as a liaison between Lafayette and General Anthony Wayne's Continentals and General (Governor) Thomas Nelson's militia also enlisted in the defense of Virginia; Anderson frequently carried messages on horseback between the various commands. In particular, he helped Nelson gather Virginia militia for active duty. Therefore, in a sense he did adjutant's work for Nelson as well as Lafayette. Anderson was on Lafayette's staff during the siege of Yorktown, obviously having no combat role for himself.[12] Cornwallis' surrender punctuated the end of Anderson's Revolutionary War career.

The war's end did not mean that Richard Clough Anderson completely severed his ties with the revolutionary cause. On January 13, 1784, he began a 42-year association with war veterans when he was appointed surveyor general for the Virginia Continental Line pertaining to the military land districts in Kentucky and Ohio. The Kentucky military land grants were located between the Cumberland and Green rivers, and the Ohio between the Scioto and Little Miami rivers.[13] Anderson's job was to supervise surveyors who laid out lots based on land warrants made out to Virginia servicemen of the Revolutionary War. Veteran's land allotments varied from 100 acres for a private up to a maximum of 1,000 acres for a major general.[14]

On July 20, 1784, Anderson opened his Kentucky land office in Louisville, and in 1787 he began taking entries for the Ohio lands.[15] Anderson held on to the surveyorship until his death, despite several attempts to oust him from office. Not only was the surveyorship difficult because of the flood of applications and complexities from overlapping jurisdictions of the state and federal governments, speculators created pressures and persons sometimes sought confirmation of lands claimed by others. In 1798, George Washington pleaded with Anderson to take measures to prevent lands from being "wrested from me."[16] Anderson often avoided legal and administrative details. When he refused to abide by the Virginia law of February 25, 1818, requiring him to move his office to Chillicothe, Ohio, the Virginia legislature dismissed him from his position as principal surveyor. Two years later the U.S. Supreme Court in *Wallace* v. *Anderson* overturned the state law on grounds that Anderson was primarily a federal official and therefore could not be denied his office by state authority. During his long tenure Anderson aided the concentration of land ownership by speculators.[17]

On November 24, 1787, Anderson married Elizabeth Clark (born 1768), sister of George Rogers Clark. Elizabeth died in childbirth on January 15, 1795. Anderson married Sarah Marshall (born 1779 and died 1854) on September 17, 1797. With his first wife he had three daughters and one son, including Richard Clough Anderson, Jr. (1788–1826), congressman and diplomat; with his second wife he had five daughters and seven sons, including Robert Anderson (1805–1871), the defender of Fort Sumter in April 1861.[18]

In April 1789 Anderson purchased 500 acres, one half of the Linn Station land, ten miles east of Louisville on the banks of the Ohio River at Beargrass Creek. Here he built a stone mansion of 16 large rooms, which he named Soldiers Retreat. He owned 12 slaves.[19] Soldiers Retreat became known for its hospitality. A succession of visitors included President James Monroe, Andrew Jackson, frontiersman Simon Kenton, and Miami Indian chieftan Little Turtle.[20] Anderson liked to depict himself as a member of the aristocracy—even in old age he still wore a wig, knee buckles, silk hose, and silver buckles.[21]

Although Anderson carefully excluded himself from the boisterous Kentucky politics, he does appear on the fringe of the state's political life. Of course, in a sense, being a dispenser of military land allotments was enough politics in itself. General James Wilkinson, whose machinations included conspiracy with Spain and seeking to establish a western separatist movement, won the confidence of Anderson, passing off Anderson as a supporter even without Anderson's knowledge.[22] In 1787 Anderson served as an Indian commissioner, along with Wilkinson and Harry Innes.[23] He served as a delegate from Jefferson County to the Kentucky statehood convention of July 1788 held at Danville. The convention's provision of statehood was, however, held up largely because the Confederation Congress did not want to usurp authority of the incoming government under the new U.S. Constitution.[24] In November 1788, Anderson was named first master of the Masonic lodge in Lexington and, in 1793, a county judge.[25] He served as a member of the Electoral College in 1793.[26]

Except for one occasion, Richard Clough Anderson stayed away from the frequent incursions of the militia into the Indian territory of the Ohio country. When Indians massacred occupants of the Richard Chenoweth home and fortress (five miles east of

Anderson's home) on July 17, 1789, Anderson swung into action. The only persons to survive the massacre were Mrs. Chenoweth, who was left for dead after being scalped, and two young children, one of them seriously wounded. Responding to the alarm which he received in the middle of the night, Anderson quickly assembled neighbors to give chase of the culprits. After going for about one hundred miles, the trail went cold and the pursuers returned home.[27]

Although he never re-entered the army after the Revolutionary War, Anderson retained a reputation as a hero and capable military officer. In 1798 President Washington nominated him among others for command in the army expected to be raised in a war that was threatening with France.[28]

Engaging in substantial agriculture and livestock production, Anderson, like other Kentuckians in the bluegrass region, had an ample stake in wresting the Mississippi from Spanish or French control in order to ship cargo abroad. In 1797 he built a merchant vessel, a two-masted schooner. Intended to ply trade in the Caribbean and in Europe, the *Caroline* wrecked in the Bahamas after only one voyage to New Orleans and Europe.[29]

To the end of his life Anderson was an avid land speculator. He died on October 16, 1826, and was buried at the family plot at Soldiers Retreat.[30] A fitting tribute to Anderson was printed in the *Richmond [Virginia] Daily Dispatch*, January 21, 1861: "There was no braver officer of the American army, and an officer [who] led a braver body of men."[31]

4. John Chilton

John Chilton's military career was cut short by enemy musket fire at the Battle of Brandywine. Although during his two-year army service he was passed over for promotion above his rank of captain, Chilton demonstrated both spunk in standing up to the arrogance of superior officers and an exceptional devotion to duty and the welfare of the men he commanded. Serving in the Third Virginia Regiment in the New Jersey–Pennsylvania campaign of 1776-1777, Chilton participated in some of the most spirited fighting of the Continental Army. Unlike other officers, he refused any lengthy furloughs.

The son of Major Thomas and Jemima Cooke Chilton of Currioman Plantation in Westmoreland County, Chilton was born in 1739. By 1765 Chilton had established his own plantation of Rock Spring in Fauquier County, and had married the 17-year-old Laetitia Blackwell. They had five children: Nancy, Thomas, Lucy, Joseph, and

George. By the time of the revolution, Chilton had served as a county surveyor, justice of the peace, vestryman, and a lieutenant in the militia.[1] Thus, moreso than many of his comrades, he had reached a level of decided maturity by the time he assumed a captaincy in the Continental Army.

In October 1775 Chilton recruited the requisite 68 members to form a minute company, of which, as was customary, he was made captain and the company's commander.[2] Initially Chilton did service at Williamsburg, which became a base for troops collected from different parts of the colony to oppose the little makeshift army of royal troops led by the governor, Lord Dunmore. Chilton served in a regiment commanded by Colonel William Woodford.

By late fall, the royal governor had built a small fort along the southern branch of the Elizabeth River. The wooden Great Bridge connected with a causeway leading to firm ground, on which the rebels constructed breastworks. On the morning of December 9, 1775, 250 of Dunmore's force (including 100 regulars of the Fourteenth Regiment and marines) burst out of the fort, running along the bridge and causeway, intending to carry a surprise assault on the rebel position. They did not go far before attracting relentless arms fire both in front and perpendicularly from a little island in the swamp below. The ranks of the attacking enemy were decimated and they had to retreat. Dunmore took his troops shipboard. The Virginians, joined by 250 North Carolina militia who had arrived a day after the battle, occupied Norfolk.[3]

For John Chilton, savoring victory was soon dampened. A few days after the battle he learned of his wife's death. Chilton immediately took leave to go home. Before he returned to the army he placed his five children in the custody of his brother, Charles, and his wife, Betsy, at their adjoining plantation.[4]

The Third Virginia Regiment, created by the Virginia Convention on December 1, 1775, to which Chilton now belonged, was accepted into the Continental Army by Congress on February 13, 1776. Colonel Hugh Mercer commanded the new unit from February 13 to June 6, 1776; Colonel George Weedon, from August 12, 1776, to February 21, 1777; and Colonel Thomas Marshall, February 21 to December 4, 1777. By April 1776 John Chilton was back in active service as captain and a company commander in the Third Virginia Regiment.[5]

The situation quieted down in Virginia after the Battle of Great Bridge. The governor's little army stayed aboard ship in the lower tidewater region. In July 1776 Governor Dunmore attempted to establish camp on Gwynn's Island, but soon found that he was "bottled-up" by Virginia troops gathered on the nearby mainland shore. Virginia artillery convinced Dunmore to abandon the island, and after sailing around in the Chesapeake his fleet exited the bay, leaving Virginia entirely in the hands of the rebels. John Chilton's company in the Third Regiment may have briefly been involved in the Gwynn's Island affair, but mostly was to be found seeking out Tory-British banditti along the banks of the Potomac River.[6]

On September 13, 1776, the Third Virginia Regiment joined Washington's army on Manhattan Island, New York. Just before the arrival, the American troops had escaped a British pincher movement on Long Island. Chilton and his comrades encamped at the northern end of Manhattan, 14 miles above New York City.[7] The American lines extended across Harlem Heights, a plateau from what is now 130 to 170th streets, and the British reached up to what is now 92nd Street.[8] On Monday, September 16, the enemy sent a detachment of troops forward to probe Washington's position. The ensuing confrontation moved from the Hollow Way (the area between the armies) uphill to a buckwheat field (roughly 116th Street today). John Chilton, in Colonel George Weedon's Third Regiment, found himself in the thick of the action, and he left the most graphic account of the Battle of Harlem Heights:

> Monday morning we marched down towards them and posted ourselves near a meadow, having that in our front, North River to our right a body of woods in our rear & on our left. We discovered the enemy army peeping from their heights near the fencing & rocks & running backward & forwards. We did not alter our position. I believe they expected we should have ascended the hill to them, but finding us still they imputed it to fear and came skipping down towards us in small parties. At a distance of about 250 or 300 yards they began their fire. Our orders were not to fire till they came near, but a young officer (of whom we have too many) on the right fired and it was taken from right to left.

Chilton himself managed to return fire three times before the enemy pulled back. Of his comrades, Chilton said "they behaved like soldiers who fought from principle alone." Pressed also by American rifle companies on their flanks, the enemy retreated a quarter of a mile. "Reinforced with men and cannon," they returned. The Americans, with only one field-piece, now themselves retreated. Chilton describes the battle as more of a "skirmish." Chilton's regiment lost three killed and eight wounded. In a postscript, Chilton noted: "Tell the old Planters in Fauquier their boys are fine fellows and soldiers."[9]

As it became clear that Howe's army intended to flank Washington's army and cut it off in Manhattan, the Americans retreated northward and established lines at White Plains. As the enemy moved toward that position, an American detachment under General John Glover contested the British landing at Pell's Point on October 18, and on October 22 the Third Virginia Regiment were among those who skirmished with Tory Rangers a few miles from White Plains. At the Battle of White Plains on October 28, 1776, the Virginians were, like most of Washington's army, hardly more than spectators to the action, which was limited mainly to Chatterton's Hill as troops, chiefly New Yorkers, fended off an enemy attack. Thus Chilton, too, was merely a spectator.[10]

Chilton's company in the Third Virginia Regiment served as the rear guard during the march of the American army through New Jersey, towards the Delaware River. Crossing the Delaware on December 7–8, Washington's army bided their time until crossing the river back into New Jersey for a surprise attack on one of the British winter garrisons, namely Trenton. The crossing began at sunset on Christmas Day and was accomplished by dawn the next day. Marching the nine miles to Trenton, the Americans gained position at the heads of the two main streets and opened artillery fire on Hessian troops as they scrambled out in the open in dazed confusion. Most of the Hessians fled to an apple orchard, trapped by Assunpink Creek. Upon surrender, the Hessian captives were escorted to Philadelphia by the Virginia Third Regiment. It may be assumed that Chilton was with his company on this mission. He probably did not return to the army in time for the Battle of Princeton on January 3. This was the day that Chilton began writing in his diary, and, though he gives a brief description of the Battle of Princeton, it is inexact, indicating his probable absence from the battle.[11]

For its winter encampment the American army established itself at Morristown on January 6, 1777, and stayed there until a move to Middlebrook on May 4. During this period the Third Virginia Regiment was among those troops detached to form a covering screen in the countryside between the two opposing armies. Chilton was acting commander of the whole regiment for about two months after the regimental commander, Colonel George Weedon, was promoted to brigadier general and all the regiment's field officers and senior captains were absent for one reason or another.[12] Writing to a friend on March 19, Chilton reported "skirmishing every day or two where two or three Britons knocked up will do."[13]

Chilton's diary, meticulously kept during the spring and summer of 1777, contributes a rare, inside view of the army, its personnel, and local conditions and people. His letters are even more candid. Occasionally his comments were a bit caustic. He noted in his diary that he "saw some fine Girls not much unlike our first Virginia Nymphs."[14] Chilton took the full measure of his colleagues and did not hesitate to voice his disapproval. He intensely disliked General Adam Stephen, who once reprimanded him for being five minutes over curfew and also Lt. Col. William Heth, whom he referred to as "imperious to the last degree."[15]

From July to early August 1777 Washington's army tramped up and down from mid–New Jersey to the New York Highlands. The furthest north for Chilton and the Third Virginia Regiment was the Clove, a hostile, barren defile where the Ramapo River empties into the Hudson. Washington would change the direction of the march of his troops every time he heard that the British army, soon aboard ships, was headed either up the Hudson, to Chesapeake Bay, or to Charleston.[16] Chilton himself commented, "From 10th of July we have been continuously marching, we have made a complete tour of the Jerseys."[17]

In mid–August, British warships bearing 14,000 troops sailed into the Chesapeake Bay. It was now clear that the enemy's destination was Philadelphia. Washington directed his army at northeastern New Jersey to make a forced march of 95 miles in four days to reach the lower Delaware River. On August 24 the American army paraded through Philadelphia on its way to seek out the enemy. A day later the huge British force debarked at the northern tip of Chesapeake Bay.[18]

While on the relentless trek through New Jersey, John Chilton worried about how his young children were doing. In writing to his brother, Charles, on August 17, less than a month before his rendezvous with fate, John Chilton expressed satisfaction that his son Joseph had undergone a shift in education:

> The old saw of telling no tales out of school has as great a tendency to slavery as any thing I know. A child may be brought up a slave, many parents wonder to see their sons turn out a silly lad and sometimes a cowardly, foolish, man, but never consider it is by cramping their genius at school where tyrants of masters leave such an impression on their tender minds that seldom they get over it. I am glad Joe is taken from that school and will not have to go to that master again on any account; for should the master promise to behave better and do so, the boy then in his turn will usurp — at any rate, don't let him go to the same master again. I should rather he should never know another letter than have the least taint of Scotch slavery, or any other kind, inculcated into him, and as I think him a generous boy and with a generous education will make a smart man.[19]

Washington drew up his army along the banks of Brandywine Creek in Delaware, in the path of the enemy's march on Philadelphia. At Chadd's Ford, expected to bear the main brunt of the attack, the American commander in chief positioned the bulk of his army: Stephen, Sullivan, Stirling, and Greene's divisions and General William Maxwell's new light infantry corps of 800 men. The Third Virginia Regiment of Woodford's brigade was positioned at the far right of the American lines, 100 yards from Birmingham Meetinghouse. Washington miscalculated that the enemy's main attack would come at Chadd's Ford. After the enemy initiated the attack there under the command of General Knyphausen, Washington belatedly discovered that the greater part of the British army was headed to engulf the American army on its right flank. Troops from the Chadd's Ford area were hastily shifted to the sweeping British attack.[20]

Captain John Chilton and 170 men of the Third Virginia Regiment found themselves occupying an orchard at the American extreme right and in the direct path of the oncoming enemy. As Henry Lee later reported, the Third Regiment "bravely sustained itself against superior numbers, never yielding one inch of ground and expending thirty rounds a man in forty-five minutes."[21] Finally, fearing that the Third Regiment was about to be surrounded, General Woodford ordered a retreat. Some fighting, however, continued until the rest of General Greene's division arrived and provided adequate cover. In the battle the Third Regiment lost about one-third of its men, including seven officers.[22]

As British infantry poured into the woods defended by the Third Regiment, a musket ball tore into John Chilton's side, leaving a gaping wound. His comrades could do no more than prop him up against a tree. During the retreat the dying Virginia captain was brought to a field hospital at the Concord Meetinghouse on the Chester Road. There, John Chilton immediately died. Chilton, as one observer noted, was "brave as Wolfe, and imitated his manner of death, inquiring about the success of the day as he expired."[23]

John Chilton's will, written on August 24, just days before his death, bequeathed estates to all his children, leaving his eldest son, Thomas, the main plantation of "Rock Spring." As a fitting testament he simply signed his will: "John Chilton of the Third Regiment of Virginia."[24]

5. Peter Francisco

Regarded as the most heroic private during the Revolutionary War — indeed in the whole history of the U.S. Army — Peter Francisco is almost unknown in our own time. Dubbed the "Paul Bunyon of the Revolution" or the "Hercules of the Revolution," Francisco, 6'6" and weighing 260 pounds, had prodigious strength. Though wounded severely four times, in battle he could work himself up to enormous rage, becoming a one-man killing machine, easily claiming the lives of the enemy. Yet Peter Francisco was also a gentle giant, a trait noticeable especially later in his life, when he exuded friendliness and grace. We know a great deal of Peter Francisco and many of his superhuman exploits have been amply corroborated.

Peter Francisco first appeared in America as an abandoned waif, five years old, at a wharf at City Point (now Hopewell), Virginia, in June 1765. The two sailors who rowed him ashore quickly returned to their main ship and disappeared. The boy's clothing, thought of fine quality, was tattered from extended wear. He had silver buckles on his shoes. Later in life he revealed that he had been kidnapped while playing in the yard of his family's mansion with his sister, who escaped. The boy, not speaking English, could only give his name as Pedro Francisco, indicating he was either Portuguese or Spanish.

What is most certainly the baptismal record of Peter Francisco was meticulously tracked down in the mid–20th century. A baptismal entry at Porto Judeu on the island of Riberirinha in the Azores group, reads in translation from the Portuguese:

> PEDRO, son of Francisco Machado Luis and his wife Antonia Maria, natives and parishioners of this parish of St. Anthony of the place of Porto Judeu [Jewish Port], was born the 9th day of the month of July of the year of 1760, and was baptized by me, Antonio Gardoza de Castro, the Vicar of the Parish....[1]

The marooned Portuguese boy at City Point was placed in the Prince George County Poor House. Judge Anthony Winston, visiting the neighborhood, learned of Peter's plight, and took him home with him to his plantation, Hunting Tower, in nearby Buckingham County. Though legend has it that Winston adopted Peter, this was probably not the case since Peter received no schooling of any kind and did not learn to read or write until relatively late in life. He did not legally become a bond servant, but for all practical purposes he was in status much like an indentured servant, and learnt the blacksmith trade.[2]

With no further record of his childhood, we find Peter Francisco, at age 16, enlisting on October 10, 1776, in Captain Hugh Woodson's company in the Tenth Virginia Regiment. On December 15, 1776, this unit was taken into the Continental Army.[3]

Details of much of Peter Francisco's army experience in the northern campaigns are lacking. But, as he himself pointed out to the Virginia General Assembly in a petition of November 11, 1820, he participated in the major engagements at Brandywine, Germantown, Monmouth, Stony Point, and Paulus Hook. Peter first showed up at Washington's army at Middlebrook, New Jersey, in May 1777, joining other members of his regiment already there. He fought with conspicuous bravery, even while wounded, at the Battle of Brandywine, especially at the Hollow Gap, holding back Cornwallis' advance to help Washington's army extricate itself. So impressed was Washington (who usually let deeds by enlisted men go unnoticed), that he had a six-foot sword, with a five-foot blade, presented to Francisco. A captain's commission was also proffered, but Francisco declined because he thought an officer should be literate, which he was not. Although not fully recovered, he was with his Tenth Regiment in Greene's division in the Battle of Germantown, three weeks after Brandywine.[4]

At the Battle of Monmouth, June 28, 1778, Francisco received a musket ball through his right thigh. In September 1778, after he recuperated, he was transferred from the Tenth to the Sixth Virginia Regiment, and was present at the army's encampments in northeastern New Jersey and the Hudson Valley through summer 1779.[5] At the storming of Stony Point on July 16, 1779, Francisco was the second over the fort's wall, and as he moved forward he received a nine-inch stomach wound, but killed the soldier who gave him the injury and two others. As a fellow soldier noted, Francisco was "the first man who laid hold of the flagstaff and being badly wounded laid on it that night and in the morning delivered it to Colonel Fleury." Such actions brought Francisco "into great notice and his name was

Peter Francisco. **By unknown artist. Courtesy of the Cook Collection, Valentine Richmond History Center.**

reiterated throughout the whole army." Francisco was carried to Fishkill, New York, where he stayed in recovery for six weeks before returning to the army.[6]

At Paulus Hook, on August 19, 1779, Francisco, though wounded in the thigh, continued in the fighting, killing several of the enemy. As he himself stated years later in reference to this occasion, "he never felt satisfied nor thought he did a good day's work, but by drawing British blood."[7] With his three-year enlistment up in December 1779, Francisco went back home.[8]

It was not long before Francisco learned of the British invasion of the southern states. He enlisted in a militia company commanded by Captain William Mayo, and was soon off to join General Horatio Gates' Southern Army. Despite his bravery, Francisco was caught in the rapid tide of fleeing Continentals and militia at the Battle of Camden, August 16, 1780. During this chaos a British grenadier was about to bayonet Captain Mayo. Francisco rushed up and shot and killed the grenadier. One of Tarleton's cavalrymen charged against the two militiamen. Francisco stepped aside, but on a second charge ran through the grenadier with his bayonet, lifting him out of the saddle. Francisco then mounted a horse and rode through the enemy lines. When he reached an American artillery battery, he discovered that the artillery horses had been killed and a cannon was about to be captured. Francisco then untied the 1,100-pound cannon from the gun carriage and carried it on his shoulder to safety. This deed was commemorated by a U.S. 18-cent postage stamp in 1975.[9]

With the Southern Army dissolved for all practical purposes, by its disastrous defeat at Camden, Francisco again returned home. Upon the raising of a new army, Francisco decided to reenlist as a cavalryman instead of infantryman. He was recruited into a troop from Prince Edward County, commanded by Captain Thomas Watkins, and this unit was soon off to join Colonel William Washington's cavalry in South Carolina.[10]

Just before linking up with Washington's cavalry, Francisco and his comrades had an encounter with the enemy, about which Francisco himself reported, many years afterward:

> We then fell in with the British army of about five or six hundred at a place called Scotch Lake. About a hundred yards from the lake they fortified themselves in upon the top of a hill resembling a sugar loaf; as soon as he got in sight of the lake, he tied his horse and ran under the bank thereof to discover the situation that the enemy were in, and, after getting opposite to the fort, he discovered there was no danger under the foot of the mount where all of their tents and marquees as they stood pitched, and where there were several hogsheads; and after walking about for some time ... went into one of their marquees, threw down one of the hogsheads ... and rolling some distance, placed himself upon his belly, with his head under cover of the hogshead, and, by drawing it down gently by each chime, got it to the lake, the British ... firing several balls through the hogshead. The British, being surrounded by our cavalry and infantry, they could not come out of the fort. When he arrived at his journey's end, General [Thomas] Johnson and his picquett being placed there, the General opened the hogshead, and the contents were shirts and overalls, and other clothing, which he divided

amongst Washington and Lee's men, who were bare for such necessaries; General Johnson himself wore some of the pantaloons. He then mounted his horse and rode around the north side of the mount, where he discovered eight horses belonging to British officers, about one hundred yards from the fort. He borrowed a whip and rode between the fort and the horses under fire, and brought them safe into the camp and gave them to Colonel Washington.[11]

Though it hadn't resulted in any kills, Francisco's heroic actions had brought in much needed clothing and horses.

At the Battle of Guilford Courthouse, March 15, 1781, in Colonel William Washington's cavalry, Francisco was in the thick of the action. In close combat with British guardsmen, Francisco killed 11 of the enemy. Then he road towards a British square formation, and as he did so, a guardsman firmly held his bayonet upward, and it caught Francisco's knee and sliced his leg clear up to his hip. Francisco helped his attacker extract the bayonet from his leg, and then, as the British soldier turned to ride off, Francisco mightily wielded his long sword and came directly down on his opponent's head, cutting it in two, with "a half falling on each shoulder." Francisco's horse reeled and threw off its rider. Terribly wounded, Francisco managed to crawl to the side of a giant oak tree. Using pieces of clothing, he unsuccessfully attempted to stop the bleeding, and lapsed into unconsciousness. Francisco was left on the field of battle for dead, but after the fighting ceased, he was discovered by an old resident of the area named Robinson, who carried Francisco to his nearby house. After recuperating sufficiently from his wound, Francisco, without money or a horse, walked to his home in Virginia.[12]

The heavy British losses at the Battle of Guilford Courthouse made it a turning point of the war. General Cornwallis commented, "Such fighting I have not seen since God made me. The Americans fought like demons."[13] A monument completed in 1910 on the spot where Francisco and his fellow cavalry charged during the battle has a plaque on its 30-foot shaft that notes:

TO PETER FRANCISCO
A GIANT IN STATURE
MIGHT AND COURAGE — WHO
SLEW IN THIS ENGAGEMENT ELEVEN OF THE
ENEMY WITH HIS OWN BROADSWORD
RENDERING HIMSELF THEREBY PERHAPS THE MOST
FAMOUS PRIVATE SOLDIER OF THE REVOLUTIONARY WAR.[14]

In July 1781 Francisco happened to be at the house of Benjamin Ward (also known as Ward's Tavern), in Amelia County (part of which is now Nottoway County), when a "plundering party" from Tarleton's dragoons came up and Francisco did not have time to escape. What happened next is best told by Francisco himself:

One of the British demanded his watch and some other jewelry that he owned, and also at the same time placed his sword under his right arm, whilst disposing of other property. He stepped back one pace in the rear, seized his sword by the hilt, cut off a large portion of his skull and killed him. He had then neither sword nor pistol of his own, but fought with his adversary's own weapons, which he took from him. He wounded and drove off the others, and took eight horses with their trappings, out of nine; the ninth man escaped with a large cut upon his back. They all joined Tarleton, who was about a mile off, except the slain man. This is the last favor I ever did for the British.[15]

When Tarleton and his 400-man force arrived at the scene and saw what had happened, he offered a large reward and sent 100 men in pursuit of Francisco, who "made his escape when he heard their horses' feet, by calling the horses he had taken to a halt and turning them down an obscure road."[16]

Yet there was to be one more occasion that served as a finale to Francisco's army career: acting as a bodyguard to Lafayette at the siege of Yorktown.[17] Francisco himself probably did not participate with 400 of Lafayette's troops in the capture of Redoubt #10 on October 14. After the surrender at Yorktown, Francisco returned to the Hunting Tower plantation. For some reason the relationship between Francisco and Judge Winston became estranged, and after the war he left the estate, never to return.[18]

Soon after Yorktown, the gigantic hero met the 16-year-old Susannah Anderson, daughter of James Anderson of the Mansion estate in Cumberland County. Susannah's family did not approve of a match between the two, largely because Francisco was still illiterate. To remedy this situation Francisco enrolled in a neighborhood school conducted by Frank McGraw. Of course, the gentle giant stood out among the school children. McGraw attested to Francisco's strength and his character:

> Francisco could take me in his right hand and pass me over the room, playing my head against the ceiling as though I had been a doll. My weight was one hundred and ninety pounds. He evidently inherited eloquence ... and he possessed the rare but simple formula of originality and directness. His ability was striking, his personality charming. He possessed a high sense of honor and vast physical courage with a gentleness whose foundation was fixed.[19]

From 1785 to 1790 Peter and Susannah Francisco lived in a log cabin in Charlotte County. Susannah died in 1790, leaving a son and a daughter.[20] Soon thereafter Francisco moved to Cumberland County where he had purchased 500 acres on both sides of Dry Creek.[21] Francisco occupied himself with farming and blacksmithing.

Peter Francisco married Catherine Fauntleroy Brooke on December 8, 1794. She hailed from Farmer's Hall on the Rappahannock River. The couple had two sons and two daughters. They made their home at Locust Grove, an estate inherited from Francisco's first wife. Catherine Brooke Francisco died on October 23, 1821.[22] At age 63, Francisco, in July 1823, married the 41-year-old widow of Major Charles West, a wealthy planter, whose maiden name was Mary Beverly Grymes. For several years the couple resided at Planterstown in Buckingham County.[23]

Not many details are known of Francisco's business and farming life. He ran a tavern for a while at New Store, Buckingham County, during the first decade of the 19th century. He and his family resided at the site. He lost his tavern license, however, in

1808 for some infraction of the law. In 1807 Buckingham County personal property tax records listed Francisco as having 17 slaves, five horses, and one carriage. Congress awarded Francisco an $8-per-month pension, commencing on January 1, 1819.[24]

Francisco was a frequent visitor to Richmond. Attending a play at the Richmond Theatre along with 600 other patrons, he was present when the theater became a blazing inferno on the night of December 25, 1811. The fire claimed the Virginia governor among its 72 victims. Francisco managed to exit the building, and outside caught 30 or more attendees leaping from a window.[25]

For six years, from 1825 to his death in 1831, Francisco served as sergeant-at-arms of the Virginia House of Delegates. Only once was he asked by the speaker to eject a trouble-maker. Francisco seized the person by the seat of the pants and neck and shoved him out of the door.[26] Though he kept his residence at Planterstown, Francisco stayed at the Columbian Hotel while in Richmond during legislative sessions.

The stories of Peter Francisco's legendary feats of strength are legion. One of the favorites is one that Francisco related to Henry Clay when the two were together at the Bell Tavern in Richmond in 1826. Francisco related the tale when Clay asked if Francisco had ever met his equal. It seems that a strong bully named Pamphlet from Kentucky came all the way to Virginia in 1806 to whip Francisco:

> When Francisco learned the object of his visit, he handed him a bunch of willow switches and told him to whip away to his heart's content. The strong man was taken aback by this demeanor and asked to feel his weight. He lifted Francisco from the ground, and remarked he was quite heavy. "Now, Mr. Pamphlet," said Francisco, "let me feel your weight," and lifting the sportive visitor twice in the air, the third time threw him over a failing fence four feet high into the public road. Pamphlet was mightily surprised at this exhibition of strength, and called out as he lay in the dust that Francisco would do him a favor if he would pitch his horse after him, as he wanted to go home. The story goes that Francisco led the horse to the fence, and with his left arm under the horse's breast and the right one behind him, put him over as requested. The discomfited Mr. Pamphlet mounted and took his way back to Kentucky.

Clay laughed and reportedly said, in allusion to hostile political pamphlets printed against him, "I am glad to know one of the mischievous Pamphlet family has been conquered."[27]

On January 16, 1831, Peter Francisco died at the Columbian Hotel, probably from appendicitis. The funeral procession wound its way from the House of Delegates, with the governor and all the legislators in the march, to burial, with full military and Masonic honors, at Richmond's Shockoe Cemetery.28 The House of Delegates passed resolutions commemorating Francisco, during which occasion many delegates spoke. Delegate James Barbour of Culpeper County was among those who eulogized Francisco. Barbour declared: "Peter Francisco was no common man. By nature he had been endowed with extra-ordinary strength, the most determined intrepidity, and the warmest patriotism." Furthermore, "as a private soldier he gave a striking example of bravery and performed exploits that have scarcely ever been excelled.... By the arms of such men the liberty of our country was achieved ... an achievement of vast moment to the whole world. To such men, honor is due."[29]

6. Nathaniel Gist

Explorer, Indian agent, diplomat, and trader, perhaps a renegade, and a daring army officer in two wars, Nathaniel Gist (pronounced "Guest") had a remarkable career, chiefly along Virginia's far frontier. In many ways his life aped that of his father, Christopher Gist, the famous scout and associate of George Washington. Nathaniel, however, did one better, living off and on with an Indian tribe.

The eldest son among six children of Christopher and Sarah Howard Gist, Nathaniel Gist was born on October 15, 1733, near Baltimore, Maryland.[1] With little or no education, Nathaniel Gist grew up on frontier life. The elder Gist, enduring financial failure as a merchant and planter in Maryland, moved his family to the Yadkin River frontier in North Carolina in 1745. Entering the hire of the Ohio Company in 1750, Christopher Gist moved his family to Opeckon, a trading post in Virginia on a tributary of the Potomac River, near Winchester. On land granted by the Ohio Company, the Gists, along with other pioneer families, settled at the "Plantation," 43 miles east of Pittsburgh and near present Uniontown, on Laurel Hill. This was the first permanent English settlement west of the Appalachian Mountains. The "Plantation" became a popular frontier post. The Gist estate, at the time, lay in Augusta County, Virginia. From this location, Christopher Gist, usually accompanied by Nathaniel, set out on exploring missions for the Ohio Company that took him into the Ohio country, including portions of southwest Pennsylvania, the Kanawha Valley of West Virginia, and Kentucky. On a trip into the Ohio country in 1751 to 1752, Nathaniel Gist had a bad case of frostbitten feet. George Washington was a companion on Christopher Gist's the journey of 1752 to 53. Nathaniel Gist, a swarthy, dark complexioned teenager, 6'2" and weighing 200 pounds, missed the latter trip by visiting the Cherokee country; upon his return he took sick and had to recuperate for a while at the Conegocheague River.[2]

By 1754 Nathaniel Gist was actively engaged as an Indian trader. Governor Dinwiddie of Virginia deputized him in 1755 to go into the Cherokee and Choctaw Indian country to obtain warriors to fight on the side of the British in the war against France. Gist's associate, a South Carolinian named Richard Pearis, quarreled with Gist and falsely told the Indians that Gist had no authorization for his mission, and as a result the Indians that Gist managed to raise went home.[3] Subsequently, Gist entered George Washington's Virginia Regiment as a lieutenant in a company of scouts commanded by his father.[4] In this capacity, Gist participated in Braddock's defeat of July 9, 1755. Just after the battle Gist was sent by his father to Fort Cumberland to report the disaster.[5]

During the summer and fall of 1756, Nathaniel Gist was frequently on a scouting mission. In May, Gist, with 18 soldiers and seven Nottoway Indians and a slightly larger group led by Colonel Thomas Cresap, set out scouting. Cresap's men soon mutinied, and Gist and his party proceeded on alone. They encountered a French scouting party, which led to a skirmish, where Gist lost four men, and the French six. As one historian has noted, Gist, facing a larger enemy force, "brought off his men with great skill and after some difficulty returned to Fort Cumberland, where he was given credit for unusual courage."[6]

In 1757, Governor Dinwiddie gave Gist a commission as a captain. About the same time, Christopher Gist's scouting company was disbanded, and Nathaniel Gist joined the newly formed company of rangers employed in protecting the Virginia frontiers.[7]

In May 1758, Gist, with six soldiers and 30 Indians, was sent to spy on Fort Duquesne. After much difficulty crossing snowy mountains, Gist reached the mouth of Redstone Creek, but was injured by a fall from a steep bank. Unable to continue on, Gist had his men proceed without him. They came back with the scalps of two Frenchmen.[8] The following month Gist was able to join the military expedition of General John Forbes as it made its way slowly into western Pennsylvania to confront the French at Fort Duquesne. Gist went out briefly to obtain Cherokee Indians to assist in the expedition, but the warriors he secured soon drifted away. Gist may have been with the Virginia troops under Major James Grant who were savagely beaten back by the French and Indians on September 14, 1758. Gist marched with General Forbes into the ruins of the evacuated Fort Duquesne.[9] The victory over the French in the war served as revenge for Gist since the enemy had destroyed the buildings and other property at the Gist family estate, the Plantation.

In 1760, during the Cherokee War along the Virginia and Carolina borders, Nathaniel Gist, while deputy superintendent of Indian Affairs for Virginia, accompanied colonels William Byrd and Adam Stephen's expedition against the Overhill Cherokee towns.[10] Before any major fighting could occur, the Indians and the Virginians came to peace terms. The Cherokees, who regarded Nathaniel Gist as a friend and one of their own, presented to him as a gift Long Island, in the south branch of the Holston River (present site of Kingsport, Tennessee). Gist did not make public this gift until 1777.[11]

While some of the Gist family (Nathaniel's father died in 1759) returned to the Plantation site in western Pennsylvania, Nathaniel Gist settled for a while at the old family environs on the Yadkin River in North Carolina. There he became close friends with a neighbor, Daniel Boone. The two went out on long hunts together. In December

1760 Gist and Boone went as far as the Tennessee River. A year later, again in westward exploration, the two men almost met their end when attacked by a pack of wolves. Gist and Boone had a disagreement, and the two men separated, with Boone moving on to the Long Island and Gist following an Indian trail to the Cumberland Gap, one of the first white men to reach that destination.[12]

Nathaniel Gist was now employed as a full-time Indian trader, becoming friends with Cherokee leaders. Like other traders who found success in the Indian country, Nathaniel Gist tapped into a kinship network. He formed a sexual liaison with Wurteh, sister of the Cherokee chief, Onitositah (Old Tassel). Gist was the putative father of Wurteh's son, the great craftsman and genius, Sequoyah. Although unschooled, Sequoyah invented the Cherokee written language. He has been referred to as "the only man in history to conceive and perfect in its entirety an alphabet or syllabary" and the "ablest intelligence produced among the American Indians." Sequoyah went by his English name, George Guess.[13]

In the opening of the trans–Appalachian west, Gist became a prominent figure. He helped negotiate the Treaty of Sycamore Shoals on the Watauga River in March 1775, whereby Cherokees ceded to the Transylvania Company territory in Kentucky and part of northeastern Tennessee.[14]

At the start of the Revolutionary War, with his loyalty to the Cherokee Indians, who veered from neutrality to hostility towards the patriot cause, Gist was equivocal as to his patriotism. Being in the crown employ as a deputy Indian agent, Gist at first appeared to support the royal cause. In 1775 he journeyed to West Florida to seek out lands that could be awarded to white Loyalists living among the Cherokees. He returned from the mission in the company of Henry Stuart, himself a deputy Indian agent.

Gist accompanied Cherokee warriors on their attack of the Watauga settlements in July 1776. He was greatly repulsed by the savagery of the Indians, and desired to escape back to his own kind. Gist persuaded the Indians to allow him to go under a flag of truce to state that the Indians would not permit a militia force under Colonel William Christian to go any further than the Little Tennessee River.[15] Christian wrote Governor Patrick Henry on October 15, 1776: "I judge the flag was only an excuse for him to get with me. I believe he is sorry for what he has done. I did intend to put him in irons, but the manner of his coming will prevent me."[16] Rebel feeling, however, ran high against Gist. Virginian John Page wrote the president of Congress that Gist and others "have committed Murders or Robberies on our Frontiers."[17] One author notes that but for the intervention of Colonel Christian, Gist would have been scalped by the soldiers.[18] Gist, nevertheless, deflected to the American side. The question of Gist aiding the Cherokees in war against frontier settlers came up before the Virginia General Assembly. On December 17, 1776, the Virginia Council absolved Gist of any treason. It was a full vindication, and in short order, on January 11, 1777, Gist was commissioned a colonel in the Continental Army and commander of an "Additional Continental

Regiment of Infantry," subsequently designated as Gist's Regiment or Gist's Rangers. The new unit consisted of three Virginia companies and two from Maryland.[19]

Washington ordered Gist that before he joined the main army he recruit four companies of rangers and 300 Cherokees to serve as scouts. Simultaneously he was given the task by the Virginia government to join commissioners from North Carolina to conclude a treaty of peace with the Overhill Cherokees. Gist arrived at the Overhill capital, Chota, on March 28, 1777. After several false starts, negotiations began in earnest in June, and on July 20, 1777, the Treaty of Long Island was agreed upon. The Cherokees surrendered all lands east of the Blue Ridge and the Cumberland Gap corridor. The Cherokee leaders also confirmed the earlier grant of Long Island in the Holston River to Nathaniel Gist. After the war, Gist tried to sell the island, but failed to do so because of opposition from other claimants. In January 1806 the Cherokees officially ceded Long Island to the U.S. government.[20]

Gist and his regiment probably linked up with Washington's army sometime during spring 1778. At the time of the Battle of Monmouth, Gist's rangers were part of Daniel Morgan's light infantry that skirted the flanks of the contending armies. As a cavalry officer reported on July 2, 1778, "Morgan's and Gist's men, with the parties of Horse, have Saved a fine Country from being pilaged."[21]

In summer 1778, Gist's regiment was assigned to a new light infantry corps commanded by General Charles Scott. This special unit acted as a search and attack force operating between the lines along the Hudson River. About 8 A.M. on August 31, 1778, Gist "fell in with a partie of the enemy," about two miles below Philipsburg Manor (in present-day Yonkers, New York), along the east bank of the Hudson. Gist's men, without incurring any casualties themselves, drove the enemy off the field, killing one and taking three prisoners. But, as General Scott reported, the enemy quickly retaliated. The rebel captain, John Stewart, and 20 soldiers accompanied by 60 Wappinger Indians from Stockbridge, Massachusetts, led by Captain (Chief) Daniel Nimham, went out on patrol. The Indians became separated from the rest, and were attacked by a combined force of Lt. Col. Simcoe's rangers and Tarleton's dragoons at the foot of Valentine's Hill. The Indians were herded into a field, and all of them were killed or "desperately wounded."[22]

Scott's light infantry went out in various patrols from outposts.[23] Gist's men, in mid–September, 1778, while holding up at the Rev. Luke Babcock's house, were attacked by Simcoe and Tarleton's special forces and some Hessians. Though they faced an encirclement movement, Gist and his troops were able to escape "through a passage which had been so unaccountably left open."[24] Through the remainder of autumn 1778 Gist's rangers did double duty — skirmishing with enemy "flanking parties" and reconnaissance/intelligence work.[25]

On April 22, 1779, the Additional Continental Regiments of William Grayson and Charles M. Thurston were incorporated into Gist's regiment. This consolidated unit, keeping the designation of Gist's Additional Continental Regiment, was assigned to the First Virginia Brigade, commanded by General Muhlenberg.[26]

Like other members of the officer corps, Nathaniel Gist had a high sensitivity towards any slight infringement upon his status as a commanding officer. He resented that Major Henry Lee used some of Gist's troops, without Gist's knowledge, in a successful assault during the night of August 18 to 19, 1779, upon British-held Paulus Hook on the west bank of the Hudson River opposite New York City. Other officers were also resentful of Lee's Paulus Hook affair, but Gist went so far as to press charges against Lee, necessitating a court martial. The foremost charges leveled against Lee by Gist were: not informing Gist of General Stirling's instructions for the assault on Paulus Hook; obtaining 300 men from a detachment then under charge of Gist and not paying heed to the fact that Major Jonathan Clark, who was among those men so appropriated, had seniority over Lee and should have led the attack; Lee keeping his troops in "disorder and confusion"; Lee ordering a retreat before all the vanquished enemy had been made prisoners; and generally Lee "behaving in a manner unbecoming an officer and a Gentleman." The court martial acquitted Lee of all charges.[27] Lee's vindication enhanced his reputation as a hero, and conversely did not bring any plaudits to Gist. Both generals Greene and Weedon weighed in on the affair. Greene wrote: Lee "has been arrested, and brought to tryal, for misconduct, but there is not a shadow of evidence against him.... After passing through the furnace of afflection, he will come out, like gold seven times in the fire."[28] Weedon directed his comment to Greene:

> I am made very happy at being informed of my much Esteemed friend Major Lees Honorable Acquittal of every Charge brought against him for his conduct in the Palus Hook enterprise. And nothing so much astonishes me as to find Colo Gist was his persecutor. For the Lordsake what could induce that head of Wrongheads to Calumnite so Splendid, So Galant, so brave, and Officerlike conduct as that little Hero displayed in that affair. For which he Ought to be loved, Honored and adored, instead of being Arraigned and brought to Trial. I am sorry for the Colo as it must hurt him in the Opinion of all good men.[29]

On December 9, 1779, Gist's regiment, along with other troops from the southern states, set out from the main army's encampment at Morristown, for the Southern department. Gist led a detachment of 224 men, one of three forming a new brigade under General William Woodford, totaling 750 men. The destination was General Benjamin Lincoln's army in Charleston. The other two detachments in the brigade were commanded by colonels John Neville and William Russell. The new brigade had a difficult march. From New Jersey through Pennsylvania the troops trudged through deep snow, ice, and mud. They crossed the Potomac on January 30, 1780, and went on to Fredericksburg and Petersburg. Leaving the latter place on March 9, they continued on through Camden, South Carolina, and finally reached their destination at Charleston on April 7. By mid April, Lincoln's army in the city was totally penned in.[30]

Nathaniel Gist was made a prisoner of war with the surrender of Charleston on

May 12, 1780. His regiment was disbanded on January 1, 1781.[31] Gist retired from the army on January 1, 1783.[32]

Nathaniel Gist received ample rewards for his military service in two wars. For the French and Indian War he collected, in 1780, 8,000 acres on his own behalf and 3,000 acres designated for his deceased father (Nathaniel was the chief beneficiary of Christopher Gist). In February 1783, he received 3,000 acres for his three years in the Continental Army. In March 1786, Gist bought 780 acres in Buckingham County, and apparently made his home on this property, as he represented the county in the Virginia General Assembly in 1788. In 1792, for his military lands in Kentucky, Gist paid taxes on 4,000 acres in Bourbon County, 2,000 acres in Logan County, and 2,000 acres in Green County. At the time he owned 15 slaves, seven head of cattle, and 18 horses.[33]

In 1793 Gist moved to Kentucky, establishing a plantation named Canewood, on 3,000 acres in Clark County (carved from Bourbon and Fayette counties in 1792). He did not bring his family to Kentucky until the next year.[34] Nathaniel Gist died at Canewood in 1796 a the age of 63, and was buried there.[35]

Few men who lived at the time of the nation's founding can claim as illustrious an extended family as can Nathaniel Gist. In 1783 he married Judith Cary Bell, daughter of Archibald Cary — planter, industrialist, legislator, speaker of the Virginia Senate, and leading contributor to the Virginia Declaration of Rights. Gist was the father of the renowned Sequoyah and the grandfather of Francis Preston Blair, Jr. — Civil War general, senator, and Democratic vice-presidential candidate (1868). Both men are represented in Statuary Hall of the U.S. Capitol. Gist is the only person to have two descendants thus honored (Sequoyah–Oklahoma and Blair–Missouri). Four daughters of Nathaniel and Judith Gist had distinctive marriages: Anna Maria married rising politician Nathaniel G. S. Hart, who was killed at the Raisin River massacre (Battle of Frenchtown, January 22, 1812); Eliza Violet married Francis Preston Blair, Sr., a member of Andrew Jackson's Kitchen Cabinet; Sarah Howard married Jesse Bledsoe, Kentucky secretary of state and U.S. senator; and Maria Cecil married Benjamin Gratz, whose grandson was the Democratic candidate for vice-president in 1872; Maria's sister-in-law, Rebecca Gratz, was the model for the Jewish heroine in Sir Walter Scott's *Ivanhoe*.[36] In 1807 Gist's widow married General Charles Scott of Revolutionary War fame and governor of Kentucky (1808–12).

7. William Grayson

"His abilities equalled by a few; His integrity surpassed by none," was a fitting public appraisal of the life of William Grayson at the time of his death.[1] William

Grayson, a neighbor and frequent companion of George Washington in Virginia, performed at the highest level of leadership in the conduct of the war and afterwards in establishing the republic. During the war, in between serving as an aide to Washington and as a member of the Continental Board of War, he commanded an infantry regiment during three of the fiercest engagements. After the war, Grayson briefly served as acting president in the Confederation Congress, and also served as Virginia's first U.S. senator.

Grayson was regarded as one of the most handsome of the founding fathers. At over six feet tall and 250 pounds, with a broad forehead, black and deep-seated eyes, large and curved nose, white teeth, and a "fine complexion," he struck a "symmetry of figure" that exuded a balance between a democratic and aristocratic aura.[2]

The third son of four children of Benjamin Grayson, an immigrant Scottish merchant, and Susannah Monroe, William Grayson was born in 1736 at the family estate of Belle Air, overlooking the Potomac River near Dumfries, Virginia. One of the best educated among the founding fathers, Grayson matriculated at the College of Philadelphia (later the University of Pennsylvania) but did not graduate. Entering England in 1760 he later graduated from the University of Oxford, pursuing classical studies, and afterwards studied law at the Middle Temple, London. In 1765, back at Dumfries, Virginia, he established a law practice; on various occasions he had George Washington as a client.[3] Grayson married Eleanor Smallwood, sister of William Smallwood, Maryland general and governor.[4]

From the beginning of the revolutionary movement, William Grayson assumed an active role in protest against British authority. In February 1766 he joined 115 other Virginians of the Northern Neck in issuing a written denunciation of the Stamp Act.[5] An Independent Company of Cadets, formed in Prince William County on November 11, 1774, chose William Grayson as its captain and commander.[6] In 1775 Grayson was made a colonel in the Virginia militia. He and his troops performed guard duty along the shores of the lower Chesapeake Bay. He resigned his commission in March 1776.

Grayson began his Continental Army

***William Grayson.* Courtesy of the Library of Virginia.**

service by being appointed an assistant secretary to George Washington on June 21, 1776. He officially entered the army on August 24, 1776, as a lieutenant colonel in the Continental line and as an aide-de-camp to Washington, serving in the latter capacity until January 11, 1777.[7]

As an aide, Grayson was at Washington's side during the battles of Long Island, White Plains, Trenton, and Princeton.[8] On January 11, 1777, Grayson, as colonel, was given the command of one of 16 new regiments authorized by Congress; his unit became known as Grayson's Additional Regiment. Grayson's regiment was not fully recruited until summer 1777.[9] For the next year and a half Grayson's regiment was part of General Charles Scott's brigade. Grayson's troops participated in the battles of Brandywine and Germantown.[10] The regiment encamped at Valley Forge with the main army during winter 1778–79. While at Valley Forge, Grayson served as commissioner along with Alexander Hamilton, Robert H. Hanson, and Elias Boudinot, the commissary general of prisoners, to negotiate a prisoner exchange with General William Howe; the negotiations failed to accomplish a general exchange of prisoners, but did secure the release of General Charles Lee from British custody.[11] Because of his legal experience Grayson was Washington's favorite choice to preside over court martials.

William Grayson was in the thick of the Battle of Monmouth, but miraculously his troops came off relatively unscathed. Just before the battle, General Charles Lee dispatched Grayson, along with 600 men and Ebenezer Oswald's artillery battery, to annoy the rear of the marching British Army. Henry Jackson's detachment of 200 men joined with Grayson's force, all of whom were placed under the command of General Anthony Wayne. Grayson mainly took position in and around the "west morass," located between the Tennent Meetinghouse and a causeway. After some skirmishing, Grayson's men and other participating troops were neutralized by stop-and-go orders of General Lee. After Washington assumed for himself the direct command of troops in the battle, Grayson's men, posted on a hill overlooking the "west morass," were mostly spectators to an ongoing artillery duel.[12]

After the Battle of Monmouth, Grayson stayed with Washington's army until April 22, 1779, when his regiment was incorporated into Nathaniel Gist's Additional Regiment, and Grayson, without command, was retained only as a supernumerary.[13] From December 7, 1779, to September 1781 Grayson was a member of the Congressional Board of War.[14]

While the Board of War had no authority from Congress to engage in independent policy formation, it served a useful purpose in presiding over most logistical aspects of the Continental Army, military appointments, recruiting, and frontier defense.[15] Several months before assuming duties in the war office, Grayson had a close scare in what is known as the "Fort Wilson Riot" of October 1779, when a "most furious mob of several hundred persons" marched on the Philadelphia home of James Wilson. Grayson, caught in the midst of the fracas, would have been "torn to pieces" had not city militia rescued him. Grayson then helped arrest some of the leaders, which had the effect of quelling the disturbance.[16]

After leaving the Board of War, Grayson returned to Dumfries to practice law. He served in the Virginia House of Delegates 1784 to 1785, and was member of the Confederation Congress from 1785 to 1787. In Congress Grayson served on the committee that drafted the Ordinance of 1785. He had a hand in adopting the New England process for settlement—a land acquisition that was democratic, yet paved the way for land speculation.[17]

As acting president of the Congress, Grayson pushed for passage of the Northwest Ordinance of 1787, and was instrumental in securing for that document an anti-slavery clause. It was not that Grayson was an anti-slavery activist but that he wanted to prevent the midwest from emerging as a competitor to Virginia for the tobacco market.[18]

In the Congress Grayson opposed giving the national government authority to effectively regulate trade, for fear this would enhance the already overreaching power of the northern states. He derided northerners for allowing the proposed Jay-Gardoqui Treaty between the United States and Spain to exclude provision for opening the Mississippi for free navigation.[19] Grayson voted for Congress to send troops under General Josiah Harmar to provide defense in the Ohio country.[20] He represented Virginia on the Committee of the States, which consisted of one member from each state to fulfill the perfunctory duties of Congress during intervals between sessions.[21]

Grayson's health began to fail. He suffered intensely from gout. The first major attack occurred in July 1786. James Monroe wrote James Madison that Grayson had "an extraordinary disease—the physicians differ in name—he is often delirious, is afflicted with strange fancies and apprehensions. The disease is supposed by some to be floating gout. Shippen calls it a bilious affection of the nerves." The "laborious exercise of the mind" and the "very close attention" he gave to his congressional service, Monroe pointed out, was the cause.[22]

William Grayson's splendid education was put to use during his legislative tenure and especially as a delegate to the Virginia Ratifying Convention of June 1788. As author Hugh Grigsby declared, from his study at Oxford Grayson not only acquired "a correct knowledge" of Greek and Latin and science, but also, from delving into English literature and history, an "excellence" in "conversational debates" and "speeches at the bar and in public bodies."[23]

At the convention Grayson "warmly opposed" adoption of the Constitution. He felt that the Articles of Confederation offered greater protection to southern interests than did the Constitution. That the northern states had already showed willingness to give up rights to navigation on the Mississippi was evidence enough that seven northern states would seek measures "to oppress the rest of the Union." The treaty-making power of the Senate should require a greater majority vote than two-thirds. Grayson also thought there was need for a bill of rights amendment and restraining federal taxation and the reach of a national judiciary. In alliance with Patrick Henry, James Monroe, and other anti–Federalists, Grayson made numerous speeches at the convention. Grayson warned his fellow convention delegates, "We are yet too young to know what we are fit for" and that the Constitution was "too weak for a consolidated and too strong for a confederate government."[24]

On November 8, 1788, the Virginia legislature chose its first U.S. senators. Of three candidates—James Madison, Richard Henry Lee, and William Grayson—the latter two, nominated by Patrick Henry, were elected, indicating the anti–Federalist preference. Grayson began attendance in the Senate on May 21, 1789, and returned home upon adjournment, September 29, 1789.[25] During his brief tenure in the new Congress Grayson most notably worked unsuccessfully for the submission of all the Virginia amendments to the states and led the fight against passage of the Judiciary Act.[26]

William Grayson died at the home of his brother, the Rev. Spence Grayson, in Dumfries on March 12, 1790.[27] At the time of his death he owned 102,000 acres in Kentucky. In 1793, Grayson County, Virginia, was named after him.[28]

During the war, William Grayson proved his military merit more in administration than in the field, where he had little opportunity to draw attention. During the latter part of his life he is said to have characterized a "search of that perfect balance between power and liberty." Although he opposed centralization, he supported the new government.[29]

8. William Heth

William Heth's military experience was rather unique: he started the war as a lieutenant in a rifle company, immediately lost an eye, but rose quickly through the ranks of colonel and regimental commander. He served two long stints as a prisoner of war. As ambitious as he was courageous, Heth inspired either intense antipathy or admiration from colleagues. He did not hesitate to cast aspersion on the competence of superior officers.

Born in Pennsylvania on July 19, 1750, the eldest of 12 siblings, Heth grew up in the vicinity of Winchester, Virginia, then on the colony's middle-western frontier. His parents were John and Mary Mackey Heth, who had emigrated from Northern Ireland.[1] Nothing is known of Heth's youth, although it is evident he had some formal education from his facility for written expression.

At age 24, Heth was initiated into military service as a second lieutenant in a rifle company formed by Daniel Morgan from militia of Frederick County for a purpose to go out and fight the Indians in the so-called Dunmore's War of 1774. This conflict had resulted from the accelerating terrorism between Ohio Country Indians and ruthless frontiersmen. Two columns of Virginia militia went into the upper Ohio River area — one led by Colonel Andrew Lewis of Southwestern Virginians, which eventually fought the Indians at the Battle of Point Pleasant along the Ohio River on October 10, 1774, and the other conducted by Governor Lord Dunmore, which veered more northerly and was poised to enter the Ohio Valley via Pittsburgh. Heth served with Dunmore, and hence avoided the battle. Both Lewis and Dunmore's divisions united to conclude a treaty with the Indians at the army's forward camp at Fort Gower.[2]

Heth was ill when he returned to Winchester, Virginia, from the Indian expedition. Eventually he was awarded, 7,777 acres for his military service.[3]

With the Revolutionary War breaking out, Heth, again as a second lieutenant, joined Daniel Morgan's rifle company of 96 men and set out for Washington's army at Cambridge, Massachusetts. Arriving there on August 6, hardly a month passed when the new company was attached to a force of 600 men commanded by Benedict Arnold, and were on their way to participate in the invasion of Canada. In their long trek through the Maine wilderness, provisions ran out, and Arnold's troops had to eat their dogs. More than one-third of Arnold's men died before reaching Point Levi, located across the St. Lawrence River from Quebec, the point of rendezvous for linking up with a force from Montreal led by General Richard Montgomery.[4] Once across the river the American troops could attack the Lower Town or move further up the river, following the path of General James Wolfe's victory of 1759.

On the way to Quebec, a Pennsylvania private observed what he considered a humorous incident. Lt. Heth, who "seemed to think all others were inferior" to Virginians, was apparently at one time assigned to the lead boat as the army flotilla passed through several ponds and a lake. The private and his companions came up to Heth and decided "to push him." They "went up" to Heth " with much force; poor Heath [sic] labouring like a slave to keep his place." The mischievous volunteers were giddy that "at the moment of our passing (for we went up on the outside of him, towards the middle of the current,) his pole stuck, upon which he gave us a few hearty curses."[5]

Heth participated in the ill-fated assault on

William Heth. **Courtesy of the Library of Virginia.**

Quebec on December 31, 1775. He was among the men led by Daniel Morgan who went over the protective wall of the Lower Town. Once inside the city, the attackers became trapped in the narrow streets and had to surrender. One of the problems the Americans faced was that their rifles and muskets were too wet to fire.[6]

During the fighting Heth exhibited uncommon bravery. Sergeant Charley Porterfield noted that Heth "distinguished himself, running through the streets in the course of his duty, when almost every man had gotten into the houses."[7] Heth was wounded in the right eye, which left him blinded in that eye.[8]

Four hundred of the invading troops were made prisoners of war. Morgan, Heth, and other officers were incarcerated at the Seminary in the Upper Town, and the enlisted men were put up at the Jesuit College and then at the City Jail. Heth kept a diary, chronicling the lighter side of imprisonment. There were plenty of cards and other games, congeniality with the British officers, and strolls in the garden.[9]

One time Heth noted his own playful side in his diary:

> The Glances we now & then have from the sparkling Black Eyes of the "*Bell Petit Madamoi-selles*" cannot avoid affecting in a very tender part.... Vanity got the better of discretion so far that last Sunday I riggd myself out in such a Brilliant manner, that I thought I could not but attract the Eyes of *any Lady* of Penetration or Taste — & I was determined — (if possible) — to support myself under the Consequences. — Upon the whole when I was fitted out am persuaded "*I cut such a figure*" ... I should have been pronounced a "*Wonderous fine Man*" ... having on a Tiny Short red Coat, turnd up with yellow reaching at the utmost not above an Inch below the wasteband of a pair of corded Breeckes, that was once white — but had seen better days — a pair of gingerly Shoes ... a close motiond white Vest ... a Neat cock'd Hat & Feather & an Epaolet (golden colored).... Thus equipt — I hung out at the windows Sunday & Monday — But what conquests I made are known only to the conquerd — It would be unnecessary to give other reasons for not joining them in a walk & playing the Gallant — than not being sufficiently acquainted with the French Language to keep up a Tete a Tete.[10]

At last, the officer prisoners were granted parole. Although boarding transports on August 10, Heth and the other officers did not disembark at New York City until September 24, 1776.[11] Heth was released from his parole when he was exchanged on November 13, 1776. Upon returning to the army, he was made a lieutenant colonel in the Third Virginia Regiment on April 1, 1777. In December he would be made acting commander of the Third Virginia Regiment, and on April 30, 1778, received a commission as full colonel.[12]

Stationed at Middlebrook during June 1777,[13] Heth found himself making what seemed like useless treks up and down New Jersey and into the New York Highlands west of the Hudson River. Somehow he grated on the nerves of some colleague officers, who were getting as impatient as he. Heth, the regiment's new lieutenant colonel, perhaps had his ego inflated by being regarded as a hero at Quebec and having won early promotions. Captain John Chilton of the Third Virginia Regiment became so exasperated with Heth that he considered leaving the army. Chilton wrote his brother:

We have one gentleman in our Regmt. A Col. Wm. Heth who takes great things to himself. Heth does not lack sense but is imperious to the last degree. I was never tired of the Service till he joined the Regmt. I have a small notion of joining the Sea Service. If I could have the command of some clever little Brig or vessel, for I have no notions of Colonels, they are too overbearing to inferior officers and remarkably mean and cringing to their superiors. Heth has greatly the ascendancy over [Thomas] Marshall [the regiment's commander], which I could not have believed. Anything clever done in the Regmt. Heth takes credit for it, what is not well done is thrown at Marshall. Which will sink his credit as Heth's rises.[14]

As Washington prepared to contest the march of the British army towards Philadelphia, he formed a light infantry corps under General William Maxwell, consisting of a selection from among the best soldiers from various units. This new group went to harass the British advance, while at the same time serially withdrawing until recrossing Brandywine Creek. Lt. Col. Heth and others from the Third Virginia Regiment were selected for this special duty.

On August 30, 1777, Washington ordered Maxwell's 800-man light infantry to move close to the British army and prepare to make a stand at Cooch's Bridge (Iron Mill). In a confrontation that lasted seven hours, Maxwell's men made persistent contact with the enemy, conducting a running fire from woods on the side of a road and withdrawing to the high ground in the vicinity of Cooch's Bridge. There the American light infantry held their own. A swamp around the hill prevented the enemy from attacking the rear of the American light infantry. Maxwell's troops, however, ran out of ammunition and few of them had bayonets. A British bayonet charge drove the American force down the hill. Maxwell's troops went into the only escape route, between Christiana Creek and the swamp; by discarding their firearms and blankets they managed to keep ahead of their British pursuers. The enemy gave up pursuit, and the Americans moved back several miles, setting up an advanced guard post at Red Clay Creek.[15]

The American light infantry rejoined Washington's army at Brandywine Creek. Soon, three detachments of the light infantry, one of which was led by William Heth, were sent to reconnoiter the approaches to Chadd's Ford and annoy British advance units. As the enemy came on, the light infantry fired a round or two and hastily retreated, successively pausing to repeat this function until finally withdrawing back across the Brandywine at Chadd's Ford. The American troops had only to contend with a detachment under General Wilhelm Knyphausen; the main British force would surprise Washington on his right flank.[16]

Meanwhile, without him, Heth's Third Regiment suffered the heaviest casualties of the battle fending off Cornwallis' troops on the American far right flank. As the American right was forced into retreat, Maxwell's light infantry and a division under Anthony Wayne held back the assault of Knyphausen's troops at Chadd's Ford. Eventually these units joined in the retreat, with the army in late evening crossing the Schuylkill River and encamping near Germantown.

The Battle of Brandywine stirred in Heth another personal animosity. He despised

General William Maxwell, a rather brusque, New Jersey farmer with a Scottish brogue, who for a decade before the war had served as a commissary to a British regiment on the far frontier. Heth filed against Maxwell "charges for Misconduct, and unofficer-like behavior."[17] In his diary, Heth declared that "Maxwell's Corps 'Twas expected would do great things — we had opportunities — and any body but an old woman, would have availd themselves of them — He is to be sure — a Damnd bitch of a General."[18]

Immediately after the Battle of Brandywine Heth rejoined his Third Virginia Regiment. He may have been at the Battle of Germantown on October 4, 1777, with other Virginians in Greene's column in Stephen's division. Although he wrote a brief account of the battle, he did not place himself in any part of the battle, and, therefore, it may be assumed that he played no significant role in the engagement. Interestingly, he did comment, "We gave away a complete victory." The enemy itself was retreating when the American force left the battlefield.[19]

On November 22, 1777, Heth is on record as serving on a general court martial[20]; there is no indication in the orderly books that he stayed with the army at Valley Forge. He probably went home on furlough as did most of the Virginia officers. In any event, he was probably back in April at the time of his promotion to full colonel and commander of the Third Virginia Regiment. Colonel Thomas Marshall had resigned this position in December 1777.

Heth's Third Virginia Regiment was with Washington's army at the Battle of Monmouth on June 28, 1778, but since it incurred no casualties it may be presumed it was among those troops the commander in chief held in reserve or only marginally entered into the action.[21] At the encampment at White Plains in November 1778, the Virginia Continental Line was re-arranged, with changes including the combination of the Fifth Regiment with Heth's Third.[22] 1779 was a year of relatively little action for the main army commanded by Washington, and all southern troops in the north on a staggered basis were sent to join forces with the Southern Army, then commanded by Benjamin Lincoln. Heth's Third Regiment went southward in the fall, and along with a detachment led by Richard Parker were posted at Augusta and vicinity. In December 1779 these troops linked up with Lincoln's main force preparing to withstand a siege by the British at Charleston.[23]

On April 1, 1780, the enemy began establishing their first parallel for the siege, then tightening the vise in stages. Finally Lincoln surrendered the city on May 12, 1780, and the American army of some 5,000 Continentals and militia were made prisoners of war. Militiamen were allowed to return to their homes. Continental enlisted men were put on prison ships in the harbor, and Heth and all the other captured officers were interned at Haddrell's Point (Mount Pleasant), five miles east of Charleston across the harbor). Eventually Heth and the other officers were allowed to go home on parole. Heth, however, remained in the status of prisoner of war until the end of the war.[24]

With the war over, Heth gave full attention to his farming interests. He lived at

Curles, a plantation just outside Richmond, Virginia, and maintained three other farms: Bremo and Shileta in Henrico County and Wales, in Dinwiddie County. Heth married, as his second wife, Eliza Briggs, and they had four children, as well as an adopted son.[25]

Heth remained a close friend of Daniel Morgan, and the two men planned to form a partnership to market flour in Alexandria, but the scheme never materialized.[26] Heth also maintained close contacts with other veterans by being an active member of the Society of the Cincinnati, formed in 1784 as a hereditary organization of former Revolutionary War officers and their direct descendants. Heth was a delegate to the formative meeting of the society in Philadelphia, and served as treasurer in its state chapter.[27]

Politics had some attraction for Heth, but he preferred to seek appointments to office rather than declare candidacy. In 1787 he was named to a three-year term as a member of the Virginia Council of State. His duties consisted largely of providing advice on constitutional issues and appointments to state office and examining state accounts.[28]

William Heth and David Henley were named by the Virginia government to join with John Pierce, the commissioner of army accounts appointed by Congress, to determine the amount of reimbursement due Virginia for expenses in providing defense of the frontier from the British and Indians during the war. George Rogers Clark's 1778-79 expedition into the Illinois country and the maintenance of western garrisons constituted most of the outlays. In the course of negotiations Heth traveled to the capital, New York City. His offer for a settlement of $500,000 was rejected by Congress as too excessive. Ironically, the sum that Virginia was asking was upped to $1,253,877 in 1791. This latter amount was included in Congress' eventual assumption of all Virginia's war debt —$28,000,000.[29]

Although not elected a member, William Heth, as one of the numerous spectators, attended the Virginia Convention for Ratifying the Constitution in Richmond in June 1788. He left a diary of his impressions of the debates during 20 of the 23 days of the session. Of the moment of the final count of 89–79 members in favor of the Constitution, he commented that "the scene was truly awful & solemn."[30]

George Washington, among his first actions as president, bestowed on Heth the collectorship of the ports of Richmond, Petersburg, and Bermuda Hundred, Virginia. Heth could be as abrasive in the customs service as he had been regarding colleague officers during the war. Alexander McDonald complained to Thomas Jefferson in March 1790, "I received the most abusive letter from Colo. Heth I ever saw, and this is the more surprising, that I never spoke ten words to the man in my life."[31] McDonald pointed out to Jefferson "the notoriety of Mr. Heth's conduct" regarding a person as a non–U.S. citizen while in actuality the person was a citizen. Heth's designation thus meant that the person alluded to had his ship and goods discriminated against in the entry into a Virginia port. Heth's "Pique and Malice" made him "an inveterate enemy" of McDonald, who considered challenging Heth to a duel, but then decided against it.[32]

Heth, a staunch Federalist, ardently supported the presidencies of George Washington and John Adams. He disliked Thomas Jefferson, and so irritated that statesman in writing poetry that cast aspersion on Jefferson's character that Jefferson's supporters saw to it that Heth's collectorship was divided and reduced. Heth resigned from his collectorship in 1802.[33]

William Heth died suddenly from apoplexy sometime during the first week of April 1807. Despite a propensity for arousing personal enmity towards himself, the one-eyed hero was well regarded. His home in Henrico County frequently received guests and visitors. Heth's will mentioned a son, Henry G. (who drowned in a boating accident in 1816), daughters Mary Andrewetta, Ann Eliza Agnes Pleasants, and Margaret Thomas Jacquelin Heth, and an adopted son, William H. Heth. Heth's widow married Lightfoot Janney.[34]

9. Josiah Parker

Similar to other officers of the Revolutionary War, Josiah Parker had a dual military career. Known for his impulsiveness, he resigned from the army in 1778, in part because he was denied a furlough. He distinguished himself in combat in the Continental Army. In 1780 he surfaced again in military command of Virginia militia for defense against the British invasions of the state.

Josiah Parker was the son of Nicholas and Anne Copeland Parker. Born on May 11, 1751, Josiah Parker grew up on the family plantation of Macclesfield on the James River in Isle of Wight County, near Williamsburg. Nothing is known of his childhood or education. In 1773, Parker married Mary Pierce Bridger, widow of Colonel Joseph Bridger. They had two daughters, only one living to maturity. The marriage brought Parker "an enormous estate."[1] Besides being an agriculturalist, Parker partially owned several merchant ships and traded in the European market.

At age 23, Parker was elected to the Second Virginia Convention that convened in March 1775, and subsequently also to the Third, Fourth, and Fifth conventions. His most significant role in the convention was to join with George Mason in drawing up "an ordinance for a general test." The convention, however, was reluctant to pass a loyalty oath and the matter was postponed; not until May 1777 did the Virginia legislature enact a law to require all free male inhabitants to swear an oath of allegiance.[2] Military service intervened, which prevented Parker from attending the later convention sessions.

Around December 1, 1775, Parker joined an embodied militia force commanded by Colonel William Woodford. In early December he was a part of a detachment stationed at Smithfield,[3] and probably was not at Woodford's fight with the governor's little army at the Battle of Great Bridge on December 9. Appointed major in the Fifth Virginia Regiment on February 13, 1776, Parker served under Charles Lee and then under Andrew Lewis in helping to drive Dunmore's force out of Virginia, and then he and his unit were transferred to the main Continental Army, hooking up with Washington's troops at New Brunswick as they retreated across New Jersey.[4] Parker was now a lieutenant colonel (as of August 13, 1776) and was second in command of Colonel Charles Scott's Fifth Virginia Regiment.[5]

On the Pennington Road above Trenton, New Jersey, on December 26, 1776, Lt. Col. Josiah Parker and the rest of Charles Scott's Fifth Virginia Regiment in Adam Stephen's brigade started the Battle of Trenton by assaulting a Hessian outpost. The enemy, caught by surprise, hastily turned out in the streets of the town, but with a snowstorm beating in their faces much of their ammunition was too wet fire; there was some exchange of arms fire, however, which lasted for about an hour, until the Hessian colors were struck, signifying surrender. Parker had the honor of receiving the sword of the mortally wounded commander of the garrison, Johann Gottlieb Rall.[6]

The Capture of the Hessians at Trenton, December 26, 1776. **By John Trumbull. Standing, at far left, in white, is Josiah Parker: at far right, with bandaged hand, is William Washington. Courtesy of Yale University Art Gallery, Trumbull Collection.**

Of the 1,586 Hessians in Trenton, 918 surrendered, while the rest made their escape. Washington's army crossed the Delaware River back into Pennsylvania, and on December 30 re-crossed the river to Trenton, encamping on the hills above the town. On January 2, 1777, the Fifth Virginia Regiment and other units contested a march of British troops coming down the ten miles from Princeton. The Americans harassed the oncoming troops under General Cornwallis and fell back into Trenton and across the Assunpink Bridge to safety among Washington's army. Cornwallis elected to withhold further attack until the next morning, at which time he discovered that Washington's army had vanished and were heading to Princeton to engage the British troops left behind there.[7] After the Battle of Princeton, January 3, 1777, Washington's army headed for winter encampment at Morristown.

While the army encamped at Morristown, Parker and the Fifth Virginia Regiment performed screening duty from the outer lines. On January 23, near Woodbridge, Parker led an "advanced party" ahead of a 400-man detachment commanded by Colonel Mordecai Buckner who were sent out to attack a wagon convoy guarded by 500 British troops on their way from New Brunswick to Amboy. Parker and his forward party fought with the enemy for 20 minutes, expecting assistance immediately from Buckner's detachment. Only about half of Buckner's men came up, and Buckner inexplicably fled the scene. Had Parker and his troops gained the full reinforcement, "we should have put them to the rout, as their confusions was very great and their ground disadvantageous."[8]

At the Battle of Brandywine, Parker served in General William Maxwell's light infantry which prodded the oncoming British army. On the morning of the battle, September 11, Maxwell placed three small detachments of Virginia troops along the road just beyond Chadd's Ford to harass the British van. Parker commanded one of the detachments, Colonel William Heth and Major Charles Simms the other two. With the British army coming on in force beginning at daybreak, these Virginia light infantrymen, as instructed, fired one round at the enemy and then retreated a certain distance and repeated the same until recrossing Brandywine Creek to the heights above Chadd's Ford, where they later engaged troops under Wilhelm Knyphausen before again retreating. One unnamed general reported in a Virginia newspaper two weeks after the battle that "Col. Josiah Parker behaved like a hero."[9]

While fighting in Greene's division at the Battle of Germantown on October 4, Parker was wounded, but not seriously.[10] In November he was able to take charge of a brigade "on command" duty in New Jersey. In early December he went home on furlough.[11]

Feeling the pressure to attend to plantation and business matters and unhappy in being unable to receive an extended furlough, Parker resigned from the Continental Army on July 12, 1778.[12] With his own privateers, Parker commented that "my business is mostly at sea."[13]

The war came close to home for Parker. Living at the upper rim of the Tidewater region, he witnessed five British invasions of Virginia: Collier-Mathew, May 1779; Alexander Leslie, October 1780; Benedict Arnold, January to March 1781; William Phillips, April 1781; and Cornwallis, May to October 1781. During the Collier-Mathew incursion, Parker refused to accept command of Virginia militia in the field, although he acted as a volunteer under Colonel Robert Lawson, who was given the command.[14] Similarly, when General Alexander Leslie, who was leading a reinforcement for Cornwallis' army in the Carolinas, stopped for several weeks to commit depredations in Virginia's lower Tidewater area, Parker was asked by Governor Jefferson to command militia in the field "to expel the invading enemy from among us."[15] It is not known whether Parker was prepared to accept this offer during the short-lived emergency.

With Benedict Arnold's invasion of January 1781, all the militia of certain counties south of the James River were placed under the command of Josiah Parker; the troops came from the counties of Isle of Wight, Nansemond, Princess Anne, and Norfolk. This appointment was made by General Steuben, who at the time was in charge of all American troops in Virginia. Parker could "arrange, officer and regiment" the militia under his command "as he may think fit."[16] Parker was also expected "to embody a troop of militia cavalry."[17]

Arnold's force, which invaded central Virginia, boarded transport ships on January 10 and headed back down the river. Reaching Isle of Wight County on January 15, Arnold and his troops disembarked and trekked southward toward Portsmouth. Just outside Smithfield, at Mackie's Mill on Cypress Creek, Parker, with 200 men and two cannons, contested the march. Arnold sent a detachment of Queen's Rangers and Hessians to attack Parker frontally while the Eightieth Regiment went downstream to assault Parker's flank and rear. The Virginians were able to stand their ground briefly, but then fled. A Hessian report noted that Parker lost 11 men dead, eight wounded, and nine men made prisoners. The British detachment loss three killed and five wounded.[18]

At Portsmouth Arnold kept his troops immobile until the arrival of a large reinforcement under General William Phillips from New York. In April the combined forces of Arnold and Phillips invaded central Virginia, eventually becoming stalled at Petersburg. Parker's militia helped to checkmate the British troops left behind at Portsmouth.

The final stage of the British invasions of Virginia began when Cornwallis' army from the Carolinas linked up with the Phillips-Arnold force at Petersburg on May 20 (Phillips had died on May 13). It was clear that Cornwallis, now in charge of all of the invading army, would seek to scour central Virginia for supplies and hopefully engage the smaller-in-size American army in the state, now commanded by Lafayette. During this emergency Governor Thomas Nelson ordered Parker to call out militia from the southeastern Virginia counties of Isle of Wight, Nansemond, Norfolk, Princess Anne, and Surry. Again Parker could "arrange" the militia as he thought necessary.[19]

Staying in the lower Tidewater region, Parker operated separately from Lafayette's army. He faced the possibility of facing detachments spun off from Cornwallis' force or sent out from Portsmouth. As it was, Lt. Col. Banastre Tarleton's dreaded dragoons were sent on raids westward and could follow up this activity with raids southeastward. Indeed, Tarleton's dragoons visited Parker's plantation of Macclesfield, but did no real damage there.[20] Lafayette advised Parker that "you are acting the partisan, with a handful of men against a large army, and will, of course, be directed by the principles which govern such corps."[21] With Cornwallis' whole army heading southward toward Portsmouth after the Battle of Green Spring on July 6, Parker's situation became more dangerous. Although he did not have a commission from the Virginia government, in effect Parker was acting as a brigade commander. Other militia officers endorsed Parker as de facto commander out of deference to Parker having served with distinction as a field officer in the Continental Army.[22] Parker went by the title "acting colonel, commanding."[23]

On August 18 the British evacuated Portsmouth, and the next day at 5 A.M. Parker and his militia occupied the town. He successfully restrained his troops from plundering. Parker reported that "the town of Portsmouth is a mere heap of rubish & what remained of Norfolk is very little better"; moreover "a Number of Negroes are left dead & dying with the Smallpox."[24]

By the end of August 1781 Parker had exhausted himself. He was suffering from "a monstrous cold" and generally "very unwell." He had slept with his "coat, Hat & Boots" on since Cornwallis had dropped down the James and all the while the British Army was at Portsmouth before going over to Yorktown.[25] He was unhappy with Governor Jefferson's proclamation that British sympathizers be sent behind British lines and refused to enforce it on grounds that such persons would be useful to the enemy. Actually, Parker favored sending Loyalist-prone citizens into the western country. He did not like the lack of cooperation from both the civilian population and the Virginia government. Too often he had to use force to secure supplies. Moreover, the government did little to implement recruitment.[26]

Parker continued to command militia at the Portsmouth and Smithfield sector on the eve of the allied siege of Yorktown. He was ill and expressed to Lafayette an intention to leave the service and journey to France to take care of some business affairs.[27] It is reasonable to conclude that Parker left military service at this time. Although he quit the field, Parker still had a hand in contributing to the war effort. Three privateers, of which Parker was half owner, were active in plundering merchant ships, blockade running, and patrolling in the Chesapeake Bay and along the Atlantic coast. These ships were the brigantine *Governor Nelson*, with 12 carriage guns and 40 men; the *Intrepid*, with one carriage gun, six swivel guns, and 35 men; and the *Swift*, a whaleboat with one carriage gun and 30 men.[28]

After the war, Parker gave attention to public affairs in addition to plantation management and trade. He served as a member of the House of Delegates from 1778 to

1779 and from 1782 to 1783.[29] He was a justice of the peace for Isle of Wight County 1783 to 1797, 1799 to 1801, and 1806 to 1809.[30] He served as a trustee for the Uzell Methodist Church,[31] and during the 1790s for the Pennsylvania Society for Promoting the Abolition of Slavery.[32]

Parker served as the naval officer for the Port of Norfolk, 1786 to 1788, resigning to take his seat in the U.S. House of Representatives. He had the reputation, along with other Virginia naval officers, of not paying strict attention to the state's laws for regulating trade.[33]

As an Anti-Federalist supporter of Patrick Henry, Parker opposed ratification of the Constitution. He ran unsuccessfully as a candidate for membership of the Virginia Ratifying Convention of the Constitution in 1788.[34]

Elected to Congress in 1789, Parker served until 1801. He chaired the naval committee. He changed from representing the Republican interest to representing the Federalist interest. Parker voted against Hamilton's excise liquor tax, incorporation of the Bank of the U.S., creation of the State Department, reduction of the army, and appropriations for the Jay Treaty.[35] He supported the location of the seat of the federal government on the Potomac River.[36]

Parker was a member of the Democratic Society (pro–Jefferson Republican) in Virginia, and helped to legitimize it in the state. He voted against Thomas Jefferson for president in the House of Representatives during the disputed election of 1800.[37]

The fighting colonel of the Continental Army and state militia died at his home, Macclesfield, on March 10, 1810. No marker on his grave on the estate survived, and hence the site is lost.[38]

10. Richard Parker

The branches of the Parker family in Virginia gave full measure in the cause for independence, providing at least 22 Continental and militia officers.[1] One of the youngest men to became a full colonel was killed in action at the age 28 — Richard Parker, Jr. Henry "Light-Horse Harry" Lee said of him:

> He was one of that illustrious band of youths who first flew to their country's standard when she was driven to unsheath the sword. Stout and intelligent, brave and enterprising, he had been advanced from the command of a company in the course of the war to the command of a regiment. Always beloved and respected, late in the siege [of Charleston] he received a ball in the forehead, and fell dead in the trenches, embalmed in the tears of his faithful soldiers, and honored by the regret of the whole army.[2]

Born in 1752 at Lawfield in Westmoreland County, he was the eldest of five sons of Richard Parker, Sr. The elder Parker, one of the wealthiest men in Virginia, was king's attorney for Westmoreland County (and after the war, a judge); he joined the independence movement early on and served on the county Committee of Safety, 1775–76.

Richard Parker, Jr., entered the war as a captain in the Second Virginia Regiment on September 28, 1775. He was probably among Colonel William Woodford's troops at the Battle of Great Bridge, December 9, 1775. Woodford, the acting commander of Virginia forces in the field, appointed Parker brigade major.[3]

During most of 1776 Richard Parker and other Virginia troops kept up pressure on Governor Lord Dunmore's little flotilla of ships carrying sailors and soldiers as they jockeyed for position in the lower James River and Chesapeake Bay. With General Charles Lee in command of all Virginia forces at the time, Captain Parker, Major Josiah Parker (no immediate relative), and Major Robert Lawson, led 40 men to try and set fire to some of Dunmore's ships. They were unsuccessful because a spy for the governor uncovered the plot. But the mission proceeded far enough for Parker and his associates to row out in small boats ready to border the enemy vessels. During this time Captain Parker inquired what should be done if they encountered any Tories. "Damn them!" Major Josiah Parker shouted. "Tomahawk Them all and throw them over Board, and give yourself no further trouble about them." If the testimony of the spy is to be believed, the raiding party, failing in their mission, upon their return "Shot a Negro going a Shore in a Canoe with a bottle of rum, which they drank to his health as he was expiring." The two Parkers and rebel troops were more successful in bringing about the evacuation of Portsmouth, as ordered by General Lee, according to the Virginia Committee of Safety's Resolution of April 10. A number of houses in the town belonging to notorious Tories "were totally demolished."[4]

With Dunmore and his royals finally driven out of Virginia, Richard Parker found himself promoted to major in August 1776 and transferred to the Sixth Virginia Regiment, which was taken into Continental service along with other Virginia regiments.[5] Although he joined Washington's army just in time for the Battle of Trenton, nothing specific is known of his participation in that affair.

At the so-called Second Battle of Trenton, January 2, 1777, Parker was assigned to help cover the retreat of an American detachment that was sent out to dispute the advance of Cornwallis' army along the Princeton Road towards Trenton. He was charged especially to defend the bridge over the Assunpink Creek (above which the American army had taken position after again recrossing the Delaware River to the New Jersey side) "to the last extremity." Parker allegedly told his commander in chief, "Sir, we intend to sleep on it."[6] The American forward troops made it safely back to the main army, which during the night stole away to fight the rear guard of Cornwallis' army at Princeton. Parker undoubtedly was also in that engagement and then went with the army to winter cantonment at Morristown. On February 10, 1777, Parker was promoted to lieutenant colonel.[7]

In late August of 1777, Washington received word at Wilmington, Delaware, that the enemy had disembarked at Head of Elk, Maryland, at the northern tip of Chesapeake Bay, and evidently were preparing to march on Philadelphia. Parker was one of 800 select troops the commander in chief appointed as a "temporary establishment" of light infantry to act as a screening force against the advancing enemy. General William Maxwell commanded this special unit.[8] These troops performed admirably up to the Battle of Brandywine, harassing the van of the enemy, and during the engagement itself absorbed some of the shock of the oncoming Hessians at Chadd's Ford.[9]

Parker and his First Virginia Regiment were in Weedon's brigade in Greene's division as they (having taken a circuitous route) made a tardy entrance into the Battle of Germantown on October 4, 1777. But once into the fighting, these troops pushed the enemy back two miles. A "horrid fog," along with other factors, led to confusion and hampered any success, with a general retreat the eventual result. General Weedon noted, however, that "our men behaved with the Greatest intrepidity for three hours."[10] Afterwards, Parker stayed with the army at Valley Forge during winter and spring, and was promoted to colonel and commander of the First Virginia Regiment on February 10, 1778.[11]

After the British evacuated Philadelphia and were marching across New Jersey, Parker and his regiment were among a 5,000-man detached force under General Charles Lee, assigned to attack the enemy's rear while the main army "followed in supporting distance." Lee's troops made contact, but unexpectedly the enemy turned about in defense, which caused Lee to order a retreat instead of a charge. Lee's force was driven "back upon the main army in confusion." Washington then came forward with his troops and ordered most of Lee's force to the rear.[12] Parker and his First Regiment, however, remained with Washington's troops. Both the Americans and the British halted to establish firm positions. A severe cannonade between both sides proceeded for several hours. Then some of "our Infantry began to advance." A select "corps" primarily carried on this action; in late afternoon a party of 650 men were dispatched to cross a morass and attack the enemy's right flank. This special detachment of Americans, consisting of 400 men under Colonel Joseph Cilley and 250 men under Colonel Richard Parker, "were within 100 yards of the Enemy before they were discovered; they immediately directed their fire so well & so briskly that the British & Royal Highlanders were obliged to show their backs."[13]

After the Battle of Monmouth the British shifted the war to a southern strategy. On November 27, 1778, Lt. Col. Archibald Campbell left New York with 3,500 troops. Arriving at the mouth of the Savannah River on December 23, this expedition moved up the river and captured Savannah on December 29. In January General Augustine Prevost led British troops up the coast from Florida and assumed command of British military operations in the South.[14] To counter this development, Washington was compelled to send that part of his army from the southern states to reinforce the new Southern Army, commanded from 1779 until 1780 by General Benjamin Lincoln.

On May 7, 1779, the commander in chief ordered Colonel Richard Parker and his First Virginia Regiment southward to link up with General Charles Scott's brigade in Virginia. These troops were delayed in completing the journey southward because of a brief invasion of the Tidewater region of the state by British troops and then by difficulty in securing sufficient supplies and recruits. Furthermore, some of the Virginia regiments were held up, remaining with Washington's army until December 1779. At last, by the end of June, Richard Parker and his regiment of 400 men started their march southward from Virginia. By mid–August this unit was encamped at Augusta, and on September 14 they joined Lincoln's army at Ebenezer near Savannah, which was garrisoned by British troops. Parker's regiment was brigaded with a South Carolina Continental regiment and three South Carolina militia regiments. This brigade connected with Lincoln's army, which now had also linked up with a French marine-land force under Admiral Charles comte de d'Estaing. On September 23 these allies began a siege of Savannah. Bad weather and logistical problems impeded the siege operations, and the siege was called off in favor of storming the garrison. The full French-American attack came on October 9. Parker and his regiment were involved in the main assault, occurring at the Spring-Hill (or Ebenezer Road) redoubt, which had the added protection of formidable earthworks on its right flank. The assault failed, causing 450 casualties; three of Parker's officers were wounded.[15]

After the disaster at Savannah, Lincoln's army went to Charleston, and d'Estaing took his naval force to the West Indies. Parker and his regiment went back to Augusta, where they stayed until Lincoln summoned them to Charleston. For the Augusta stay, the Georgia Executive Council voted a resolution of gratitude to Parker for his "respectful deportment towards the civil authority; the good order in which he has kept the Troops under his Command and for his unremitted services in defence of the State."[16]

General Henry Clinton, with a flotilla of transports bearing 3,000 troops, landed on the South Carolina coast in early February 1780 and in late March encamped several miles from Charleston. The British general determined to capture Charleston by standard siege tactics. On April 1, Clinton's army advanced and established the first parallel, which reached across the Charleston peninsula, 600 to 1,000 yards from the American lines.[17] General Benjamin Lincoln, chose to defend the city, and, with the arrival of Parker and William Heth's two Virginia regiments and the rest of General Charles Scott's brigade, had about 5,000 troops (2,200 of whom were regulars and the rest, militia.)[18]

Until the arrival of General Scott in Charleston in April, Colonel Richard Parker was placed in charge of a brigade consisting of the two Virginia regiments and a North Carolina regiment.[19] Parker's brigade was assigned to "garrison & keep up a sufficient guard at the Half Moon Battery, placing the necessary sentries within the abatis, so as to secure most effectually that part of the lines."[20] The men at the Half Moon Battery were there to essentially control the left part of the lines bordering the Ashley River; the lines included both a canal dug by the Americans and two rows of abatis.[21] Besides regular duty for Parker's men, there was occasionally an odd fatigue assignment. On March 29, 100 soldiers from Parker's brigade were ordered to "patrol the several streets & alleys in the town, & kill all the dogs they shall find. They shall destroy them in any way whatever, saving that of shooting"; for this task a soldier would receive one dollar for each dog they killed.[22]

As the British pushed closer to the city, duty on the American lines became increasingly hazardous. By April 21 the enemy had begun their third parallel, now so close to the American defenses that small arms fire could easily take out targets peering over the American works. Actually, as a Hessian officer noted, most American soldiers killed during the siege were shot by rifle bullets.[23]

On the evening of April 24 at about 8 P.M., while directing grapeshot fire upon a nearby enemy working party, Richard Parker leaned over from an opening on the parapet at Half Moon redoubt, and was instantly struck in the forehead by a rifle ball. He tumbled over into the ditch below.[24]

11. Charles "Charley" Porterfield

The young lieutenant colonel, a lifelong bachelor, from Virginia's Shenandoah Valley, mortally wounded at the battle of Camden, was one of the most respected officers of the Revolutionary War. Charles Porterfield performed heroically in the northern army, Washington's main army, and in an activated Virginia state regiment. Of Porterfield, Washington said that he was "universally esteemed by his acquaintances in the Army, as an Officer of very extraordinary Merit."[1]

Born in 1750 in Frederick County, Virginia, nothing is known of his early life. His father, Charles Porterfield, and family were of Scotch-Irish stock and migrated into the valley from Pennsylvania. Charles Porterfield the younger must have been of some means since he would equip a rifle company at his own expense. Porterfield was very close to a younger brother, Robert, who also distinguished himself in military service and was made a prisoner of war at Charleston in May 1780.[2]

On June 22, 1775, the Frederick County Committee of Safety appointed Daniel Morgan to raise a rifle company. Morgan quickly enlisted 96 men from Winchester and vicinity. Included among the recruits was Charles Porterfield, a man known for few words and described as being 6'2" and 210 pounds, "round limbed and fleshy, but not corpulent."[3] Evidently, he had a reputation as an expert marksman because of his selection in the frontier rifle company. Porterfield signed on as a cadet. A cadet carried no official rank, and was regarded as an "officer in training."[4] A cadet was considered below an ensign or lieutenant, and this explains why during his early military career Porterfield was referred to as Sergeant Porterfield.

On July 14, 1775, Porterfield and Morgan's troops departed Winchester to join Washington's Continental Army outside of Boston. On August 6, 1775, the new Continental riflemen arrived at Washington's headquarters at Cambridge. Porterfield had come to the main army just in time to be included in an invasion of Canada. General Orders for September 5 authorized the forming of a detachment of nearly 800 men to be commanded by Colonel Benedict Arnold for an ascent to Quebec, where they would be joined by troops coming from further up the St. Lawrence led by General Richard Montgomery. Morgan's riflemen and two similar companies from Pennsylvania formed the core of Arnold's expeditionary force. The march to Quebec exhibited terrible suffering; one writer notes that "no army known to the annals of ancient and modern warfare was ever subjected to such misery."[5] The group traveled through tangled forests, swamps, mountains, and snow. Provisions ran out. One-third of Arnold's men died on the way.[6]

At last, the would-be attackers reached the vicinity of Quebec, and during a snow storm of December 31, just before dawn, they began scaling the walls of the Lower Town of the city. Porterfield noted that "if there was any honor in being first over the barrier, I had it." The rebels captured some 30 men from the defending guards, but valuable time was lost with Arnold's force being drawn up in parade formation. With daylight appearing, a British reinforcement arrived, and the Americans huddled together in the narrow streets were easy prey for musketry and cannon fire. The only choice was to surrender. Only 26 of Morgan's riflemen survived the affair. In another quarter of the attack General Montgomery was killed and his men withdrew.[7]

The American captives remained prisoners of war for eight months. They enjoyed rather compassionate treatment from their captors and were relegated to the fourth story of the Seminary of Laval, where they had access to the adjacent gardens. "Sergeant" Charles Porterfield kept a diary for the period of March 3 to July 10, 1776; there is little of interest recorded concerning the actual experiences of the prisoners of war.[8] Porterfield and the officers were released on parole in August 1776, and, boarding transports, were sent to New York Harbor, debarking at Elizabethtown, New Jersey, on September 24. The prisoners gained their complete freedom by exchange in January 1777. Porterfield spent the period of his parole at his home in Virginia.[9]

Charles Porterfield returned to field duty as captain in the Eleventh Virginia Regiment in February 1777. To obtain his commission he had to recruit 28 men. Porterfield's former close associate, Daniel Morgan, commanded the new regiment. By April 1777

Porterfield and his comrades had rejoined Washington's army in New Jersey.[10] He had the honor to be selected to command a company of a specially constituted light infantry corps, commanded by General William Maxwell, who were employed to harass the British army as it marched on Philadelphia during the first week of September 1777.

With Washington's army poised on September 3 along Brandywine Creek, the light infantry was ordered to cross the creek and move closely as possible to the oncoming British army. Participating in several skirmishes from the cover of woods, Maxwell's force slowly withdrew to high ground at Cooch's Bridge (Iron Mill). Making a stand for a while on the hill, with the enemy preparing to surround them, the American troops managed to extricate themselves. As they retreated they paused to return fire, made it to a safe distance.[11]

On the day of the Battle of Brandywine, September 11, the light infantry was again given the role of annoying British advance units. In this capacity, as an American officer observed, "our Friend Porterfield began the action with day light — he killed (himself) the first man who fell that day — His conduct through the whole day — was such as has acquired him the greatest Honor."[12]

During a lull in the afternoon during the Battle of Brandywine, small parties of Maxwell's light infantry again crossed the creek. Men commanded by Captain Porterfield were among those who drove enemy troops from woods and were about to capture a cannon, according to Lieutenant John Marshall, when "the sharpness of the skirmish soon drew a large body of the British in that quarter, and the Americans were again driven over the Brandywine."[13] By very late in the afternoon, Maxwell's light infantry and Porterfield had joined up with the rest of Washington's army in retreat.

On October 4, at the Battle of Germantown, Porterfield was most likely in General Greene's column on the left flank. Nothing is known of his involvement in the battle. Porterfield himself was getting rather restless serving merely as an infantryman and commanding only on the company level. He sought appointment at the rank of major or lieutenant colonel to the command of a new artillery regiment. Washington wrote Governor Patrick Henry of Virginia that he did not have sufficient knowledge to recommend Porterfield for this position. The commander in chief, however, did note that Porterfield was an invaluable officer and was well regarded by his colleagues; furthermore, Porterfield had "made Mathematics his particular Study."[14] In January 1778 Captain Porterfield became interim commander of the Eleventh Virginia Regiment.[15]

At the Valley Forge encampment, beginning in December 1777, Porterfield, his brother Robert, Captain Philip Slaughter, and Lieutenant John Marshall (the future chief justice), lodged together in a log hut. Slaughter wrote of the experience: "We were without bedding of any sort ... almost naked and many times half rations. We suffered more than I can describe."[16] At Valley Forge, Porterfield participated in his share of infantry patrols; occasionally his company skirmished with a forward British unit.[17]

At the Battle of Monmouth in June 1778, Porterfield probably did not see any direct action. No member of his Eleventh Virginia Regiment is listed on the casualty list. Most likely Porterfield himself was selected for Daniel Morgan's special corps, which hovered only on the periphery of the battle action, or perhaps was part of Washington's army, which was held in reserve.[18]

Remaining in the ranks as a captain, Porterfield became brigade major to General William Woodford's brigade on July 13, 1778,[19] and the following September was given the command of a rifle company in the new Seventh Virginia Regiment.[20] With Washington's army becoming increasingly inactive and the war having moved to the southern states, in July 1779 Porterfield resigned his Continental captaincy and accepted an appointment as major in the Virginia State Garrison Regiment.[21] Although normally prohibited by law from leaving the state, the Virginia government decided to make an exception and send a substantial force of state troops to assist the Southern Army in confronting a wholescale British invasion in the Carolinas and Georgia. On March 29, 1780, Porterfield received notification that he was to lead a detachment, under his "absolute controul and Command," upon short notice southward; Porterfield's troops consisted of "volunteers of the State Garrison Regiment, the greater part of Marshalls Corps of Artillery and two Troops of [John] Nelsons horse."[22] In all, Porterfield had charge of nearly 500 troops.[23]

In early May 1780, Porterfield's select corps headed southward to join the Southern Army. Fortuitously they just avoided two debacles. Upon arriving at Hillsborough, North Carolina, Porterfield learned of the surrender of the whole of the American army at Charleston. Then soon thereafter Porterfield received news that a detachment of Virginia troops under Colonel Abraham Buford had been cut to pieces at the Waxhaws at the border of North Carolina and South Carolina.

Linking up with Continentals under General Baron De Kalb and the North Carolina militia, Porterfield finally caught up with General Horatio Gates' replacement Southern Army in South Carolina. Colonel Armand's dragoons were added to Porterfield's command. Shortly after the reinforcements arrived, Gates decided to move his army towards Lord Cornwallis' nearby redcoats. On August 13, from Rugeley's Mills, 13 miles north of Camden, Gates' army, with Porterfield's troops in the advance, began their slow march to seek out the British Army. On the night of August 15, both armies unknowingly steered toward a collision course; Gates, seeking a battle, hoped to gain a favorable position to receive a British attack. The Americans, under strict orders, marched in complete silence.[24]

Under a full moon, which was said to make visibility as clear as daytime, the battle began with the initial contact between Porterfield's light infantry and oncoming British dragoons. Lt. Col. Guilford Dudley of the North Carolina militia, who was riding with Porterfield, gives a remarkably detailed narrative[25] of the agony of the heroic Lt. Col. Porterfield, who was mortally wounded during the opening volleys of the battle. Col. Armand, who had been posted far ahead, spotted the oncoming British troops. He "put spurs to his horse, and at full speed dashed from the road to the front of our right flank of infantry; and leaning over his saddle, in an audible whisper said to Col. Porterfield, 'there is the enemy, Sir—must I charge him.' Porterfield, who was a serious man, of few words, and slow of speech, gravely replied in the tone of Armand, 'by all means, Sir.'"[26]

> Porterfield's infantry and Armand's cavalry gave Tarleton's dragoons a heavy "velocity of a flash of lightening [sic]" that forced the enemy to back off. Soon a column of about five hundred British infantry approached, and fired "at close distance." With only about fifty men, Porterfield "maintained his ground with great firmness and gallantry" for about five rounds of ammunition. The two opposing groups moved even closer together and Porterfield, on horseback, received "a horrid wound in his left leg, a little before the knee which shattered it to pieces." Falling forward on his saddle, Porterfield ordered a retreat while his horse, severely injured, threw him to the ground. Twenty-four year old Lt. Col. Guilford Dudley, who had ridden with Porterfield, tried to put him on his own horse, but was unable to do so, given Porterfield's 210-pound frame and mangled leg.[27]
>
> Fortunately, two soldiers camp up and assisted in putting Porterfield on a horse and moving off away from the fighting. The relief party, with Porterfield unconscious most of the time, entered a "little thicket of persimmon bushes," about waist high. A bundle of twigs and a bandage was placed around Porterfield's wounded leg. The three men with their patient were able to move another mile away, and placed Porterfield under a shady tree. Dudley dispatched the two soldiers to find the American army and return with help. At break of day on August 16, the two emissaries returned with three or four surgeons and about a dozen soldiers. Unfortunately, the surgeons did little more than change the bandage and splint. Porterfield was put on a litter and carried away by four men, just as the artillery boomed, signaling the beginning of the main engagement at the Battle of Camden. Dudley left Porterfield to join the fray.[28] [See Appendix for Dudley's full account.]

With the American army breaking into full retreat, Porterfield was captured in a house near Rugeley Mills. On August 30 he wrote General Gates asking that a surgeon be sent to attend him. "My life in this season depends on speedy relief."[29] Of course, Gates, who himself fled from the battlefield and now was many miles away, could not do anything immediately to assist Porterfield. His British captors were kind but were also short on surgeons. It can be assumed, however, that Porterfield's leg was amputated.

Despite what was evidently a mortal wound, Lt. Col. Charles Porterfield lingered on for five months. Granted quick parole because of the severity of his condition, Porterfield attempted to visit his brother Robert, a prisoner of war in Charleston. On January 10, 1781, as he journeyed to that place, he died, and was probably buried in an unmarked grave—as one writer notes, "another forgotten hero of the American Revolution."[30]

12. Thomas Posey

Unlike many Virginia revolutionary leaders, Thomas Posey did not have the support of family wealth but had to make it on his own. Yet, he typified the Revolutionary War participant who availed himself of the benefits and opportunities that war service afforded, ending up as a distinguished western statesman. In personal appearance Posey was described as "powerfully built," with "noble appearance and courtly manners," 6'2" tall, with light brown hair and blue eyes.[1]

Thomas Posey was born on July 9, 1750. His formative years are obscure—so much so that he is regarded as probably having grown up only in the foster care of his alleged father, Captain John Posey. It is certain, however, that until age 19, Posey lived at John Posey's plantation, Rover's Delight, in Fairfax County, Virginia, adjacent to George Washington's Mount Vernon. His paternity has been in doubt, and attention has been called to his close physical resemblance to his neighbor, George Washington, who, incidentally, paid young Posey's tuition at a local subscription school. Thus it is not surprising that in the 19th century, rumor surfaced that Posey was fathered by George Washington during his bachelor days. The rumor lacks any conclusive evidence, but so does its disproval. Posey, who exhibited a polished, aristocratic air, himself said that he had "a tolerable english education."[2]

Thomas Posey. Courtesy of the Library of Virginia.

At the time that John Posey had to divest himself of most all of his real estate to satisfy debts, owed mostly to George Washington, Thomas Posey set off for Virginia's frontier, settling at Staunton in Augusta County. There he learned the saddler trade, eventually establishing his own shop. In 1772 he married Martha Matthews.[3]

The 24-year-old craftsman joined other western Virginia volunteers for service in Dunmore's War, which involved a two-prong expedition for the punishing of Ohio country Indians. Posey served as a commissary (arranging for provisions) for the column led by Colonel Andrew

Lewis. It was Lewis' troops who fought the Indians at the Battle of Point Pleasant in October 1774.[4]

Posey quickly adapted to the revolutionary movement. He was a member of the local committee of correspondence. On March 20, 1776, he received a commission from the Virginia Committee of Safety as captain of a company of the Seventh Virginia Regiment of the Continental Army.[5] When Governor Dunmore established a post on Gwynn's Island in Chesapeake Bay near the mouth of the Rappahannock River, Posey and the Seventh Regiment were rushed to the shoreline there to resist a mainland landing by the enemy. Other rebel troops moved into the area, and, finally, effective rebel artillery batteries compelled Dunmore to leave the island and his flotilla of shipboard troops eventually sailed out of the bay.[6]

Posey and the Seventh Virginia Regiment, after spending the early winter at Williamsburg, started their march on January 16, 1777, to link up with the main army. After serving with Washington's army in New Jersey during spring and early summer, Posey was among soldiers selected for Colonel Daniel Morgan's corps of 500 riflemen and dispatched to join General Horatio Gates's Northern Army, soon confronted by a British force from Canada led by General John Burgoyne. Posey was in the thick of the two battles of Saratoga (Freeman's Farm and Bemis Heights). He recorded an impression of the fighting at Bemis Heights. During the heat of the battle, with troops under Colonel Benedict Arnold having been twice repelled, Morgan's rifle regiment

> march'd under cover of a thick wood, and a ridge, which ridge the enemy were about to take possession of as Morgan gainfed the summit of it, the enemy being within good rifle shot, the regiment poured in a well directed fire which brought almost every officer on horseback to the ground.[7]

Captain Posey stayed with Morgan's rifle corps, which after Saratoga made its way back to Washington's main army at Middlebrook, New Jersey. During the encampment at Valley Forge from December 1777 to June 1778, Morgan's riflemen guarded the camp's perimeters, and, assisted by cavalry, skirmished with enemy armed foraging and scouting parties. When Morgan went home on leave in March 1778, Posey, as senior captain, became temporary commander of Morgan's rifle corps. On April 30, 1778, Posey was promoted to major.[8]

Morgan was back with the army to take charge of a special corps designed to keep watch and harass outward units of the enemy's army. The group included Morgan's rifle corps, to which Posey was still attached. Morgan's troops saw little or no action during the Battle of Monmouth, June 28, 1778, as General Charles Lee, who commanded the American troops during the first phase of the battle, failed to call upon Morgan's unit. After the battle, with Morgan's special detachment being dissolved and his rifle corps greatly diminished in numbers, Morgan moved on to command a newly constituted Seventh Virginia Regiment, and Posey assumed charge of the remnant rifle corps. Posey and his men were deployed to chase after Indians on the New York frontier;

not much was accomplished except to destroy several Indian villages. In December 1777, upon orders from Washington, Posey rejoined the Seventh Virginia Regiment.[9]

On June 12, 1779, Washington ordered the creation of a new Light Infantry Corps. The one previous, commanded by General William Maxwell in relation to the Battle of Brandywine, had been disbanded. For the new unit, now led by General Anthony Wayne, four regiments of light infantry were composed of proficient soldiers from all 46 regiments in the main army. Major Thomas Posey commanded one of the 350-men regiments.[10]

Near midnight on July 15–16, Wayne was ready to execute a carefully planned assault on Stony Point, a fort on the Hudson River. Posey and Lt. Col. François de Fleury each led a column of 150 shock troops in the vanguard of the attack. Posey, with a sword in one hand and a spontoon in the other, led his men in driving the enemy from gun ports. So rapid was the American assault that the defenders were caught wholly by surprise and did not have time to form en masse. From the fierce hand-to-hand combat the British troops surrendered. During the action Posey was wounded in the lower part of a leg. The injury was not deemed serious enough for Posey to refrain from fighting, but in his last years it partially disabled him.[11] Although Anthony Wayne irritated Posey for not publicly recognizing Posey's heroism at the attack on Stony Point, Colonel Christian Febiger, who fought alongside Posey at Stony Point, referred to, in regard to the attack, "the gallant, a most valuable Posey."[12]

By December 1779 Posey was back with the Seventh Virginia Regiment. He was among Virginia troops sent to the Southern Army in the spring of 1780. Posey's regiment unfortunately arrived to join General Benjamin Lincoln's forces at Charleston just in time to be captured by the enemy. Posey himself, however, had delayed his march and hence avoided the catastrophe. During most of 1781 Posey had charge of some militia in eastern Virginia, vainly anticipating combat with invading British forces, and was also involved with recruiting in the Shenandoah Valley.[13]

Promoted to lieutenant colonel on September 8, 1781, Posey performed as acting commander of the Second Virginia Regiment in Lafayette's right wing of the army at the siege of Yorktown. Like most all of the soldiers of the allied armies, Posey won no special distinction on the siege lines. Present for the capitulation, he wrote, "I had the happiness to see the two forgoing armies (Burgon and Cornwallace) defeated and lay down their arms."[14]

Posey led a detachment of new recruits to join General Nathanael Greene's army in South Carolina. On the march south orders were changed and Posey's troops were directed to link up with General Anthony Wayne's force ready to begin a siege of Savannah. In late May 1782, Posey arrived at Wayne's camp about five miles from Savannah. During predawn, June 24, 150 Creek Indians, under Emistesequo, by complete surprise rushed into the American camp. The Indians were trying to break their way through to join the city's defenders. Wayne's troops were driven from camp. In the hand-to-hand combat that ensued Posey led a bayonet charge that pushed the enemy into a swamp and routed them. Chief Emistesequo was killed, and Posey proudly acquired 12 prisoners, whom Wayne had summarily shot.[15]

Spending the winter of 1782 to 1783 in Virginia, Posey was transferred to the reconstituted First Virginia Regiment on January 1, 1783. Soon thereafter he left the army, resigning his commission on March 10, 1783.[16]

With the war over, the veteran hero could attend to family life. He had lost his first wife, Martha, during childbirth on August 4, 1778. Posey married Mary Alexander Thornton on January 22, 1784, and moved to one of the Thornton estates, Greenwood, in Spotsylvania County. Posey would now become the patriarch of a large family: nine of ten children by Mary survived; there were also three children from the first marriage and three stepchildren from Mary's previous marriage. During the 19 years Posey resided in Spotsylvania County, he participated in local public affairs, which included acting as justice of the peace and county lieutenant.[17]

The Indian wars of the Northwest beckoned Posey out of military retirement. On March 11, 1793, he was named a brigadier general of the Legion of the United States, a special federal striking force to punish the hostile Indians. Claiming the need to take care of his large family, but probably mostly from resentment about being caught in the middle between the vicious rivalry of the army's two top commanders, Anthony Wayne and James Wilkinson, Posey did not remain long in the field, resigning his commission on February 28, 1794, six months before the victory at the Battle of Fallen Timbers.[18]

Posey sought out opportunities in the national political realm. Although a nationalist, he did not affiliate with the Federalist Party. In the Congressional election of 1797 Posey lost to John Dawson. The following year President Adams appointed him U.S. commissioner for the 11th District of Virginia to determine the enumeration of slaves and property evaluation.[19]

In spring 1802 Posey and his family trekked 1,000 miles, crossing the Cumberland Gap and on to western Kentucky, settling at his new homestead, Longview, along the Green River, near Henderson.

In 1804 Posey was elected to a two-year term in the Kentucky Senate. He was almost instantly elected speaker and presiding officer of the Kentucky Senate as a replacement for the lieutenant governor, John Caldwell, who had died. On November 23, 1805, Posey was elected to serve out Caldwell's unexpired term as lieutenant governor.[20] Posey completed this service in 1807 and prepared to run for governor. He withdrew from this race, preferring not to contest the governorship with General Charles Scott, who, like Posey, was one of the last surviving top officers of the Continental Army and had come to Kentucky from Virginia. Scott won the election and served until 1812.[21]

Sometime in late 1811 or early 1812 Posey and his family moved to Baton Rouge, Louisiana. In October 1812 Posey accepted a recess appointment from the Louisiana governor to serve in the U.S. Senate. On December 7, 1812, he took his seat—even though the state General Assembly refrained from ratifying the appointment. Posey left the state Senate on February 5, 1813. During his brief tenure as senator Posey, staunchly backed the war with Great Britain.[22]

The War of 1812 opened a new avenue for Posey. When William Henry Harrison resigned as governor of the Indiana Territory to accept command of the Northwest Army, President Madison named Posey as Harrison's successor for a three-year term. Posey was confirmed by the U.S. Senate on March 3, 1813, and he assumed his duties at Vincennes on May 4. Although the territorial capital was located at Corydon, Posey lived and conducted business at Jeffersonville, on the Ohio River across from Louisville; this move allowed Posey, whose health was now failing, to be close to his physicians. At Jeffersonville Posey built a 16-room mansion overlooking the Ohio River.[23]

President Madison reappointed Posey to another term in 1816. This year, however, Indiana achieved statehood. In the 1816 state election Posey was defeated for the governorship by Jonathan Jennings by a tally of 5,211 votes to 3,934. William Hendricks defeated Posey for the U.S. House of Representatives in August 1817. Although Posey had political appeal as one of the last surviving Revolutionary War heroes, his health and age and political demographics worked against him. A frontier constituency was not too enthralled with Posey's reputation for aristocratic demeanor and his having opposed statehood. On the latter issue Posey thought that the immigrant population in the state was unprepared to determine state affairs intelligently. Furthermore citizens were not especially attracted to an aristocrat and former slave holder.[24]

As a territorial governor, Posey's administration was vigorous in attempting to give Indiana an identity of its own. Although not accomplishing the extensive militia reform as he had hoped, Posey was able to separate Indiana's militia system from its previous control by Kentucky authorities. Among other developments, Posey presided over the restructure of the court system, the revision of territorial laws, and secured only "moderate taxes." In his honor, a new county created in 1814 was named after him.[25]

After losing the 1816 gubernatorial election, Posey, upon application to the secretary of war, was appointed U.S. agent for Indian affairs for lower Indiana and Illinois. He set up his office at Vincennes in November 1816. For 18 months he served as Indian agent, primarily concerned with negotiating land purchases and dispensing annuities to the Kickapoo and Wea tribes.[26]

While abiding ill-health, including recurring infections in his old leg wound, Posey managed to stay on the job as Indian agent. He moved his residence to the Westwood home of his daughter in Shawneetown, Illinois, on the Ohio River. There he died of pleurisy and typhus fever on March 19, 1818.[27]

Posey (like Charles Scott, also a self-made Virginian-war hero transplanted to Kentucky and governor of Kentucky 1808 to 1812) was a transitional figure in providing leadership from winning independence to building a new nation. Posey's very able biographer gives a fitting tribute in summarizing Thomas Posey's war experiences:

What kind of soldier was Thomas Posey? His personal bravery in battle, demonstrated many times over, cannot be questioned, and his record attests to his dedication and steadfastness in the noble quest pursued by his revolutionary generation. As an officer and leader, without any military background or training other than by example and experience, he was competent and technically proficient. As a commander, he was caring and solicitous of his men, active in procuring their provisions and clothing, heedful of their health and well-being, and deeply concerned when they fell ill or wounded in the field. As a human being, he was compassionate to his defeated British and Indian enemies. He was perhaps self-centered, too absorbed in having his exploits duly recognized, and overly preoccupied with his place in history, but these were qualities shared by many, if not most, of the revolutionary army's officer class. On balance, he may be fairly assessed as a good and courageous fighter in the best of causes.[28]

13. Gustavus "Gusty" Brown Wallace

Gustavus Brown Wallace won a reputation simply for solid leadership during seven years of the war. He was around for Washington's northern campaigns until transferred to the Southern Army, where he was made a prisoner of war after the capture of Charleston, South Carolina. If "Gusty" Wallace never left a splash in the record books for extraordinary heroism, he nevertheless was recognized as an outstanding officer who inspired his comrades and enlisted men alike. He shared in the hardships of his men so as to bolster morale.[1] Wallace, as one historian notes, "was a mild, but firm, disciplinarian, and was several times transferred to build up morale of new regiments to which he was assigned."[2]

Wallace had many friends in the army. A lifelong bachelor, he was known to be somewhat of a womanizer. An army colleague wrote from the encampment at Pompton Plains, New Jersey, in November 1778, that Wallace was quartered in a house "where there is a fine little Dutch girl, and he is determined to lay close seage to her." The reporter added that

> he says he thinks he shall be able to starve her out in four or five days — but if he should fall through in that manoeuvre, he is determined to raise a light apron and harass her parties in that way; which he thinks will most certainly complete his designs.[3]

All five Wallace brothers enlisted for military service. Besides Gusty there were Michael, William and twins John and Thomas, who in 1776 at age 15 ran away from home to join Gusty's regiment, but were sent back home. Thomas reenlisted, and as a lieutenant was captured, as was Gusty, at Charleston in May 1780. William started the war as an infantry lieutenant, and later, as a captain in the Continental artillery, became a prisoner of war at the Battle of Camden, remaining thus until the end of the war.[4]

Born on November 9, 1751, one of nine children of Dr. Michael Wallace, a physician from Scotland, and Elizabeth Brown Wallace, Gusty grew up on his father's large estate Ellerslie, in Stafford County, five miles from Fredericksburg. The elder Wallace died in 1767, leaving the major part of his estate to Gustavus Brown Wallace.[5] Gusty studied in one of the small private schools in Fredericksburg. His pursuit of a law education was interrupted in 1775 when he journeyed to Glasgow, Scotland, to settle the estate of his aunt, Rebecca Wallace (his father's only sister). Gusty inherited two-sevenths of Rebecca's property, and his brothers the rest; ironically when the estate was finally settled, Gusty had only two diamond rings to show for his inheritance.[6] In fall 1775 Gusty returned to Virginia.[7]

On February 20, 1776, Gustavus Brown Wallace was commissioned a captain of the fifth company of Colonel George Weedon's Third Virginia Regiment.[8] Wallace participated in the checkmating of the small royal force commanded by Governor Lord Dunmore, which concluded with the enemy's departure from Virginia in August 1776.

Wallace and Weedon's Third Regiment joined Washington's army on Manhattan Island, New York, on September 11, having traversed 400 miles from Virginia in a little more than three weeks. Gusty was disappointed to find only 1,500 troops in Washington's army instead of the 10,000 he had been told of. Actually, Washington had 16,124 effectives. Wallace probably took into account the American troops on Harlem Heights, where the Third Regiment was stationed.

The enemy, moving up the East River after securing Brooklyn, debarked at Kip's Bay on September 15. General William Howe was intent upon pushing the Americans out of New York City instead of, as originally considered, cutting them off in the rear at the northern tip of Manhattan. Washington barely managed to extricate the American troops in lower Manhattan and bring them to the Harlem Heights plateau, which extended about four miles from what is now 130th Street to 170th Street.[9] Most of the soldiers who evacuated the city were New Englanders. Wallace commented bitterly, "Our Regiment had been out of camp under arms for two nights before we were ordered to cover the retreat of the cowardly yankeymen"; fortunately, however, General Greene, Wallace's division commander, countermanded the order.[10]

On the morning of September 16, the Third Virginia Regiment "formed in the woods on the side of a hill just above a meadow that was 50 yards wide." The enemy was sighted on the other side of the meadow also on a wooded hill. Some of the Virginia troops and a Maryland rifle company crossed a swamp above the meadow to flank the enemy. Soon "a pretty hot engagement" ensued. New England troops were sent in to attack the front of the enemy and suffered heavy casualties. With the full play of American fire from several directions, the enemy was forced to retreat. A British reinforcement came up, and the Americans halted pursuit. The Battle of Harlem Heights lasted nearly three hours. The Third Virginia Regiment had four enlisted men killed and several officers and 12 privates wounded. As Colonel George Weedon, Wallace's regimental commander, said of the battle, "upon the whole," the enemy "got Cursedly thrashed." As Wallace himself noted, "all of our officers and soldiers behaved with the *greatest* bravery."[11]

Wallace and the Third Virginia Regiment, along with other Virginia and Delaware Continentals, skirmished with 500 Tory rangers five miles from White Plains, New York, on October 22; the Americans came out victors, returning with the enemy's colors and inflicting many more casualties than sustained. At the Battle of White Plains, on October 28, with only a small part of the American lines engaged, Wallace and the Virginians were merely spectators.[12]

Presumably, Gusty Wallace was with his regiment at the Battle of Trenton. He was with the army through the summer of 1777.[13] He probably missed the Battle of Brandywine, as he did the Battle of Germantown, when he was incapacitated at Trenton with an "old disorder." Gusty's brother, Dr. James Wallace attended him during his illness,[14] and Gusty soon recovered. On October 4, 1777, Wallace was promoted to major in the Fifteenth Virginia Regiment (renumbered as the Eleventh in March 1778).[15]

Gustavus Brown Wallace endured the whole stay of the army at the Valley Forge encampment.[16] On March 20 he was promoted to lieutenant colonel. On March 28, 1778, he began a stint as brigade major to General William Woodford's brigade. In this position he had the assistance of two adjutants.[17] Undoubtedly, Wallace was with the army during the Battle of Monmouth, June 28, 1778, in Woodford's brigade, but most likely he himself was not engaged in the action—probably held back among reserves, as none of his regiment were listed among the casualties. Wallace was probably with Woodford's brigade during the encampment at Middlebrook in the winter of 1778 to 1779.[18]

In May 1779, Gustavus Brown Wallace was ordered to join a special force of 2,200 men, commanded by General Charles Scott, to march southward and link up with General Lincoln's Southern Army in Charleston. Recruitment for this mission made little headway, but on December 5, 1779, 300 troops led by Colonel Richard Parker, with Lt. Col. Wallace second in command, arrived at Charleston.[19] Wallace and his younger brother, Lt. Thomas Wallace, had the misfortune to be captured along with the rest of Lincoln's army at Charleston on May 12, 1780. Gusty Wallace and other surrendered officers of the American Army were interned at Haddrell's Point across from Charleston.[20]

Wallace's release from imprisonment came slightly ahead that of his fellow captives. In fall 1781, the Virginia militia's General Thomas Nelson arranged with General Cornwallis for Wallace to return to Virginia to line up some 400 hogsheads of tobacco as payment for debts incurred by the captive officers for their keep while confined at Haddrell's Point. Thus Wallace gained his parole, which lasted until the close of the war.[21]

After the war, Gustavus Brown Wallace settled in at his White Hall mansion in Stafford County, which his father had willed him.[22] In 1784 he solicited Congress for a military "command of Detroit and the Lakes of Canada."[23] Of course, at the time America's new national government had neither the resources nor the will to establish a wide-ranging military establishment. In 1789 Wallace unsuccessfully sought Congress to appoint him a collector of the federal tariff for the "port of Rappahannock."[24]

In 1802 Gustavus Brown Wallace again visited Scotland to look into inherited property. Aboard ship on his return, he contracted typhus, sometimes called jail or hospital fever, at the time often confused with typhoid fever.[25] Upon reaching America, because of the contagiousness of his usually lethal disease, he was unceremoniously dumped into the swamp grass along Potomac Creek, five miles below Fredericksburg. A servant of Wallace's cousin, Frances (Moncure) Daniel, discovered the dying Wallace, who refused to be brought to his cousin's home at Crow's Nest for fear of giving his hosts the disease. Wallace, however, consented to be taken to Fredericksburg, where, several days later, on August 17, 1802, he died. He was buried at the Masonic cemetery in Fredericksburg.[26]

14. George Baylor

Destiny summoned the 25-year-old Virginia aristocrat to the command of a cavalry regiment during the Revolutionary War. His father, John Baylor, a long-time and close friend of George Washington, was one of the wealthiest of the Virginia gentry and probably the most prominent horse racing enthusiast and breeder in the colony. At his plantation seat, Newmarket, along the Rappahannock River in Caroline County near Fredericksburg, John Baylor cared for 100 horses. Among his equine prizes were stallions and mares imported from England. John Baylor could boast ownership of Fearnaught, the premier stud horse in Virginia's history. When John Baylor died in 1772, 20-year-old George Baylor, as the third eldest son, inherited part of the plantation estate and blooded racehorses, most notably Godolphin, a celebrated racer, a descendant of other famous thoroughbreds in England and America by the same name. Godolphin was a progenitor of many famous thoroughbreds, not the least being Man of War and Secretariat. Young George Baylor was known as an accomplished horseman and a "spirited" youth, ideally suited as a leader of dragoons (cavalrymen).[1]

George Baylor was born at Newmarket on January 12, 1752, one of 12 children of John and Frances Walker Baylor. He received his education from tutors on the plantation and from several years study in England, although he took no college degree abroad. Upon his father's death in 1772, young George Baylor engaged in plantation management and assumed his father's role as horse breeder.[2]

On November 10, 1774, George Baylor was elected to the 20-man Caroline County Committee of Safety, one of the many local associations being formed in the colonies to implement a commercial boycott against Great Britain called for by the Continental Congress. Committee members inspected account books of merchants concerning compliance, conducted hearings, and punished violators.[3]

From visits to John Baylor's home and their long-standing friendship going back to the time that they were comrades during the French and Indian War, George Washington had known George Baylor all his life and liked him. Thus, with recommendations from Edmund Pendleton and other Virginia illuminaries, Washington, only a month after assuming command of the Continental Army, named George Baylor an aide-de-camp at the rank of lieutenant colonel.[4] George Baylor stayed in this capacity until he gained a field command as a cavalry officer in January 1777. With George Baylor as an aide, Washington soon discovered that his 23-year-old appointee was not at all a "penman," a skill, of course, necessary for the secretarial duties of Washington's "military family." But the commander in chief remained impressed with Baylor's enthusiasm and eagerness for service.[5] Washington wrote General Charles Lee that young Baylor "is as good, and as obliging a young Man, as any in the World, and as far as he can be Serviceable in Riding & Delivering verbal Orders as useful, but the duties of an Aid de Camp at Head Quarters cannot be properly discharged by any but Pen-men."[6] Hence Baylor found himself limited to duties requiring horse riding, such as carrying messages and escort assignment, including acting as the official escort of Martha Washington.

George Baylor, despite his lack of skills as a military aide, had an active role in the Battle of Trenton of December 26, 1776. He seems to have been the American officer who, under a flag, approached the hard-pressed Hessians and, speaking to several German officers, persuaded the Hessians to surrender. Washington himself was nearby as the Hessians stacked their arms. The commander in chief had just prior to the act of surrendering ordered American artillerists to shift from firing shot to canister. Washington rode through the ranks of the Hessians and soon troops of both sides were commingling. That Baylor may have had even a more important role at the Battle of Trenton is suggested by the fact that Washington chose him to deliver the news of the victory to Congress sitting in Philadelphia. A grateful Congress, on January 9, 1777, voted Baylor "a Horse properly caparisoned" and a promotion to full colonel. Congress also recommended to Washington that he appoint Baylor to the command of a cavalry regiment. The commander in chief accordingly obliged, naming Baylor to the regimental command of the Third Continental Light Dragoons.[7]

Most of Baylor's new cavalrymen came from Virginia; a few were drawn from Pennsylvania. From January until late fall of 1777, Baylor and his officers stayed in Virginia recruiting and acquiring horses and supplies for the new cavalry regiment.[8] Although George Baylor himself did not return to the army until late 1777 many of his recruits were with Washington's army for the parade through Philadelphia on August 23, 1777 and at the battles of Brandywine, September 11, and Germantown, October 4.[9]

By December 1777, Baylor and his cavalry regiment were included in the right wing of the army,[10] and were deployed, along with the First Dragoons, in small detachments to scout the enemy and seek intelligence, particularly to make sure the enemy did not gain position along the flanks of the American army. Baylor and his dragoons accompanied Washington's army as it moved into encampment at Valley Forge on December 19, 1777. A short time, however, was spent at the new winter quarters, as the enlistments of Baylor's dragoons expired. Baylor himself was soon back in Virginia recruiting and seeking to outfit his regiment.[11]

George Baylor did not return to Valley Forge. Meanwhile, many of his dragoons had rejoined Washington's army, and under acting commander of the regiment, Major Alexander Clough, fought a skirmish against some 600 British troops guarding wood and forage details near Bordentown, New Jersey, on May 8, 1778.[12] Congress, on May 27, 1778, prescribed the size and structure of dragoon regiments. Each troop company contained 62 dragoons. A field officer commanded two troops. The total complement for a regiment consisted of 408 cavalrymen. During the subsequent course of the war, however, no dragoon regiment ever measured up to its allocated size, and more often than not actually contained one-fifth to one-third of the maximum.[13]

George Baylor continued with his recruiting and logistical duties in Virginia until early September 1778. On May 30, 1778, he married Lucy Page, daughter of Mann Page of Mansfield, located near Fredericksburg. They had only one child, John Walker Baylor.[14]

Without George Baylor himself being present, the Third Continental Light Dragoons, consisting of men Baylor had forwarded from Virginia, had a peripheral role in the Battle of Monmouth, June 28, 1778. The regiment, originally placed at the rear of Lafayette's detachment, was especially of service in badgering outer units of the British army as it progressed on its retreat across New Jersey for transport to New York City and environs.[15] With the war in the north subsequently stalemating, the commander in chief envisaged the main use of dragoons to "keep the Enemy from foraging or drawing other supplies from this part of the Country."[16]

The luck of the Third Continental Light Dragoons ran out. First, however, on September 27, 1778, there was a joyful moment before tragedy struck. Baylor's dragoons received an issue of 200 new uniforms. Baylor's cavalrymen could now wear flashy attire befitting daring cavalrymen. The uniforms con-
sisted of black leather caps with brown horsehair crest and red turban, a white coat faced with blue collar, a vest, lapels, cuffs, and coattails, silver buttons, white breeches, and black boots with silver spurs. A trooper also carried a silver-hilted sword with a black leather scabbard rimmed with silver and held by a white leather belt over the right shoulder. To top off this arrangement was a white sling over the left shoulder with a silver sling to hold a carbine. The dragoon officer wore a crimson waist sash and silver-colored epaulets.[17]

Sunday, September 27, was the same day that Baylor's regiment moved several miles away from major army units to take post at the Cornelius Haring farm near Old Tappan in Northern Bergen County, New Jersey, adjacent to the border with New York. Baylor's troopers had been conducting widespread scouting, and it was considered that for a night's encampment they had distance enough to prevent attack by any of General Cornwallis'

George Baylor. From Orval Baylor and Henry Bedinger, *History of the Baylors* (LeRoy, IL: Letter Journal Publishing Company, 1914).

large detachments scouring farms west of the Hudson River for forage and livestock. Baylor miscalculated the mobility of the enemy, and he failed to establish a sufficient guard, putting out only a sergeant and 12 men at a nearby bridge. For the night of September 27 to 28 Baylor's 120 dragoons bedded down in three barns, and the officers, at the Haring residence. Tories abounded in the area, making for the greater possibility that Baylor's isolated troop position might readily be revealed to the enemy.[18]

Cornwallis, commanding the grand forage detachment, received word that Baylor and his dragoons encamped not far distant at an exposed position, and he responded by ordering General Charles "No Flint" Grey to attack Baylor's dragoons. First, Grey's troops slaughtered the American guard at the bridge before they could sound an alarm. The enemy crept into Baylor's camp and rushed into the buildings with drawn bayonets. The order went out to give no quarter, and the redcoats proceeded to butcher the sleeping dragoons, who were able to give either no or feeble resistance. At the Haring house officers trying to escape up the chimney of a huge Dutch oven were pulled down and bayoneted. George Baylor sustained an all but fatal wound to the lungs. In all, 50 dragoons were killed, 17 wounded, and 50 captured.[19] Thomas Jones, Loyalist judge, gave a glum description of the debacle:

> The whole corps were massacred in cold blood, and to the disgrace of Britons. Many of them were stabbed while upon their knees humbly imploring and submissively begging for mercy.... An act inconsistent with the dignity of honor of a British General, and disgraceful to the name of a soldier.[20]

The American dragoons killed at the massacre at Old Tappan were thrown into mass graves in tanning vats at the site. The exact location of the interment was not revealed until excavation occurred in 1968. Baylor explained to the commander in chief that tragedy had resulted from the guard having been wiped out at the bridge, thus preventing any alarm.[21] A major factor in the easy success of Grey's troops at Old Tappan had been the lack of any infantry support for Baylor's dragoons, an oversight that Washington remedied in 1781 for all dragoon units. Baylor, who was made a prisoner of war, was treated for his wound by the dragoon surgeon, but never fully recovered. Because of the continuing severity of his wound, the British allowed Baylor to be exchanged after a short period of time.

The Third Continental Light Dragoons never fully recouped. Baylor himself was unable to assume actual field command, and the Third Dragoons were placed along the 1st and 4th Dragoons under the command of Lt. Col. William Washington. Each of the individual dragoon units still kept their identity. The remnant of the Third Dragoons fought well at Cowpens and Guilford Courthouse. At Eutaw Springs, on September 8, 1781, the Third Dragoons met disaster, losing all their officers except two; one half of their members were killed or wounded, and their commander at the time, William Washington, was wounded and captured.[22]

In June 1782 George Baylor received the command of a legionary corps, which consisted of the remnant of the Third Dragoons and what was left of cavalry that had been commanded by Henry Lee and Stephen Moylan. In the following November a few more fragments of dragoon units were added to the group, now dubbed Baylor's Dragoons.[23] It is probable that George Baylor, because of the lingering critical condition from his wound, never resumed, on a sustained basis, actual field command of his troopers. In fall 1782 Major John Swann, Baylor's second in command, had charge of Baylor's dragoons, stationed near the Combahee River, where they had the assignment to keep a check on Tory partisan raiders from St. Augustine, Florida.[24]

Actually there was soon lack of opportunity for military action, with the British army's complete withdrawal from the south, signified by the evacuation of Savannah on July 11, 1782, and Charleston on December 14, 1782. The war was over. Yet Congress hesitated to discharge any troops for fear that unpaid and hungry soldiers might resort to armed resistance against the Continental and state governments. There was unrest among Baylor's dragoons, who had suffered from lack of pay and insufficient food.

In May 1783 Baylor's troopers mutinied and set out for Virginia's capital at Richmond to demand redress. This occurred several weeks before Pennsylvania soldiers marched on Congress at Philadelphia.

Leading the Baylor mutineers was Sergeant Major William Dangerfield. Baylor himself was at Fredericksburg, Virginia, at the time. General Nathanael Greene, who never harbored any sympathy toward mutineers, and who feared a general uprising in the Southern Army, wrote General Charles Scott, who was at his home in Powhatan County, Virginia, 40 miles west of Richmond, to collect militia to apprehend the mutineers. Greene insisted that the mutineers had only false pretensions of having suffered deprivation. The mutineers, as they progressed, sent ahead a petition to Governor Benjamin Harrison stating their grievances. The governor passed the document on to the Virginia Council of State, who gave it a sympathetic hearing. In the end, it was agreed to call General Daniel Morgan back into military service to go out and meet the mutineers and persuade them to go an additional 150 miles to Winchester, Virginia, where at a Continental military depot and barracks there the dissidents could find succour. This was done without incident and not long after the mutineers arrived at their destination they were sent home.[25] Most likely Baylor met with his unhappy cavalrymen as they passed through Fredericksburg.

George Baylor exited the army with a brevet commission of brigadier general, conferred on September 30, 1783.[26] The wound he had suffered at the Tappan massacre in September of 1778 continued to plague him, becoming over the years even more bothersome and painful. In May 1784 George Baylor traveled to the Bahamas. He resided at Bridgetown, where he died on November 9, 1784. He was buried in the churchyard of St. Michael's Cathedral.[27]

Like his neighbor, Alexander Dick, George Baylor had all the makings of a military hero. He was more fortunate than Dick in gaining the personal friendship of George

Washington. At age 23 he became an aide to the commander in chief, and one and a half years later was promoted to full colonel, and assumed the command of one of the army's prestigious units, a regiment of light dragoons. Though he was reinstated to his command after being released as a prisoner of war and being critically wounded at Old Tappan in September 1778, for the most part he avoided actual field duty for the remainder of his military career. With Baylor's death at age 32 from the lingering effects of his wound, Virginia was denied further service from a young man of great potential as a leader.

15. Theodorick Bland, Jr.

Tall and imposing, though somewhat shy and reluctant to engage in public speaking, Theodorick Bland, Jr., was a man of extraordinary energy and talent. For a while he was one of Virginia's most wealthy planters. Named to command a cavalry regiment early in the war, Bland would normally have been in the major battles, north and south, had not competing service intervened: Bland was a military policeman in charge of the British army captives from the battle of Saratoga and also a member of the national Congress. Actually, Bland's active military duty in the field lasted only about two years, and much of that time was spent remaining in Virginia for recruitment and obtaining horses and supplies for his regiment. Once entering into legislative service, Bland was a member of state and national assemblies. He was one of only two Virginia physicians who left the calling of a practicing doctor to become a field officer in the Continental Line during the war—Adam Stephen was the other. The versatile Bland kept close watch on agricultural production at his plantations, and, in a different vein, tried his hand at writing poetry and prose.

The son of Theodorick Bland, Sr., and Frances Bolling Bland, Theodorick Bland, Jr., was born on March 21, 1742, at his father's tobacco plantation, Caesons, located at the confluence of the Appomattox and James rivers in Prince George County, just southeast of Richmond. Later in life, Theodorick Bland, Jr., made his residence at Farmingdell, a plantation also in Prince George County.

At the age of 11 Bland was sent to England. There he studied six years at the Wakefield School in Yorkshire. He did well pursuing a classical education, although according to the headmaster, Theodorick, along with other students, performed "wretchedly" in composition, especially in Latin.[1] Deciding upon a career in medicine, Bland studied at the Liverpool infirmary from 1759 to 1761, and thereupon entered the University of Edinburgh, from where he received his doctorate in 1763. Along with a half dozen other Virginians pursuing a medical degree at Edinburgh, Bland formed the Virginia Club, and wrote the club's constitution. This fraternity was mainly aimed at promoting the licensing of physicians in Virginia. Each member pledged "for the honor of his profession not to degrade it hereafter mingling the trade of an apothecary or a surgeon with it."[2] In 1764 Bland returned to Virginia. The 22-year-old physician set up practice at Blandford, a hamlet adjacent to Petersburg, Virginia. In 1768 he married Martha Dangerfield; there were no children from this union.

Dr. Bland, as the editor of his papers notes, "with a constitution from the cradle delicate and infirm, and with a strong natural bent towards a life of rural quiet and studious repose," found being a physician for a sparse and scattered population too demanding on his time and health. Physicians at the time were expected to make rounds of house calls. He retired from actively practicing medicine in 1771, which occurred about the time that he inherited a plantation through his mother, which he named Farmingdell. Bland now gave full attention to agricultural production at Farmingdell

and also at another plantation he owned in Amelia County. He raised principally tobacco, wheat, and corn and tended to husbandry. As a favor to his neighbors, Bland gave medical advice and prescriptions upon request.[3]

On June 24, 1775, Bland was one of the 24 young men who broke into the governor's palace in Williamsburg and stole 200 weapons (pistols and muskets), most of which had been displayed in the front hall. These arms were deposited in the town's magazine under Bland's charge. Bland became a member of the Prince George County Committee of Safety on May 8, 1775.[4]

Bland pressed the Virginia Convention, the interim governing body for the state during the developing revolutionary crisis, for an army commission, and on

Theodorick Bland Jr. By unknown artist. Court House, Baltimore. Courtesy of the Frick Art Reference Library, New York City.

June 13, 1776, was rewarded with appointment as captain of the first troop of Virginia cavalry of six companies. This unit was made into a regiment in December 1776, with Bland as colonel and commander, and it was brought into the Continental Army. In January 1777 Bland led his First Continental Light Dragoons into the army's winter encampment at Morristown and joined General Lord Stirling's division. Bland's dragoons saw field duty during spring and summer 1777 in reconnaissance and providing security for foraging parties.[5]

As the British Army headed from the Head of Elk at the upper end of Chesapeake Bay for Philadelphia, Bland was charged by Washington with "keeping small guards and constant patrols, both of horse and foot, on the flanks and in front of the enemy." The commander in chief expected from Bland "immediate notice" of "every matter of importance."[6] Although it appears he waited too long to do so, Bland discovered that the enemy was mainly avoiding Chadd's Ford on Brandywine Creek where the attack was anticipated, and was instead heading upstream to a point near Birmingham Friends Meetinghouse Hill, which was to become the major battle site.[7] Sullivan, Greene, and Stephen's divisions were shifted to the far right of the American lines to engage the British offensive directly. It is not known whether Bland's dragoons were able to get into the battle, but they probably did so on the fringe of the action.

The weaknesses of the young dragoon commander during the preliminaries of the Battle of Brandywine did not go unnoticed by one of Bland's fellow troopers, Captain "Lighthorse Harry" Lee, who later commented that Bland was a "noble, sensible, honorable, and amiable" officer but one who was "never intended for the department of military intelligence."[8] Bland may himself have felt disappointed in his role as intelligence gatherer, and this may have been one of the reasons he asked Washington for permission to resign his commission. The commander in chief refused but allowed Bland to return to Virginia in March 1778 for the purpose of procuring horses and supplies for his troopers. During his long furlough Bland made an excursion into North Carolina to procure horses. By mid–August he had rejoined the main army at its encampments along the Hudson River.[9]

The young Virginia cavalry commander had seen his last military action. Through fall of 1778, Washington's army experienced relative quiet while encamped in and around White Plains, New York. Soon Bland faced a new turn in his military career — one that would make him a military police commander. The British troops, under General Burgoyne, who had surrendered along the Hudson River in October 1777, had been enduring their captivity in barracks at Cambridge, Massachusetts. This Convention Army, as the captives were styled, had been detained in America in violation of the terms of their surrender, which had provided for their return to England. Congress decided to move the Convention troops far away from population centers and from proximity to British forces, north or south. Hence Congress,, in October 1778 ordered Washington to have the prisoners sent to the Piedmont section of western Virginia, at Charlottesville.

Washington, who highly respected Bland's intellect and reputation as a good disciplinarian, instructed the Virginia cavalry colonel, on November 5, 1778, to take charge of the procession of the captives from Massachusetts to their Virginia destination. The commander in chief directed that the march begin November 8 and prescribed for Bland the route: by way of New Windsor, New York, Newton (in western New Jersey), York in Pennsylvania, Frederick in Maryland, and Leesburg, Virginia.[10] Continental troops provided the escort to the Hudson River, whereupon state militia belonging to the state being traversed supplied the subsequent escorts.[11]

The march of the prisoners began November 9, and on November 17, the group crossed into Connecticut and into New Jersey on December 5. On December 20 the marchers reached Lancaster, Pennsylvania. Six days later they crossed into Maryland, and on the 31st crossed the Potomac into Virginia. The prisoners came to their destination in Albemarle County, Virginia, on January 9, 1779, and began building huts. Food was scarce at first. The British generals resided at nearby homes, and other officers were allowed to find lodging within a 100-mile radius. Upon arrival Bland turned over command of the prisoners to Colonel Charles Lewis.[12]

Difficulty arose in maintaining discipline at the Albemarle prisoner internment site. Theodorick Bland was tapped again, this time as the commandant of the detention complex. In justifying this appointment to the Board of War, Washington stated that Colonel Bland "answers the description of the Officer which you think that duty requires, and has already had some acquaintance with the Conventioners." To Bland himself, Washington pointed out that Bland fully met the expectations of the Board of War, who

> having received disagreeable Accounts, of the situation of matters at the Convention Barracks, are of opinion that order can be restored only by the presence of a sensible, discreet officer charged with the general direction of their affairs, and having sufficient weight and knowledge of business to regulate the uneasy and discordant spirits among the prisoners.[13]

Bland formed friendly relations with the British generals William Phillips and Baron Friedrich von Riedesel and other officers. In a short time the Albemarle County prisoner of war compound had the appearance of a prosperous community. Bland, however, had some difficulty in shaping effective discipline among his Convention Guards Regiment, consisting of 600 Virginians enlisted for one year or until the prisoners left the state. Some of the guardsmen were very young—one was only 13 years of age. Their insufficiency of training was underscored when a sentry accidently shot one of his officers. An "intended mutiny" among the guardsmen was uncovered in August 1779. The plot was nipped in the bud by Bland's decisive action. Washington praised his prisoner commandant for inflicting only "light" punishment and expressed confidence that Bland could eradicate the main cause of the conspiracy—the want of certain "necessaries." Bland, however, was informed that he could not expect any reinforcements from the main army.[14]

To thwart the high desertion rate of soldiers from the Convention army proved to be Bland's major challenge. Almost every day deserters set out into the countryside hoping to link up with a makeshift underground "railroad" of Tories which would take them to the New Jersey coast and on to British headquarters in New York City.[15] Deserters from the German regiments could find refuge among kinsmen in the backcountry. In one week, 400 Convention troops deserted. Many were able to obtain forged passports and state loyalty certificates.[16] Eventually Bland was able to curtail escapes from the Convention Army. He followed Washington's advice to allow less freedom to roam in the vicinity of the encampment, and he kept out patrols to intercept fleeing prisoners.[17] In November 1779 Bland received permission from Washington to resign his prisoner of war command and to resign from the army, which he did in December. Colonel James Wood replaced him in the prison of war command.[18]

Bland was elected a delegate to the Continental Congress on June 21, 1780, and subsequently reelected for two more terms, serving until 1783.[19] A colleague in Congress depicted Bland as a "man of Moderate Talents, of firmness & Candor and Much Attached to the Constitution of the States — Tho not very Systematical nor always of the best Judgment and is rather rustic in debate."[20] A nationalist, Bland favored giving powers to Congress to tax. He proposed the establishment of a national bank, or rather a central agency controlling several different banks.[21] Bland supported the compromise that led to the commutation of pensions for officer veterans at five years half pay.[22] He advocated negotiating with Spain for opening navigation on the Mississippi River.[23] On June 5, 1783, he introduced a motion, seconded by Alexander Hamilton, for creating a large military reserve in the Virginia western land cession for satisfying land bounties given to the Revolutionary War soldiers. Nothing came of this at the time but it paved the way for the Northwest ordinances of 1785 and 1787.[24]

On January 3, 1781, Bland was appointed to a five-man congressional committee to join with two Pennsylvania commissioners to settle the grievances of the soldiers of the Pennsylvania line who had mutinied. On January 8 an accord was reached with the mutineers's Board of Sergeants whereby persons would not be held in service beyond their terms of enlistment and solutions were found for pay and clothing issues.[25] Several weeks later, as Bland reported, a mutiny of part of the New Jersey line was "nipped in the Bud." Bland discerned a lesson from the mutinies that American citizens "should turn their thoughts from Party Aminosity and Private gain to replenishing the Public Coffers with the Sinews of War and opposition."[26]

The British invasions of Virginia during the spring and summer of 1781 brought Bland severe economic hardship. In June 1781, he wrote to Governor Jefferson: "My Finances are as well as my Credit entirely exhausted, my Private resources in Virginia Cut off by the Enemy, and I am at this moment without the means of buying or of procuring money even to purchase a bait of oats for my horses." Furthermore, he could not find a buyer for his horses. Hence it was hard to just find "subsistence for my family." He had been unable to pay toward money he had borrowed, and was "exhausted to the last Shilling."[27] Two months later, Bland reported that at the hands of the enemy

> my House has been plunderd of the whole of my Furniture, and my Plantation Stript of every Negro and all my Stock which added to my loss I have suffered by the destruction of the Tobacco in the Warehouses and all my Crops of grain &c. cannot amount to less than four thousand Pounds Specie.[28]

Adding to his misfortune, during the period of his congressional service Bland endured several ailments, namely headaches, "broke Bone fever," and "rheumatic Pain in the Shoulder."[29]

Back home after his congressional stint in Philadelphia, Theodorick Bland became even more attuned to politics. In 1785 he was named the county lieutenant (commander of the militia) for Prince George County.[30] He was a candidate for governor, along with Henry Lee and Edmund Randolph, in November 1786. A joint ballot of the state Senate and House of Delegates overwhelmingly elected Randolph.[31] As a delegate to the Virginia Convention for Ratifying the Constitution in 1788 (although he was a backbencher and did not give any major speech), Bland made his presence felt as an ardent Antifederalist. He voted against ratification chiefly on grounds that the document lacked a bill of rights.[32] From 1787 to 1788 Bland served in the Virginia House of Delegates.

Bland was elected to the first U.S. Congress in 1789, taking his seat in the House of Representatives on March 30. He pushed for amendments to the Constitution guaranteeing basic rights. Despite being a staunch Antifederalist, he supported Alexander Hamilton's plan for the national government to assume the state's wartime debts. His position was not that he actually favored this measure but that its passage would underscore the supposition that the framers of the Constitution were seeking a consolidated government.[33]

While in New York City attending Congress, Bland became seriously ill from influenza during an epidemic, and died on June 1, 1790. He was buried in the churchyard of Trinity Episcopal Church in New York City. His widow afterwards twice remarried. Except for small grants to his nephew and land donated for the establishment of a college, Bland's widow was the sole beneficiary of his estate. Bland's remains were reinterred at the Congressional Cemetery in Washington, D.C., on August 31, 1838.[34]

Theodorick Bland was a man of accomplishment: physician, plantation manager, soldier, and legislator. He retained the friendship and confidence of George Washington. Bland had two important military commands: that of a cavalry regiment and the superintendence of a captive British army. His legislative service occurred at five levels; local committee of safety; Continental Congress; Virginia Convention for Ratification of the Constitution; Virginia House of Delegates; and the U.S. House of Representatives. A tribute to Bland by the editor of his papers notes that "his career was distinguished rather by the usefulness of plain, practical qualifications, than by any extraordinary exhibitions of genius." His "patriotism was not an impulse, but a principle."[35] A less charitable estimate of Bland states:

> Possibly the greatest irony of his life is the timing of his death, coming within weeks after he finally realized that the Antifederalist cause was futile. Bland, unable to face this harsh reality, turned his face to the wall and died.... After a lifelong metamorphosis designed to preserve the idyllic world of Virginia's golden age. Theodorick Bland, aware of his failure, departed this life, an unrepentant Antifederalist and a committed member of the tobacco elite.[36]

16. William Washington

No other Continental Army officer was more relied upon or endured more combat than William Washington. As cavalryman par excellence he was constantly in the field participating in a succession of military engagements from skirmishes to major battles. A superb and inventive tactician, he was always sporting for a fight. Few patriots of the Revolutionary War had as rightful claim to the status of hero as did William Washington.

William Washington. **By Charles Willson Peale (1781–82). Courtesy of Independence National History Park.**

Born in Stafford County, Virginia, on February 28, 1752, the second son of Bailey Washington and Catherine Storke Washington, and second cousin of George Washington, William Washington studied under the rector of St. Paul's Parish, Dr. William Stuart, to become a clergyman, but events propelled him away from that calling.[1]

At age 23, on September 12, 1775, William Washington was elected a captain in a company of Stafford County minutemen commanded by Colonel Hugh Mercer. On February 25, 1776, Washington was commissioned a captain in the Third Virginia Regiment of the Continental Army. Arriving with his regiment in New York City not long after the Battle of Long Island, Washington joined George Washington's main army.[2] Participating in both the battles of Harlem Heights (September 16) and

White Plains (October 28), Washington appears not to have taken a particularly active part in either.

At the Battle of Trenton on December 26, 1776, Captain William Washington commanded the advanced guard. He made an important contribution during the opening moments of the battle. Along with Lieutenant James Monroe he led a bayonet charge that captured the Hessian artillery battery. Wounded on both hands, Washington had to be carried from the field. Though his injury was painful Washington was able to participate in the honor afforded his Third Regiment—accompanying the Trenton prisoners of war to Philadelphia.[3]

Promoted to major on January 27, 1777, Washington began his long career as a cavalry officer in the Continental Light Dragoons. Initially he served in the Fourth Light Dragoons, and later in the Third Light Dragoons.[4] Recuperating from his battle wound probably in Philadelphia, Washington joined his new unit in late spring, and during the course of the summer performed scouting missions. Washington and his dragoons did not play an important role at the Battle of Brandywine on September 11, 1777, but after the engagement ended in a British victory all of the army's cavalry were employed unsuccessfully in the attempt to delay the British entry into Philadelphia.[5] At the Battle of Germantown, October 4, Washington's dragoons, on the American right in Sullivan's division, did not see much action because of the fog, but in the aftermath significantly protected infantry in their retreat.[6]

From October 1777 through June 1778 Washington and his dragoons were busy with various scouting duties and spent some time in Maryland and Virginia purchasing horses. At the time of the Battle of Monmouth on June 28, 1778, Washington and his men rode reconnaissance and were part of General Daniel Morgan's right wing. Morgan's force did not participate in the main battle.[7] On November 20, 1778, Washington was promoted to lieutenant colonel and commandant of the Third Light Dragoons.[8]

The remainder of 1778 through 1779 turned out to be a period of frustration for the action-oriented dragoons. Attached mainly to General Stirling's division, Washington's troopers performed utility duty, chiefly in providing escorts. Although under orders as early as spring 1779 to join the Southern Army in the Carolinas, Washington and his dragoons did not arrive in Charleston, South Carolina, until mid February 1780. Subsequently Washington's dragoons, now numbering about 125 men, connected with General Benjamin Lincoln's army in Charleston and had the assignment of protecting the northern line of supply into the city.[9] Lt. Col. William Washington now entered a period of a year and a half of frequent combat as a dashing cavalry commander. More often than not he faced his brilliant and brutal counterpart, Lt. Col. Banastre Tarleton, who led the British Legion, a Loyalist cavalry and mounted infantry unit.

Washington's first encounter with Tarleton came at Rantowle's Mills, northeast of a bridge that spanned the Stono River, South Carolina, on March 27, 1780. There Washington attacked Colonel John Hamilton's North Carolina Royalist Regiment of

Tory infantry, killing seven men and capturing eight. Tarleton and his legion came up and attempted to rescue the prisoners. Washington's dragoons charged and drove Tarleton back. Tarleton, lacking any infantry support, decided to withdraw.[10] At Middleton's plantation, on April 5, Washington, who had learned the value of hit-and-run tactics, attacked Tarleton's rear guard, took a few prisoners, and then quickly disappeared.[11] A larger engagement occurred on April 14 while Washington's dragoons and 500 troops under General Isaac Huger were posted guarding Bacon's Bridge over the Cooper River near Monck's Corner. The Americans were completely surprised and routed. Many of Washington's and Huger's troops were taken prisoner. Washington and Huger both were made prisoners, but both men escaped — according to some accounts of participants, by running into a swamp during the darkness; or, as a biographer of Washington states more credibly, Washington rode away on his fast horse which his captors had failed to take away.

During the Camden campaign and until the end of September 1780, Washington visited Virginia to procure horses, arms and other equipment for his Third Dragoons.[12] By November, Washington had rejoined the Southern Army, operating in advance reconnaissance and ready for a fight.

On December 4, 1780, an "incredible coup launched Washington and his Third Dragoons upon their ride to glory in the south." Learning that 112 of the enemy's cavalry under Colonel Henry Rugeley were encamped in a barn at Rugeley's Farm, Washington decided to attack "by Strategm." With his 90 dragoons, Washington found that because the log barn was occupied by the enemy and there was a surrounding abatis, successful assault would only be possible with the use of artillery. Washington, therefore, obtained a pine log, fixed it to resemble a cannon, placed it on a carriage, sent a flag to his opponents and demanded immediate surrender. The ruse worked, and "to prevent the Shocking Scene of bloodshed & Slaughter that must follow the first discharge of this Mighty Cannon," Washington quickly made the whole garrison captive. Washington's ploy is known as the use of a "Quaker gun."[13] General George Washington, who generally was very reserved in praise of his officers, enthusiastically declared that "the stratagem of Colonel Washington" deserves "great commendation; it gives me inexpressible pleasure to find that such a spirit of enterprise and intrepidity still prevail."[14]

General Nathanael Greene created a Corps of Light Infantry, commanded by General Daniel Morgan. On December 16, Washington and his dragoons were attached to Morgan's new force.[15]

To squelch the plundering by a band of 250 Loyalists led by Colonel Thomas Waters, Morgan sent Washington's troops and Colonel James McCall's North Carolina mounted militia to seek out and destroy this Tory force. At Hammond's Stores on December 28 at noon, the American detachment caught their prey by surprise while they were dismounted and preparing their noon meal. The Americans and the enemy were on opposing hills. Washington charged down one hill and up the other and the mounted militia delivered rifle fire from the flanks; Waters's men desperately tried to escape on foot. Despite Washington's attempts to restrain the American troops, the cavalrymen, angered by previous British massacres such as the one at the Waxhaws in May, cut down the enemy, giving no quarter. Killing 150 and taking 40 prisoners, Washington's dragoons did not lose a man.[16] The defeat and massacre of Loyalist militia at Hammond's Stores convinced General Cornwallis, the British commander in the south, not to place reliance on Loyalist militia and also to postpone invasion of North Carolina until he secured his western flank. Cornwallis, therefore, sent Tarleton to seek out Morgan and defeat him.[17]

Washington stayed with Morgan, who withdrew from Tarleton's rapid advance. The Virginia Continental general carefully chose a position from which to encounter Tarleton: at Cowpens, a former pasture for cattle, on a small rise about five miles south of the unfordable Broad River, which would prevent his troops from retreating. On each side were swampy woods and cane bogs, preventing any wide flanking. Morgan's force consisted of 900 men in two lines of Georgia, North Carolina, and South Carolina militia, a third line of Maryland and Delaware Continentals with 200 Virginians, and William Washington's 80 dragoons and 40 mounted militia on Morgan's left flank out of sight below the rise. When the American front lines gave way as planned after firing initial volleys, Washington's cavalry surprisingly charged against the oncoming enemy. Washington's men penetrated through the enemy's ranks and then completely wheeled around and did the same thing again.

As Tarleton's troops began to retreat, Washington ordered another charge, himself, his sergeant-major, and a trumpeter riding far ahead of their comrades. What happened next, as one historian notes, "was probably the most famous hand-to-hand duel of the war." Eager to catch up with Tarleton, Washington first encountered a British officer. Slashing at his enemy, Washington's sword broke off at the hilt. As the British officer prepared to administer the coup de grace to Washington, the latter's trumpeter rode by and shot the British officer through the shoulder, rendering his sword arm useless. Another British officer then struck at the all-but-disarmed Washington, but had his sword blunted by the American sergeant major. Tarleton now saw his opportunity to finish off Washington. He swung his huge sword at Washington, but the American dragoon commander managed to parry the blow with his broken sword, severely crippling Tarleton's right hand. Tarleton then wheeled around and fired a pistol ball at Washington, which merely grazed a knee but wounded Washington's horse. The other American dragoons quickly came up, and Tarleton had no choice but to join his own troops in flight.

In the one-hour battle, of Tarleton's some 1,000 troops, 100 were killed, 200 were wounded, and 600 were made prisoners. Only Tarleton and a corporal's guard escaped the astounding defeat. The American losses were only 12 killed and 60 wounded.[18] Following the battle, Washington and his dragoons gave pursuit of the remnant of Tarleton's troops, but soon returned to join Morgan's force.[19]

Washington reaped laurels for his bravery and skill at the Battle of Cowpens. Congress struck a medal in his honor. One side of the medal depicted an officer riding in front of cavalry troops, above which flew an angel with a laurel leaf in her right hand and a palm branch in the other. The legend read: "Guiliema Washington Legionis Equitus Praefecto." On the reverse side appeared the inscription: "Quod Parva Militum Manu Strenus Prosecutus Hostes Virtutis Ingenitae Praeclarum Specimen Dedit Im Pugna Ad Cowpens XVII Jan. MDCCLCCCI." (Translation: "Because having vigorously pursued the foe with a small band of soldiers, he gave a brilliant specimen of innate valor in the battle Cowpens, 17th of January, 1781."[20]

While Cornwallis found that the British cause fared poorly on the western Carolina frontier, namely at Kings Mountain and Cowpens, he felt he could successfully engage Greene's army and defeat it. The big test shaped up at the battle of Guilford Courthouse on March 15, 1781. Greene drew up his troops for battle in exactly the same way Morgan had at Cowpens: two militia lines backed by Continentals, with cavalry on the flanks. The militia held more firmly than they did at Camden, but, as permitted, after firing one volley at the oncoming redcoats they pulled back. On the American right, Washington's dragoons, initially concealed from view from the British soldiers, covered the retreating militia and became heavily engaged, along with Colonel Charles Lynch's Virginia riflemen, in bearing down on the advancing British Second Battalion of Guards, the 33rd Regiment, and a Jaeger unit. The attackers soon shifted to the American left with the intention of gaining the American rear. Washington, seeing this development and the Maryland Continentals struggling to hold position, ordered his trumpeter to sound a charge.

Washington's dragoons rushed down a hillside and clashed with the Guards. As one of Washington's dragoon captains reported, "Leaping a ravine, the swords of the horsemen were upon the enemy, who were rejoicing in victory and safety, and before they suspected danger, multitudes lay dead."[21]

Washington's dragoons charged through the whole British ranks and wheeled around and did the same again. Riding with Washington was Virginia's great Portuguese immigrant, Private Peter Francisco, 6'6" and 260 pounds. Relentlessly wielding his specially-made five-foot-blade sword, Francisco dispatched 11 enemy soldiers. A Maryland Continental regiment helped hold off the British Guards. In the charges, Washington came across a British officer accompanied by aides, whom Washington determined to be General Cornwallis. Washington immediately raced toward his intended quarry with some of his dragoons. Becoming aware of this development, the British officer and his party rode back to the security of a large body of British troops. While in the chase, Washington lost his leather helmet, and went back to retrieve it; in so doing, he left another officer to lead the dragoons on the charge. Unfortunately, that officer was shot through the body, which rendered him incapable of reining in his horse; the mount bolted a different direction, with the dragoons following, thus guaranteeing the British officer's escape.

Cornwallis, back within his lines, ordered the firing of artillery grapeshot into the third line of American Continentals. While this endeavor stopped Washington and other American troops in their tracks, it also, being aimed too low, wreaked a heavy toll of casualties on the British troops. As Greene's army pulled away, some fringe fighting occurred, mostly between "Light Horse Harry" Lee's mounted Legion and Tarleton's dragoons, who had arrived at the battle scene late.[22]

It is generally concluded that from the spirited performance of Washington's dragoons and others, Greene could have afforded to delay a retreat a bit longer and secured a decisive victory. As it was, Cornwallis took possession of the battlefield, but in reality he had a hollow and costly triumph.[23] Washington's dragoons' loss in the battle amounted to four killed, seven wounded, and seven missing—very slight compared to the British casualties.[24]

After Guilford, Washington and his band of horsemen performed various mopping-up activities, from pursuing enemy stragglers to rounding up livestock and destruction of Loyalist property.[25] By mid–April 1781, General Greene positioned his army two miles from Camden, South Carolina, where British troops under Lt. Col. Lord Rawdon were garrisoned (Rawdon had succeeded General Cornwallis, who was now about to invade Virginia, as commander of British forces in the southern theater). At Hobkirk's Hill, Greene arranged his army for combat should Rawdon attack; Washington and his Third Light Dragoons, along with some North Carolina militia, were placed as a reserve in the rear. The battle commenced on April 25. Washington's cavalry swung around a flank to attack the British rear, but because they circled too widely and had to go through a thicket, they arrived too late to directly participate in the fighting. Several miles from the battlefield Washington's men ambushed 60 enemy cavalrymen and dispersed them. With Greene pulling away from the battlefield as usual, the fight at Hobkirk's Hill ended with both sides each suffering about 250 casualties.[26]

For most of the summer of 1781, Washington's dragoons helped scour South Carolina from the Piedmont to the outskirts of Charleston, often in conjunction with other cavalry led by Henry Lee, Thomas Sumter, Francis Marion, Wade Hampton, and Peter Horry. From mid–May through June 22, 1781, Washington's dragoons operated in the vicinity of Fort Ninety-Six, and assisted in the unsuccessful siege of that post. The wide-ranging actions against isolated enemy units and foraging parties during the summer of 1781 were styled the "Dog Days" expeditions.[27]

At the same time that American and French forces readied for a siege of the British army at Yorktown, Virginia, General Greene decided to rein in British forces in the vicinity of Charleston, South Carolina. The ensuing battle between the two equal forces of 2,300 men each—commanded by Greene on one hand, and the British Lt. Col. Alexander Stewart on the other—proved to be the most disastrous engagement in the long experience in combat by Washington's dragoons. The Battle of Eutaw Springs on September 8, 1781, was fought at a site about 40 miles north of Charleston. Much of the fighting occurred in the woods. Greene's deployment of his troops resembled his other recent battle plans, with Washington's cavalry again arraigned in the rear as a ready reserve. The main action saw the front-line militia being pushed back by a British bayonet charge, which brought a counter-bayonet charge by Continental troops. Washington's dragoons, far ahead of any supportive troops, ran across on the flank a strong British unit, commanded by Major John Majoribanks. At this moment Washington's troops, now in an open field, were caught in withering musket fire, which, Washington's biographer notes, "turned this gallant cavalry unit into a screaming, disordered mass of wounded and dying men and horses." Majoribanks then conducted a brutal bayonet charge, leaving one-half of Washington's men casualties; of the ten dragoon officers only one was not killed or wounded. Washington himself was wounded in the side and made a prisoner.[28]

Washington's Third Regiment of Light Dragoons never regrouped after the Battle of Eutaw Springs.[29] The war was definitely winding down, and there was not much need for bolstering military strength. British forces in the south could not afford to remain in the field and withdrew to Charleston; Savannah was the only other southern site to remain in the enemy's hands. Washington stayed a prisoner of war in the Charleston area until the evacuation of Charleston by the British on December 14, 1782. During his captivity, Washington could not be exchanged because the British had no other prisoner equal to his rank in the south. Admired by his captors, Washington was allowed much latitude in his prisoner of war status — he was employed as a go-between in negotiations involving the contending armies and was occasionally allowed to visit the new estate he had acquired through the inheritance of his wife, whom he married during the period of his captivity. One reason that Washington was not freed from captivity was that he was regarded as a hostage in case the American military command decided to retaliate for the British army's hanging of Colonel Isaac Hayne for a parole violation.[30]

William Washington had fully recovered from his wounds by January 1782. He married Jane Elliott, daughter of a wealthy planter, on April 21, 1782. They had two children: Jane, born August 1, 1783, and William Jr., born September 17, 1785. The Washingtons made their home at the Sandy Hill plantation, ten miles west of Charleston. Besides the Sandy Hill plantation (inherited by his wife), which contained 4,975 acres, Washington in all had possession of 12,650 acres, involving six plantations. Washington principally cultivated rice, which brought high prices after the war, and he became one of the wealthiest people in the state. The Washingtons owned nearly 500 slaves. In December 1785, the Washingtons purchased a large mansion in Charleston, which served as home for four summer months as well as during February racing season. Located at Church and South Battery streets, the edifice is still standing.[31]

The dashing cavalry lieutenant colonel adjusted quite well to civilian life. In addition to becoming an enterprising planter, William Washington involved himself in a myriad of public responsibilities. Enjoying high regard and popularity among fellow citizens, he could have become governor but refused to go that route because he felt that he lacked the requisite speaking ability. Among the varied local positions he held, Washington served as road commissioner, vestryman, justice of the peace, college trustee, and sat on special committees such as the one formed to seek repudiation of the Jay Treaty of 1794. A member of both the South Carolina conventions for ratifying the U.S. Constitution in 1788 and 1790, Washington strongly favored adoption, having only such minor suggestions as shortening the presidential term from four years.[32]

Washington served three consecutive terms in the state House of Delegates, 1787 to 1790. During the same period he was a member of the state's Privy Council, which advised the governor on legislation. Washington was a member of the state's Senate, 1792 to 1804. Most notable in his legislative career, Washington voted against the "importation of Negroes" for slaves and the moving of the state capital to Columbia. He served as a presidential elector in 1796 and 1800.[33]

On occasion, during the postwar years Washington offered himself for military service during emergencies. In 1784 he headed a volunteer cavalry unit to quell riots by radicals protesting aristocratic rule in South Carolina.[34] From 1791 to 1798 he held a reserve command as brigadier general of the state militia.[35] During 1798 to 1800, in connection with the Quasi-War with France crisis, Washington held a commission as brigadier general in the proposed federal army expansion, which, however, never materialized.[36]

William Washington died in Charleston on March 6, 1810. His wife, Jane, survived him until December 14, 1830. Both are interred in the Magnolia Cemetery, a private Elliott family burial ground, seven miles from the Sandy Hill plantation.[37]

In all of America's military history, William Washington deserves to rank among the foremost war heroes. Embodying unsullied character and self-effacing, he exhibited determined and compassionate leadership and extraordinary courage and skill in combat on numerous occasions. Another esteemed cavalryman of the Revolutionary War, "Light Horse Harry" Lee, described Washington as six feet tall, "broad, strong, and corpulent." As to temperament, "he was good humored; in disposition amiable; in heart upright, generous, and friendly; in manners lively, innocent, and agreeable." As for being a man of arms, he "preferred the heat of action" rather than "the drudgery of camp and the watchfulness of preparations. Kind to his soldiers, his system of discipline was rather lax, and sometimes subjected him to injurious consequences, when close to a sagacious and vigilant adversary."[38] One of the speakers at the dedication of a 17-foot-high marble monument to Washington in Magnolia Cemetery on May 5, 1858, noted that Washington, while a prisoner of war at the close of the Revolution, had "the consolation of knowing that from the beginning to the end of the great contest, he had served his country bravely and indefatigably — that his prowess had helped to turn the tide of battle on many a glorious field — and that he played a brilliant part in the very closing scene in the great war-drama of Liberty."[39]

CONTINENTAL ARTILLERY

17. Charles Harrison

The artillery battery is often the single most important component of an army in battle. Its weaponry softens up an enemy and turns the tide of battle, but it also has symbolic value in combat. As a Confederate artillerist observed: "The gun is the rallying point of the detachment, its point of honor, its flag, its banner. It is that to which men look, by which they stand, with and for which they fight, by and for which they fall. As long as the gun is theirs, they are unconquered, victorious; when the gun is lost, all is lost."[1] It is an irony, however, that while artillery wins battles, artillerists are unsung heroes. Of course, there is the heroic gender exceptionalism of Margaret Corbin and Molly Pitcher as canoneers and General Henry Knox as commander of the artillery corps of the main army and as confidante of George Washington. But generally, the artillerist from the lowly matross to commanding officer has not garnered much recognition.

Colonel Charles Harrison was one of those whose accomplishments as an artillerist has escaped the laurels bestowed by history. Though he was present in only a few battles, during seven years of the war he performed distinctive service as both an artillery regimental commander and as chief of artillery for the Southern Army.

The youngest son of the nine children of Benjamin Harrison IV and Anne Carter Harrison, the daughter of one of the most prominent upper Virginia gentry, Robert "King" Carter, Charles Harrison was born in 1744 at the new mansion house on Berkeley Plantation on the James River, about 20 miles east of Richmond. Among the first settlers of Virginia, the Harrisons over a century had amassed a fortune from land and trade. Charles' oldest brother, Benjamin Harrison V, a signer of the Declaration of Independence, was the father and great-grandfather of U.S. presidents. Like his brothers, Charles was part of the new trend among the gentry's sons to forgo educational opportunities in Great Britain and opt instead for American institutions. Charles Harrison was educated at William and Mary College.[2]

In a bizarre twist of fate, Charles's father, Benjamin Harrison IV, and two of his sisters were killed by a lightning strike on July 12, 1745, as they stood in the north doorway at Berkeley.[3] Charles grew up at Berkeley and probably lived there most of his life. His father left him ample property; in 1780 he sold a plantation in Surry County, on which he may have lived for a while.[4]

Charles Harrison married Mary Claiborne in 1763; he was 19 years old at the time, she was 16. Mary was the daughter of Augustine Claiborne of "Windsor," Sussex County. The couple had three daughters and three sons. Mary died on July 25, 1775.[5]

Charles Harrison entered military service by being placed in charge of the artillery for a Virginia brigade commanded by General Andrew Lewis. Harrison's battery of two 18-pounders and another of lighter guns bombarded Governor Lord Dunmore's ships and royalist troops at Gwynn's Island in July 1776, near the mouth of the Rappahannock River in Chesapeake Bay. Harrison's gunnery "almost beat the *Dunmore* [ship] to pieces, & drove off the whole Fleet." As John Page observed to Thomas Jefferson, Harrison and his artillerists "behaved admirally well on that Occasion, so well that no one seems to regret the Lost of [Captain Dohickey] Arundell, who lost his life by a bursting of a wooden Mortar."[6]

With the initial enlistments in the Continental Army about to expire, Congress, responding to Washington's urgent request, on November 26, 1776, authorized raising a Virginia regiment of artillery, to consist of a colonel and a major to oversee ten companies. Each company would consist of a captain, three lieutenants, a sergeant, four bombardiers, eight gunners, four corporals, and 48 matrosses. Charles Harrison, who was given the command of a Virginia state regiment of artillery on November 30, 1776, was appointed colonel and commander of the new Virginia Continental Regiment of Artillery on January 1, 1777, with rank retroactive to November 30, 1776.[7]

Because enemy war, transport, and provision ships were "hovering" in the Chesapeake Bay near Hampton Roads, Congress assigned Harrison and his artillerists to the southern department, which meant they did mainly garrison duty at Portsmouth and Yorktown. Besides firing on enemy vessels, Harrison's men were available to intercept British landing parties.[8]

In March 1778, Harrison's regiment was ordered to join Washington's army. It was first entered on an army return at Valley Forge in May 1778.[9] At this time Harrison's First Continental Artillery Regiment consisted of ten Virginia companies (600 men) and two Maryland companies (120 men), for a total of 720 troops. Harrison's regiment was one of four that made up the Brigade of Artillery, commanded by General Henry Knox, Washington's chief of artillery. Supposedly, the artillery brigade was to have 3,000 rank and file; in fact, most of the companies were never more than 30 to 45 men. Since artillerymen were not assigned to a state's quota, the regimental officers had to use some of their own men as recruiters. A continuing problem was that artillery companies were expected to furnish two to three detachments of their men to infantry brigades.[10]

At the Battle of Monmouth, June 28, 1778, Harrison most likely saw intense action as his regiment assisted General Lord Stirling's west wing of the American troops on high ground, overlooking a ravine. The First Continental Artillery Regiment provided heavy shelling against British troops pressing forward. A contemporary recalled that this encounter brought the "severest artillery fire ever heard in America."[11] As the historian of the battle noted, "The artillery hurled the round shot and shell upon the charging ranks of the enemy and the volleys of the foot soldiers carried death into the British columns."[12]

From December 1778 to June 1779, Charles Harrison was most likely stationed with his artillery regiment at an artillery park located in Pluckemin, New Jersey, 15 miles south of Morristown. The main army itself was posted at Middlebrook. The First Continental Artillery Regiment (as it was now styled — minus reference to Virginia) would encamp at Morristown with the army for the 1779 to 1780 winter season. The artillery park at Pluckemin was a hub for all things relating to gunnery. Sixty pieces were there for training purposes. A military stores department distributed thousands of muskets, bayonets, cartridges, and flints. An armorer's shop repaired hundreds of weapons. In June 1779, the artillerists were moved out to accompany infantry units as the army again took to the field. The military buildings in Pluckemin were subsequently used for a hospital.[13]

In April 1780 Harrison and his regiment were ordered to rejoin the Southern Army.[14] After pausing in Virginia to raise recruits,[15] Harrison and his artillerists linked up with General Horatio Gates' Southern Army. An accident, however, prevented Harrison from being involved in the inglorious defeat by the British at Camden. As General Gates wrote Governor Jefferson of Virginia on August 3, 1780:

> Col Harrison of the Artillery, has been severely Wounded in the Leg by a Kick from a Horse, which Splintered the Bone. He was left at Buffalo Ford, on Deep River, and I am this day inform'd is Worse than when I parted from him.[16]

Meanwhile, Harrison's regiment was posted in front of the American center at the battle of Camden, and was eventually swept away as was the rest of Gates' army. Governor Jefferson, however, wrote Washington that Harrison's artillerists at the Battle of Camden "very much distinguished themselves."[17]

Harrison went home to Virginia to recuperate from his broken leg. He returned to active duty on March 4, 1781, as the chief of artillery for the Southern Army, now commanded by General Nathanael Greene.[18] On the mend before going southward, he took on the assignment of putting the Virginia Ordinance Department on a "well regulated footing." With this responsibility, Harrison visited arms depositories in the state to make arrangements for the supply of both Continental and militia troops.[19]

At the Battle of Guilford Courthouse, March 15, 1781, Harrison's guns held a position in the front line between the two North Carolina militia brigades, commanded by generals John Butler and Thomas Eaton. Although they gave an effective account of themselves, the American artillerists had no choice but to join in the retreat ordered by General Greene, leaving their cannon in the field to be captured by the British.[20]

In the Battle of Hobkirk's Hill on April 25, 1781, Harrison led a small force of only 40 artillerists with three six-pounders. Positioned along the sides of the main road and between the first and second Maryland regiments, they "kept playing upon the front of the enemy, who began to give way on all sides, and their left absolutely to retreat." Unfortunately the militia in the front were "thrown into disorder." Other American troops rallied too late, and the enemy "gained the Hill and obliged the Artillery to retire." Both the Americans and British withdrew. As General Greene noted, "we retired about two or three Miles without any loss of Artillery [being only light cannon were used] or Ammunition Waggons."[21]

For summer and fall of 1781 there was a far-ranging, non-glamorous mission. General Greene sent Harrison on a tour for inspection of stored arms and ammunition and also installations, such as laboratories and armories. According to orders, Harrison was to report on military stores at Oliphant's Mill, North Carolina, inspect the armory and establish a laboratory at Salisbury, North Carolina, and have arms and bayonets made at the Moravian towns in North Carolina, then go to Virginia, reporting on military stores en route. He was to put the armories and laboratories "in a proper way" for service to both Lafayette's army in Virginia and Greene's in the Carolinas. Harrison was also to arrange for the employment of 15 good armories to repair arms "with the army." Furthermore, he should recruit men to serve as artillerists; for the latter endeavor Harrison secured only 50 artillerists. Harrison assiduously pursued his assignment, keeping Greene informed of the status of weaponry and military stores at the various locations.[22]

Washington ordered Harrison to establish a laboratory (magazine) in Virginia for the support of the Southern Army. For this assignment Harrison traveled to Philadelphia to work out funding and other arrangements for the new facility. On his return, Harrison suffered from a "violent complaint in my bowels," which detained him from resuming active military duty for five weeks. Thus, he missed the siege of Yorktown, in which some of his artillerists participated.[23] By early January 1782 Harrison had recovered, and for the next six months he completed his task of seeing that "all matters [relating to military stores and artillery] were "regulated in Virginia and North Carolina."[24]

On June 14, 1782, Harrison, led a small detachment of artillerists and arrived at Greene's headquarters near Bacon's Bridge, South Carolina.[25] Harrison stuck it out with the Southern Army until the end of the war.[26] Before leaving the army he was often addressed as "General," although there is no record of such a promotion. After his official retirement from the army (January 1, 1783), however, Congress gave him the brevet rank of brigadier general on September 30, 1783.[27]

From 1783 to 1786, Charles Harrison resided in London, England, attending to business affairs. He expected to reap huge profits by handling tobacco contracts — the price of tobacco had spiraled because of scarcity during the war. He also traded in "the first blooded horses, mares and colts."[28]

Harrison never remarried after his wife's death in 1775. While she was alive, a contemporary commented that Charles and his wife Mary Harrison were known "for their many accomplishments, their high, noble, modest & genteel deportment & her extream Beauty, & his manly & polished Manners."[29] Charles Harrison died in 1794.

MILITIA

18. James Innes

If heroism is judged not by heroic deed, but rather by competent and energetic leadership in various capacities, James Innes performed heroic service. During the war he served in the state artillery, Continental infantry, and as militia commander. As a field officer he participated in Washington's military campaigns of 1776 to 1777 and in the resistance to the British invasions of Virginia during 1781. He was a commissioner of the Virginia Navy and president of the state's Board of War. Despite eschewing the national office proffered him after the war, Innes became one of the foremost leaders in Virginia society and politics. He was a long-term legislator and the state's attorney general. Innes won laurels for his magnificent oratory and debating skills, allegedly even exceeding the abilities of Patrick Henry. Governor Littleton W. Tazewell later said that Innes was the most elegant and eloquent orator he had ever heard.[1]

Later in life, Innes, at six feet tall, became enormously overweight, and was regarded as the "largest man in the State." He could not ride a normal horse or sit in a regular chair. As Hugh Grigsby comments, "In speaking when he was in full blast, and when the tones of his voice were sounding through the hall, the vastness of his stature is said to have imparted dignity to his manner. His voice, which was of unbounded power and of great compass, was finely modulated."[2]

Born in 1754, the youngest of three sons of the Reverend Robert Innes, a Scottish clergyman, and Catherine Richards, Innes grew up in Caroline County, Virginia. He received his elementary education

James Innes. **Miniature by Charles Willson Peale. Courtesy of Virginia Historical Society (1993.11. A-B).**

from his father, rector of Drysdale Parish, and attended a school conducted by Donald Robertson in King and Queen County. The elder Innes died in 1765.[3]

In 1771 Innes entered the College of William and Mary, where he excelled as a student and as a leader. He was especially active in the F.H.C. (Fat Hat Club), founded in 1750 as the first college fraternity in British America. The club professed to encourage learning and virtue.[4] Innes' authorship of articles published in the *Virginia Gazette* condoning the independence movement and his participation in "military engagements" cost him the position of head usher at the Grammar School of William and Mary, a position he depended upon for compensation towards his tuition. He was a leader of a group of students who seized military stores from the governor.[5] As the war came, Innes organized a military company known as the "Williamsburg Volunteers."[6]

In February 1776 Innes was elected captain of an artillery company of Virginia militia and participated in hounding out the governor and his small military force from Virginia.[7] On November 13, 1776, Innes was appointed lieutenant colonel of the Fifteenth Virginia Infantry Regiment to be raised for the Continental Army. He and his regiment linked up with Washington's army in time to participate in the battles of Trenton and Princeton. Innes marched in the funeral procession for General Hugh Mercer in Philadelphia on January 16, 1777.[8] Later in the year Innes fought at the battles of Brandywine and Germantown. An officer commented that at Brandywine, Innes was one of three colonels who "distinguished themselves."[9] At Germantown, Innes is credited for rallying troops.[10]

In late 1777, Innes was assigned as second in command of Virginia's Sixth Continental Regiment.[11] Though piqued by the poor quality of his regiment and its dwindling size, Innes stuck it out in the army. He returned to Virginia on furlough in early 1778. Overstaying his leave, he resigned from the army on June 12, 1778. About this time Innes married Elizabeth Cocke of Williamsburg. They had two children.[12]

In October 1778, Innes accepted an appointment by the Virginia General Assembly as one of the commissioners of the Virginia Navy Board.[13] This agency had difficulty in recruiting seamen for the state's warships. The government failed to extend the size of the navy. The Collier-Mathew invasion of Virginia during May 1779 knocked out the capital warships.[14] In summer 1779 the Navy Board was abolished; the subsequent five-member Board of War, with Innes as its president, had jurisdiction over all state army and navy affairs.[15]

During 1780 to 1781, Innes represented James City County in the House of Delegates, and during 1781 to 1782 and 1785 to 1787 he sat as a delegate from Williamsburg.[16] Innes served concurrently as a legislator and as a member of the Board of War. In the latter position he shared in the responsibility for oversight of all Continental and militia troops in Virginia; as the board's president, whose duties including clerking, Innes concerned himself mainly with recruiting and training.[17] In July 1780 the Board of War was disbanded and succeeded by a commissioner of war in charge of the "war office."[18]

James Innes had a major role in leading militia versus the British invasions of 1781. With General Benedict Arnold's British waterborne troops heading up the James River toward the capital, Richmond, Governor Jefferson appointed Thomas Nelson to command militia in defense; Innes was named the second in charge. Nelson and Innes had some 60 men drawn up at Jamestown to offer token resistance to Arnold's 800-man force. Partially because Arnold thought this group was larger than it was and partially due to George Wythe and two others out partridge hunting who took "a pop" at the passing enemy, Arnold's flotilla proceeded on, not disembarking until reaching Westover Plantation near Richmond. One contemporary credited "Colo. Innes's good management" as a reason the enemy avoided Jamestown.[19]

In February 1781, Nelson took sick "with a violent pleurisy" and turned over the militia command to Innes. The legislature was remiss in making out a commission for Innes, but despite this negligence Innes continued in command.[20] It turned out, however, that he did not have much to do, as Arnold's raid into central Virginia was conducted with lightning speed, and within several days he and his invaders headed back down the James, taking post on the coast at Portsmouth. Innes and his militia waited to join forces with the few Continentals being raised in Virginia by General Steuben, officially the commander in chief in the state during early 1781, and Muhlenberg. With Lafayette arriving with Continental troops in April 1781 and with a further reinforcement under General Anthony Wayne in June, Innes was placed in command of the buildup of militia at Gloucester at the mouth of the York River, across from Yorktown, to be in position to counteract British maneuvers in the Tidewater region. In mid–April, however, Innes was unable to prevent British detachments from Portsmouth from destroying the state's shipyard at the mouth of the Chickahominy River.[21]

Innes and his militia were deployed as a vanguard of the other American troops in Virginia. As an invasion force in April 1781, under the British general, William Phillips, they moved from Portsmouth up the James toward Richmond. Innes' force went all the way to Richmond, while Phillips' troops debarked at City Point (Hopewell), headed northwestward to destroy rebel munitions at Chesterfield County Courthouse, and then marched on Richmond. During his foray, Phillips and Steuben fought the Battle of Petersburg, on April 25. Four days later, Phillips was deterred from crossing the James to attack Richmond by the sudden appearance of Lafayette's reinforcement and some militia stretched out on the hills of Richmond overlooking the river. Phillips dropped back to Petersburg, where he died. His troops were soon joined with General Lord Cornwallis' force which arrived from North Carolina. Apparently Innes and his militia accompanied or stayed near Lafayette's force as the Frenchman played tag with Cornwallis' maneuvers in central Virginia. As Cornwallis moved down the James to Portsmouth and then established his army at Yorktown, Innes and his militia were repositioned at Gloucester.[22]

While Washington's troops and their French ally tightened the vise about Yorktown,

Virginia militia and French soldiers under General Duc de Lauzun did the same with British troops commanded by Lt. Col. Banastre Tarleton at Gloucester. For this venture General George Weedon superseded Innes in the overall militia command. Besides containing the Gloucester post, the Virginia militia had the important duty of creating obstacles for any attempted escape of Cornwallis' army towards Maryland. The one heated engagement between Tarleton's men and the allies was met primarily by Lauzun's troops.[23]

The victory at Yorktown-Gloucester signaled a finale to Innes' military career. In July 1782, Congress elected Innes to be Judge Advocate General of the Continental Army. Innes, already entering a civilian legal career, declined the appointment.[24]

Innes soon achieved status as one of Virginia's most prominent and successful lawyers. He turned away from riding the rural law circuit and joined the Richmond bar, where he could concentrate on practice before the state's superior courts. His most famous case, *Ware* v. *Hylton*, which he argued on behalf of Virginia debtors along with other members of the defense team (including Patrick Henry and John Marshall) before a federal circuit court and the Supreme Court, resulted, contrary to Innes' position, in the landmark decision that the Virginia law of 1777 confiscating pre–Revolutionary War debts due British creditors was invalid. Judge James Iredell commented regarding the circuit phase of the trial that he had never before witnessed the "ingenuity, a depth of investigation, and a power of reasoning ... with a splendor of eloquence" as he did on this occasion.[25]

As the single delegate from Williamsburg, Innes attended the Virginia Convention for Ratifying the Constitution in June 1788. He waited until the last day of the session before entering the debates. Innes excused himself for the delay by saying that, as the state's attorney general, he had been occupied in preparing cases coming up in the state's Court of Oyer and Terminer.[26] As one observer put it, Innes "closed the debates with a very forceful speech."[27] Patrick Henry, Virginia's most ardent opponent of ratification, though he took Innes to task for not supporting amendments to the Constitution, said of Innes that he was "endowed with great eloquence,—eloquence splendid, magnificent and sufficient to shake the human mind! He has brought the whole force of America against this State."[28] A celebrant of independence a few days after adjournment of the convention, in Norfolk on July 4, 1788, stated: "Demosthenes was eminently great in his and our days, but Innes has no obligation to pebbles to correct defect, or to extend his voice by contention with the ocean, in order to habituate himself to the tumult of popular assemblies."[29]

In his speech at the convention, adhering to the issue at hand — ratification with or without amendments, Innes declared:

> This question is as important as the revolution which severed us from the British empire. It rests now to be determined whether America has in reality gained by that change which has been thought so glorious — and whether those hecatombs of American heroes, those blood so

freely shed at the shrine of liberty, fell in vain; or whether we shall establish such a Government as shall render America respectable and happy. I wish her not only to be internally possessed of political and civil liberty, but to be formidable, terrible, and dignified in war, and not depend on the ambitious Princes of Europe for tranquility, security or safety.[30]

Innes felt there was too much diversity among the states on the question of amendments, and this could cause delay in granting the Union effective government. He denied that liberty was endangered in America.[31] It would be vain "to look for a perfect Constitution."[32]

In the period of establishing the national government, Innes refrained from soliciting federal office, both because he was essentially a localist (despite being a Federalist in politics), who preferred state service, and because of his recurring ill health, brought on partly by his enormous weight. He declined running for Congress despite Virginia leaders urging him to do so.[33] John Marshall and Edward Carrington nominated Innes for the U.S. Supreme Court. Innes was also considered for appointment as the nation's attorney general.[34] Had his health permitted, Innes would probably have been appointed as an envoy to France.[35]

Innes did accept two lower-level appointments from Washington. In 1794 he served as an agent for the president to Kentucky to inform citizens of the government's impending treaty with Spain concerning free navigation of the Mississippi. In 1796 Innes received another diplomatic-type assignment, as one of two commissioners who were to ascertain details of damages awarded to U.S citizens under Article 6 of the Jay Treaty.[36]

While serving as a Jay Treaty claims commissioner in Philadelphia, Innes, at age 44, suddenly died of "a dropsy of the abdomen" on August 2, 1798. He was buried in the cemetery at Christ Church, near the tomb of Benjamin Franklin. The epitaph, in part, reads:

> To the memory of James Innes, of Virginia, formerly Attorney-General of that State. A sublime genius, improved by a cultivated education, united with pre-eminent dignity of character and greatness of soul, early attracted the notice and obtained the confidence of his native country, to whose service he devoted those conspicuous talents, to describe which would require the energy of his own nervous eloquence. His domestic and social virtues equally endeared him to his family and friends, as his patriotism and talents to his country.[37]

19. Robert Lawson

As a Continental officer and brigadier general of Virginia militia, Robert Lawson had a major role in the military campaigns, north and south, and in the defense of

Virginia from the British invasions. He also gave distinguished service as a public official. Despite Lawson's prominence and influence in Virginia, his life remains in obscurity. Nothing is really known about the early and final periods of his life.

According to tradition, Lawson was born in 1748 in Yorkshire, England, and came to Virginia with his parents. He emerges, by 1773, as a planter-lawyer-businessman. Although he definitely practiced as an attorney, there is no indication that he ever underwent any qualifying process. He formed a business partnership with John Nash.[1]

Lawson's public life began with his election to the Prince Edward County Committee of Safety on June 19, 1775. The committee expressed loyalty to the crown and hope for reconciliation. It approved, however, of Patrick Henry and his militia forcing the royal governor, Lord Dunmore, to make compensation for power seized from the Williamsburg magazine. The committee also endorsed the revolutionary activity of the Virginia Convention in putting the colony under arms. Lawson himself was elected to the second, third, and fourth Virginia conventions (meeting in March, July, and December 1775). On November 20, 1775, Lawson was elected to the colony's 21-member committee of safety, which substituted as an executive body. The Virginia Committee of Safety confirmed the resolutions of the Continental Congress, which put the colonies on a war emergency.[2]

War interrupted Lawson's budding public career. On January 12, 1776, Lawson was elected major of the Fourth Virginia Continental regiment, an appointment ratified by the Continental Congress on February 13, 1776. Not much field action followed for Lawson and his regiment other than combining with other Virginia troops to intimidate the ship-bound governor, Lord Dunmore, who finally realized that his cause was hopeless and left the colony in August 1776. On August 19, 1776, Lawson received a promotion to lieutenant-colonel.[3] Finally, his regiment, in the brigade commanded by General Adam Stephen, embarked from Portsmouth for Head of Elk (Elkton), Maryland, on the way to join forces with George Washington's main army, which was stationed in New York City and vicinity.[4] While the Fourth Virginia Regiment, along with Stephen's other troops, managed to link up with Washington's army in New Jersey and fight in the two battles of Trenton, December 26 and January 2, it seems that Colonel Lawson remained in Virginia to attend to recruitment; possibly, he may have gone northward and returned to Virginia for this duty. Through July 1777, Lawson continued to superintend "the recruiting service for the completion of the Fourth Virginia Regiment."[5]

Somewhat frustrated by not being with his troops in the field, Lawson sought to resign his commission in July, but when no immediate action on his request was taken, he rejoined his unit in New Jersey by early August 1777, and found himself there as acting commander of the regiment. He was promoted to colonel and regimental commander on August 19, 1777.[6]

Although there are no recorded instances of individual actions by Lawson, it may

111

be assumed that he was present at the Battle of Brandywine on September 11, 1777, fighting only late in the engagement on or around Birmingham Hill in the Fourth Virginia Regiment of Charles Scott's brigade in Adam Stephen's division. Similarly, he partook in the piecemeal combat at Germantown on October 4, 1777.[7]

A month after Germantown, at the army's encampment at Whitemarsh, Colonel Lawson joined seven other field officers in submitting a petition to Washington containing "hints and observations" for reform in the Continental Army. The officers complained of insufficiency of pay, scarcity of "every necessary of life," the "unlicensed chicanery of the Staff," and the "eccentric promotions" without regard for merit.[8] Lawson again stated his intention to resign. Congress granted his request on December 17, 1777.[9]

Lawson's leaving the army had much to do with his decision to enter the political arena. He was elected to the Virginia House of Delegates in 1778, and served in both the May and December sessions. The highlight of this service was being a member of a committee that passed a bill, written largely by Thomas Jefferson, condemning Josiah Phillips. The bill condemned Phillips, an outlaw leader in the Tidewater region, to death unless he turned himself in for trial. In general, the bill offered pardons to those persons who had "levied war" against any of the states or otherwise had aided the enemy, providing they surrender themselves before June 10, 1778, and take the "oath of fidelity."[10] Lawson was reelected to the House of Delegates for 1779 and 1780. During his three successive terms he, at different times, served on the standing committees of courts of justice, religion and morality,[11] and propositions and grievances. From June 18 to September 27, 1779 Lawson sat on the state's board of war.[12]

As the war turned southward, Lawson, like many other Virginians, made himself available to defend his country by taking to the field with fellow militiamen. In this capacity Lawson saw some of the significant fighting in the south.

First of all came the initial British invasion of Virginia — a naval-army force on a raid in tidewater Virginia from May 9 to 26, 1779, led by Commodore Sir George Collier and General Edward Mathew. Anchored at Hampton Roads, 1500 enemy troops debarked and plundered in the area, sacking Portsmouth, setting the town of Suffolk aflame, and destroying shipyards, naval vessels, military stores, tobacco and provisions, and stealing slaves. Virginians and their government were extremely alarmed, afraid that the British intended conquest of the state. Lawson left his home in southside Virginia and went to Richmond, where he secured a quick appointment as brigadier general of volunteers. He then collected some 700 militia "in order to oppose the progress of the Enemy, which it seems saved Smithfield."[13]

With the enemy's rapid withdrawal from land operations in Virginia, Lawson again had respite from military duty. No one, however, was under the illusion that British forces would stay out of the state. The thrust of the British war effort was now in the southern theater, and Virginia, with its prosperous economy, served as a hub for supplying patriot forces in the Carolinas and Georgia, and it would see other British invasions.

A year and a half after helping to thwart the Collier-Mathew incursion, Robert Lawson found himself replicating the same role that he had performed during that crisis.

On October 15, 1780, a British fleet of 60 sailed into the mouth of the James River, and near Portsmouth landed some 1500 men. Governor Jefferson called upon General Muhlenberg, who commanded Continental recruiting in Virginia, to take command of all militia forces in Virginia. Militia generals George Weedon, Thomas Nelson, Edward Stevens, and Robert Lawson were expected to give assistance. Until the Virginia troops could take to the field, the enemy brought "fire and sword" at will along the James River.[14]

Six days after the enemy's landing, General Muhlenberg brought up 800 regular troops to the vicinity of Portsmouth where the enemy began now "entrenching themselves." General Alexander Leslie, commander of the invading force, intended, according to Muhlenberg, "to penetrate the country, and form a junction with Lord Cornwallis." The defeat of British loyalists at Kings Mountain on October 7 forced a delay in this possibility. Meanwhile, reinforcements for Muhlenberg, consisting of Lawson's 800 militia volunteers and 100 horsemen and 1,000 men each under generals George Weedon and Thomas Nelson, sealed any ambition for any further inward invasion of Virginia. A request to bring in a French fleet to join in on siege operations by the American troops before Portsmouth did not materialize. Leslie, nevertheless, grasping the seriousness of his situation, embarked his troops on November 25 and headed southward to link up with Cornwallis in the Carolinas. The American regular troops returned to their previous encampment at Cabin Point, and then went to Petersburg for discharge.[15]

The Virginia Assembly passed a resolution expressing their "high sense of the patriotic exertions of the Volunteers under General Lawson and wish to render them every proof of their approbation." It was expected that Lawson's troops would soon be dispatched to reinforce the Southern Army. The new commander of the Southern Army, General Nathanael Greene, wrote General Baron von Steuben, who had arrived in Virginia to take command of all American forces there, that Lawson's "corps of horse and foot should march immediately and join the Southern army." Problems were that Lawson's militia volunteers (brigaded with 538 men at the end of November, consisting of 465 infantry and 73 cavalry) had served out their tours of duty and there was a scarcity of provisions. Hence the legislature directed the governor to discharge Lawson's militia force.[16]

Robert Lawson was back at his "Rosedale" plantation, near present-day Farmville in Prince Edward County, when startling news came that General Benedict Arnold, with a flotilla from New York City carrying 1600 soldiers, on December 30, 1780, had sailed into the Chesapeake Bay. Word soon also arrived that Arnold, leaving half his force at Portsmouth, took the remainder up the James River. Reaching Richmond, the invaders put government officials to rout and destroyed supplies; they set the town ablaze and also wiped out the munitions at the Westham foundry, eight miles west of

Richmond. Governor Jefferson, about to flee Richmond on January 3, 1781, called out militia from several counties, including Prince Edward, to form resistance to the invasion. Lawson and his militia did not get into the field until Arnold had returned to Portsmouth after his lightning raid into central Virginia. Lawson's 830 militia joined with 500 men under Colonel Josiah Parker, taking position at Smithfield.[17]

Through January and early February of 1781, Lawson stayed with the American forces and the stalemate resulting from locking Arnold's little army in Portsmouth. Other militia besides his own came and went. Occasionally Lawson sent out detachments to contest with any British scouting or forage parties. Eventually his militia settled into a camp at Dr. Thomas Hall's plantation on the road between Suffolk and Portsmouth.[18] Among the difficulties that Lawson's militia faced were that many of his men were sick, "without medication, physicians, and necessaries," and that huts to shelter his troops could not be erected because of lack of axes.[19] When General Muhlenberg left to take charge of recruiting at Chesterfield County Courthouse, Lawson was placed in command of all the American troops around Portsmouth.[20]

Lawson did not find the relative inactivity in his lower Tidewater command much to his liking. He was eager to join General Greene in the Carolinas. Meanwhile, he decided to take a brief leave of absence. Writing to General Steuben, who was still the overall American commander in Virginia, Lawson declared, "My present state of Health requires this respite."[21]

Greene applauded Lawson's leadership in the defense of Virginia, and wrote Lawson that the militia were fortunate "to have so good a leader."[22] Lawson bided his time for the opportunity to bring militia troops to Greene's army. At the end of February he was given the go-ahead authority to raise militia for the Southern Army from central Virginia south of the James. Governor Jefferson re-designated Lawson's military status from that of brigadier general of volunteers to brigadier general of militia.[23] By the first week of March, General Lawson and his new militia brigade were on the march to join Greene's army.[24]

On March 10, 1781, General Robert Lawson brought 1,000 Virginia militia into General Greene's camp at the junction of Troublesome Creek and the Haw River, seven miles southwest of present-day Reidsville, North Carolina. Greene had been moving his camp almost every day to avoid contact with Cornwallis' army until sufficient reinforcements arrived. He had sent South Carolina and Georgia militia southward. The American southern commander very much desired a battle with Cornwallis and he had even picked out a site: Guilford Courthouse. Arriving about the same time as Lawson's men, were General Edward Stevens' Virginia militia, 1,000 North Carolina militia, 530 Virginia Continentals, and 400 riflemen from western Virginia and North Carolina. In all, Greene now had an army of 4,500 versus Cornwallis' 2,000. Greene was now ready to accept battle, and Cornwallis (oddly, as he had the definite numerical disadvantage) was all too willing to oblige.

Greene's army reached Guilford Courthouse on the afternoon of March 14. The British army was encamped only about 12 miles distant at Deep Run Meeting House. Greene intended to attack Cornwallis the next day but the British general instead took the initiative and headed towards Greene's army. Lighthorse Henry Lee's Legion skirmished with the enemy's outer units, and confirmed the advance of the whole of Cornwallis' army. Anticipating combat, Greene arranged his troops on a slight slope, using Daniel Morgan's successful battle disposition at Cowpens two months before. The American general formed three lines. In front he placed North Carolina militia, flanked by Continental cavalry. He put a second line 300 yards to the rear in a dense woods: a brigade each of Lawson and Edward Stevens' Virginia militia. The Virginians had some discharged Continentals in their ranks, providing a steady hand to raw militia. A further 500 yards to the rear were Greene's 1,400 Continentals.[25]

The North Carolinians in the first line were instructed to fire two volleys and then fall back. The Virginians in the second line were to allow the men retreating to pass through their ranks. At 1 P.M. the redcoats began to come on through 400 yards of open ground of a wet corn field in order to make contact with the American force. Cannonading proceeded from both sides. As the enemy's infantry closed in, they met withering fire from the militia. The redcoats pressed forward with fixed bayonets. That was enough for the Carolinians to flee through the Virginia militia line. Riflemen and Continental cavalry caught the British soldiers in a deadly crossfire. This determination and the brief, stiff resistance of the militia, served to break up the British formation. Some British troops got to the rear of Lawson's men, some of whom fled without firing a shot, but most of the Virginians held ground effectively, for awhile thwarting the advance of the enemy. With the enemy penetrating the third line and these Continentals giving way, General Greene ordered a general retreat. It has been said that if the American general had delayed this action, the Continentals might have turned around and re-engaged the enemy.[26] Although Cornwallis retained the battlefield, heavy casualties to his troops proved a devastating blow.

Lawson and Stevens' Virginians received plaudits for their gallantry and effectiveness at the Battle of Guilford Courthouse. A British officer commented that "the Virginia militia, who composed the second American line, did not quit the ground, it is said, until their commander, seeing them no longer able to withstand attack of regular troops, and ready to be overpowered, gave orders for a retreat."[27] Lt. Col. Henry Lee noted that his compatriots stood firm "against the wave of flight" of the North Carolinians and "battle that rolled impetuously toward them ... the resistance of the Virginians was rude and resolute ... and being better marksmen than soldiers, their fire, though not regular, was fierce and fatal."[28] General Greene himself said, "The conduct of the Virginia Militia deserves my warmest approbation. General Stevens and Lawson with all the Officers under them did themselves great honor."[29] The American adjutant general's report after the battle revealed light casualties among the Virginians: for Lawson's brigade, one killed, 16 wounded, and 87 missing. Interestingly, the report declared that many of the missing Virginians "are expected to return, or to be found at their homes."[30]

Lawson's battle-scarred militia had enough of war for a while and refused to extend their brief tours of duty and by the end of March had returned home. For the time being Lawson furloughed himself from Greene's army. Greene commented that he was "sorry General Lawson was leaving so soon." The role of both Lawson and Stevens at Guilford Courthouse was "important," and "the public are under great obligations to them for their services."[31]

With the war in the South unfolding aggressively on two fronts — Virginia and the Carolinas — Lawson, as a true patriot, could not rest on his laurels, and back in Prince Edward County he again set about accumulating another militia force. General Greene asked Lawson to come to Salisbury, North Carolina, to take charge of 2,200 militia expected to rendezvous there.[32]

Lawson was due in Salisbury on May 14, 1781, the same day that Cornwallis' army reached Petersburg, Virginia. Because of this development Governor Jefferson did not permit Lawson to lead Virginia militia to the Carolinas. Instead, Lawson was now entrusted with the command of all Virginia militia south of the Appomattox River, preparing to join Lafayette's troops in Virginia to form resistance to the enemy.[33] For a while Lawson and 600 men were stationed along the James west of Richmond to "prevent the Enemy from ravaging the Country in small parties";[34] this was largely in response to Lt. Col. Banastre Tarleton's dashing raid through central-western Virginia the first week of June.

Cornwallis decided to give chase to Lafayette's army in central Virginia, all the while seeking to destroy American supplies and military stores. From June 16 to 21 he occupied Richmond and then dropped down the James, with Lafayette's troops hovering nearby. Lawson now brought his militia into Lafayette's little army. The Frenchman did not feel he had enough military strength to bring Cornwallis into combat. By early July, Lafayette's situation had improved somewhat. He had been reinforced by Pennsylvania Continentals commanded by Anthony Wayne and the Virginia militia. Of Lafayette's 4,000 troops, 3,000 consisted of three little brigades, commanded by Robert Lawson, Edward Stevens, and William Campbell.[35] Lawson's men did not take part in the fighting between detached units of both Lafayette and Cornwallis' armies (at Spencer's Tavern, June 26 and Green Spring, July 6) near Williamsburg. As the British Army crossed the James heading towards Portsmouth, however, Lawson's militia were placed in the American front column as far as Byrd's Tavern.[36]

Although commanding troops in the field off and on to help form resistance to the British invasions of Virginia, Lawson managed to continue in civilian public service. During 1782 to 1783 he was a member of the Council of State (sometimes referred to as the Privy Council), which shared executive power with the governor.[37] While serving on the Council of State, Lawson gave up his law practice as "incompatible" with his public duty.[38] In 1783 he resumed service in the House of Delegates, membership in which he had given up after the 1780 term.

Lawson's southside militia remained with Lafayette throughout summer 1781.[39] During the lull of activity Lawson undoubtedly went to Richmond from time to time for public business or his own; while in Richmond, he probably left his law practice temporarily in abeyance. At the siege of Yorktown, Lawson's brigade was one of three, part of a militia division commanded by General (Governor) Thomas Nelson. Lawson and Stevens' brigades shared holding the right wing of the siege, while General George Weedon's Virginia militia were posted across the river at Gloucester. The Virginia militia brigades constituted 3,500 of Washington's total American force; the French contingent amounted to 7,800 men.[40]

Since the siege of Yorktown was primarily an artillery bombardment and the seizure of several redoubts by the allied forces was accomplished by Continentals and French troops, the militia on the south side of the river at Yorktown experienced almost no military engagement with the enemy. After the surrender, however, Lawson was entrusted with the major responsibility of escorting the captured British troops northward to holding stations.

On the day after the capitulation at Yorktown, Lawson received orders from General Nelson:

> take Command of the Militia ordered to conduct the British Prisoners to their Stations. At Fredericksburg you will meet with the Garrison of Gloucester of which you will take Charge, together with the Command of their Guard. One half of the Prisoners are to be stationed at Winchester, the other at Frederick Town in Maryland. Those allotted for Maryland, you will deliver to a Guard of that State on its Border; The others you will conduct to Winchester & so soon as Col. John Smith, County Lieut. of Frederick, can call out a sufficient Guard of the Militia of that & the adjacent Counties, for which he has my Orders, you will deliver them to him, & discharge the Troops.[41]

Lawson was also advised:

> If you shall find the Militia under your Command inadequate for the Duty they are upon, you are hereby authorized to call on the commanding officer of the Counties through your Route as contiguous to your Station for such a Proportion of their Militia as you shall think sufficient; & they are required to comply with your requisition.[42]

In all, Lawson would lead 6,000 prisoners of war. Except for 180 British officers selected to remain with their troops, only the enlisted men were involved in the prisoner of war march. Lawson and his charges set off from Yorktown at 10 A.M. on Sunday, October 21, 1781. At the front of the long column, Lawson, his staff, and certain other militia officers rode on horseback. Also mounted were those British and Hessian officers who could procure horses. The prisoners marched by regiment, usually accompanied by women and children. In front, behind, and occasionally on the sides marched Lawson's militia, who were drawn from units from the Piedmont and Shenandoah Valley counties. Large numbers of local folk greeted the three-mile long line of marchers, sometimes selling goods to prisoners who had hard cash.

By nightfall of October 23, the prisoners and their escort reached Bird's Tavern, 18 miles above Williamsburg. The next day some English soldiers mutinied, and so serious was the situation that the militia had to fire on them. At this time, too, individual soldiers began to straggle and desert. Subsequently, the march went smoothly. After a week's journey, the deadline allotted by Governor Nelson for the caravan to be supplied along the way, at Fredericksburg on the Rappahannock River, was reached. The next day, the 30th, prisoners from the Gloucester post arrived. On Thursday morning, November 1, the prisoner train waded across the cold waters of the Rappahannock and began moving up the Potomac Path, the main thoroughfare northward. On November 2, at Fairfax Courthouse, the troops destined for Maryland were headed northward while the rest began marching for Winchester. Expecting scant accommodations at Winchester, Lawson left behind 100 prisoners in the custody of local militia. On Monday evening, November 5, after covering nearly 240 miles, the prisoners were quartered at the New Frederic Barracks, four miles beyond Winchester.

Located on a hillside, the New Frederick Barracks was a series of connected cabins in two wings, one above the other. The prisoners were crowded in their quarters, with as many as 36 men to a cabin, barely leaving enough room to stand. The arrival by mid–November of additional British prisoners and convalescents caused further distress. Finally, on January 27, 1782, two columns — one each of the British and Hessian troops — marched out, later crossing the Potomac River, with the British prisoners ending up at Lancaster and York, Pennsylvania, and the German captives at Fort Frederick, Maryland. Lawson, who had to deal with a complexity of personnel and logistical problems, had completed his mission.[43]

After Yorktown, Lawson could expect that the orders so often countermanded to march to reinforce Greene in the Carolinas would be renewed. Various factors, however, intervened. His governmental duties received priority; in spring 1782, illness prevented him from taking to the field,[44] and the British had abandoned or had been driven out of all interior territory in the South.

It is not known whether Lawson returned to his law practice after the war. When he finished out his Council of State term in 1783 he was back in the legislature, and was in it again in 1788. As a member of the House of Delegates, Lawson labored for a more equitable real estate tax base for Southside counties, and he opposed the payment of prewar British debts.[45] From 1784 to April 1789 Lawson served as deputy attorney general, and in 1785 he became county lieutenant for Prince Edward County,[46] a position which made him the chief local militia officer.[47]

Along with Patrick Henry and the Rev. John Blair Smith, Lawson prevailed upon the legislature to re-establish Prince Edward Academy (founded 1776) in 1783 as Hampden-Sydney College. Lawson became a trustee of the new institution.[48]

Lawson demonstrated a community spirit in other ways. He was a long-time vestryman for St. Patrick's parish. This office ended however, when the parish ceased to exist when the state divested it of its property by virtue of the Statute of Religious Freedom of 1786. It has been said that by 1792 there were no persons in Prince Edward County who called themselves Episcopalians.[49]

Lawson and Nathaniel Venable induced a former French army surgeon, Dr. Francis Joseph Mettaurer, to reside in Prince Edward County. Lawson and Venable arranged for part of the confiscated glebe lands to be given to the new doctor for his use.[50] Lawson was also a member of the Virginia branch of the Society of the Cincinnati, an organization for ex–Continental army officers and their direct descendants.[51]

Lawson and Patrick Henry represented Prince Edward County at the Virginia Convention for Ratification of the Constitution held in Richmond during June 1788. Both men, along with George Mason, Richard Henry Lee, and others, formed a faction presenting "a violent and determined opposition" to ratification. These "anti–Federalists" opposed the Constitution largely because it called for a too-consolidated government that derived its power from the people and operated directly on the people rather than the states; a bill of rights was also desired. Lawson had little if anything to say on the floor of the convention, unlike Henry, who was on his feet almost constantly and at one time spoke for seven hours straight. Lawson, needless to say, cast his vote against ratification.[52]

From 1789 on, Lawson's life is completely shrouded in mystery. This is odd because he was one of the most prominent leaders in the state. It seems that in 1789 Lawson moved with his family to Lexington, Kentucky. General Adam Stephen wrote Lawson in that year, saying, "My congratulations on your Safe arrival with your family." The letter was addressed to Lawson at Lexington.[53] Lawson wrote Vice President Jefferson from Lexington on June 27, 1797, requesting an army commission for his son. Jefferson replied that he would see what he could do, but it would help if a recommendation were secured from General James Wilkinson, a founder of Frankfort, Kentucky, an officer whom Jefferson regarded as "the head of the military."[54]

There is a strong possibility that Lawson returned for long periods to his old home in Prince Edward County, even while his family remained in Kentucky. Sarah Meriwether Pierce Lawson (b. 1750), presumably Robert Lawson's wife, wrote Edward Carrington in March 1804 that she had received a letter from her husband the day before "informing me his father wishes to come to this country" and that her husband wanted to know "whether I could educate Columbus (name of a son of Robert Lawson) for a professional character, it is the only thing I long life for."[55]

If the letter just mentioned is indeed from the wife of Robert Lawson, it contradicts an astonishing assertion by Thomas Jefferson. Jefferson, at Alexandria on his way to Philadelphia in March 1790 to assume his office of secretary of state, wrote William Short, in Paris:

> For small news I have only *the murder committed by Genl. Lawson on his wife and his escape* [italics mine], the death of Grayson now hourly expected ... and the marriage of my daughter with T. Randolph of Tuckahoe.[56]

That such an event might explain Lawson's posthaste move to Kentucky is not likely as Kentucky at the time was still part of Virginia. There is no corroboration in the newspapers or elsewhere, for Jefferson's mention of Lawson having murdered his wife. Could Jefferson have been mistaken?

Three of Robert Lawson's children are known to have resided in Kentucky: Columbus Lawson, who was killed at the battle of New Orleans; daughter America, who married John Lewis of Harrodsburg in 1789 (Lewis became a judge in the Territory of New Orleans); and Jeremiah Lawson, who became a popular Methodist preacher in Kentucky, Missouri, and Ohio.[57]

Tradition has it that Lawson died in Richmond, Virginia, in April 1805.[58] There are no extant obituaries. Lawson was certainly held in high esteem by compatriots. In 1787, George Mason wrote of Lawson to Charles Cotesworth Pinckney: "My friend General Lawson being called on some Business to Charles Town" was "a very worthy and brave Officer of our late Army."[59] A modern writer has noted that Lawson "possessed a mind that was clear and orderly, he was an excellent militia officer, and he was energetic."[60]

20. Edward Stevens

Sturdy patriots from Virginia's Piedmont area answered the call from the Virginia Convention to turn out minutemen — organized militia ready at an instant's notice — to go into combat. The Culpeper Minutemen, recruited from a district consisting of Culpeper, Orange, and Fauquier counties, appeared as a regiment of 350 men in the fall of 1775. Lt. Col. Edward Stevens was second in command to Col. Lawrence Taliaferro. The regiment marched to join other Virginia forces collecting at Williamsburg for the purpose of doing battle with a motley group of sailors, Loyalists, and slaves whom Governor Lord Dunmore had assembled under the royal standard. Thus began the military career of Edward Stevens, who went on to win great distinction as a commander in combat in both the northern and southern theaters of the war.

Although he rose to military and civilian prominence, very little is known of Stevens' early life. Of British descent, Stevens' parents were among the first settlers during the early 18th century on the Virginia frontier as it edged from the Piedmont to the Blue Ridge Mountains. The British and Scots-Irish immigrants that came to the region mixed in with German pioneers. Fifteen percent of the Culpeper militiamen were of German extraction.[1]

Born in 1745, Edward Stevens lived all his life in the area of the village of Culpeper, in the central part of Culpeper County, of which it was the county seat. Whether Stevens was a merchant or a farmer is not known, but most likely, he was both, as were many of his neighbors. Culpeper, was founded as a county in 1749 and as a town ten years later. Situated amidst hills and piney woods, it represented a crossroads between the backcountry and river ports such as Alexandria on the Potomac and Fredericksburg on the Rappahannock. Before 1769, Stevens, married Gizzell (Gilly) Coleman, daughter of Robert Coleman and Sarah Ann Saunders.[2]

Stevens and his fellow minutemen had a snappy appearance at the Williamsburg encampment. On October 20, 1775, the *Virginia Gazette* announced that the "Culpeper Battalion of minutemen, all fine fellows, and well-armed (near one half of them with rifles)," had arrived in Williamsburg.[3] One minuteman was impressed by the reception given them by the local folk. "The people hearing that we came from the backcountry," said Captain Philip Slaughter, and "seeing our savage-looking equipments, seemed as much afraid of us as if we had been Indians. We took pride in demeaning ourselves as patriots and gentlemen, and the people soon treated us with respect and great kindness."[4]

By the end of October 1775, Governor Lord Dunmore was prepared to wage open warfare in Virginia. A mainstay of his military endeavor was to operate out of Fort Murray near the little village of Great Bridge. The Virginia Convention in Richmond entrusted the command of patriot troops in Tidewater to Colonel William Woodford. In late November the Convention ordered Woodford to send five companies of the Culpeper regiment to Norfolk and other of the minutemen to Hampton to assist in warding off any attack by Dunmore's force.[5] Unfortunately, one-half of the Culpeper minutemen were discharged. But the remaining 200 minutemen soon had further work cut out for them. On December 4 Woodford sent Stevens "over the river" with 100 men for a probing of British positions at Fort Murray. Stevens' men encountered "a guard of about 30 men, chiefly Negroes," and in the ensuing brief fight, Stevens's men killed two of the enemy and took two prisoners.[6]

As a result of Stevens' mission, the British commander at Fort Murray sent out a scout to reconnoiter the strength of the patriot force. On his return, the scout reported that the opposition consisted of several hundred "shirt men," so called because of the green linen shirts of the minutemen, emblazoned with the motto "Liberty or Death." Thus emboldened, the British commander at the fort ordered an assault on the rebel position, breastworks which Colonel Woodford had constructed at the end of the short causeway that connected to the fort. In the meantime, Stevens' and some of his minutemen were placed in the swampy area on the left flank of the causeway. As soon as the British detachment started across the causeway, it was caught in deadly frontal and crossfire from Stevens' troops. In the fight, which lasted less than a half hour, 15 of the attackers were killed and 75 wounded. Woodford's troops did not pursue the British survivors as they retreated back to the fort because of artillery fire. Nevertheless, the battle of Great Bridge was a convincing stand by the rebels and the enemy abandoned Fort Murray. Stevens' minutemen suffered no casualties, and overall the rebels had only one man wounded.[7]

After the Battle of Great Bridge, Stevens and his minutemen joined other Virginia militia and recently-arrived North Carolina troops commanded by Colonel Robert Howe in patrolling the shores at and around Norfolk. On January 1, 1776, Dunmore's naval units bombarded the waterfront buildings of the city, and landing parties went ashore and set fire to warehouses, with the flames eventually engulfing the entire city.[8] During the British assault,

> the intrepid Stephens still added to his fame. At the head of his hardy, indefatigable, and irresistible band, he rushed, with the rapidity of lightning to the water-side, struck a large party of British, who had just landed there, and compelled them to retire, with slaughter and in dismay, to the protection of their wooden walls. In general, during the whole of this afflicting scene, both officers and men evinced a spirit worthy of Veterans.[9]

By April 1776 the short-term enlistments of the Culpeper regiment had expired and its members went home, where they remained until early 1777. Other militiamen, under the command of Brigadier General Andrew Lewis and colonels Charles Scott and William Woodford, were adequate in containing the aggression of Governor Dunmore's motley crew and ultimately forced them out of Virginia in August 1776.

The Virginia regiments that were still in service in September 1776 were dispatched to the vicinity of New York City to be incorporated into George Washington's Continental Army. Meanwhile, Edward Stevens was made a colonel on November 12, and in January 1777 was placed in the command of a new regiment (the 10th), consisting of men from ten northwestern Virginia counties. Taken into General George Weedon's brigade, Stevens' tenth regiment spent spring and early summer 1777 in Continental Army encampments at Morristown and Bound Brook, New Jersey.[10] Stevens presided over a general court martial at Middlebrook in June.[11] On August 23, as the army prepared for a march through Philadelphia on its way to engage General William Howe's advancing army as it moved northward from having debarked at the northern tip of Chesapeake Bay, Stevens served as brigade field officer of the day.[12]

The second pitched battle of the Revolutionary War began in the early afternoon of September 11, 1777, as General Cornwallis, leading 6,000 troops of Howe's army, crossed Brandywine Creek and surprised the American army on its right flank. Stevens' regiment, in Weedon's brigade in Greene's division, was posted at the time at the center of the American line near Chadd's Ford, where Washington had expected the main British thrust. As it turned out, only a Hessian detachment attacked the American force there. With the enemy pressing his right flank, Washington sent Weedon's Virginians to the vicinity of Birmingham Meetinghouse Hill, and there at the base of the hill in the "Ploughed Field" occurred the bloodiest fighting of the battle. During this phase of the battle, Stevens and his men were only engaged on the perimeter of the action, but when the American troops began a general retreat, his regiment and that of a Pennsylvania regiment commanded by Colonel Walter Stewart provided cover, which hotly contested the advance of the British pursuers. At dusk, Cornwallis called a halt in the action.[13]

There was only scant pause for recuperation. Washington, who had spent a frustrating summer unsuccessfully trying to lure Howe's army into battle in New Jersey on terms favorable to the Americans, had confidence that he could still pull off a victory, especially if he could engage only part of the British Army opposing him in the field. The opportunity came when Howe, having captured Philadelphia, sent part of his army out of the city along the Schuylkill River. An encampment at Germantown provided a tempting target for Washington's troops. On the foggy morning of October 4, the Americans attacked. The whole force of which Stevens' regiment was part — Weedon's brigade in Greene's division — through a mistake in calculating the route to Germantown, arrived at the battle well after the action was underway. Stevens' men nevertheless pushed British troops back to the banks of the river before an American retreat was called. One officer recalled after the battle that he was wounded at the Battle of Germantown "and carried off the field by Col. Edward Stevens."[14]

Edward Stevens did not relish enduring a cold winter at the army's next encampment at Valley Forge. There would not be much opportunity for military action during the usual winter stalemate between the two armies. On January 20, 1778, however, a rather freak incident occurred. A party of 200 enemy dragoons came to the house where Stevens was staying temporarily in Radnor, Pennsylvania, and expected to break down the doors and seize Stevens. As the intruders "attempted to force their way into the house," with Stevens' men manning their weapons at the windows and doors, they were "baffled by the bravery of my men," noted Stevens. After the attackers had two men killed and four wounded, they "desisted and sheered." Stevens' troops in pursuit managed to "intercept" some of the enemy. So effective was Stevens' effort that his men raided the stables of the dragoons and captured all their horses. The only casualty for Stevens' troops was a "slight wound" inflicted on Lt. William Lindsay.[15]

Not only was there the dreary prospect of winter encampment, there were also many other causes for complaint among the officers. These included the inadequacy of pay, inflexibility of granting furloughs, and overall incompetence in army administration. Stevens, however, did not have the grievance that so disrupted the officer corps at Valley Forge: disgruntledness over criteria used in promotions. Stevens requested a furlough, but was denied.

On January 24, 1778, at Valley Forge, Stevens sent a letter requesting his resignation from the army to Washington and to the president of congress, Henry Laurens. Washington refused to comply, informing Stevens that he would not grant any resignation without the approval of Congress. Fortunately for Stevens, Congress, acting on a recommendation from the Board of War, accepted Stevens' resignation on January 31.[16]

Edward Stevens waited more than two years to re-enter military service. He was not among the militia called out to rally against a British incursionary force in the Tidewater area during May 1779. Nor was he among the Virginia Continentals who went to reinforce General Benjamin Lincoln's army in South Carolina, only to be swept up in the American surrender at Charleston on May 12, 1780. Just before the Charleston disaster, the Virginia legislature voted to call up 2,500 militia to be sent to the Southern Army. Edward Stevens was designated a brigadier general and commander of the new levies. In mid–June 1780 Stevens appeared at Hillsborough, North Carolina, with 700 militiamen. Here he would stay, adding more men to his force as they came in. Stevens' militia were now brought into a new Southern Army being raised by its commander, Horatio Gates, who had replaced the captured Benjamin Lincoln.[17]

After accustoming his militia brigade to military life and training for over a month, Stevens, on August 13, 1780, led his troops out of Hillsborough for Rugeley's Mills to link up with Gates' new army. Stevens' brigade consisted of 1,625 men, almost two-thirds of the militiamen called out. General Gates grossly miscalculated his situation. He thought he had a force of 7,000 men; in actuality only 3,000 were present and fit for duty. Stevens' force was not only deficient in manpower, but the militia soldiers, according to one contemporary report, were "raw and ignorant of discipline and under officers as undisciplined."[18]

Gates was confident that his untried troops would outmatch Cornwallis' force of 3,000. The American general did not solicit advice from his senior officers, and ordered a march toward the enemy known to be about 15 miles away. At 10 P.M. on August 15, Gates' little army set out, with the intention of taking post at a creek about six miles from where the British were encamped. Meanwhile, unknown to Gates, Cornwallis put his army in motion toward his opponent. Halfway between Camden and Rugeley's Mills the two armies met. Any full-scale combat awaited until dawn. During the brief lull before battle, Gates again had opportunity to decide whether to go into battle or withdraw. Gates put the question to his officers: "Gentlemen, what is best to be done?" There was no immediate response, as officers who favored a retreat were reluctant to be the first to speak up. Then, "The brave, but headlong" Stevens exclaimed, "We must fight! It is now too late to retreat. We can do nothing else. We must fight!"[19]

With the decision to fight now irreversible, the respective field officers attended to the disposition of their men for battle. Johann De Kalb's division of two Maryland brigades and a Delaware regiment held the right; General Richard Caswell's North Carolina militia was positioned in the center; on the left were Edward Stevens' Virginia militia and Charles Porterfield's 100 Virginia light infantry. Some Maryland troops made up a reserve. Both flanks were bordered by swamps. Stevens' troops were placed in the position which would be attacked by the best troops in the British army led by Colonel James Webster.[20]

At daybreak the enemy came on strong. Stevens himself said at that moment, "I was flushed with all the hopes Possible of Success as our left where I was had gained such an Advantage over the Enemy in outflanking their Right." But "alas on the first Fire or two they Charged and the Militia gave way, and it was out of the power of Man to rally them." The on-rushing Britishers, brandishing their flashy steel bayonets, terrified both the Virginians and North Carolinians of Gates' front lines. Stevens shouted, "We have bayonets, too! We can charge! Come on, men! Don't you know what bayonets are for?" But these American troops so panicked that most of them did not get off a single shot. In the panic, the Virginia and North Carolina troops fled through the ranks of Marylanders held in reserve. General Gates himself three times tried to rally the fleeing troops to return and fight. As the Virginia and North Carolina militia disappeared in the woods to their rear and then in flight far beyond, General Gates himself suddenly abandoned his army and fled as fast and far as he could. Only the Maryland and Delaware Continentals held their ground as long as possible. Stevens himself was far removed from the battlefield. As he said afterwards, "The whole was in the utmost Confusion, and the greatest Panic prevailed that ever I had an Opportunity of seeing before." So precipitous had been the flight of the Virginians that not more than three men were wounded or killed.[21]

Stevens was able to collect only about 400 of his militia as they fled northward towards Hillsborough. Four days after the battle Stevens paused at Spink's Farm on the Deep River in North Carolina 40 miles southwest of Hillsborough. Here he wrote Governor Jefferson that "we had to retreat through a Country of upward of hundred Miles which may be truly said to be Inhabited by our Enemies." What arms his men had not discarded, the Tories took away. As to his fleeing troops, Stevens lamented, "From their Rascally Behaviour they deserve no pity. Their Cowardly Behaviour has indeed given a Mortal Wound to my Feelings. I expect that near one half of the Militia will never halt till they get Home."[22]

By August 30, Stevens, along with the small remnant of his troops who had not deserted, reached Hillsborough. He again had bad news for Governor Jefferson. "Great Desertions has taken place," he wrote. "Judge what my Situation must be. My Pen cannot describe the trouble and Feelings I have had since I took Charge of them. Such disgraceful behaviour I believe was never Instanced before.... If every Man Deserts me I will remain till I hear from you on the Subject."[23]

As soon as the news of the rout at Camden reached the Virginia legislature, it immediately called up 2,000 more militia. Of the 881 men regarded as delinquent for not joining up with Stevens' force before the battle of Camden as they were supposed to, they were now to serve an additional eight months of their enlistments as punishment. The remainder 1,100 plus men were to be new levies. Virginia also drafted 3,400 men for 18 months service as Continental Army troops. Thus the state's proposed contribution to the Southern Army for fall and winter 1780 amounted to 6,000 men.[24] During September and October Stevens was busy receiving the incoming militia at Hillsborough and Taylor's Ferry, North Carolina.[25]

The new Southern Army under General Nathanael Greene marched out of Hillsborough in late December. On January 1, 1781, it went into winter encampment along the north side of the Pee Dee River "near the Cheraw hills," South Carolina. In February, Stevens' "eight months Company," as the Camden fugitives were called, were discharged.[26]

For a while, Stevens' military service was rather confused. In October 1780 Governor Jefferson ordered Stevens to return to Virginia to "assist in command" of militia being assembled to thwart a British incursionary force that had landed in the Tidewater area and was causing havoc to property. The invaders pulled out on November 23, 1780, and Stevens appears not to have entered this special assignment.[27]

Stevens had difficulty getting his militiamen into fighting shape. More than one half of his men were unfit for duty because of scarcity of clothing. He was given the double assignment of marching back to Virginia a large group of his militiamen who were allowed to be discharged and at the same time taking charge of prisoners of war from the Battle of Cowpens of January 17, 1781, for internment at Charlottesville, Virginia. Stevens set out on his double mission from Greene's camp on January 25. On his way, on February 2, Stevens met General Daniel Morgan and his detachment crossing the Yadkin River near Salisbury with Cornwallis' army in pursuit. Stevens paused for two days, sending his prisoners on without him, to assist Morgan in carrying supplies across the swollen river. Stevens tried to get his militia to reconsider accepting discharge and stay in the Southern theater a bit longer. Almost to a man they refused.[28]

Meanwhile, Stevens went on with his retiring militia to Virginia. In mid–February Greene's army and Morgan's troops also entered Virginia by crossing the Dan River, hotly chased by Cornwallis. Denying boats on the river to the British, the American troops had a temporary safe sanctuary in Virginia. Cornwallis pulled back to Hillsborough, and the American army recrossed the Dan River on February 23, to begin a war of maneuver until the size of the army increased. As a first step, Stevens returned to Greene's army with 600 militia.[29]

At the end of February Greene made camp along Alamance Creek, 15 miles distant from Cornwallis' army. Militia now joined the Southern Army in fairly large numbers. Stevens and Lawson formed two militia brigades. In addition there were Delaware, Maryland, and Virginia Continentals. Greene's army totaled 4,200 compared to Cornwallis' 2,000. On the morning of March 15, Greene moved his army near Guilford Courthouse and stationed his troops on wooded rising ground, thus inviting Cornwallis to do battle — an event the British commander welcomed, despite the inferior number of his troops.

Greene aligned his troops in three lines: first North Carolina militia, then the Virginia militia, and thirdly, the Continentals. Generals Lawson, with his brigade on the north side of the road, and Stevens, on the south side, held the second line extending 1,000 yards. Stevens, well remembering the precipitous flight of his troops at Camden, sought insurance against the recurrence of such behavior by placing behind the Virginia militia line a second line of guards instructed to shoot any militiaman attempting to run away. The Virginia militia line had no flank support, but depended on the flank support of the North Carolinians as this front line expectedly fell back. The third line consisted of two Continental brigades. American cavalry troops, especially those of William Washington, waited to strike from the rear flanks.[30]

Just past noon on March 15, the Battle of Guilford Courthouse began with cannonading by both sides for a half hour. The British advanced in three columns, somewhat hindered by not being able to use bayonets to advantage because of the woods. The North Carolinians, as though expected, quickly fled backwards, with Stevens' and Lawson's men opening ranks to let them pass. A British account describes the course of the battle:

> The Virginia militia, in the second line were by no means influenced by their [the North Carolina militia] example; they, on the contrary stood their ground for a considerable time, and fought with great resolution.... It was indeed an action of almost infinite diversity. The excessive thickness of the woods, had rendered the bayonet in a great measure useless; had enabled the enemy, however, broken to rally, to fight in detachment, and to make repeated and obstinate stands; it had necessarily and entirely broken the order of battle, and separated and disjoined the British corps, who could know no more of each other, than what they gathered from the greatness, the continuance, or the course of the firing, to different quarters. Thus the battle degenerated into a number of irregular, but hard fought and bloody skirmishes.[31]

Facing brutal action from the front, Stevens' troops were finally forced to retreat by the added factor of Lt. Col. Banastre Tarleton's British dragoon attacking from the flank. During the heat of the fighting Stevens sustained a musket ball through a thigh, and had to be removed from the battlefield; it was exactly at this point that his men gave way.[32] Eventually, at the Battle of Guilford Courthouse, in the words of a British officer, the American troops "gave way on all sides, and were routed with confusion."[33] Although the British held the battleground, their victory came at a high cost in casualties, and Cornwallis was reluctant thereafter to re-engage until he had a more substantial fighting force. The American casualties were also relatively high. Of 1,310 total casualties and missing, Stevens' militia brigade lost 11 killed, 36 wounded, and 141 missing, for a total of 188.[34]

Stevens' militia merited praise for their heroism at the battle of Guilford Courthouse. A British source said that the Virginia militia "fought with bravery, and greatly weakened the British line before it reached the continentals."[35] General Greene lauded the role of the Virginians. To the president of Congress, he wrote: "The Virginia Militia gave the Enemy a warm reception and kept up a heavy fire for a long time, but being beat back, the action became general almost everywhere."[36] In also noting the praise to Governor Jefferson, Greene added, "I sensibly feel the loss of General Stevens"; he and General Lawson "have been important and the public are under great obligations to them for their exertions."[37]

Stevens was soon on the mend from his wound, as it proved to be only a flesh injury. His militiamen went home when he did and were discharged. Stevens, however, was eager to return to active duty. General Greene wrote him that he was glad that the wound had not been of "greater misfortune," and said that he wanted Stevens back in active service as soon as possible.[38]

The British kept a sizeable army in Virginia, beginning in January and continuing through the summer and fall, first with the invasion of Benedict Arnold, and then General William Phillips and finally General Cornwallis. Stevens occasionally checked with the legislature about calling up militia that he would again command. So it happened that in early June 1781 Stevens was in Charlottesville, where the legislature had fled from Arnold's raid of Richmond, the capital. Cornwallis set out from Petersburg to prod General Lafayette's little army of Virginia militia and some Continentals into combat, something that the Frenchman skillfully avoided. Cornwallis detached Lt. Col. Banastre Tarleton and his feared dragoons into western-central Virginia, with one objective being to capture legislators at the makeshift capital, Charlottesville, and Jefferson from his home at Monticello. As it was, Jack Jouett spotted Tarleton's legion, which had taken the back roads in order to effect a surprise, trotting by Cuckoo Tavern in Louisa County near Charlottesville, and hurried off to warn Jefferson and the legislators. Except for capturing a few members of the House of Delegates who had delayed their flight, Tarleton's mission was unsuccessful. Stevens was in Charlottesville when Tarleton and his dragoons appeared. He rode by Tarleton and his men, and being in plain clothes and on a shabby horse, he went unnoticed. The capture of a rebel general would have been a major coup for Tarleton. Needless to say, Stevens did hightail it out of town.[39]

By early July 1781 Stevens was back in command of a new militia unit attached to Lafayette's Virginia army. He did duty primarily at the army's encampment at Malvern Hill, 17 miles south of Richmond.[40] He did not directly participate in the skirmish at Spencer's Ordinary on June 26, or at a major confrontation at Green Spring (Jamestown Ford) on July 6—both instances involving mainly Pennsylvania troops attached to Lafayette's army. In August the Virginia government, to show its appreciation for his heroic service, awarded Stevens a handsome horse.[41]

Stevens' and other militia encamped with Lafayette's army at Williamsburg. In mid–September Washington's main Continental Army and General Rochambeau's French troops were added to the mix. For the time being the American Continentals formed the right wing and the French, the left wing; the militia occupied a "second line." The "advanced line" was three miles below Williamsburg.[42] On September 28, the combined allied army, consisting of 8,845 American troops (3,200 militia) and 7,800 French troops headed toward Yorktown.[43] Of all the Virginia militia during the siege of Yorktown, only Weedon's 1500 militiamen across the York River at Gloucester saw any action.[44] Stevens' and other militia were held in reserve.

Further military opportunity awaited Stevens. Governor Harrison wrote him on June 25, 1782:

> The removal of the French Troops from this State renders necessary that a body of troops should be sent immediately to Garrison the Town of York, and as the Post is of consequence an Officer of distinction & merit must be fixed on to command. I have to request of you Sir to take on this important trust.[45]

A day later Harrison informed General Rochambeau:

> I have appointed General Edward Stevens to the command of the Garrison which I hope will be agreeable to you. He is an old Continental Colo. is a Gentleman of great prudence and of considerable abilities in his profession & has distinguished himself greatly on many occasions. I am led to this appointment from a full conviction that the Garrison being chiefly Militia ought to be under one of our officers who is acquainted with the Laws of the State, and will govern them as they direct.[46]

There is no indication that Stevens accepted this appointment. The governor was after him a month later to assume another command. Governor Harrison ordered 150 militia "to strengthen Fort Pitt" at the western border of Pennsylvania, and another 1700 men "under the command of Gen. Edward Stevens to hold themselves in readiness to march at the shortest warning" for the relief of Fort Pitt "should it be invested" by the British and/or Indians. Unfortunately, the militiamen had to agree to go beyond the state's borders for them to be sent to Fort Pitt. Moreover, General William Irvine, the commander of the garrison at Fort Pitt, requested that the Virginia militia not be sent because feeding them at the post "is almost impossible." The 150 militia were ordered discharged by the governor, and the other contingent not raised.[47] Thus Brigadier General Edward Stevens' military career concluded.

Politics had some allure for Edward Stevens. He was elected to the first state Senate in 1776 and subsequently consecutive terms from 1779 to 1790, representing Culpeper, Orange, and Spotsylvania counties.[48] Being a senator did not much interfere with Stevens' military service, as the Senate had little to do other than ratify or reject bills passed by the House of Delegates, and the Senate met only briefly during the October and May sessions. Stevens served on the usual standing committees, for example in 1787 on the claims and elections committees. He favored court reform and voted for a bill for the speedy recovery of debts.[49]

Stevens sought election as a delegate to the Virginia Convention for Ratification of the Constitution in 1788. In a five-way contest for two seats from Culpeper County, he, along with James Pendleton and James Walker, lost out to French Strother and Joel Early.[50]

With a recommendation submitted on his behalf by Thomas Jefferson, Stevens accepted in March 1792 an appointment by President Washington as an excise inspector. Among his duties was to report to the secretary of treasury on the status of manufactures in Virginia.[51]

Stevens was an ample owner of urban property. Six houses that he owned in the town of Culpeper were still standing in the 1970s.[52] Stevens donated land toward the building of St. Stephen's Episcopal Church and also for a Presbyterian Church in Culpeper.[53] The town of Stevensburg, incorporated by the General Assembly in 1782, was named for Edward Stevens. The town, which became the largest in the county, was located on a direct route from Fredericksburg to the mountains.[54]

Stevens died August 17, 1820, in Culpeper.[55] By his will he left property to his widow, Gilly Stevens (who died January 27, 1821): daughter-in-law, Polly Williams (widow of his only son, John — the couple were childless); and to children of his sister and friends.[56]

21. John "Jack" Jouett

Jack Jouett performed a daring feat similar to that of Paul Revere: Both rode off to sound the alarm to state leaders gathered at an interior village of the state that the "British are coming!" Though Revere did not accomplish his mission, his ride was celebrated in a poem, and he has come down through history as a legendary hero. Jouett, on the other hand, was successful, but no poets of post war Virginia documented his deed. Jack Jouett stands out from the other subjects of this volume in that he is lauded for a single accomplishment in contrast to the recognition of the accumulated endeavors of the others.

An imposing 6'4" and weighing 220 pounds in adulthood, Jack Jouett was descended from French Huguenots who came to Manakin, a village just outside of Richmond and then to nearby counties of Louisa and Albemarle. Jack Jouett was born in Charlottesville (in Albemarle County) on December 7, 1754, one of three sons of John Jouett, Sr., and Mourning Glenn Harris. The senior Jouett was sub-sheriff of Louisa County, 1763–66, and primarily a tavern keeper.[1]

Father and son signed the Albemarle Declaration of 202 citizens renouncing allegiance to George III. Both men were militia captains. Jack's brother Matthew was killed at the Battle of Brandywine, and his other brother, Robert, a captain in the Continental Army, was wounded at the Battle of Eutaw Springs.[2]

Until 1781, Jack Jouett, as a captain in the militia, did not see much in the way of military action, as the war had avoided Virginia since the departure of Governor Lord Dunmore in August 1776, with the exception of the very brief enemy incursions into the state in May 1779 and October 1780. The Benedict Arnold invasion, which began in January 1781 and was complemented by reinforcements under General William

Phillips in April, mainly elicited activity from only the southeastern and central counties of Virginia. Louisa and Albemarle counties were only marginally affected. But in May 1781, Cornwallis began to lead an army up from North Carolina to join forces with Phillips/Arnold in May 1781, which became a matter of utmost importance to all citizens. In its southern strategy, the enemy was determined to take Virginia out of the war and also had a subsidiary objective of setting free the captive Convention Army (prisoners from the battle of Saratoga) interned near Charlottesville.

While taking his army towards Fredericksburg in pursuit of General Lafayette's small army and then engaging in a retrograde movement, Cornwallis dispatched Lt. Col. Banastre Tarleton with his legion of 180 men and 70 mounted infantry beyond his right flank. Tarleton had orders to capture Thomas Jefferson, the outgoing governor, at his home, destroy military stores at Charlottesville, Old Albemarle Courthouse, and Point of Fork, and disperse (or capture) members of the Virginia Assembly then convening at Charlottesville.[3] Tarleton's dragoons, consisting of Loyalist cavalry from New York and Pennsylvania, had a reputation for brutal acts, such as the massacre of members of a Virginia detachment in South Carolina in May 1780 when they attempted to surrender.

On the night of June 3, 1781, Jack Jouett was in the vicinity of Cuckoo Tavern, seven miles east of Louisa County Courthouse and 40 miles from Charlottesville. John's father is reputedly to have once owned the tavern, but at the time he was the proprietor of Swan Tavern in Charlottesville. Jack Jouett, who himself lived in Charlottesville, was in Louisa County—probably to look into his father's real estate there.[4] At 10 P.M. Tarleton's troopers came up on the main road and rode past the tavern. Jouett instantly realized Tarleton's objective, including the seizure of Jefferson. Tarleton did not pause until 11 P.M. when he stopped at a plantation near the Louisa County Courthouse. After three hours, the enemy was again on the march, whereupon they captured a wagon train of 11 vehicles carting arms and clothing destined for General Greene's Southern Army. At daybreak Tarleton and his men halted at Castle Hill, the home of Dr. Thomas Walker, where they had a hearty breakfast and ensnared "some of the principal gentlemen of Virginia." Before he himself headed out, Tarleton detailed Captain McCloud and a party of troopers to Monticello to capture Jefferson.[5]

Meanwhile, Jack Jouett responded quickly to Tarleton's advance. By setting out on a thoroughbred horse and exchanging it for a fresh mount at Dr. Walker's and because of Tarleton's pauses, Jouett eventually put a three-hour difference between himself and Tarleton. Jouett's journey, however, was not an easy one; He was imperiled by hilly terrain, woods, underbrush, and roadways that were hardly more than paths. Jouett's ride took him across the Rivanna River and through the little village of Milton.[6]

Jouett's arrival at Monticello just before dawn at 4:30 A.M. awakened Jefferson and his guests: Archibald Cary, speaker of the Virginia Senate, Benjamin Harrison, speaker of the House of Delegates, and several visiting legislators. After sitting down with the group for a glass of wine, Jouett set off for Charlottesville, two miles distant. Jefferson sent his wife and family to Blenheim, a nearby Carter plantation, and then on to Enniscorthy, an estate belonging to Colonel John Coles on the Staunton River. The outgoing Virginia governor himself did not want to depart from Monticello until he was sure that Tarleton aimed at his homestead.[7]

As Jefferson settled down to await further news, Captain Christopher Hudson suddenly appeared. He had ridden up the steep hill to Monticello and announced that at that very moment an enemy party was doing the same. Hudson had been in Charlottesville when someone told him that Jouett had sounded the alarm. Not knowing whether Jefferson had learned of the oncoming enemy, Hudson took it upon himself to bring the tidings. At Monticello, Hudson found Jefferson "tranquil, and undisturbed." Convinced that the enemy was only a few minutes away, Jefferson fled down the back of the mountain, and rode off to join his family at Blenheim.[8]

On June 4 Jouett succeeded in alerting the Virginia legislators, most of whom fled. The General Assembly had adjourned on January 2 at Richmond in the face of the British invasion, and had convened again at Charlottesville on May 28. The legislative refugees re-established the General Assembly at Staunton on June 7.[9]

Jack Jouett. By unknown artist. Courtesy of the Jack Jouett Chapter of the Daughters of the American Revolution, Charlottesville, Virginia

One delegate who did not flee Charlottesville when Tarleton's raiders appeared was Daniel Boone, who represented a district of Virginia-controlled Kentucky. He and Jouett had stayed behind to secure wagons and horses. As Tarleton's dragoons arrived, Boone and Jouett took their leave. Before they could get away, however, they were apprehended, examined, and released by the enemy troopers. Both men were plainly dressed, and Boone, in his usual buckskin attire, did not incite suspicion that he was a member of the House of Delegates. As both men departed they came to a fork in the road and Jouett said to Boone, "Wait a minute, Captain Boone, and I'll go with you." A British officer was heard to say, "Ah, he is a captain," and Boone and Jouett immediately were placed in custody, and detained several days. Both captives had to give their parole not to take up arms against the British. A primary reason Boone was released, as his son later mentioned, was that "he very probably explained his title of captain by referring to his old Dunmore commission [1775]."[10]

After the Monticello–Charlottesville raid and destruction of some military stores in the area, Tarleton's detachment reunited with Cornwallis' army at Elk Hill on the James River. The British army occupied Richmond from June 16 to 21 and then dropped down the river to Williamsburg, eventually stationing themselves at Portsmouth and then Yorktown. Tarleton made one more wide-ranging raid for 16 days in July into southwestern Virginia.[11]

The Virginia legislature did not wait long to officially recognize Jack Jouett's heroic ride of June 3 to 4. As soon as it reconvened in Staunton it resolved

> that the Executive be directed to present to Captain John Jouett an elegant sword and pair of pistols as a memorial of the high sense which the General Assembly entertain of his activity and enterprise in watching the motions of the enemy's cavalry on their late incursion to Charlottesville and conveying the Assembly timely information of their approach, whereby the designs of the enemy were frustrated and many valuable stores preserved.[12]

Jouett received the jeweled sword (purchased in France) in 1783, but it was not until 1803 that he came into possession of the two French pistols.[13]

Jack Jouett was among the first pioneers in Kentucky. In 1782 he settled at Harrodsburg. On August 24, 1784, he married his childhood sweetheart, Sally Robards, sister of Lewis Robards, husband of Rachel Donelson, who was later the wife of Andrew Jackson.

As a member of the Virginia House of Delegates in 1787 and 1790, Jouett was a strong supporter for Kentucky statehood. He served in the Danville Convention of 1788, in which he helped draft in committee a petition to the Virginia General Assembly "for obtaining the independence of Kentucky." Jouett was a member of the Kentucky legislature from Mercer County in 1792 and from Woodford County in 1795, 1796, and 1797. His final place of residence was in Bath County.[14]

Jack Jouett figured in the controversy involving Andrew Jackson and his wife, Rachel. Jouett served on a special committee for empowering the court of appeals in Kentucky to act on a petition of Lewis Robards, Jouett's brother-in-law, for divorce from Rachel Donelson. The General Assembly granted Robard's right to sue in the Kentucky courts for divorce, which Robards neglected to do. Under the false impression that divorce had been granted, Jackson and Donelson married illegally.[15]

Kentucky is indebted to Jack Jouett for helping it to become a livestock raising state. He imported thoroughbred cattle and horses from England. Jouett was a judge at the first cattle show in Kentucky, held in Fayette County in 1816. Sallie, the bay mare that Jouett first mounted on his famous ride, became the progenitor of a long line of thoroughbreds in Kentucky down to the present time.[16]

Jack Jouett died on March 1, 1822, and was buried at his Bath County farm, Peeled

Oak.[17] He had 12 children; his second son, Matthew Harris Jouett, who studied with Gilbert Stuart, achieved fame as a portrait artist.[18]

A fitting tribute is given to Jack Jouett by the preeminent historian of Kentucky:

He was a man of note in his day, "physically and mentally a *man*"; full of humor, fond of fun, a high liver, remarkable for hospitality, the associate and companion of Clay, Jackson, Joe Daviess, Breckinridge and the Marshalls, indeed of all the great men of early Kentucky.[19]

STATE LEGION

22. Charles Dabney

A tall, dignified and congenial aristocrat, Charles Dabney aimed to please. A life-long bachelor, he often materially aided family members, friends, and comrade veterans. He was one of the few Virginian Revolutionary War officers to serve on active duty for the entire duration of the war. Only briefly in Continental service, Dabney had about all of his military career in the Virginia army — the Virginia State Line, which was employed mainly for intra-state defense, but on occasion was borrowed for use in conjunction with the Continental Army.

The third son of Colonel William Dabney, Charles Dabney was born in 1745 at the family's Aldingham plantation on the South Anna River in Hanover County near Richmond. The Dabneys in Virginia date back to the Huguenot immigration of the mid–1650s.[1]

May 1775 saw Charles Dabney active on two revolutionary fronts. He was serving on the 13-man Committee of Safety for Hanover County[2] and was among local rebels who were led by Patrick Henry to Williamsburg to seek amends from Governor Lord Dunmore, who had whisked powder away from the town's magazine to a royal ship in the James River.[3] Instead of returning his prize, the governor made compensation for it.

For the next year and a half Dabney stayed on as a captain of local militia.[4] On December 20, 1776, Dabney was appointed major in the Third Virginia Continental Regiment, and subsequently, on June 23, 1777, became a lieutenant colonel in the Second Virginia Regiment.[5] There is no indication that Dabney saw any action along with the Virginia and North Carolina Continentals and militia in the several military engagements in Virginia that forced the royal governor and his motley troops to evacuate the state finally in August 1776. Nor is it known if he was present with Washington's army during the northern campaigns up through the battles of Brandywine and Germantown.

Dabney is identified as being at Valley Forge in early 1778; there is a marker at the park designating his campsite.[6] He served in Christian Febiger's Second Virginia Regiment in General Muhlenberg's brigade.[7]

During the Battle of Monmouth, June 28, 1778, Dabney and his regiment were attached to General William Smallwood's brigade. Toward the end of the battle, as the British began their retreat, a French officer rode up to Smallwood to advise him that Washington had given orders to advance along a causeway over a swampy morass to attack the enemy. The movement would have been virtually suicidal. Smallwood, however, dutifully obeyed, despite his officers calling for a halt. Halfway across the morass, an aide-de-camp to Washington rode up and declared that no order to advance had been issued and directed a countermarch.[8]

In late summer of 1778 Dabney resigned from the Continental Army, and on September 30 of the same year accepted an appointment as lieutenant colonel in the second Virginia State Regiment.[9] Virginia needed to shore up its immediate defenses. For the first time since the departure of Governor Lord Dunmore's force in August 1776, the state was again susceptible to invasion. A combined army-navy flotilla out of New York City briefly made an intrusion into Tidewater Virginia in May 1779. There was not much reason to think that this feat would soon be duplicated, and therefore, Dabney and his state regiment were allowed to join Washington's army during summer 1779.

While again attached to General Muhlenberg's brigade, it seems that Dabney was honored by being one of those soldiers selected to give service in the special light infantry corps. Washington had learned belatedly the value of light infantry, which could be employed for diverse functions, ranging from reconnaissance to harassment of an enemy's advance. A special light infantry corps had been of immense worth during the preliminaries leading up to the Battle of Brandywine. During the summer of 1779, General Anthony Wayne commanded the light infantry, which drew on the best soldiers selected from the army's regiments. After the war Dabney heartily boasted of his presence with Wayne's troops in their brilliant capture of Stony Point on July 16, 1779. This post, along with Verplanck, both on the Hudson River, had been captured from the rebels in June. Both posts were of great strategic importance to the security of the Highlands and to keeping open communications and navigation. Wayne's light infantry corps of 1,200 men consisted of four specially constituted regiments, with selected Virginia troops forming one of the companies.[10]

Stony Point, surrounded on three sides by water, was garrisoned by 600 British soldiers. Two lines of abatis protected the fort on its land side. It seems that Dabney was one of the 700 troops whom Wayne sent in as a frontal assault, with a team ahead clearing away the abatis. The successful attack, carried on entirely by the use of bayonets, was a complete surprise to the enemy. The British lost almost 100 killed or wounded and 450 captured; the rebels had 15 killed and 83 wounded.[11] One of Dabney's recollections of the event was his feelings of horror upon witnessing "the agony of a British officer who had his thigh broken," and "in this condition was repeatedly trampled on by the combatants in the fury of the melee."[12] Interestingly, part of General Muhlenberg's brigade, to which Dabney was normally assigned, provided a detachment of 300 men "on the opposite side of the marsh," in reserve and ready to support the attack and cover a retreat.[13]

After Stony Point, with the rest of the Virginia troops with Washington's army headed southward to link up with General Benjamin Lincoln's Southern Army, Dabney and his state legion returned to Virginia where they would stay for the remainder of the war. For nearly a year, the enemy held ground in the state, with General Benedict Arnold's invasion of Virginia in January 1781 and culminating with Cornwallis' surrender in October 1781.

As Arnold and his invasion force settled in Portsmouth, Lieutenant Colonel Dabney was given charge of military posts below Williamsburg. Governor Jefferson, in February 1781, expected Dabney to assemble a team for the purpose of capturing the turncoat general, making use of a water approach to Portsmouth to seize Arnold at his head-quarters.[14] Taking Arnold into custody was all the more desireable since he and an 800-man detachment had raided the state's capital at Richmond. The project never materialized, partially because of the arrival of substantial British Army reinforcements in the state.

Meanwhile, Dabney looked after his state regiment, which, in spring 1781, num-bered 302 soldiers drawn from the counties of Amherst (138 men), New Kent (73), Elizabeth City (46), and Albemarle (45).[15] Dabney reported that his soldiers "have behaved very well," but he had serious problems. Four of his New Kent County officers had deserted, and many of his troops were "unfit for duty for want of shoes and clothes"; they also had insufficient ammunition.[16]

On May 20, 1781, General Cornwallis arrived at Petersburg, Virginia, with his army from North Carolina, and except for a detachment he sent to the British post at Portsmouth, he set out with the combined forces of his own and that of General William Phillips (who had just died) to cut a swathe through central Virginia. Cornwallis' com-mand now amounted to one of the largest field concentrations of British troops during the war. One of Cornwallis' objectives was to engage General Lafayette's new Virginia army of Continentals and militia. Dabney and his state troops now joined with Lafayette's force of 3,000 men. With his own army being only half the size of that of Cornwallis, Lafayette tagged along but stayed out of reach of Cornwallis' army, except for several collisions of forward units. On May 30, Dabney, with Lafayette's army, crossed the Pamunkey River, heading northward.[17]

After nearing Fredericksburg, Cornwallis' army veered westward to near Char-lottesville and then dropped down the James River, occupying Richmond from June 16 to 21, and then headed further down the James. Dabney's troops served in Lafayette's rear guard, and hence were not involved with the 800 men led by General Anthony Wayne in battling part of Cornwallis' force at Green Spring near Williamsburg on July 6. After this engagement, Lafayette ordered Dabney to look after the wounded who were brought to New Kent County Courthouse and to report on the needs for their care. Dabney was to assure the injured soldiers that Lafayette would provide "every possible relief and refreshment," which would be procured at Lafayette's personal expense. As Lafayette's army moved southward following Cornwallis' march to Portsmouth, Dabney's state troops had the duty of covering Lafayette's left flank.[18]

By mid–August 1781, Dabney had set up a recruitment headquarters at Cumberland County Courthouse. Many of the short-term enlistments of his men had expired. He managed to collect 124 new recruits, mostly for six-month terms. But, as usual, there was trouble in obtaining the necessary clothing and arms.[19]

Like many soldiers in the allied armies at the siege of Yorktown, Dabney and his troops were mostly spectators, while the respective artillerists engaged in their duel. For a while during the siege Dabney's men did service along with a detachment of Delaware and Maryland regulars and 160 Virginia militiamen as security for the army's artillery park, taking their orders from the artillery commander, General Henry Knox.[20]

A story of Dabney's rather nonchalant attitude at the siege of Yorktown is told by one of his kinsmen:

> Col. Towles and Col. Hamilton, on one occasion observed an American officer walking in fearful proximity to the enemy's lines, and exhibiting the most astonishing composure. When they discovered that officer to be Col. Dabney, they asked him why he exposed himself to such unnecessary danger; and he replied that he had gone out to reconnoiter the British works and did not imagine that he ran much risk in doing so.[21]

It may be said that Charles Dabney's most important role in the Revolutionary War occurred after the conflict ended. As the Continental and French armies returned northward and the militia called into active duty to assist repelling the British invasions of Virginia were sent home, Dabney's Second State Regiment (soon to be reconstituted as Dabney's Legion) were left almost alone to be in the front line in the event of recurring British invasions of Virginia.

On January 18, 1782, Governor Benjamin Harrison ordered that the state infantry, the state cavalry, a company of dismounted dragoons, and the state artillery company be established as Dabney's Second State Legion (simply known as Dabney's legion).[22] The new legion, consisting of 225 rank and file (to which militia were sometimes added), throughout 1782 was garrisoned at several posts — Yorktown, Hampton, and then Richmond. While at Yorktown and Hampton, the legion had the occasional duty of negotiating under flags of truce with British naval commanders off the Virginia coasts. Dabney tried to interest the Virginia government in invading Bermuda. George Rogers Clark attempted to have the legion annexed to his Illinois regiment for a campaign against the Shawnee Indians in the Ohio Valley, but the suggestion was rejected. The Legion was, however, kept in readiness for such a mission.[23] In November 1782 Dabney convinced the Virginia government to have the stockade of the garrison at Yorktown dismantled. Unfortunately, local citizens rushed to claim the stockade wood.[24]

From the end of 1782 to the official closing out of the war the next year, Dabney resided at his plantation in Hanover County. During his continued absence, two officers substituted in the command of the legion: first, Captain Windsor Brown, followed in March and April 1783 by Captain Abner Crump. On April 24, 1783, Dabney's legion was officially disbanded.[25]

While serving in the field most all of 1781, Dabney's financial affairs became disordered. Furthermore, during Cornwallis' trek north of Richmond in June, Dabney's homestead and personal property underwent significant losses from the British troops who were encamped nearby.[26]

In fall 1783, Dabney went to Kentucky to locate military lands that had been allotted him. Arriving in Kentucky he set out to explore the area of his grant, carrying only a blanket and a rifle; two persons accompanied him. For six weeks Dabney and his companions stayed in the wild, subsisting on animals they killed. There was the constant danger that Indian warriors or hunting parties might stumble upon them. Most notable during Dabney's adventure was coming upon a large buffalo herd. Much later, back in Virginia, Dabney became concerned that the Kentucky legislature had a tendency "to dispossess non-residents of their lands," and, therefore, he sold most all of his veteran claims for less than their actual value.[27]

Charles Dabney spent his years after the war tending to his plantation, and for several years he was a leading advocate for veteran pensions. He refrained from taking on public office. Though he never married, he was close to family members, and enjoyed telling them and friends war stories, in which it seems that he often embellished his role at battle scenes. Dabney, though parsimonious in his own affairs, was financially generous to his brother, sister, nephews, and others. He exhibited "unbounded hospitality." Dabney had the "knack of putting every one at their ease by an unstudied unceremonial politeness."[28]

Charles Dabney died at Aldingham on December 15, 1829, and was buried in the garden of his estate.[29] His estate was probated at $22,730.45. Dabney had given away most of his property. Aldingham itself was willed to his nephew, Charles Dabney.[30]

23. Anna Maria Lane

One of the very few military heroes certified as such by the Virginia government was an unlikely prospect. First of all, the person came from the enlisted ranks and, even then, may not have been officially inducted into the army. Both military and civil authorities paid almost no attention to outstanding merit and bold deeds demonstrated by enlisted personnel — and this was especially true as the war progressed, with most in the lower ranks throwaways — the propertyless, destitute, and often newly arrived immigrants. If such persons risked injury or death, they were deemed to have been rewarded simply by having received food and lodging while serving in the armed forces.

Another factor making for the unliklihood of hero status was that the person under consideration was a woman. Although large numbers of women could be found at any army campsite and some women actually followed their men, offering assistance such as participating in an artillery gun squad, most women with the army were there to provide support, or care for children, do laundry, mend, and cook. Some women sold market items in camp, and others served as nurses. Women deemed to be of service to the army and their children were allowed partial rations.

Anna Maria Lane, Virginia's only recognized military heroine, is especially significant in that she was not only a camp follower but by either deception or permission was allowed to put on men's clothes and bear arms as a "common soldier." While almost nothing is known of her life outside of pension and several legislative documents, the general outline of her story can be pieced together.[1]

Anna Maria Lane was born about 1735, and her husband John, in 1727.[2] They both hailed from New England; it is not concluded whether they came from Connecticut or New Hampshire. Both husband and wife were of middle age when they linked up with the Continental Army, and at the time they had a young child, Sarah. It is not certain, but it may be assumed that Anna Maria accompanied her husband at the time of the battles of White Plains, Trenton, Princeton, Germantown, and Savannah. The only thing we know of Anna Maria as an active soldier is that she fought dressed as a man and was severely wounded at the Battle of Germantown.[3]

That Anna Maria fought as a soldier at Germantown is borne out — had she been merely a camp follower she would have been left behind at the staging camp, Pennypacker Mills, as Washington's army made its sudden and intended surprise march on Germantown, and have rejoined Washington's army after the battle at the campsite at Whitemarsh.[4] A good case can be made that Anna Maria was never authentically enrolled in the army at the time of the Battle of Germantown because after the war only her husband received a federal military pension. We do not know the actual military unit in which Anna Maria or her husband served. They had by now probably transferred to the Virginia Continental line and were assigned to either generals Scott or Muhlenberg's brigade. Anna Maria could have received her wound in any one of the major confrontations of the battle; the initial pushing the enemy up against the Schuylkill River; involvement in "friendly fire" with General Anthony Wayne's troops; or during the contested general retreat. It is not likely that Anna Maria participated in the disastrous attack on the Benjamin Chew house, which was sustained mainly by New Jersey troops. The wounded Anna Maria was probably dropped off with other injured troops during the retreat at the Boehm German Reformed Church, which served as a makeshift military hospital.[5]

Anna Maria Lane may or may not have accompanied her husband in a regiment commanded by Colonel Richard Parker that joined Benjamin Lincoln's army in 1779. In October of that year he was wounded and captured at the unsuccessful Franco-American siege of Savannah. John Lane was later released as a prisoner of war by

140

exchange.[6] Otherwise, nothing is heard about the Lanes for over two years. He transferred from the Continental Army to the Virginia militia, and became a member of Major John Nelson's Light Dragoons.[7]

In January 1782, John Lane joined the Virginia State Legion commanded by Charles Dabney, and subsequently did garrison duty at Yorktown, Hampton, and Richmond. When this state legion was disbanded on April 24, 1783, John Lane was taken on as a member of the "State Guard" in Richmond, which a year later was relocated at Point of Fork (Columbia, Virginia), on the James River, near Charlottesville. The Point of Fork installation, employing gunsmiths, blacksmiths, tailors, and assorted laborers, provided arms and clothing for all the militia of Virginia. Anna Maria Lane, living with her husband and daughter Sarah, was employed for household work, including laundering, receiving only subsistence pay.[8]

The state of Virginia allowing Anna Maria Lane to be maintained at the State Guard resembled the treatment of disabled veterans in the Corps of Invalids of the Continental Army. Stationed at West Point, New York, injured veterans, in return for their keep, performed limited duty, which ranged from guard duty to giving military instruction to other soldiers. Anna Maria's counterpart at West Point as a charity case was the pauperized artillerist-heroine, Margaret Corbin.

In 1801 the magazine at Point of Fork was moved to Richmond at the Virginia Manufactory of Arms, and the State Guard was included in the move. Sixty-eight men, mostly old, disabled veterans, like the 75-year-old John Lane, made up the guard garrison. Weapons were produced at the new installation as well as repaired. John Lane, besides performing guard duty at the manufactory and other public sites in Richmond, undoubtedly assisted in the cleaning and packaging of weapons, and perhaps painting artillery carriages.[9] An early historian of Richmond described the guard-house:

> A shabby, old second-hand wooden house, occupied as barracks by the Public Guard, under the command of Captain Quarrier. The grounds immediately around it were bedecked with the shirts of the soldiers and the chemises of their wives, which flaunted on clothes-lines, and pigs, poultry and children enlivened the scene.[10]

At the Richmond Manufactory Anna Maria Lane served as a nurse to the guardsmen, and upon recommendation of the city's health officer, Dr. J. H. Foushee, Governor James Monroe granted her rations and pay. In 1804, being too old and infirm and very much lame from her old wound, Anna Maria had to forfeit her post as a nurse. Even John Lane, at 81 years old in 1807, was so decrepit that he was put merely to sweeping floors. In 1808 John Lane also was discharged.[11]

The Lanes had always been very poor, and had barely been able to get by on the scant army compensation. Now in extreme old age the times were even more difficult. Hence it is not surprising that husband and wife, both having been wounded in the service of their country, applied for special pensions from the state of Virginia.

The request came to the attention of Governor William H. Cabell, and on January

26, 1808, in his annual message addressed to Hugh Nelson, speaker of the House of Delegates, he spoke on behalf of the Lanes:

> It may be literally and truly said that they have been worn out in the public service ... and now without property or money, and their age and infirmities rendering them unable to procure either, they must be sent forth to beg or starve, unless the humanity of the Legislature shall interfere.

Furthermore, Anna Maria Lane

> is also very infirm, having been disabled by a severe wound which she received while fighting as a common soldier, in one of our Revolutionary battles, from which she never has recovered and perhaps never will recover.[12]

The legislature acted quickly on the governor's recommendation. On February 6, 1808, it enacted that John Lane receive an annual pension of 40 dollars and that Anna Maria Lane

> who in the revolutionary war, in the garb, and with the courage of a soldier, performed extraordinary military service, and received a severe wound at the battle of Germantown, shall in consideration thereof, be entitled to receive one hundred dollars per annum from the public treasury.

Both husband and wife were also authorized to receive in addition an immediate grant of 40 dollars.[13]

Four times a year the Lanes, or someone on their behalf, visited the state auditor's office in Richmond to collect quarterly payments of their pensions. Each time John received ten dollars, and Anna Maria, 25 dollars. Both John and Anna Maria, being illiterate, signed their receipts with an "X."[14]

Anna Maria Lane died June 13, 1810.[15] John became increasingly infirm, and their daughter Sarah usually collected his pension for him.[16] In 1819, he moved into the Richmond poorhouse, and in the same year applied for a federal pension.[17] John Lane died on July 14, 1822, at the age of 95.[18]

Thus, Anna Maria and John Lane pass into history with their individual heroism only scantily noticed. Since Anna Maria was lame in later life, it can be assumed that her wound at the battle of Germantown was that of a fractured thigh or leg. But her heroic action at that event is a total mystery. Her exploit must have been nothing short of marvelous because the state pension granted her recognized her "courage" and "extraordinary military service" amounted to two and a half times that which her husband, or for that matter any ordinary soldier, received. Again, it is unfortunate, but expected, that the heroic action of a common soldier, and in this instance a woman, would go almost without notice until a generation after the event.

OVERMOUNTAIN MEN

24. William Campbell

On August 25, 1781, General Marquis de Lafayette in his general orders expressed sorrow at the death of William Campbell, "an officer whose services must have endeared him to every Citizen & in particular to every American Solder." The glory that Campbell achieved at Kings Mountain and Guilford Courthouse "will do his memory everlasting honour and insure him a high rank among the defenders of liberty in the American Cause."[1]

William Campbell lived all his life on the inner edge of the Virginia frontier. A native of Augusta County who later moved further into southwestern Virginia, he established a plantation, Aspenvale, near present-day Abingdon. Six feet and two inches tall, muscular, and blue-eyed with brownish-red hair, William Campbell had an imposing presence, and was more than suited to be a military leader of Virginia frontiersmen. Born in August 1751 he was the son of Charles Campbell, a farmer, and Margaret Buchanan Campbell. A grandfather, Patrick Campbell, came from Northern Ireland and settled in central Pennsylvania. William Campbell's father moved to Augusta County in 1733. Growing up on his parent's large farm, Manor Beverly, the younger Campbell managed to acquire a solid education, first from tutors and then in Augusta Academy (later Washington and Lee University). He was masterful in self-expression, whether oral or written. After his father's death in 1767, Campbell, along with his mother and sisters, made their new home, Aspenvale, on the Middle Fork of the Holston River, in what is now Smyth County.[2]

On July 6, 1773, Campbell was appointed justice of the peace for Fincastle County, which had been newly formed from Augusta County and stretched through most of eastern Kentucky. Campbell raised a company of militia from Fincastle County and they joined Colonel Andrew Lewis' force which fought with the Indians on October 7, 1774, at the Battle of Point Pleasant, along the Ohio River. Although some of his men were in the fray, Campbell was not actively engaged. He stayed on with the army, however, until Governor Lord Dunmore, the expedition's commander, concluded a treaty of peace with the enemy.[3]

As the revolutionary movement took shape, William Campbell was elected, along with fourteen others, as members of the Fincastle County Committee of Safety. In January 1775 the group sent the "Fincastle Resolutions" to the Virginia delegates in the Continental Congress, declaring not to submit "our liberty or property to the power of a venal British Parliament or to the will or a corrupt Ministry."[4]

To defend the cause of rebellion, Campbell raised a company of militia from Bedford, Botetourt, Fincastle, and Pittsylvania counties, who were sent to rendezvous with other Virginia volunteer soldiers at Williamsburg. Campbell himself stayed in western Virginia recruiting. He did not join, as a lieutenant colonel, Patrick Henry's First Virginia regiment until the second week in December, thus missing the Battle of Great Bridge with Dunmore's little royal army. Campbell was with his troops during the enemy's bombardment of Norfolk in January 1776. On February 28, 1776, he was appointed captain of the First Virginia Regiment in the Continental Line. Doing mainly garrison duty at Williamsburg during the spring and summer of 1776, Campbell managed to be present with General Andrew Lewis' force which drove Dunmore's invaders from Virginia. The war in a distant theater had no appeal for Campbell; he preferred to be around to defend his family and home, situated precariously on the edge of Indian country. Thus as relations with the Cherokees deteriorated, Campbell resigned his Continental Army commission on October 9, 1776, and accepted the militia command of an intended expedition against the Cherokees, which, however, did not become necessary at the time. Campbell served as a commissioner for deciding the boundary between Virginia and Cherokee territory. He married Elizabeth Henry, sister of Patrick Henry, on April 2, 1776. From January 1777 to April 1780, he sat as a justice of the peace, which meant sometimes presiding over country court sessions in the new Washington County. Campbell retained leadership of local militia, and served as county lieutenant.[5]

William Campbell became known for his intense hatred of Tories and "half-hearted" patriots. Loyalists caused trouble in the neighborhoods along the Holston and New rivers. Citizens took decisive action, and many of those apprehended were fined, imprisoned, and had property confiscated.[6] Among the hazards was the solicitation by British Army officers for Indians to come to the aid of the royal cause.

In April 1779 a plot was discovered that 500 Tories planned to rise up along the New River and capture the Virginia Lead Mines in Montgomery County. Fortunately, Montgomery militia were able to nip the conspiracy in the bud, but Loyalist discontent still fomented. In neighboring Washington County, William Campbell led militia in rooting out Tories. In mid-summer 1779 he conducted patrols seeking out Tory gangs. In the field Campbell and his followers lived off stolen Loyalist livestock and provisions. Campbell and Walter Crockett at the head of 130 rebel militia invaded North Carolina. From the foray they captured a Loyalist band, of whom they promptly hanged 12 men. Campbell was acquiring a reputation for cruelty in his zero tolerance of Tory resistance. He was referred to as the "bloody tyrant of Washington County."[7]

Campbell further earned the wrath of the Tories for his mistreatment and execution of New River Tories. Repeated threats were made against his life, so much so that a neighbor said that Campbell was "in more danger from the assasin, than any other persons."[8]

One incident of William Campbell's summary treatment of Tories stands out.

Returning from Presbyterian services at the Ebbing Springs church one Sunday, carrying his infant daughter on his lap, he heard one of his companions scream, "That's Frank Hopkins!" referring to a horseman who had ridden nearby. Hopkins had come before Campbell's county court the previous year, and had been sentenced to six months in prison for various misdeeds. He had escaped and gone behind British lines, where he secured an army commission. At the time of this encounter he was on his way to deliver letters from British officers to their expected allies, the Cherokees.

Upon learning the identity of the fleeing horseman, Campbell handed his baby to his slave, saying, "Take care of her and your missus, John," and rode out after Hopkins, followed by several companions. Campbell caught up with Hopkins at the Middle Fork of the Holston and the two men wrestled each other into the river. With the aid of his companions, Campbell managed to

William Campbell. **Kings Mountain National Military Park. Courtesy of the Library of Virginia.**

secure Hopkins. After a brief drumhead court-martial, Hopkins was hanged by his stirrups from a riverbank sycamore tree. When Campbell returned to his wife, she asked him what he had done with Hopkins. "Oh, we hung him, Betsy, that's all," was the reply.[9]

In April 1780 Campbell was elected to a seat in the state House of Delegates and was also appointed colonel and commander of the Washington County militia.[10] On June 15, 1780, Governor Jefferson appointed Campbell to lead militia against renegade Cherokee Indians. Taking to the field with 400 Virginia militiamen and two companies of North Carolinians, Campbell advanced to the Nolichucky River. From there he went no further because of news of New River Tories again mobilizing for an attack on the lead mines in Montgomery County. The governor cancelled the orders for an expedition against Indians. Upon his return home Campbell found that he was in command of all the militia from Botetourt, Montgomery, and Washington counties. Heading out with 140 mounted militiamen, Campbell discovered that the rebellious Tories, forewarned and fearing Campbell, had dispersed, most of them fleeing into the mountains. Campbell had one captured Tory immediately shot. He and his militiamen went from house to house, confiscating Loyalist property. In late August Campbell again went after a hostile Tory band, which took him into North Carolina. From a confrontation with one Tory band, Campbell had the most notorious leaders shot or hanged.[11]

While Campbell and his troops were suppressing Tory insurrection in western Virginia, another menace developed: the British invasion of the Carolina piedmont, close to Campbell's home. An American army was destroyed at Camden on August 16. In an effort of the British to control the Carolina backcountry, Major Patrick Ferguson and 4,000 troops — mostly Loyalist militiamen — readied to sweep through western settlements. Hoping to strike terror, he issued a proclamation threatening to hang rebel leaders and lay waste to the countryside if there was resistance.

Overmountain Men, so-called frontiersmen from Virginia and North Carolina, rallied to form an expedition against Ferguson. In late September 1780, William Campbell and 200 Washington County militia marched out and were joined by 200 more under his cousin, Arthur Campbell. On September 25 they reached Sycamore Shoals on the Watauga River, where they were met with 1,040 men from North Carolina (including Tennessee). A council of war agreed to send on 900 mounted militia from among the some 1,400 men gathered, with the remainder to follow as infantrymen. William Campbell was chosen to command the combined forces; being the only non–North Carolinian among the field officers it was felt he would be the least one to incite jealousy.[12]

On the night of October 6, the patriot force gathered a mile from Kings Mountain, on the top of which Ferguson intended to make a stand; the site measured 600 by 70 yards, and was encircled by wooded slopes. The plan of attack was simply to surround the enemy with a "band of fire" and then tighten the vise. Campbell visited all the troops and promised that anyone who did not wish to fight could immediately leave for home. He also announced that the signal for attack would be the scream of an Indian-style war-hoop. Ferguson's position, initially thought to offer a definite advantage, actually made the defenders sitting ducks.

The battle began in late afternoon. Having tethered their horses to trees at the base of the mountain, the rebels prepared to advance up the slopes. Campbell started the action by bellowing, "Here they are, my brave boys; shout like Hell, and fight like devils!" As the attackers reached the top of the mountain they were greeted by several bayonet charges, which were repulsed. The frontiersmen fired from behind rocks and trees; their rifles had deadly accuracy. When the enemy troops did fire downhill they did so over the heads of the rebels. William Campbell, in the words of one participant, "was during the whole time busily engaged in encouraging his men, and leading them up on the mountain." Whenever his troops gave way, he "rallied them each time, and brought them again into action in the most gallant manner."[13]

The bloody fray lasted one hour; Ferguson was killed, as were 156 of his men; 163

were wounded; 698 were made prisoners. The rebels had less than 100 casualties. Enemy officers waving white handkerchiefs had difficulty in surrendering. Their efforts to gain quarter elicited the response, "Give them Buford play!" in reference to Tarleton's massacre of rebel troops at the Waxhaws five months earlier. Campbell's troops kept firing on those attempting to surrender.[14] William Campbell's record in this situation is mixed. He tried to stay the wanton killing. As a participant noted, Campbell, still with "a handkerchief tied about his head" and in shirt sleeves, was "waving his sword downward, and calling to his men to cease firing that the enemy had surrendered."[15]

Campbell boldly succeeded in restraining his followers from further slaughter of their vanquished foes. It would seem that at long last he had become compassionate. But no sooner had the shooting ceased than one of Ferguson's foraging parties returned and took a few shots at the patriots before fleeing. The cry went up that Tarleton's dreaded cavalrymen were attacking and there was fear that the prisoners would join their compatriots. Thus William Campbell ordered riflemen near him to shoot the prisoners to prevent them from breaking out. According to one rebel officer, "We killed near a hundred of them and hardly could be restrained from killing the whole."[16]

Campbell led the march with the surviving captives as far as Gilbert Town where he turned them over to Colonel Benjamin Cleveland, and he himself went to Hillsborough to confer with General Gates about the further disposal of the prisoners. With so many escapees, when the prisoners were eventually interned in a camp near Salisbury, only 130 remained.[17] But while Campbell still had charge of the prisoners there would be more killings. It was discovered that among the captives were many who had plundered property and harmed patriot families in the internecine Carolina partisan warfare. Word had also arrived that Cornwallis had condoned hangings of captive rebels. With vengeance in the air, Campbell did what he could to keep his men from retaliation on the prisoners. Four days after the battle, he mentioned in his general orders that all his officers should "endeavor to restrain the disorderly manner of slaughtering and disturbing the prisoners."[18] But on October 14, when the procession made camp ten miles northeast of Gilbert Town, Campbell himself convened a court-martial to try the most notorious of the captives. Thirty-six were convicted of crimes varying from murder to arson and was sentenced to die. Hangings of three at a time occurred at a great oak tree; after the ninth execution, the others were pardoned.[19]

William Campbell emerged as the great hero of the Battle of Kings Mountain, despite efforts by Colonel Isaac Shelby, who himself had been in the thick of the battle, to discredit him. Campbell received many plaudits, among the most esteemed of them being that from the Continental Congress, which on November 13, 1780, resolved that it entertained "a high sense of the spirited and military conduct of Colonel Campbell, and the officers and privates of the militia under his command, displayed in action of the 7 of October, in which a complete victory was obtained over superior numbers of the enemy, advantageously posted on King's [sic] Mountain...."[20]

After Kings Mountain, William Campbell returned home, and was preparing to resume his House of Delegates career when, with the stepped-up British offensive in the South, he found himself again in the field, commanding 400 riflemen attached to General Greene's Southern Army.

On the night of March 5–6, 1781, Campbell's men were on a screening mission along with Colonel Otho Williams' Maryland Continentals. Tarleton's dragoons and Cornwallis' forward light infantry under the command of Lt. Col. James Webster surprised Campbell at his camp, and drove the Virginians to the banks of Reedy Fork at Wetzell's Mill. Williams, whose troops included Henry Lee's legion and William Washington's cavalry, rushed in to assist Campbell. With the British army poised for an encircling movement, Williams, taking charge of the situation, had Lee cover a retreat by Campbell and other troops. Cornwallis, nearby, did not order pursuit. In the overall skirmishing at Wetzell's Mill both sides each lost about 30 to 40 men.[21]

As the two armies prepared for a fight at Guilford Courthouse on March 15, 1781, Campbell's riflemen and Lee's legion, acting as a screening corps on the left front of Greene's army, sparred with Tarleton's cavalry and British light infantry. Campbell led the attack against the enemy and drove them back. When the main battle shaped up Campbell's and Lee's troops again faced an assault upon the American left. For the fighting that went on for two hours, in this sector it was mainly American rifle butts against British bayonets. Momentarily, Lee's troops and "the dangerous courage of Campbell and his riflemen" repelled the British assault. Campbell was driven back to a sloping ridge, his riflemen suffering heavy casualties. Unfortunately, Lee pulled his troops out of the action, leaving Campbell's riflemen stranded against enemy fire. Lee's excuse was that he needed to reconnect with American troops on his right. According to Campbell, Lee's troops had come within 200 yards of Campbell's men without giving aid. Campbell, greatly offended by Lee's withdrawal, had no choice but give way in confusion. With other American units hard-pressed, Greene ordered a general retreat.[22]

General Greene's personal commendation did not assuage Campbell's wounded pride. Greene wrote him on March 19: "Your faithful services and the exertions which you made to second the efforts of the Southern army, on the 15th inst., claim my warmest thanks. It would be ungenerous not to acknowledge my entire approbation of your conduct, and the spirited and manly behavior of the officers and soldiers under you."[23] The next day Campbell resigned his commission. He announced that he could no longer serve in the army with honor while Lee remained an officer.[24]

Returning home, Campbell resumed his service as a member of the House of Delegates. He attended sessions first at Richmond and then, in the face of the British military invasions of central Virginia, at Charlottesville and subsequently at Staunton. Campbell sat on committees relating to elections, martial law, and amendment of the militia act. He had hardly settled into his legislative duties when the House of Delegates named him brigadier general of militia assigned to the army under General Lafayette, who commanded all American forces in Virginia. Upon joining Lafayette's troops in central Virginia, near Richmond, Campbell was placed in command of a brigade containing all 780 riflemen in Lafayette's army.[25]

When Cornwallis' army, after having swept through central Virginia, was encamped at Williamsburg before resuming their march to a Virginia seaport, Lafayette's soldiers held ground six miles away towards Richmond. Campbell and his light troops were posted at Three Burnt Chimneys, located half the distance between the two armies. Expecting to catch the enemy in an ambush, Campbell and a large detachment of mounted riflemen hid in the woods along a roadway behind a forward picket station. Campbell correctly assumed that the British would seek to drive back the pickets, who were instructed by Campbell to immediately withdraw. As British cavalry approached, the pickets, as planned, retired and were pursued, whereupon Campbell's men let go a barrage of rifle fire, killing 20 British cavalrymen and 40 horses.[26]

Campbell probably did not participate in the action at the Battle of Jamestown Ford (Green Spring) on July 6. On the American side, the battle was primarily an affair of General Anthony Wayne's Pennsylvanians, although some of Campbell's riflemen were involved. Most likely Campbell's troops formed a reserve for Wayne's troops.[27]

In mid–August 1781, William Campbell fell ill and took leave from Lafayette's army to visit Rocky Mills in Hanover County, the home of his half-brother in law, John Syme. There, he died of a heart attack on August 22. He was buried in the Syme family cemetery. In 1823 his remains were re-interred at the Campbell Aspenvale estate.[28]

Although he displayed ruthlessness towards his Tory enemies, William Campbell earned universal respect from all who knew him. Lyman Draper, the great collector and chronicler of Revolutionary War America, said of him:

> In his domestic and social relations, he was the most amiable of men. He would send his servants to aid a poor neighbor, while he would himself plow through the heat of the day in his fields, giving his spare moments to his Bible and his God, endeavoring scrupulously to live up to the golden rule in all his dealings with his fellow men. But he set his face like a flint against the enemies of his country and of freedom, proving himself almost as inflexible as a Claverhouse or a Cumberland toward those who betrayed or deserted the holy cause for which he contended, and for which he died.
>
> But it was as a military genius that he shone preeminent. He had the ability to form able plans — confidence in himself, and indefatigable perseverance to execute them; and the rare capacity to inspire all under his command with his own confidence and indomitable courage.[29]

A more succinct assessment is given by Virginian John Warwick Daniel in a 1908 presentation to the U.S. Senate of a report concerning "A Monument to the Memory of William Campbell":

> You ask me his name, and I answer, "General William Campbell of the Holston," and you reply, "Who was General William Campbell?" Let me answer: "A Virginian by birth, a

Scotch-Irish Presbyterian by ancestry and conviction, an innate lover of freedom and liberty, a sworn enemy of the Tories, a border chieftan, and the hero of the greatest military triumph of the Revolutionary War, the battle of King's [sic] Mountain."[30]

25. William Crawford

When the two 17-year-olds George Washington and William Crawford met, while Washington was on surveying duty, inaugurating a life-long friendship, little could they predict that both would become officers in an army fighting for their country's independence. Still less could they anticipate that one of them would attain everlasting glory as a conquering hero and the principal founder of a nation while the other would endure one of the most hideous fates ever recorded in human history. The story of William Crawford is a sad one.

Son of William and Onora Grimes Crawford, William Crawford was born in 1732 in Frederick County, Virginia.[1] Although he inherited the family farm upon his father's

William Crawford. From *Ohio State Archaeological and Historical Publication,* vol. 6 (1898), frontispiece.

death in 1736, William Crawford's childhood years were spent at the Bullskin Run farm of Richard Stephenson, whom his widowed mother married. Besides his full brother, Valentine, Crawford had five half brothers and one half-sister.[2] Nothing is known of Crawford's formative years. While still living in Frederick County he married Hanna Vance; they had one son and two daughters. Besides farming, William Crawford earned income as a surveyor, and in this capacity Crawford's and Washington's paths frequently crossed.[3]

During the French and Indian War, Crawford enlisted as an ensign in Captain Robert Stewart's company of light horse in the Virginia regiment commanded by George Washington. On July 27, 1757, he was promoted to lieutenant. Crawford spent much of his time doing garrison duty in Augusta County and at Fort Loudoun, Virginia, and Creasap's Old

Town, Maryland.[4] Crawford served in Washington's regiment attached to Brig. Gen. John Forbes' army, which drove the French from Fort Duquesne (Pittsburgh) and western Pennsylvania.

In 1765 William Crawford and his wife and children moved from the Virginia piedmont country to Stewart Crossings, on Braddock's Road, west of the Allegheny Mountains, on the Youghiogheny River, 40 miles southeast of Pittsburgh.[5] Here he built a cabin. Besides some farming and engaging in the Indian trade, Crawford worked mainly as a surveyor. From 1767 to 1771 Crawford served as a surveyor for 40,000 acres claimed by George Washington along the Youghiogheny, Great Kanawha, and Ohio rivers. From October 20 to November 25, 1770, the two men journeyed down the Ohio River to the Great Kanawha River viewing land claims. Washington was a frequent guest at Crawford's home.[6]

Washington successfully petitioned on behalf of himself and other officer grantees for the Virginia government to proceed with the surveying of 200,000 acres in the Ohio country as bounty lands reserved by a proclamation by Governor Robert Dinwiddie for Virginia veterans of the French and Indian War. Washington's recommendation of Crawford as "a person of good Character" and one who was "well acquainted with the Country to the Westward of the Allighany Mountains," was enough to secure for Crawford the principal surveyorship of these lands.[7] Crawford set about making surveys, placing slashes on trees, clearing some of the lands, and building cabins on lands claimed. Individual tracts were 300 acres each. By July 1773 Crawford had completed the survey project.[8]

Unfortunately, the British government declared the 200,000 acres of the Virginia French and Indian War grant null and void, on grounds that the lands lay in an area prohibited to entry by the Proclamation of 1763.[9]

In 1773 Crawford became the official surveyor for the Ohio Company.[10] Similar to the Virginia veteran lands, the claims by members of the Ohio Company would also be negated.

Because of competing Pennsylvania and Virginia jurisdictions, Crawford performed duplicated public service. In 1770 he was a justice of the peace for Cumberland, in 1771 for Bedford, and 1773 for Westmoreland counties, in Pennsylvania. In view of an expressed loyalty to Virginia, the Pennsylvania authorities dismissed him from the Westmoreland position. In December 1774 Crawford was named a justice of the peace for Augusta and in 1776 for Yohogania counties, Virginia.[11]

William Crawford re-entered military service during Lord Dunmore's Indian war of 1774; he was commissioned a captain and was soon promoted to major. He was assigned to a field column commanded by Dunmore himself. The other column, led by Colonel Andrew Lewis, fought the Indians at the battle of Point Pleasant. Crawford, meanwhile, in Dunmore's force, supervised the building of Fort Fincastle (at present Wheeling, West Virginia), renamed Fort Henry during the Revolutionary War.[12] In July and August he also led expeditions into the Indian country, destroying villages and obtaining very few captives.[13] Crawford also had a hand in building Fort Gower, on the east side of the Hockhocking River.[14] After the signing of a peace treaty at that place, Crawford stayed on duty, leading another punitive expedition, this time destroying a Mingo (western Seneca) town, killing six Indians, capturing 14, and taking plunder.[15]

In May 1775, at Pittsburgh, Crawford participated as a member of a 30-man committee of correspondence which adopted a resolution endorsing rebel activities in New England and called for the forming of minutemen companies.[16]

Crawford received a commission as a lieutenant colonel in the Fifth Virginia Regiment on January 12, 1776, and became a colonel (by act of Congress) in the Seventh Virginia Regiment on October 11, 1775 (made retroactive to August 14, 1776).[17] It is disputed whether Crawford served in any part of the New York–New Jersey campaigns of 1776–1777, although it is probable he fought in the battles of Trenton and Princeton.[18]

In the summer of 1777, Crawford obtained the command of the Thirteenth Virginia Regiment or the "West Augusta Regiment." With 200 of these troops he joined Washington's army near Philadelphia in August. Crawford led a scouting party on September 3, 1777, as the two armies prepared to do battle, resulting in a "pretty hot" engagement.[19] He certainly participated in the Battle of Brandywine. In the follow-up action, at Germantown, he was almost captured.[20]

Crawford and part of the Thirteenth Virginia Regiment were transferred to nearer their homes in the western department of the army in November 1777. General Edward Hand had the overall command at Pittsburgh. In summer 1778 Crawford constructed Fort Crawford, on the Allegheny River northeast of Pittsburgh (now the town of Parnassus).[21] Under Hand's successor, General Lachlan McIntosh, Crawford was given the command of militia from the northwest counties of Virginia. He made his headquarters at Fort Crawford. Crawford led several punitive raids into the Indian country.[22] In April 1781 Crawford and 300 of his troops joined Colonel Daniel Brodhead's excursion against Delaware Indians, with the Indian town of Cochocton, the Delawares' capital the principal objective. A factor in this operation was that the Delawares had transferred their allegiance to the British. The expedition yielded slight success. The Indians had abandoned their town, and the 15 warriors captured there were put to death.[23]

Indian relations continued to deteriorate. Attacks upon settlers increased. On March 8, 1782, Pennsylvania militiamen under Colonel David Williamson rounded up a group of peaceful Christian Indians at Gnadenhutten, massacring all 96 of those present: 35 men, 27 women, and 34 boys. The atrocity fueled a blood lust in western Pennsylvania to go back and kill more Indians, even those who were Moravian converts.[24]

For the expedition, 500 Virginia and Pennsylvania militiamen gathered at an old Mingo town on the Ohio River on May 25. Upon assembling, an election was held for commander. William Crawford won by only five votes over David Williamson. Instructions for the mission had been provided by General William Irvine, then the commandant at Pittsburgh: "The object of your command is to destroy with fire and sword, if practicable, the Indian town and settlements at Sandusky." The militia force was to traverse the 160 miles northward to the Wyandot town of Upper Sandusky, on the Sandusky River.[25]

In the afternoon of June 4, the militiamen, approaching a large grove, were greeted by a cannon volley. One hundred British Rangers, commanded by Captain William Caldwell, had joined hostile Delawares, Wyandots, Shawnees, and Mingos, led by the Delaware chief, Captain Pipe. Crawford's men drove the enemy from the woods. Intense arms fire was exchanged between the militiamen lined up at one side of the grove and the Indians and British concealed among the bushes. Crawford lost five of his men killed and 11 wounded. The battle resumed the next day. With the arrival of a band of Shawnees, Crawford, thinking he was now outnumbered, called for a council of war, which decided on a nighttime retreat. Upon their withdrawal the troops panicked. The enemy picked off and scalped stragglers. Crawford lost contact with his only son, John, his nephew, William Crawford, and son-in-law, William Harrison, who were with the expedition. Falling to the rear of his fugitive troops in search of them, Crawford became lost. He then met Dr. John Knight and nine other men, all of whom were soon separated from the body of militiamen. Crawford and his comrades wandered for two days and then were captured; four of the prisoners escaped, but two of them were taken and killed and scalped. Meanwhile, Colonel David Williamson's remaining 300 soldiers extricated themselves and made their way back to the staging area.[26]

The Ohio Indians, furious about the terrible Gnadenhutten atrocity, were bent on revenge.[27] Their wanted target was Colonel David Williamson, the author of the Gnadenhutten tragedy and now second in command of the expedition led by Crawford. Williamson, however, had fled, and retribution would have to settle on Crawford and other captives.

The victors marched their captives 35 miles to a village of the Wyandots, Half King's Town. Captain Pipe, the Delaware chief, painted Crawford black. The next day Crawford and the other captives were led to a nearby Delaware village on Tymochtee Creek. Except for Crawford and Knight the other captives were immediately tomahawked and scalped. For one of the officer prisoners, as reported by Dr. Knight, "an old squaw cut off his head and the Indians kicked it about on the ground. The young Indian fellows often came where the colonel and I were and dashed the scalps in our faces."

At 4 P.M. Crawford and Knight were led to a fire, where Crawford was stripped naked and ordered to sit down near the fire. Crawford's wrists were tied behind his back and connected to a rope fastened to a 15-foot pole. Captain Pipe gave an oration before a gathering of 40 men and 70 or so women and boys. The men shot powder from their guns onto Crawford from his feet to his neck. Then someone from the crowd came up and cut off his ears. An eye was poked out. Burning sticks were picked up and thrust into Crawford's body, already burnt from the black powder. Several women poured burning coals over him. More hickory sticks were applied to the fire surrounding the victim. This terrible ordeal went on for more than two hours. Then, a modern writer notes:

> When the fire reached its peak, two warriors cut the rawhide cord that bound the still shuffling Crawford and, one on each side, let him shuffle toward the fire. When the heat became too intense for them to advance closer, they thrust him from them and he sprawled onto the blaze. His legs jerked a few times and one arm flailed out but then, as skin and flesh blackened, living motion stopped and all that remained was a gradual drawing of arms and legs close to the body in the pugilistic posture characteristic in persons burned to death.[28]

Crawford was pulled away from the blaze and scalped and then his body was returned to the fire. The next day as Dr. Knight, who later managed to escape, was being led away, he and his captors "came to the spot where the Colonel was burnt ... I saw his bones laying amongst the remains of the fire."

Thus was the horrible and ignominious fate of a noble patriot and fighter for independence. Words uttered by George Washington in connection with a recommendation submitted to the Board of War in March 1778 are a fitting epitaph for Colonel William Crawford: "I know him to be a brave and active officer, and of considerable influence upon the western frontier of Virginia."[29]

26. James Armistead Lafayette

Recruiting slaves as spies made sense. They could move about pretty much at will behind enemy and friendly lines; as non-citizens they were expected not to have interest in the war's outcome; and, of course, they were regarded as only marginally intelligent. And why would the British suspect that a black man who desired freedom could voluntarily be an agent for the American cause which held him in thraldom? The British enlisted many southern blacks into special army units. The Americans were wont to incorporate blacks into regular armed forces, but only if they were already free. With so many slaves flocking to the British standard in the South, American commanders in that theater found it relatively easy to use slaves in espionage. Probably the most important of African Americans to spy on the British during the Revolutionary War was a 33-year-old Virginian slave, James, the property of William Armistead of New Kent County, Virginia, near the city of Richmond. He eventually took on the names of his master and General Lafayette, and became known as James Armistead Lafayette.

Although we know that James Armistead Lafayette was born in 1748, very little is on record about him before his famous military service of 1781. Despite being illiterate, he had special abilities that made him essentially a household servant. He was probably at Armistead's side in Richmond as he attended to business as a merchant and as commissary of military supplies for the Southern Continental Army. William Armistead was also a member of the state's House of Delegates.[1]

James' career as a spy was confined to the period of March to October 1781, during the British invasions of Tidewater and central Virginia. Benedict Arnold, now a British general, had invaded Virginia in January 1781 with 1,600 troops, conducting a lightning raid up the James River to the state's capital, Richmond. Arnold was succeeded in command first by General Williams Phillips in April and then by General Charles Cornwallis, both of whom brought sizeable reinforcements for the British Army in Virginia.

With the encouragement of his patriotic master, James volunteered to go behind British lines to secure valuable information. He served generals Arnold and Cornwallis as a forager, helping the enemy obtain fodder and provisions, and also as an officer's orderly, eventually ending up as a waiter on tables at British headquarters.[2] As a spy James was not only able to pick up knowledge of the enemy's operational plans but he also conveyed instructions from Lafayette to other spies behind the enemy's lines.[3]

During the spring and summer of 1781, Lafayette could not hope to defeat the British army in Virginia. When Cornwallis added his force from North Carolina to

British forces already in the state, in May 1781, the enemy's total strength in Virginia amounted to about 8,000 troops. The best that Lafayette could show was about 3,200 men under arms; the 1,200 that he himself brought to Virginia from the North, 900 more under General Anthony Wayne arriving in June, and about 1,000 militia. Lafayette's objective was to maneuver as close to the enemy as possible without engagement, giving the impression that he was aggressively hounding the enemy. Of course, he had to be very alert so as not to be attacked by the enemy in force. With the intelligence of British planned moves he could avoid this possibility.

Cornwallis was always guarded and secretive as to his plans. Hence it was all the more a challenge to obtain headquarters intelligence. Fortunately, as a waiter at headquarters James was privy to detailed conversation among Cornwallis and high-ranking officers. James, of course, pretended that he had no interest or comprehension of what was being said. But he did not hesitate to convey the essentials of the talk to other black spies in camp, and soon Lafayette had the intelligence.[4]

As Cornwallis' army moved from Portsmouth to Yorktown in August 1781, James

James Armistead Lafayette. **By John B. Martin (1824). Courtesy of Valentine Richmond History Center.**

appeared back in Lafayette's camp informing the young Frenchman that he had been sent as a spy for Cornwallis.[5] Thus James was now a double agent. Lafayette received accurate information concerning British military plans and operations, whereas Cornwallis obtained only what Lafayette wanted him to have. Once, when Cornwallis was ready to move against Lafayette, the latter conducted a ruse to prevent such action. He gave James a piece of paper, torn in half, supposedly an order to General Daniel Morgan to join his force and take position on the right flank of Lafayette's army. Back at Cornwallis' headquarters James presented the pieces of paper, but since he could not read, he indicated that he did not know if the items were of any importance. Cornwallis, however, believed the untrue report of Morgan's pending arrival and did not attack.[6]

Undoubtedly James' spy efforts

were a major factor of Lafayette being one step ahead of his opponent, able to keep pressure on Cornwallis in the field and to contribute to the British general's getting himself pinned down at Yorktown. Knowing his enemy's next moves allowed Lafayette ample leeway in maneuverability.

Two days after Cornwallis surrendered at Yorktown, Lafayette learned that the British commander desired a meeting with him. This was arranged with Lafayette inviting Cornwallis to dine with him. While they were eating, James came into the room wearing an American uniform. The startled Cornwallis thus realized that his black spy had all the while been an American counterspy and the one most responsible for outguessing him.

During a visit to Richmond a year after the signing of a treaty of peace, Lafayette penned a testimonial on behalf of James (who would now start calling himself James Armistead Lafayette). The declaration read:

> This is to Certify that the Bearer By the Name of James Has done Essential Services to me While I had the Honour to Command in this State. His Intelligences from the Enemy's Camp were Industriously Collected and More faithfully deliver'd. He properly Acquitted Himself with Some important Commissions I Gave Him and Appears to me Entitled to Every Reward his Situation Can Admit of. Done Under my Hand, Richmond November 21st 1784

> Lafayette.[7]

James Armistead Lafayette lost no time in forwarding the certificate to the Virginia House of Delegates, accompanied by his request to be emancipated from slavery. As the journal of the House of Delegates records for a meeting of December 4, 1784:

> Also, a petition of James, a negro slave; setting forth, that being impelled by a most earnest desire of gaining that liberty which is so dear to all mankind, and convinced that if he rendered any essential services to the public, that would be his reward, he often during the invasion of the enemy in the year 1781, at the risk of his life entered into the enemy's camp, and collected such intelligence as he supposed of importance, and which he conveyed in the most expeditious manner to the Marquis de la Fayette, who then commanded the American army in Virginia; and praying that an act may pass for his emancipation; and that a reasonable compensation may be made for him to his present proprietor.[8]

The legislature did not act on James Armistead Lafayette's petition at the time. Thus in November 1786 he again applied for his freedom:

> To the honorable speaker & gentlemen of the Genl Assembly

> The petition of James (a slave belonging to Will Armistead of new Kent county) humbly sheweth: That your petitioner persuaded of the just right which all mankind have to Freedom, notwithstanding his own state of bondage, with an honest desire to serve this country in its defence thereof, did, during the ravages of Lord Cornwallis thro' this state, by the permission of his master, enter into the service of the Marquis Lafayette.

> That during the time of his serving the Marquis he often at the peril of his life found means to frequent the British Camp, by which means he Kept open a channel of the most useful Communication to the army of the State. That at different times your petitioner

conveyed inclosures, from the Marquis to the enemies lines, of the most secret important Kind, the possession of which if discovered on him would have most certainly endangered the life of your petitioner.

That he undertook & performed all commands with chearfulness & fidelity in opposition & to the persuasion & example of many thousands of his unfortunate conditions.

For proof of the above your petitioner begs leave to refer to a certificate of the marquis Lafayette hereto annexed, & after taking his case as here stated into Consideration he humbly intreats that he may be granted those Freedoms, which he flatters himself he has in Some degree contributed to establish, & which he hopes always to prove himself worthy of, nor does he desire over this inestimable favor, unless his present master from who he has experienced everything which can make tolerable the state of slavery, shall be made adequate compensation for the loss of a valuable workman, which your petitioner humbly requests may be done & your petitioner shall ever pray.
Endorsed — James
Nov'r 30th 1786.[9]

The General Assembly responded on January 9, 1787, by voting emancipation for James Armistead Lafayette and provided fair value compensation to his master, William Armistead.[10]

For a while, as a free man, James Armistead Lafayette attained at least a minimum level of well-being. He soon acquired 40 acres of "broken, and much worn" land adjacent to the property of his former master and owned two horses and three slaves (the latter was not uncommon among free blacks in Virginia at the time). He married and had at least one son.[11]

Over time James Armistead Lafayette became poverty stricken. Thus, in December 1818, he went again before the General Assembly and asked for a veteran's pension. He was granted $60 for his "present relief" and a yearly pension of $40. Thereafter, twice a year he visited the office of the state auditor, James Ewell Heath, to collect a $20 payment.[12] In his request for assistance, James Armistead Lafayette, now 70 years old, called attention to his declining health and increasingly inability to perform labor.[13]

During his last visit to the United States in 1824 Lafayette went to Yorktown. From a large, enthusiastic crowd that greeted him, the Frenchman immediately recognized James Armistead Lafayette. A Richmond newspaper reported that James Armistead Lafayette was "taken into his embrace."[14] At the time of Lafayette's visit James Armistead Lafayette sat for a portrait by Richmond's foremost artist of the day, John Blennerhasset Martin. In Martin's painting, as a modern essayist has noted, the former slave and spy "is no longer clothed in fantasy." The portrait, which is located in Richmond's Valentine Museum, depicts James "proud and dignified," wearing a "white neck cloth, and his blue military coat is adorned with bright buttons embossed with the American eagle." James exudes "an individual identity earned at the repeated risk of his life and ... an unshakable faith in the ideal of democracy."[15]

James Armistead Lafayette appeared as a minor character in a romantic novel on plantation life, *Edge-Hill* (1828), written by the very state auditor, James E. Heath, from whom James received his pension payments. In the novel, James appears in the context of his spy activity.[16] James Armistead Lafayette died in New Kent County on August 9, 1830.[17]

An irony of James Armistead Lafayette's life is that he single-handedly won his emancipation from slavery by service to the cause of American freedom, which itself denied freedom to a large segment of the adult population. It is also of further significance that James Armistead Lafayette's example most probably had influence on Lafayette's decision to advocate for the abolition of American slavery. Lastly, his service itself demonstrated nobleness.

QUARTERMASTER

27. Edward Carrington

"No body ever heard of a quarter Master in History as such or in relateing any brilliant Action," lamented General Nathanael Greene about his service in that office.[1] Upon becoming quartermaster general of the Continental Army, Greene wrote a fellow general: "All of you will be immortalizing your selves in the golden pages of History while I am confined to a series of druggery to pave the way for it."[2]

Greene felt that he was taking a step down by accepting a post as a staff officer, although he was permitted to nominally keep his rank as a major general in the line. A Virginian two years later made the same decision as Greene, but with not as much regret. Lt. Col. Edward Carrington, a most valued artillerist, was in a sense moving up, while Greene, already at the height of army command, was sacrificing the inevitable laurels of victory. Both men served with great distinction in the Quartermaster Department.

It is true that on the road to military glory assignment to a staff department, separate from field duty, put a cap on one's ambition. It did not matter much that battles were won or lost on the capabilities of staff support — provisioning, logistics, engineering. After two years, Greene was able to put his staff experience behind him, and went on to become the triumphant commander of the Southern Continental Army. But behind all his success was the extraordinary energetic and competent quartermaster activity of Edward Carrington. In actuality, Carrington was no less a hero than Greene himself.

The eighth of 11 children of Colonel George and Anne Mayo Carrington, Edward Carrington was born on February 11, 1749, on his father's plantation, Boston Hill (located in the part of Goochland that later became Cumberland County). He had little formal schooling, but became masterful in written expression. From the summer of 1771 to the autumn of 1772, Carrington resided in Barbados for the purpose of collecting his father's share of an inheritance. On his return to Virginia he studied law, and was licensed to practice in Cumberland County in June 1773.[3]

At the outbreak of the war, Carrington involved himself in military affairs. As a member of the Cumberland County Committee of Safety in 1775, he was sent to Philadelphia to purchase gunpowder for the local militia.[4] In fall 1775 Carrington was named captain of a company of minutemen, and in February 1776 the Virginia Committee of Safety commissioned him a second lieutenant in a new Virginia artillery company. He was acting captain and commander of the company July through November

1776. On November 30, 1776, Congress appointed him lieutenant colonel of Colonel Charles Harrison's First Continental Artillery Regiment; he would remain in this rank in this unit until June 1783.[5]

Carrington was involved with recruiting during the first part of 1777. Subsequently, Governor Patrick Henry persuaded Congress to allow Carrington's artillery company to remain in Virginia for coastal defense. Thus Carrington missed the battles of Brandy-wine and Germantown.[6] The young artillery officer created a ruckus by declaring that Governor Henry should not select officers for the artillery regiment. The angry governor persuaded Congress that if Carrington did not apologize he should be dismissed. Car-rington conceded.[7]

In spring 1778 the First Continental Artillery Regiment reported to Washington's army at Valley Forge, and was established as part of General Henry Knox's corps of artillery.[8] In the absence of Colonel Harrison, Lt. Col. Carrington commanded the First Continental Artillery Regiment at the Battle of Monmouth, June 28, 1778. Car-rington's artillerists, with the assistance of General William Woodford's brigade, pushed back British light infantry, Forty-Second Foot, and Black Watch, as they came on after General Charles Lee ordered a retreat. The rebel cannonade gave the "severest artillery fire ever heard in America," as one contemporary noted, thereby saving the American army from defeat. As Washington, in rare praise, said, "All the Artillery both officers and men that were engaged distinguished themselves in a remarkable manner."[9]

Carrington stayed with Washington's army until summer 1780. In March of that year he and General Arthur St. Clair served as commissioners for implementing prisoner of war exchange.[10] In June 1780 Carrington temporarily left his artillery regiment to assist General Johann De Kalb in establishing an ammunition arsenal for the Southern Army in Richmond and organizing a relay system for delivering supplies to General Horatio Gates' Southern Army at Hillsborough, North Carolina.[11] This activity was interrupted when Gates ordered Carrington to assume command of the First Continental Artillery Regiment since the commander, Colonel Charles Harrison, had "been severely Wounded in the Leg by a Kick from a Horse, which Splintered the Bone."[12] On his way to join the Southern Army, Carrington happened upon fugitives from the American army fleeing from defeat at the battle of Camden, on August 16, 1780. One of the fugi-tives, Colonel John Senf, directed Carrington to return to Richmond to resume his work in facilitating ammunition and supply arrangements.[13]

In the first week of December Carrington met with the new commander of the Southern Army, Nathanael Greene, in Richmond. In Charlotte, North Carolina, Greene relieved Gates of his command. Impressed by the abilities and character of Carrington, Greene immediately requested that the young Virginia artillerist become the deputy quartermaster general for the Southern Army, in effect with full powers of chief of that department in the South. Carrington accepted the assignment on December 15, 1780.[14] Meanwhile, he went on a special mission for Greene to explore the Dan River (the upper branch of the Roanoke River) along the border between Virginia and North Carolina, to find if it would be feasible to use this route for transporting supplies to the Southern Army.[15] Having performed this task by the end of December, Carrington visited Richmond to meet with the state's quartermaster, Richard Claiborne, for the purpose of drawing up procedures and means for transporting supplies to the Southern Army.[16] As the war moved southward, Richmond became the hub for collecting supplies to be forwarded to Greene's army. With Benedict Arnold's invasion of Virginia in January 1781, Carrington remained in the state temporarily to take on the additional duty as quartermaster for General Steuben, who had command of all patriot forces in Virginia (Continentals and militia).[17]

Carrington rejoined Greene's army near Guilford Courthouse on February 5, 1781. The southern commander had a very special assignment for Carrington. With Cornwallis' army in pursuit Greene expected to take his army across the Dan River into Virginia and there wait for reinforcements. Carrington had to determine the best crossings of the river and to assemble boats for ferrying Greene's troops. This Carrington accomplished splendidly, and the American troops crossed the river just ahead of the enemy.

Edward Carrington. **Courtesy of the Library of Virginia.**

The young dashing hero Henry Lee said of Carrington's exploit: "Without a single dollar in the military chest," by "his method and seal, and indefatigable industry" he managed "to give promptitude to our movements, as well as accuracy and punctuality to the supplies of subsistence" and "to collect in due time all the boats upon the Dan, above Boyd's Ferry, at the two points designated for the passage of the river."[18] As Carrington's biographer notes, the crossing of the Dan was the "turning point" of the war in the South.[19]

In early March 1781 Carrington met with an officer of Corwallis' army, Captain Henry Broderick, to arrange a cartel for the exchange of prisoners of war. A cartel agreement was concluded May 3, 1781.[20] Subsequently, Carrington did double duty as quartermaster and artillery commander. He supervised the artillerists at the Battle of Guilford Courthouse on March 15 and also assisted General Greene in attempting to rally the troops.[21] At the Battle of Hobkirk's Hill on April 25, 1781, Carrington led a detachment of 40 artillerists with three six-pounders placed in the center of the American line, along with some other of Charles Harrison's artillery regiment, which checked the advance of Lord Rawdon's troops.[22]

Carrington took leave of his quartermaster post in July 1781 and returned to the main army in the north as acting commander of the Fourth Artillery Regiment. He also served as chief assistant to General Henry Knox. Carrington helped to direct the artillery at the siege of Yorktown.[23] Carrington expected to be named commander of the Fourth Artillery Regiment upon the resignation of Colonel Thomas Proctor. But Congress balked at selecting Carrington, on the grounds that because Proctor and most of the regiment were from Pennsylvania, that state, not Virginia (according to the rule made by Congress), had the privilege to make promotions.[24]

Early in 1782 Carrington visited Philadelphia to arrange for supplies for the Southern Army. On his return to Nathanael Greene's army he inspected supply posts in Richmond, Salisbury, the Waxhaws, and Camden. He arrived at Greene's camp at Ashley Hill, South Carolina, around August 1, 1782.[25] With the war over, while other officers took their leave of the army, Carrington stayed on in the quartermaster service to attend to the disbandment of the army. He had to oversee the evacuation of troops northward, the disposition of army stores and other goods no longer essential for military need, and the settlement of accounts. With the embarkment of the last of the troops or ships for Philadelphia on July 19, 1789, Carrington journeyed northward, catching up with General Greene for triumphal processions in various towns. By early September he had returned to his home in Richmond to stay.[26]

Carrington's duties in the Southern Army as quartermaster had been complex and varied. He was responsible for letting out army contracts. He was "bombarded with problems of transportation and supply and exerted his every resource, personal and official, to develop systems and principles of operation for greater efficiency and economy." He looked after pasturing of livestock, keeping prices reasonable, upholding standards of quality, supervising forage, and maintaining a tight grip on wagoners.[27] Among the myriad difficulties facing Carrington as the quartermaster for the Southern Army was the prohibition by law in South Carolina of army impressments of provisions and supplies and purchasing through the contract system — many individuals and firms unwilling to contract with the army, given the dismal financial performances on Congress.[28]

In June 1784 Carrington went to Philadelphia as a Northwest claims commissioner for Virginia to secure federal compensation for expenses incurred in providing military defense in the Ohio country.[29] From 1784 to 1786 he served two terms as a member of the Virginia House of Delegates, representing Cumberland County.[30]

In the Congress for two terms, 1786 to 1788, Carrington served as chairman of the committee that drew up the Northwest Ordinance, which provided for the organization of government for the territory under federal auspices. In taking a leading role in shaping this legislation, which passed Congress on July 13, 1787, Carrington indicated himself as a strong nationalist. Congress had no constitutional mandate to enact the ordinance.[31] Carrington was also the author of an act to set aside lands in the Northwest to satisfy military bounties. He served on the committees for Indian affairs in the northern and southern departments. He sought action from the federal government to bring to justice those frontier ruffians responsible for atrocities against the Indians.[32] Carrington condemned the inefficiency of the Confederation government, and feared that the "spirit of insurgency" demonstrated by Shays's Rebellion might spread and bring down state governments.[33]

Still in Congress at the time that the Constitutional Convention was meeting in Philadelphia, Carrington let it be known that although he did "not implicitly accede, in sentiment, to every article" of the proposed Constitution, he urged its ratification.[34] He introduced the motion in Congress to have state legislatures hold conventions for ratification as "speedily" as possible.[35] Carrington favored amendments to be proposed by Congress rather than by a "General Convention."[36]

Carrington returned to Virginia from his Congressional service in October 1788. Even though still a member of Congress, he was immediately elected to the House of Delegates representing Powhatan County.[37] In spring 1788 he sought election to the Virginia Convention for Ratifying the Constitution, but, largely through the influence of anti–Federalist Patrick Henry, he was defeated.[38] In 1789 Carrington won a second term in the state legislature, where he proved to be a staunch Federalist.[39]

Upon completion of legislative service, Carrington accepted President Washington's appointment as U.S. marshal for the District of Virginia. In this capacity he also had the added duty of supervising the federal census in Virginia for 1790.[40]

In 1791 Carrington was appointed the federal supervisor for the excise for Virginia, and continued in that role until June 1804 when the duties of that office were transferred by Secretary of the Treasury Albert Gallatin to the district marshal.[41] Upon the request of Alexander Hamilton, Carrington prepared a report on manufactures in Virginia.[42] Carrington remained a faithful supporter of all of Hamilton's financial programs. He declined appointments as U.S. attorney general and secretary of war.[43]

On December 8, 1792, the 43-year-old bachelor married 32-year old Elizabeth Ambler Brent, a widow and sister-in-law of John Marshall. They had no children.[44] After both of his parents died in 1785, Carrington and his family made their abode at the ancestral home in Cumberland County, 50 miles from Richmond.[45]

During the Whiskey Insurrection of 1794 to 1795, Carrington was charged, along with the Virginia governor, with assembling troops for service in western Pennsylvania. Winchester and Moorefield were designated as places for rendezvous.[46]

Like many veterans of the Continental Army, Carrington was willing to undertake further military service. He accepted a commission as quartermaster general of the army expected to be raised in 1798 to 1799 to fight what was thought to be an impending war with France.[47] The war did not materialize, nor did the army.

Carrington served one term as mayor of Richmond, 1807 to 1809, and was foreman of the jury for the treason trial of Aaron Burr in 1807. In addition, he became a wealthy banker.[48]

Carrington was not an outspoken foe of slavery, but he did recognize the institution could not last. Colonel Timothy Pickering asked Carrington at the close of the Revolutionary War "what he thought would be the final result of the Negro population, in slave-holding States. He answered — They will mingle their blood with the Whites. That, of course, would bring slavery to an end."[49]

The artillerist who ably performed in the line and who, as a staff officer, almost single-handily kept an army on its feet as it struggled to outlast the enemy in the South, died on October 28, 1810. He was buried just outside a window of St. John's Church (still extant) in Richmond where he had stood on March 23, 1775, as he listened to Patrick Henry's famous "Give me Liberty or Death" speech, declaring at the time that he wanted this to be his burial site.[50]

COMMISSIONER OF WAR

28. William Davies

One of Virginia's military officers most admired for his abilities and competence was one who almost escaped history — William Davies, whose star rose momentarily during the war and then all but disappeared. William Davies had the distinction of being the powerful second and last commissioner of war for the state of Virginia.

The son of the Great Awakening preacher and president of the College of New Jersey (Princeton), Samuel Davies, and Jane Holt, William Davies was born in Hanover County, Virginia, in 1749. His mother was the sister of William Holt, who had served as mayor of Williamsburg, and the brother of John Holt, who published a newspaper in New York and Norfolk, Virginia.[1]

That William Davies does not appear to have been much affected by his father's fire-and-brimstone sermons may be due to the fact that the elder Davies had to preach in churches at different locations among the Scots-Irish Presbyterians while the family stayed home and to the fact that after a two-year stint as college president, he died in 1761 at age 38, when William was only 12 years old. William Davies became the ward of Richard Stockton, a distinguished New Jersey lawyer. He received an undergraduate degree and an MA from the College of New Jersey. Davies then read law with Stockton and taught grammar school. Upon returning to Virginia Davies became a prominent lawyer at Norfolk.[2] Nothing further is known of William Davies until 1774 when he became active in the revolutionary movement.

On July 6, 1774, William Davies signed, as clerk for a Norfolk group of citizens, resolutions calling for a Virginia convention at Williamsburg, a Continental Congress, support for the beleaguered citizens of Boston, and a boycott of English goods.[3] In July 1775 Davies was named secretary of the Norfolk Committee of Safety.[4] Under an act of the Third Virginia Convention "for Raising and Embodying a Sufficient Force for the Defence and Protection of This Colony," in mid–September 1775 Davies was elected by a committee for the district of Princess Anne County, one of six such jurisdictions, to superintend recruitment of troops for the Continental Army.[5] Davies himself was given a commission as captain and commander of a company in the First Virginia Regiment, which was accepted into Continental service on February 13, 1776.[6] Davies was not at the Battle of Great Bridge on December 9, 1775, but remained in the Norfolk vicinity and served in the Virginia forces that drove the royal governor out of the lower tidewater region.[7]

Davies and his infantry regiment linked up with Washington's army at about the time of the Battle of Harlem Heights on September 16, 1776.[8] He was elected by the

Continental Congress to serve as mustermaster general over some 10,000 special service militia, dubbed as the "Flying Camp" on October 5, 1776, a post he declined.[9] Davies had the misfortune of being captured in the surrender of Fort Washington, November 16, 1776.[10] Apparently, within several months he was released from captivity by exchange. On March 22, 1777, Davies was named a major in the Seventh Virginia Regiment, and in November of the same year was appointed a lieutenant colonel in the Fifth Virginia Regiment.[11]

While at Valley Forge, where he stayed for the whole period of the encampment,[12] Davies received a dual appointment: he was to continue as a line officer and he was commissioned, on March 20, 1778, a colonel in the Fourteenth Virginia Regiment (later redesignated as the Tenth); he was also named one of the four subinspectors of the army on March 28, 1778.[13]

Although Washington's nomination of Davies for the post of adjutant general of the army was passed over by Congress in favor of Colonel Alexander Scammell, Davies served briefly as an acting divisional adjutant general. Meanwhile, he continued on as a subinspector until December 1779.[14]

While Davies was on a leave of absence in late 1779, Washington requested that he should accompany "the whole of the Virginia line being ordered to the Southward." But, if this was inconvenient for Davies and if he had not "completed the arrangement" of his private affairs, then Davies should inform General William Woodford, the commander of the southern-bound troops, who was authorized to appoint Lt. Col. Samuel Jordan Cabell to the southern inspectorship. Davies declined, and Cabell was appointed. There was bad blood between General Woodford and many of the Virginia officers, and Davies openly expressed a preference not to serve under Woodford.[15]

In early 1780 Washington directed Davies, who was in Virginia at the time, to join in the march of Virginia troops on their way to be attached to the Southern Army in the Carolinas and Georgia. Davies accordingly went to Petersburg as the troops came in, but found that "no command in the line had been reserved" for him and that Colonel Nathaniel Gist "without any right or justice had been given one of the regiments." Davies refused to go on with the troops.[16] As small consolation, Washington offered Davies an appointment as a temporary superintendent of the many sick and disabled Virginia troops cared for at an army hospital in Petersburg. Davies responded that as his patriotic duty he would "undertake the care of these unhappy fellows." In this position Davies reported to General Muhlenberg, who had returned to Virginia to assist in the state's defense.[17]

Davies, however, still kept his options open. In a supernumerary situation, he was practically out of the army. He applied for the position of deputy quartermaster general of the Southern Army, on the expectation that Colonel William Finnie was about to vacate this office. Timothy Pickering, the quartermaster general of the Continental Army, informed Virginia governor Thomas Jefferson:

Colo. Davies's abilities are indisputable, and I do not know that his Integrity is suspected: but whether he is industrious I am altogether uninformed. It seems too that he is of an uneasy disposition, and less accomadating than could be wished at a time when by every just means we should conciliate the affections of the people, as so much depends on their good will. Yet upon the whole, from the vast superiority of his abilities, he may merit a preference to Colo. Finnie.[18]

Finnie decided to stay in office until the war's end.

Meanwhile, Nathanael Greene, the freshly appointed commander of the Southern Army, suggested to General Steuben, now the commander of Continental troops in Virginia, that Davies might well be appointed "to superintend the Recruiting service" in Virginia.[19] Steuben agreed, and named Davies to be "superintendent of the Recruiting service."[20]

William Davies made his headquarters a central place for receiving recruits the Continental Training Depot and General Rendezvous at Chesterfield County Courthouse.[21] As superintendent at the Chesterfield depot he oversaw the procurement of clothing and provisions for the troops and wagons, to be supplied by each Virginia county and municipality.[22] Davies started a shoe factory at the depot. At times he had to provide clothing, provisions, and equipment for those soldiers enlisted and biding their time before being sent to army units. During the British invasions of central Virginia, Davies had the responsibility of moving materiél from the reach of the enemy. Steuben said that Davies deserved "great credit" for this effort.[23]

On March 27, 1781, William Davies accepted an appointment from Governor Jefferson as Virginia's commissioner of war, a post vacated by the first commissioner, Colonel George Muter.[24] The appointment came at a time the British were conducting full-scale invasions of Virginia and the Carolinas and Georgia. As a condition of acceptance, William Davies secured the privilege that he retain his rank as a colonel in the Continental line while holding this civilian office. Congress forbade the dual officeholding, and Davies opted to serve only in the civilian capacity.[25] Ironically, Davies was not officially mustered out as a colonel until January 1783, probably not so much an oversight but to ensure that he would enjoy full veteran benefits.[26]

William Davies proved to be a superb administrator, and probably was the ablest member of the Virginia government during the war. As commissioner of war, he had charge of all aspects of the war effort, particularly logistics. Davies had to secure arms, clothing, provisions, boats, "traveling forges,"

William Davies. Miniature by unknown artist, destroyed by Hurricane Hugo in September 1969. Courtesy of Jane Bockel.

and wagons.[27] He wrote Lafayette in September 1781, "I am exerting the whole of my influence to procure supplies for the army."[28] He also had to allocate supplies and munitions to militia mobilized in the field.[29] All state quartermasters, commissaries, clothiers, and the state commercial agent reported to Davies.[30] Davies cracked down on staff personnel considered negligent, and on such occasions had miscreants arrested.[31]

Davies, the "war effort" dictator, had his office in the "Senate House" in Richmond. Besides equipping army units, Davies also presided over the military draft, held in counties under local administration. Only 44 percent of the constituencies (32 counties) ever attempted to put the draft into effect in relation to inducting Continental Army troops; many of those taken into such service quickly became deserters.[32]

With the British invasions of 1781 Davies had his hands full in providing supplies and recruits to both Lafayette's army in Virginia and Greene's Southern Army. Greene, however, recognized that Davies' priority was the defense of Virginia.[33]

After Yorktown, Davies still had responsibility of supplying Virginia Continentals with Greene. Virginia frontier defense now demanded more attention. Davies had charge of sending militia to the Kentucky posts.[34]

On November 16, 1782, the Virginia House of Delegates appointed a committee to draft a bill abolishing the Commissioner of War office and transferring its duties to the executive branch. The measure became law on December 24; Davies, however, resigned during the first week of December.[35]

After the war William Davies practiced law first in Petersburg and then in Norfolk. He married Mary Murray, widow of Alexander Gordon of Petersburg. No record of the date of the marriage exists. There was one daughter, Mary Ann.[36]

In September 1788 William Davies was made a commissioner to settle accounts between the United States and Virginia; he held the post until 1799. Davies arrived in New York City on April 22, 1789, to assume his new position. When the capital moved to Philadelphia in 1790, Davies had his headquarters there.[37]

Davies was soon at odds with William Winder, a 25-year-old Baltimore lawyer who was one of the five commissioners appointed by Congress to review the work of the state commissioners. Winder refused to give any credit to Virginia's claims because of their disordered condition.[38] The issue became related to the proposal in Congress for the federal government to assume all state war debts. This goal was accomplished, thus diminishing the confusion and stress of William Davies' role as settler of the war accounts. Despite the controversy, Davies boasted that not a single Virginia claim was rejected. After many adjustments, Virginia won a credit of $19,085,981, the largest of any state. The assumption had been achieved as part of the famous compromise that located the nation's capital along the Potomac River.[39]

In December 1800 President Adams appointed Davies collector for the ports of Norfolk and Portsmouth, Virginia, and also "superintendent of the Light Houses and other Establishments ... for the protection of navigation."[40]

Almost nothing is known of William Davies' last years. In September 1801 Thomas Jefferson received a letter from Thomas Newton that said: "Coll Davies our Collector lies very ill with a paryleitic or an appoplectic affection in the head ... I apprehend he will not recover, tho I hope he may, as he is the best collector we have had at this place."[41] Davies may have resigned the collectorship around this time, but probably prevailed in the office for one or several years. On November 12, 1804, President Jefferson nominated Wilson Cary Nicholas as William Davies' successor.[42] A Norfolk newspaper of December 23, 1805, reported that William Davies "late collector of this port" had died in Mecklenberg County.[4]

Appendix: Death of Charles Porterfield at the Battle of Camden*

At length the fatal night of the 15th August, 1780, arrived, when Gates, precisely at 10 o'clock, agreeably to general orders just issued, put his army in motion — the light troops moving simultaneously, joined but a few minutes by 200 exhausted raw Virginia militia, and Col. Armand's corps of dragoons, consisting of about 60 privates, marching in order of battle after the following disposition : the foot divided into two bodies, moved by files through the open piney woods plain, 25 yards out of the great Waxhaw road ; the right flank headed by Col. Porterfield (commandant of the whole corps in person,) whilst Capt. Drew with his Virginia regulars, (about 55, and mostly raw levies,) composed the leading company of that flank. The left flank of infantry, under the care of Major Armstrong, moved in like order, having the Halifax volunteers, headed by Capt. Lockhart, for his leading company. Col. Armand, with his dragoons in column, occupied the road which was here a dead level and very spacious. It became my duty by direction, to post myself on the right side of Colonel Porterfield, as he had on several occasions before, made use of me (a private soldier) to carry his orders to other officers of his command, and in one or two instances, to repair to the main army on business. In this order we slowly advanced, to give time to the main army to approximate us in the most profound silence ; it being expressly stated in Gen. Gates's last orders, that any person speaking above his breath, should be instantly put to death on the spot where the violation occurred. Lord Cornwallis, as it was afterwards ascertained, by a singular coincidence, put his army in motion at the same hour in the night that Gates moved, to strike him in his camp at Clermont the next morning at break of day, while Gates's object was to move down upon Camden that night. The consequence of this simultaneous movement of both armies was,

*From Guilford Dudley, "A Sketch of the Military Services Performed by Guilford Dudley, then of the Town of Halifax, North Carolina, during the Revolutionary War," *Southern Literary Messenger*, 11 (1845): 146–48 and 231–35.

that we met about half way near Sutton's plantation between 12 and 1 o'clock in the night. The moon was at full and shone beautifully; not a breath of air was stirring, nor a cloud to be seen big as a man's hand. Consequently, we could see to fight in the open piney wood plains, destitute of brush wood almost, as well in the night as in the day. Tarleton, with his dragoons, (said to be 350,) with a suitable number of infantry, composed the British van. Armand's videt, who rode about 300 yards in our front, descried the enemy advancing upon him, and at that instant emptied his pistol, and came clattering in with all the speed his horse could make. The discharge of the pistol was most distinctly heard through all the American corps. A pause ensued, when Col. Armand, in the road, who discovered the British dragoons, put spurs to his horse, and at full speed dashed from the road to the front of our right flank of infantry; and leaning over his saddle, in an audible whisper said to Col. Porterfield, "there is the enemy, Sir — must I charge him." Porterfield, who was a serious man, of few words, and slow of speech, gravely replied in the tone of Armand, "by all means, Sir." I was at this moment, as I had been constantly before, riding on the right side of the American commandant, as near as I could conveniently get; and anxiously desirous of hearing Armand's brief communication to his Col. Commandant, leant over myself almost upon the withers of Porterfield's horse, and distinctly heard Armand's communication and the question it involved, together with the reply, although all was expressed only in a whisper. Armand, instantly wheeling his horse, rushed on to the head of his column, which he had left but a few seconds before, when Tarleton, sounding a charge, came on at the top of his speed, every officer and soldier with the yell of an Indian savage — at every leap their horses took, crying out, "charge, charge, charge," so that their own voices and the echoes resounded in every direction through the pine forest. Armand stood his ground and received the enemy's charge: the front sections of each party emptying their pistols before the dreadful clashing of sabers, which instantly succeeded. Col. Porterfield, now breaking silence, as soon as he heard the enemy's clamor, and saw their swift approach towards the front of Armand's column, with his usual com-posure and deliberate manner, ordered his right flank of infantry to "advance," which order was hastily executed in a step approaching to a trot, keeping our due distance from the road, and in a line parallel to it, when pretty well covering Tarleton's left flank, though we were far from seeing to its rear, by reason of the great length of his column. Porterfield ordered "halt, face to the road and fire." This order was executed with the velocity of a flash of lightning, spreading from right to left, and again the piney forest resounded with the thunder of our musketry ; whilst the astonished British dragoons, looking only straight before them along the road, counting no doubt with certainty upon extirpating Armand's handful of cavalry, and not dreaming that they were flanked on the right and on the left by our infantry within point-blank shot, drew up, wheeled their horses, and retreating with the utmost precipitation, were out of our reach before we could possibly ram down another cartridge. This firing, however, announced to the two commanding generals their certain proximity, unexpected as it was, and they both took their measures with promp-titude accordingly. But to return to the American infantry and cavalry. The shock and clangor of the charge of cavalry just mentioned, in the sight of raw, fatigued, and undisciplined militia, (except Drew's leading company on the right flank, and the Halifax volunteers, under Lockhart, on the left,) who had never before seen an enemy in arms, and within 25 steps of the road, instantly fled and retreated to our main body, and Armand's dragoons did the same — a few of the leading sections in front, who fought near the person of their Colonel, excepted. Near the whole of his column, without waiting to ascertain the success of the front sections engaged with the enemy hand to hand with the sabre, nor to see the effect of the fire of the infantry, shamefully abandoning their Colonel, and the few that fought about him, wheeled and retreated in inextricable confusion, carrying dismay and disorder into the ranks of the Maryland troops, composing the front division of Gates's army, advanced, it seems, to within a mile of the ground where the light troops were engaged — such, I mean, as maintained their posts, who were indeed but few out of 450 who composed our front. Armand bravely maintained the onset at first against vastly superior numbers, was forced to save himself by flight with the loss of his horseman's cap, and followed his dispersed troops to the main body. What gave me infinite pain, at this critical juncture, was to see the left of Drew's company of regulars, with his subalterns, on whose firmness and prowess I had made sanguine calculations, fall back in much disorder upon the first meeting of the cavalry, and before we had fired a single musket. Watching the motions of our own troops, as well as those of the enemy, with eyes eagerly bent in every direction, and seeing the shameful defection of this portion of our infantry, without saying a word to Col. Porterfield, or Capt. Drew, who were side by side, and too much engaged in other matters to see it, I turned my horse, and galloping down the line along the rear of those who stood firmly, and rushing among the confused men who had fallen back, with the authority of an officer who had a right to command, in a loud tone of voice, called to them to "halt, rally and form the line," without appearing to recognize any individual, or calling upon any name, although I knew them all, having served day and night with them from the time Col. Porterfield took the command of the light corps, until that moment. My command was instantly obeyed, and thus order was promptly restored; when wheeling my horse again, I hastened back and resumed my post by the side of the Colonel. Whilst these things were transacting on the right flank of infantry, the left, under Major Armstrong, were equally panic struck, by the charge of Tarleton's dragoons, and all fled, except the Halifax volunteers, under Captain Lockhart, who, taking their part with decision, poured in a heavy fire upon the British Colonel's right flank of cavalry, which must have done great execution, although we were never able to ascertain the enemy's loss, as we were shortly after compelled to yield the ground upon which we fought without entering the road at all. No sooner had Tarleton received one destructive fire on his right and on his left, and retreated out of our reach, than the British infantry, who were close at hand, advanced in column to the number, it was said, of about 500, but which, probably, did not exceed 350. Porterfield, holding up his fire until he saw his enemy between our two flanks of infantry, commenced his fire at close distance, which was answered by our left flank, under Capt. Lockhart, with equal spirit and deliberation. The enemy seemed for an instant to pause, but conscious of their superiority in numbers as well as discipline, facing to their right and left, returned upon us a heavy fire, which

173

enveloped us from our right to left, in consequence of the recession of so large a number of troops in the commencement of the action, leaving us only 100 or less on both flanks to contend with the unbroken, undismayed column of the enemy; but soon the remains of our left flank, under Capt. Lockhart, receded also, and hastily falling back in an oblique direction from the road, formed on the extreme of the left wing of our army, now forming, and composed of Stephen's brigade of Virginia militia, who had only reached head-quarters late in the preceding afternoon. The conflict on our right, where Porterfield in person commanded, became, therefore, more unequal and destructive; yet Porterfield maintained his ground with great firmness and gallantry for about five rounds, with this handful of men, not more than 50 at this time. The enemy, without leaving the road and advancing upon us as he might have done, pushed his column along until he passed our left, when giving us a cross-fire from both his flanks, as well as from his centre directly in our front, he threatened instant extermination to our brave little band.

At length both sides being simultaneously prepared, poured in upon each other the heaviest fire that had been yet exchanged during the conflict. At this fire, Porterfield, with horse's head reined directly to the enemy, received a horrid wound in his left leg, a lit-tle-below the knee, which shattered it to pieces, when falling forward upon the pommel of his saddle, he directed Captain Drew, who was close by his side, to order a retreat, which was done in a very deliberate tone of voice by the Captain, and instantly our little band retreated obliquely from the road, which was wholly secluded from us by the enemy. At this moment I was ten or twelve yards down the line from the Colonel, with my horse's head reined also directly to the enemy, and his nose touching the shoulders of our rear rank. Glancing my eye from left to right as the enemy poured in his fire, I fixed it upon Porterfield at the instant he received the ball and fell upon the pommel of his saddle, when wheeling my horse I dashed up to the Colonel, while Drew having given the order for retreat, was on his left side, in the act of wheeling his horse from the enemy, with the intent to carry him off. Locking my left arm in the Colonel's right to support him in the saddle on that side, and having completely turned his horse, we received another hot fire from the enemy, directed solely upon us at the distance of thirty yards or less. Upon this the Colonel's horse, very docile and standing fire with the same steady composure as his master, having no doubt been grazed by a ball which he sensibly felt, reared, plunged forward and dropt his rider on the spot, who had a severe fall in his maimed condition, and had liked to have dragged me off my horse with our arms locked, and the horse going off with his accoutrements at the top of his speed, followed the track of the retreating soldiers. At the very instant Porterfield's horse reared and plunged forward, Captain Drew fell prostrate on his face, and that so naturally, that I entertained no doubt but he was killed. The Captain, however, receiving no injury, and being an active, nimble little man, was presently on his feet again, and wheeling round the stern of my horse, was in a moment out of sight. Thus left entirely alone with the Colonel, who was flat upon the ground with his head towards the enemy and his shattered leg doubled under him, entreat-ing me not to leave him, I sprang from my horse and seizing him with an Indian hug around the waist, by a sudden effort jerked him up upon his well leg. Then again the

Colonel, in the most pathetic manner, apparently dreading instant death, brave as he was, or captivity, entreated me, as he had done before, not to forsake him; the blood, in the meantime gushing out of his wound in a torrent as big as a large straw or goose-quill, which presently overflowed the top of his large, loose boot and dyed the ground all around him. Pale as a piece of bleached linen, and ready to faint with the loss of blood and anguish of his wound, he made another appeal my feelings in the manner above described, from an apprehension, as I then believed, that I would not have firmness enough to stand by him under the trying circumstances I had then to encounter, knowing also that this was the first of my battles, and that every man, under his command, even his main depend-ence, Captain Drew, who had fought many battles, had all fled and were totally out of view,—when I replied the second time, as I had in the first instance, with much earnestness and energy, "that I would carry him off or perish with him." Upon this assurance, twice repeated, the Colonel became tranquillized and seemed patiently to wait his doom, which he expected would be nothing less than instant death or captivity, the latter of which, at that moment, in his miserable situation, I believe to have been as appalling to his mind as the first. While we stood thus in front of the enemy, with my horse uncommonly gentle and no ways alarmed at the firing, drawn up close by my side, we received another fire from a platoon of the enemy just in our front, whilst the rest of their line seemed to have slackened theirs, and in no wise annoyed us. Still clasping Colonel Porterfield in my arms and supporting him upon his well leg, his back to the enemy, my face and right shoulder above his left, looking intently at the enemy to see if a file or section would leave the road and advance upon us with charged bayonets, I made three violent essays to throw him upon my horse, which was tall, and thus endeavor to carry him off. My efforts were per-fectly fruitless. I was then young and light, and Colonel Porterfield was a man of the largest size, perhaps 6 feet and an inch or two in height, round limbed and fleshy, but not corpulent, although he weighed perhaps 210 pounds and was about 30 or 32 years of age. Although I several times poised him and raised him a little from the ground, yet as he could only stand upon one leg with my support, the other dangling from side to side and sometimes behind as I moved him, and incapable of bounding in the least from the earth, I was incapable with my utmost exertions of throwing him into my saddle. In this dilemma I ceased to make any further efforts to throw him upon my horse and resolved calmly to wait the result whatever it might be, nor did Porterfield attempt to give me any direction in this emergency, or express an opinion how I ought to act for his relief or my own preservation, but appeared to be entirely resigned to whatever fate might await him in his exhausted and fainting condition. Still holding up the Colonel upon his well leg, watching the motions of the enemy and not infrequently turning my head over either shoulder, casting a wishful and exploring eye on every side and in the rear, to see if no friendly assistance could be obtained, however improbable, (for all was silence; not a living soul to be seen but the enemy in the road, occasionally giving us a scattering but ineffectual fire.) I was at last so fortunate as to fix my eyes upon two men at the distance of about 150 yards in my rear, running back with great speed, half bent and with trailed arms, towards where they supposed the main body, under Gates, was by this time halted.

Although I could not at the moment divine where these men came from, I yet, nevertheless, with joy as well as surprise recognized them for American troops by their garb, their manner and by their clumsy wooden canteens slung over their shoulders upon their blankets and knapsacks, all which I could plainly discover by the brilliant light of the moon, casting her beams with great luster over the open piney wood plain. Believing this providential discovery would be the last resource I should be favored with to save Porterfield and myself, I was determined to avail myself of it if possible at every risk, and therefore endeavoring somewhat to modulate the tone of my voice, with great eagerness I called out to them, "come here, come here," without saying for what purpose or mentioning any names. Whether they had seen us before or not I cannot say, but hearing my voice, they instantly turned their heads in the direction where Porterfield and myself stood, though without slackening their pace, and kept on with rather increased speed and bodies lower bent, with no obstruction before them but the yielding wire-grass which was profusely spread over the piney plain about waist high. Seeing them no ways disposed to come at my call to our assistance, and knowing that we should be lost without it, I resolved to make one desperate effort to draw them to us before they should get out of my sight or hearing. I therefore in a very loud tone of voice and with much energy, regardless of the immediate proximity of the enemy, cried out, "by G — d, come and help me away with Colonel Porterfield." This name, pronounced with so much emphasis, operated on the feelings of these two honest young soldiers like magic, and they instantly wheeled and came running to us with all their speed, no longer half bent to conceal themselves among the wire-grass, but with erect countenance and a determined air. No sooner had they reached us and laid down their muskets and fixed bayonets by my direction, than they seized Porterfield by both his arms and around his body to sustain him in the position they found him in upon coming up. Then I sprang into my saddle and ordered them to lift him up carefully over the stern of my horse and place him close to the hind tree of my saddle, (the Colonel instantly clinging to me with both arms around my waist,) and then directing them to resume their muskets with one hand and each with the other to sustain him in his seat across the loins of the horse, taking care to steady his shattered leg so as to keep it from swinging about under the flanks of the horse, and to prevent his falling off behind. All these instructions were obeyed with an alacrity and cheerfulness that instantly won my affections and confidence; and thus fixed, with the reins of the bridle in my own hand, I moved slowly off in a direction perpendicular to the road, not daring to oblique to my right or march parallel to the road to gain our main body, lest I should be intercepted by the enemy, who had pushed the front sections or files of their light infantry along up the Waxhaw road, for some distance beyond the spot where we had fought, and gave us all in a group as we were, a scattering, parting fire, with no more effect than if it had been made with little boy's pop-guns, constructed of the joint of an alder stalk and charged with tow wads; so wretchedly did they take aim, as I had discovered from the first fire at the commencement of the action, for at the distance of only 25 yards from the road many of their balls whizzed along six feet above our heads, while others struck the ground before they reached us, and rebounding passed off without doing much injury that I could perceive, whilst others that were better directed produced, as might be supposed, the most destructive effects, the lamented Porterfield being one instance.

But to resume: thus fixed, with the Colonel clinging around my waist, we marched very slowly off to save him all the pain we possibly could in his melancholy situation. We had, however, scarcely progressed more than 30 or 40 yards before he fainted with loss of blood and the anguish of his wound, and was very nearly falling off backwards over the stern of my horse, but was sustained in his seat by my two faithful companions. We were then compelled to halt, although still in sight of the enemy, to give the Colonel time to breathe a little, I ordering the soldiers to dash some water they fortunately had in their awkward wooden canteens in his face, when, clasping his arms around my waist the second time, for he had unconsciously unlocked his hands when he first fainted, we moved quietly off again, but had scarcely proceeded more than 40 yards further when he fainted the second time, but was soon revived by the use of the same means as were first applied. He then, in the most pathetic and moving accents, entreated me to lay him down and let him abide his fate, whatever it might prove; but this I refused, and exhorted him with all the energy and force of reasoning that I was master of, to bear his miserable situation a little longer and he should be safe, telling him that the enemy was yet in view, although he did not pursue at that moment; yet in all probability, nay, to a certainty, his discomfited cavalry would, in a few minutes, return and scour the whole plain in our front, rear and all around us, when we should all be inevitably lost. Yielding to these arguments, the Colonel became passive, and then directing my companions to hold him fast in his present seat, (finding there was great danger of his falling off as he became more exhausted,) I sprang from my saddle upon the ground and joining with them, directed them to assist me to lift the Colonel over the hind-tree into the seat of the saddle that I had just left, and then springing up myself behind him and clasping my arms around his waist, I directed one of the men to take the reins of the bridle and guide the horse himself, as I could no longer do it in my changed position, both my hands and arms being employed in this manner. With the same alacrity as they had manifested upon all occasions before, my order was obeyed, and thus we moved on the third time as before. But unfortunately, although the Colonel's new position was more safe and easy than before, yet, nevertheless, growing more weak and exhausted every moment, he presently fainted the third and then the fourth time, while I pressed him around the body with both my arms and sustained him in his seat without his saying another word or entreating to be laid down as he had done before. But in both these last cases he revived by the free use of the contents of the wooden canteens, which contained nothing but warm, dead water, only drinkable from necessity. Most fortunately, at the last instance of his fainting, we were emerging into a little thicket of small persimmon bushes, about waist high, growing among the wire-grass, a phenomenon I had never before seen in the open piney wood plains. At first it had been impracticable to place a bandage around his leg, as we had neither time nor means to accomplish it, though it would evidently be attended with advantage to the unfortunate Colonel, but there was no brush-wood or other growth from which a handful of twigs could be cut for the purpose of splintering his leg before the bandage was applied.

No sooner, therefore, did I cast my eye over the aforesaid cluster of little persimmon shrubs, than the idea of availing myself of their use occurred. And directing the soldier who had the bridle-rein in his hand and was guiding the horse to halt, I slipped off from behind Porterfield and requested him to tear off a bandage from one side of his blanket its whole length, whilst I should, pulling out my pocket knife for the purpose, cut a bundle of twigs 10 or 12 inches in length and hastily trim them to apply all around the Colonel's leg before the bandage was wrapped over them. This request was also instantly complied with, and the bundle of pliant twigs being expeditiously prepared with the assistance of this soldier, whilst the other held Porterfield fast in the saddle, I very soon bound up his leg in many folds of the strip of blanket as tight as I could draw it, which almost entirely stanched the blood, and then resuming my seat behind him we soon moved on again for the last time, steering our course as before, due West as near as possible. This surgical-like operation was of infinite advantage to Porterfield, who no more fainted or complained. And thus we moved on without any further interruption or delay, perhaps a mile and a half from the road where we fought, when we were stopped by one of those large, flat, impassable morasses, that so frequently occur in the pine plains of South Carolina, extending an unknown distance from North to South and nearly parallel to the road we had recently left. Here, of necessity, we were obliged to halt, and fortunately striking the margin of the morass, where grew a large laurel sapling with its dark green and glossy leaves just in the edge of the marsh, with a wide spreading bushy top which cast a deep shade upon the ground eastward, I determined to lay the exhausted Colonel down, and stretching him at full length in the shade of the laurel with his leg and thigh bolstered up with my great-coat which was fastened to the pommel of my saddle, and taking time to tie my horse to a limb of the same laurel with his fore feet in the water and mud to conceal him as much as possible in the dark shade of the sapling, as well as Porterfield and myself, resolving to remain alone by Porterfield's side, I sent off my two faithful companions, with directions to search for Gates' army, where or at what distance we knew not; nor did Porterfield offer a conjecture on the subject, or give a single order from first to last respecting the premises, seeing that every thing was done by ardent friends that mortal man under existing circumstances could accomplish for his relief and safety. The order I gave them was, upon finding the army, to bring up two or three surgeons and as many men as would afford a relief or two to bear off the Colonel on a litter. No sooner did I deliver this request, than these two willing, generous soldiers, with their arms in their hands and their knapsacks and canteens slung upon their backs, departed almost in a run to execute the order just received, upon the speedy execution of which depended the life of the Colonel as well as my own. Porterfield was lying in the shade of the laurel on the edge of the morass with his feet towards Camden. I laid my unsheathed sabre and pistols on the ground by his side and within a few feet of my horse. It now being about two hours before day-break, I laid myself down along-side of the Colonel, feeling weary after fatiguing marches in the hot season.

July, but especially for the last seventeen or eighteen days after the volunteers were placed in the light infantry corps, where, in the midst of starvation, we spent sleepless nights, and consumed the long days of July and August in fatiguing marches over scorching bald sand hills and burning piney wood plains, often without a drop of water to slake our thirst or cool our parched lips and tongues; never remaining in one position ten min-utes at a time, often only five, but were continually shifting our ground from one undu-lation of the plain, and from one copse of black-jack shrubs to another, to be safe from surprise, or the charge of British dragoons, always to be expected and easily effected by their overwhelming superiority, while we had literally none; Armand's dragoons never acting with us, and the few militia light-horse from the upper country of North Carolina sticking close to Major General Caswell's division, which, as well as the continental troops, was always out of supporting distance. Thus prostrate on the earth, Porterfield being indisposed to talking from natural taciturnity and from exhaustion, a painful silence ensued, which, however, was sometimes interrupted first, by our own light-horse in full gallop sweeping along the plain within thirty or forty yards of the spot where we lay close to the ground in the shade of the laurel, and then bearing to their left further off the morass into the plain 'till we lost sight of them and then the British dragoons, who were all in motion, coming in the other direction and scampering over the plain, sometimes at a considerable distance, but the tread of whose horses' feet, lying as we were, flat on the ground, we could distinctly hear as well as the confused voices of their riders, patrolling in every direction. On these occasions, Porterfield, in a feeble voice, would make some remarks as well as myself, but finding from the direction they took as I reported it to him, (for he never raised his head,) that they would not be upon us, he sank again into a state of silence and apathy. At last a large patrol of British dragoons came from the South in the direction of Camden, and in a brisk gallop came on pressing close in upon the margin of the swamp, coming, apparently, directly upon us, when, as before, I was aroused first by the trampling of their horses and then by a full view of them, after raising myself up upon my left elbow, at the distance of thirty or forty yards, when seizing my pistols, I hastily cocked one and was about to stand upright, but Porterfield, who now himself expected we should be discovered and consequently lost, feebly stretched out his right arm and laying his hand upon mine, entreated that I would not fire, alleging that if I did they would cut us to pieces without mercy ; for being in a desperate situation, and feeling no inclination to fall into their hands and trust to the clemency of British dragoons, I had resolved to sell my life as dear as possible, and after emptying both my pistols, to resume my sabre and defend myself to the last extremity as long as possible, announcing, however, at the same time, the name of Porterfield and asking quarter for him, and then with my arms in hand, leaving my horse behind, plunge into the morass and scramble over as well as I could, knowing that further pursuit was impracticable. These resolves were formed with the rapidity of thought, and the execution of them would have been attempted as far as practicable but fortunately, the same kind Providence who had so wonderfully protected and shielded us during the various past scenes of the night after Porterfield was wounded, did not forsake us now; for almost in the same instant that I descried them, they bore away to their right and I presently lost sight of them among the lofty pine trees of the forest. This was the last patrol that made its appearance on either side, and as soon as we felt safe from further search, we sank down again in our sleepless repose. In fifteen or twenty minutes after his last occurrence, as the Colonel and myself were lying in profound silence and the day beginning to break we heard most distinctly the report of a cannon, fired in the direction of Camden, which echoed through the plains at the distance of six miles, when asking the Colonel the meaning of it, he informed me in a feeble voice, that it was their morning gun. From which circumstance I learned that a garrisoned town always fired a morning gun about break of day. This was not only a morning gun fired to awaken the garrison, but was also designed, as I believed, to serve as a signal for Lord Cornwallis to put his army in motion and prepare for the battle just at hand, both armies having formed in the night and lain upon their arms within two hundred and fifty yards of each other. Just at this crisis, at break of day, my two faithful companions returned, bringing with them three or four surgeons, one of which was the surgeon of the Halifax volunteers; the rest were of the Maryland line, together with Capt. Drew, Lieut. Vaughn, Ensign V —, and eight privates of Drew's company, and several more, who, hearing of Porterfield's situation and the place where he lay, followed after them. The surgeons immediately fell to work upon the Colonel, but did nothing more than to take off my bandage and twig splinters and put on their own boards and bandages, whilst the rest of us were busily engaged in cutting down small pine saplings of which to form a litter to carry him off. These things being speedily accomplished, the Colonel was carefully placed on the litter, which was raised up from the ground and placed on the shoulders of four men, when the procession began to move off in solemn silence. The dawn of day then appearing, I stepped back a few paces and putting up my arms and mounting my horse, accompanied them thirty or forty yards in the direction they were going, when suddenly the stillness of the dawn was startled by one of our parks of artillery, which at once served as a signal for battle and as a guide to direct me to the spot where our army was formed, of which I was before, as well as Colonel Porterfield, entirely ignorant, not having time to ask any questions about the matter of my two companions, or any other person whom they brought up with them. Upon this firing, the meaning of which I was at no loss to understand, I wheeled my horse and riding back a few paces to the side of the litter, took an affectionate farewell of Colonel Porterfield, telling him at the same time, that I hoped to join him again in the course of an hour or two, which was in sincerity my expectation, so sanguine were my hopes of immediate victory, notwithstanding the disasters of the past night. Vain hope! I never more set my eyes on Porterfield, for here we parted — I steering my course to the army by the roar of our cannon, and the rest of the company, with the surgeons, falling back northwardly and shaping their course in a direction where they hoped to find some plantation at which to leave the Colonel with the necessary attendants, until the battle should be over.

Notes

Abbreviations in Notes

ANB   John. A. Garraty and Mark. C. Carnes, eds., *American National Biography* (New York: Oxford University Press, 1999).

ARE   Richard L. Blanco, ed., *The American Revolution: An Encyclopedia* (New York: Garland Publishing, 1993).

AWP   W. W. Abbot et al., eds., *The Papers of George Washington*, Revolutionary Series (Charlottesville: University of Virginia Press, 1983–); Colonial, Confederation, and Presidential Series are also cited under *AWP*.

CSP   W. P. Palmer et al., eds., *Calendar of Virginia State Papers* (Richmond, VA: 1875–).

DAB   Dumas Malone, ed. *Dictionary of American Biography*, 11 vols. (New York: Charles Scribner's Sons, 1957).

DVB   John Kneebone et al., eds., *Dictionary of Virginia Biography* (Richmond, Library of Virginia, 1998–).

EAR   Harold E. Selesky, ed., *Encyclopedia of the American Revolution*, 2d ed. (Farmington Hills, MI: Thompson Gale, 2006).

EARW   Gregory Fremont-Barnes and Richard A. Ryerson, eds., *The Encyclopedia of the American Revolutionary War* (Santa Barbara, CA: ABC-Clio, 2006).

FWW   John C. Fitzpatrick, ed., *The Writings of George Washington* (Washington, DC: Government Printing Office, 1931–).

JCC   Worthington C. Ford, ed., *Journals of the Continental Congress, 1774–1789* (Washington, DC: Government Printing Office, 1904).

JP   Julian P. Boyd, ed., *The Papers of Thomas Jefferson* (Princeton, NJ: Princeton University Press, 1950–).

LD   Paul M. Smith, ed., *Letters of Delegates to Congress, 1774–1789* (Washington, DC: Library of Congress, 1976–).

LP   Stanley J. Idzerda, ed., *Lafayette in the Age of the American Revolution: Selected Letters and Papers, 1776–1790* (Ithaca, NY: Cornell University Press, 1977–).

LV   Library of Virginia

MadP   William T. Hutchinson et al., eds., *The Papers of James Madison* (Chicago: University of Chicago Press, 1962–).

MP   Herbert A. Johnson et al., eds., *The Papers of John Marshall* (Chapel Hill: University of North Carolina Press, 1974–).

NDAR   William B. Clark and William J. Morgan, eds., *Naval Documents of the American Revolution* (Washington DC; Naval Historical Center, 1964–).

NG   Richard K. Showman et al., eds., *The Papers of Nathanael Greene* (Chapel Hill: University of North Carolina Press, 1976–).

OL   H. R. McIlwaine, ed., *The Official letters of the Governors of the State of Virginia* (Richmond, VA: 1926–).

PCC   Papers of the Continental Congress, National Archives

RV   William J. Van Schreevan et al., eds., *Revolutionary Virginia: The Road to Independence* (Charlottesville: University Press of Virginia, 1973–).

VFOB   *Valley Forge Orderly Book of George Weedon* (New York: Arno Press, 1971, orig. pub. 1902).

VHS   Virginia Historical Society

VMHB Virginia Magazine of History and Biography

WD   Donald Jackson and Dorothy Twohig, ed., *The Diaries of George Washington* (Charlottesville: University Press of Virginia, 1976–).

WMQ   William and Mary Quarterly

Introduction

1. Quoted in Ewen, 344.
2. Wecter, 4.
3. Gerson, 3.
4. Carlyle, 239.
5. Wecter, 11.
6. Paul Johnson, 280.
7. Riley, 8, 10, 12.
8. Ralph Waldo Emerson, "Heroism," in Slater, 148–55.
9. Herold, 43 and 220; Riley, 200.
10. Quoted in Wecter, 15.
11. Thomas Paine, "American Crisis I," in Philip, 69.
12. "Army Officer Who Refused Iraq Duty Is Allowed to Resign," *New York Times*, September 27, 2009.
13. Wyllie, 7–8; Norton, xviii.
14. John C. Fitzpatrick, *The Spirit of the Revolution*, 190–91.
15. Wyllie, 40.
16. Norton, xx.
17. Zeleny.
18. Letter of Lt. Gen. Ron Christmas, Marine Corps Heritage Foundation, Dumfries, VA., January 4, 2010, http://www.marineheritage.org.
19. George Dudley Seymour quoted in Wecter, 89.
20. Norton, xiv.

1. Alexander "Sawney" Dick

1. *Oxford English Dictionary*, 14: 538.
2. John Marshall to Mary W. Marshall, February 23, 1824, in *The Papers of John Marshall*, ed. Charles F. Hobson (Chapel Hill: University of North Carolina Press, 2000), 5:5; "Library of Charles Dick" *WMQ* 1st series, 18 (1910) 112–13.
3. L.H. Butterfield, ed., *Diary and Autobiography of John Adams* (Cambridge: Harvard University Press, 1961), 2:354.
4. George H. S. King, 153; T. E. Campbell, 394.
5. T.E. Campbell, 403; Fall, 221, 249; Duke, 14; Felder, 54, 56, 60–61, 263.
6. Washington to Dinwiddie, Sept. 6, 1755, *AWP*, 1: 222; Jackson et al., 2:31n., 32, 54, 58.
7. Felder, 61.
8. Jackson, et al., 3:13, 41; Harry M. Ward, *Duty, Honor or Country: General George Weedon and the American Revolution*, 31–32.
9. Duke, 14, 85, 87.
10. Spotsylvania County Committee Petition, May 7, 1775, in *RV*, 3:113; Resolution, July 7, 1775, in *RV*, 3:761.
11. Spotsylvania County Committee Resolution, October 17, 1775, in *RV*, 4:230–31.
12. Virginia Committee of Safety, Sept. 22, 1775, in *RV*, 4:138; William R. Siener, 119–21; Coleman, 41–42.
13. Dean C. Allard, "The Potomac Navy of 1776," *VMHB* 84 (1976): 412–16.
14. Virginia Committee of Safety Proceedings, March 29, 1776, in *RV*, 6:267; Virginia Convention Ordinance, Jan. 1, 1776, in *RV*, 7:41n.
15. Sanchez-Saavedra, *A Guide to Virginia Military Organizations in the American Revolution*, 175.

16. Virginia Committee of Safety, April 23, May 23, and June 15, 1776, in *RV*, 6:451, 7:243, 528; Claghorn, 90–91.
17. Receipt, June 17, 1776, in *RV*, 7:539; Journal of the Virginia Navy Board, October 12, 1776, in *NDAR*, 6:1242.
18. Virginia Navy Board to Capt. Richard Taylor, Sept. 12, Journal of the Virginia Committee of Safety, Sept. 13, and Journal of the Virginia Navy Board, Sept. 25, 1776, in *NDAR*, 6:790, 808–9, 995, resp.
19. Journal of the Virginia Committee of Safety, Aug. 3 and Journal of the Virginia Navy Board, Oct. 15, 1776, in *NDAR*, 6:44, 1282; Claghorn, 97.
20. Virginia Navy Board to Capt. John Harris and to Alexander Dick, Dec. 4, 1776, in *NDAR* 7:371–72; Journal of the Council, Jan. 10, 1777, in *OL*, 1:91; Petition of Alexander Dick to Governor and Council, Nov. 2, 1779, in *JP*, 3:152; Campbell, *Colonial Caroline*, 291; Robert A. Stewart, *The History of the Virginia Navy of the Revolution*, 35.
21. Cross, 40–41.
22. "George Catlett," in *Virginia Pension Applications*, comp. Dorman, 17:16; Walter D. McCaw, "Captain John Harris of the Virginia Navy: A Prisoner of War in England, 1777–1778," *VMHB* 22 (1914): 161, 163; McManemin, 390.
23. "Journal of the H.M.S. Ariadne," in *NDAR*, 9:19; Dorman, *Virginia Pension Applications*, "George Catlett," vol. 17, 17; Campbell, *Colonial Caroline*, 272–73; McManemin, 391.
24. McManemin, 391.
25. Alexander, 369.
26. Gen. William Howe to Washington, Jan. 18, 1778, in *AWP*, 13:272; Washington to the Board of War and to Gen. William Howe, Jan. 2–3 and Jan. 8, 1778, in *AWP*, 13:110, 177.
27. Archibald Cary and George Wythe for the Virginia Assembly to Henry Laurens, Jan. 12, 1778, quoted in *AWP*, 13:112n–13n.
28. Alexander, 371–74, 378–79.
29. *Ibid.*, 370–71.
30. Parramore, 353–54.
31. Cohen, "Thomas Wren: Ministering Angel of Forton Prison," 279, 282, 287; John S. Barnes, 19; quoted in Alexander, 370.
32. Cohen, *Yankee Sailors in British Gaols*, 115, 279, 282.
33. Catherine M. Prelinger, "Benjamin Franklin and the American Prisoners of War in England during the American Revolution," *WMQ*, 3d ser. 32 (1975): 261–94.
34. "List of American Prisoners in Forton Prison," in *NDAR*, 11:890; Parramore, 354; Alexander, 381.
35. Cutter, 73.
36. John S. Barnes, 13–14; Parramore, 354–55.
37. Cohen, *Yankee Sailors in British Gaols*, 83, 109–10.
38. Frank Gaynor, 273; John S. Barnes, 13; Prelinger, "Benjamin Franklin and American Prisoners of War," 283.
39. Alexander Dick to Arthur Lee, Sept. 30, 1778, Lee Family Papers, University of Virginia Library, microfilm.
40. John Adams to J. D. Schweighauser and Others, Nov. 7, 1778, in Line, et al., 200–201.

41. Alexander Dick to Arthur Lee, Dec. 10, 1778, Lee Family Papers.

42. *JCC*, Sept. 17, 1779, 15:1075; Paullin, 119; Claghorn, 187.

43. Charles R. Smith, 226–27; Morison, 198–205; John S. Barnes, 23.

44. John Paul Jones to Alexander Dick, Feb. 26, 1779, John Paul Jones Papers, ms. Microfilm, ed. and pub. by Chadwyck-Healey Ltd.

45. Arthur Lee to John Paul Jones, May 8, 1779, *ibid.*

46. L.H. Butterfield, vol. 2, 320.

47. *Ibid.*, 37.

48. Alexander Dick to John Paul Jones, April 19, 1779, John Paul Jones Papers.

49. *Memoirs of Rear Admiral Paul Jones*, vol. 11, 161; Joseph Callo, 72–73.

50. Alexander Dick to Arthur Lee, May 5, 1779, Lee Family Papers.

51. Dick to Lee, May 26, 1779, *ibid.*

52. Dick to Lee, June 10, 1779, *ibid.*

53. Charles R. Smith, 226–28.

54. Morison, 200, 203; L.H. Butterfield, vol. 2: 370–71.

55. Charles R. Smith, 228.

56. Benjamin Chew to Benjamin Franklin, Aug. 19, 1779, in Lopez, 178.

57. Alexander Dick to Speaker of the House of Delegates, Dec. 18, 1779, Legislative petitions, LV; *Journal of the House of Delegates of the Commonwealth of Virginia for 1779* (Richmond, VA: 1827), Nov. 22, 1779, 66; Dorman, 17:18.

58. Dorman, 7:65–66, 36:46–47; Hocker, 107–9; Muhlenberg, 210–212.

59. Alexander Dick to House of Delegates, Dec. 18, 1780, Legislative Petitions, LV; George Weedon to Greene, Dec. 21, 1780, extract in *NG*, 6:604.

60. Harry M. Ward, *Invasion: Military Operations near Richmond*, 3–4.

61. Greene to Steuben, Jan. 8, 1781, in *NG*, 7:76–77.

62. *Ibid.*, 78; Tustin, 266.

63. Alexander Dick to Steuben, Jan. 4, 6, 26, Steuben Papers, microfilm ed.; Thomas Nelson to Jefferson, Jan. 4, in *JP*, 4:30.

64. For the full story of Arnold's seizure of Richmond, see Harry M. Ward, *Invasion*.

65. Emory G. Evans, *Thomas Nelson of Yorktown*, 93–94; Muhlenberg, 223–25.

66. Muhlenberg to Steuben, Jan. 27, 1781, and Return of the Militia under the Command of Brig. Gen. Muhlenberg, Feb. 4, 1781, Steuben Papers.

67. Muhlenberg to Steuben, Feb. 19, 1781, *ibid.*

68. Steuben to Lawson, Feb. 2, 1781, Robert Lawson Papers, Duke University; Robert Lawson to Jefferson, Feb. 15, 1781, in *JP*, 4:617; "Edward Cooksey," in Dorman, 22:59.

69. Alexander Dick to Steuben, Feb. 26, 1781, Steuben Papers.

70. Muhlenberg to Steuben, March 11, 1781 and Lafayette to Weedon, March 20, 1781, Steuben Papers.

71. Harry M. Ward and Harold Greer, 83; Muhlenberg, 229–30.

72. Dorman, "Charles Cooksey," in *Virginia Pension Applications* vol. 22, 59; "Micajeh Francis," in *Virginia Pension Applications* vol. 40: 5; "Joseph Baugh," *Virginia*

Pension Applications vol. 5: 47, and "Phillip Crowder," *Virginia Pension Applications* vol. 25: 31.

73. Alexander Dick to Jefferson, April 10, 1781, in *JP*, 5:397.

74. John G. Simcoe, 188–91.

75. Steuben to Muhlenberg, April 20, 1781, Steuben Papers.

76. John Banister to Theodorick Bland, May 16, 1781, in "Phillips and Arnold's Invasion and Capture of Petersburg in April 1781," *Virginia Historical Register* 4 (1851): 199–201; Muhlenberg, 249–52; Robert P. Davis, 145, 151–52; Young, 99–102.

77. Robert P. Davis, 167.

78. Quotes General Orders and letter to Congress, in Muhlenberg, 250–51.

79. Tarleton, 335–37; Young, 103–5.

80. Alexander Dick to Speaker of the House of Delegates, May 11, 1781, Executive Communications, LV, quoted in McDonnell, 441–42.

81. Alexander Dick to General Nelson, Aug. 8, 1781, in *CSP*, 2:305; "William Allen," in Dorman, 1:70; "Wiltshire Caldwell," in Dorman, 15:71; "Moses Fleshman," in Dorman, 38:15–16; "William Cutts," in Dorman, 26:17.

82. "William Cole," in Dorman, 21:9.

83. Alexander to the Governor, Nov. 22, 1782, in *CSP*, 3:377–78.

84. Alexander Dick to William Davies, Dec. 8, 1781, in *CSP*, 2:645; Dorman, 21:9.

85. Alexander Dick to Col. Davies, Dec. 26, 1781 and Jan. 14, 1782, in *CSP*, 2:670–71 and 3:20.

86. Berg, 120; Sanchez-Saavedra, *Guide to Virginia Military Organizations*, 135.

87. Alexander Dick to Charles Dabney, Oct. 25, 1782, Charles Dabney Papers, VHS; Dick to the Governor, Nov. 17 and 22, 1782, in *CSP*, 3:373, 377; Dick to the Governor, —1782, in *CSP*, 3:414.

88. Alexander Dick to Gov. Harrison, Jan. 1, 1783, in *CSP*, 415–16.

89. Berg, 120.

90. John W. Gwathmey, 222.

91. Felder, 296, 302.

92. *Ibid.*, 250–51; Alexander Dick to Gov. Harrison, Jan. 7, 1783, in *CSP*, 3:418; Siener, 11–12; Kathleen Bruce, 38–39.

93. "Henry Allen," in Dorman, 1:65; Gov. Harrison to Alexander Dick, Jan. 14, 1783, in *OL*, 3:437–78, 432n.

94. Gov. Harrison to Dick, Jan. 14, in *OL*, 3:432n., 437–38.

95. Taliaferro, 219–20.

96. Alexander Dick to the Governor,— Feb, 1783, in *CSP*, 3:438.

97 Siener, 124; Felder, 296; Coleman, 47.

98 Taliaferro, 220.

99. Harry M. Ward, *Duty, Honor or Country*, 250–51. Although he was a major in the Virginia Militia only, and never had a commission in the Continental Army, Dick, nevertheless, became a member of the Virginia branch of the Society of the Cincinnati ("Virginia Society of the Cincinnati" [List of Members], *Virginia Military Records*, Baltimore, 1983, 899).

100. Taliaferro, 220.

101. Alexander to Governor Harrison, Nov. 7, 1784, in *CSP*, 3:622.

102. Crozier, 404; "Fredericksburg District Court

Deed Book A," *Virginia Genealogist* 37:57; "Library of Charles Dick," *WMQ*, 1st ser. 18 (1909–10):112; Burgess, 3:1101–2.

2. John "Jack" Cropper

1. Alton B. Barnes, 5; Jon G. Kolp, "John Cropper," in *ANB*, 3:568.
2. Hast, 35.
3. Kolp, "John Cropper," 568–69; Charles H. Russell, "Inscriptions on Tombs at Bowman's Folly, Accomac," *WMQ*, 2d ser. 5 (1925):272.
4. Alton B. Barnes, 12; Kolp, "John Cropper," 569.
5. Berg, 128; Heitman, 364.
6. Wise, 278; Catesby W. Stewart, 1:809.
7. Washington to Woodford, April 29, 1778, in Catesby W. Stewart, 1:926; Heitman, 179; Wise, 278.
8. Kolp, "John Cropper," 569; Wise, 285.
9. General Orders, July 22, 1778, in *AWP*, 16:121, 593n.
10. Excerpt of Diary of Cropper, in Wise, 284–85; Hast, 137–38; Robert A. Stewart, *History of the Virginia Navy*, 61–63.
11. Wise, 285, 287; Cropper to John Jay, Aug. 16, 1779, in Catesby W. Stewart, 1:1070–71; Robert A. Stewart, *The History of the Virginia Navy*, 63.
12. George Corbin to Jefferson, May 31, 1781, in *JP*, 6:47; Wise, 296.
13. Wise, 96–97.
14. *Ibid.*, 297; Footner, 49.
15. Cropper to William Davies, Dec. 6, 1782, in McManemin, 63–66; Cropper to Gov. Paca, Dec. 6, 1782, in "Action between American and British Barges in the Chesapeake Bay, November, 1782," *Maryland Historical Magazine*, 4 (1909):124–26; Gaines, 33–34, 36–37; Alton B. Barnes, *Cropper*, 77–80; McBride, 204.
16. Wise, 303, 309: Kolp, 570.
17. Wise, 303–4; Kolp, 569–70.
18. Kolp, 570.

3. Richard Clough Anderson

1. Robert B. Lancaster, *A Sketch of the Early History of Hanover County, Virginia and Its Contributions to the American Revolution* (Richmond, VA: Whittet & Shepperson, 1976), 38; "Historical and Genealogical Notes," *WMQ*, 1st ser. 21 (1913):292; "Anderson," *WMQ*, 2d ser. 10 (1930):214.
2. Tischendorf and Parks, xv-xvi.
3. Coulter, 270.
4. Edward L. Anderson, *Soldier and Pioneer*, 14.
5. Richard Peters to Washington, Oct. 24 and Greene to Washington, Nov. 7, 1776, in *AWP*, 7:26–27, 109; "Austin Corley," in Dorman, 23:25; Harry M. Ward, *Charles Scott and the "Spirit of '76,"* 20–24.
6. Harry M. Ward, *Charles Scott*, 24–26; Samuel S. Smith, *The Battle of Princeton*, 13–17; "New Jersey Campaign," in *EAR*, 2: 811–12; Fischer, *Washington's Crossing*, 295; Barr; Edward L. Anderson, 19; Dorman, 2:39; Stryker, *The Battles of Trenton and Princeton* 258–61; Smith, *Battle of Princeton*, 13–17.
7. Deposition of Sally (Sarah) Anderson, widow of Richard Clough Anderson, in Dorman, 2:39–40; Samuel

S. Smith, *The Battle of Brandywine*, 20–22; Thayer, 192, 194–95.
8. Donald W. Gunter, "Richard Clough Anderson," in *DVB*, 1:151; Samuel S. Smith, *The Battle of Monmouth*, 16–28; C. Ward, 2:572.
9. Uhlendorf, 167–69; Lumpkin, 34; Cashin, 100; Edward L. Anderson, *Soldier and Pioneer*, 25–26; Alexander A. Lawrence, *Storm over Savannah: The Story of Count d'Estaing and the Siege of the Town in 1779* (Athens: University of Georgia Press, 1951), 101–107; Ferling, 388–90; "Savannah, Georgia," in *EAR*, 2:1038–40.
10. Boatner, 512; Borick, *A Gallant Defense*, 42; Uhlendorf, 183.
11. Harry M. Ward, *Charles Scott*, 75, 77; Heitman, 71; Gwathmey, 15–16.
12. Gunter, "Anderson," 152; Coulter, 270; Edward L. Anderson, *Soldier and Pioneer*, 27; Barr, 5; Evans, *Thomas Nelson*, 114; *LP*, 4:510; Anthony Wayne to Lafayette, June 6 and 7, in Gottschalk, 171–72, 220n.
13. *MP*, 1:166n.; Collins, 1:370; Abernethy, 336.
14. Tischendorf and Parks, xvi.
15. Collins, 2:179; Rubenstein, 79.
16. Washington to Richard Clough Anderson, July 30, 1798, in *FWW*, 36:377–78.
17. Rubenstein, 47, 71, 78–79.
18. Gunter, "Anderson," 152–53; "Historical and Genealogical Notes," *WMQ*, 1st ser., 21 (1913): 292; Mrs. J. E. Warren, "Thompkins Family," *WMQ*, 2d ser. 10 (1930): 234.
19. Dicken-Garcia, 84; Hammon and Taylor, 185; Tischendorf and Parks, xvi.
20. Kenton, 296; Hay, 478–79; Edward L. Anderson, *Andersons of Gold Mine*, 18–19; Edward L. Anderson, *Soldier and Pioneer*, 54.
21. Barr, 15.
22. Bodley, 383, 403.
23. Abernethy, 325.
24. Thomas D. Clark, ed., *The Voice of the Frontier*, xxxiv; Talbert, 236; Lowell H. Harrison, 62.
25. Barr, 6.
26. Collins, 1:354, 357, 367, 376; Talbert, 262.
27. The Chenowell Affair"; Barr, 15.
28. "Proposed Arrangement of General and Other Officers," July 14, 1798, in *FWW*, 36:353–54.
29. Gunter, "Richard Clough Anderson," 152; Tischendorf and Parks, xvi.
30. *Richmond Enquirer*, 7 Nov. 1826; Barr, 9.
31. *Richmond Daily Dispatch*, 21 Jan. 1861.

4. John Chilton

1 Russell and Gott, 16, 25, 41, 62 and n., 63, 249.
2. *Ibid.*, 66.
3. *Ibid.*, 89; Harry M. Ward, *Duty, Honor or Country*, 46–47; Cecere, *They Behaved Like Soldiers*, 5–6.
4. Cecere, *They Behaved Like Soldiers*, 7.
5. *Ibid.*; Harry M. Ward, *Duty, Honor or Country*, 47; Berg, 125–26.
6. Cecere, *They Behaved Like Soldiers*, 8; Harry M. Ward, *Duty, Honor or Country*, 53–54.
7. Cecere, *They Behaved Like Soldiers*, 13–14.
8. Harry M. Ward, *Duty, Honor or Country*, 59–60.
9. Chilton to Martin Pickett, Thomas Keith, or

Charles Chilton, Sept. 17, 1776, in Cecere, *They Behaved Like Soldiers*, 81–83.

10. Champagne, 116–18; Harry M. Ward, *Duty, Honor or Country*, 64; Billias, 115–16.

11. Cecere, *They Behaved Like Soldiers*, 24, 31–35, 37; Russell and Gott, 146, 151, 156.

12. Cecere, *They Behaved Like Soldiers*, 37, 44.

13. Chilton to Maj. William Pickett, March 19, 1777, in Lyon G. Tyler, ed., "The Old Virginia Line in the Middle States," 116.

14. "John Chilton's Diary," in Cecere, *They Behaved Like Soldiers*, 121, Aug. 28, 1777. The diary is published in full here, pp. 113–23, and in Tyler, "The Old Virginia Line in the Middle States," 283–89.

15. Chilton to Charles Chilton, Aug. 17, 1777, in Cecere, *They Behaved Like Soldiers*, 109–10.

16. See "Chilton's Diary," passim.

17. Chilton to Charles Chilton, Aug. 17, 1777, in Cecere, *They Behaved Like Soldiers*, 109.

18. "John Chilton's Diary," Tyler, "The Old Virginia Line in the Middle States," 284–87.

19. Chilton to Charles Chilton, Aug. 17, 1777, in Cecere, *They Behaved Like Soldiers*, 108.

20. *Ibid.*, 61–63; Harry M. Ward, *Duty, Honor or Country*, 100–101.

21. Henry Lee quoted in Cecere, *They Behaved Like Soldiers*, 65.

22. *Ibid.*, 65–66.

23. Letter from a General Officer, Sept. 22, 1777, in Catesby W. Stewart, 2:873; Russell and Gott, 206, 443.

24. Russell and Gott, 110.

5. Peter Francisco

1. Daniel, 37–38; John E. Marshall, "Discovery of Peter Francisco's Birth Certificate," in Moon, 53–54.

2. Hamilton, 10–20; Moon, 1–2.

3. Hamilton, 35.

4. James H. Bailey; Moon, 5, 8; Daniel, 38.

5. Moon, 9.

6. "Letter of Peter Francisco to the General Assembly, Nov. 11, 1820," *WMQ*, 1st ser. 13 (1905): 217; Porter and Albertson, 28–29; quote in Moon, 10.

7. "Letter of Peter Francisco … Nov. 11, 1820," 217.

8. Moon, 10.

9. *Ibid.*, 11–12.

10. *Ibid.*, 12.

11. "Letter of Peter Francisco … Nov. 11, 1820," 218.

12. Hamilton, including quote of Lt. Philemon Holcombe, 72–73; Porter and Albertson, 34–35; Daniel, 38.

13. Moon, 14.

14. Hamilton, 79–80.

15. "Letter of Francisco … Nov. 11, 1820," 219.

16. Peter Francisco to the Speaker and Members of the House of Representatives and the Senate of the United States, Feb. 28, 1828, in "The Revolution in Virginia — Peter Francisco"; Hamilton, 83–85. For an extended narrative of the Ward's Tavern encounter, see also Henry, 2:131–32.

17. Alexander Hamilton to Lafayette, Oct. 15, 1781, in *LP*, 4:418–20n.

18. Moon, 20.

19. Quote in "Francisco Marries Francis Marie Savannah Anderson," in "The Revolution in Virginia."

20. *Ibid.*

21. Moon, 23.

22. Goodwin and Brook, "Sketches from the Life of a Favorite Soldier," typescript, Aug. 22, 1970, VHS; Hamilton, 106–08.

23. Moon, 37–38; Porter and Albertson, 76.

24. Moon, 24, 31.

25. *Ibid.*, 27; Ward and Greer, 67–68.

26. Hamilton, 117.

27. Quote in Moon, 25; Porter and Albertson, 60–61.

28. Pap, 16; Daniel, 39.

29. Quote in "Francisco Gains Post in Virginia Assembly," in "Revolution in Virginia"; Hamilton, 119–20.

6. Nathaniel Gist

1. Dorsey and Dorsey, 29; Kenneth P. Bailey, 24; Orrill, 195; Thomas D. Clark, "Christopher Gist," 443; "Christopher Gist," in *EAR*, 1:435; Freeman, 6:17n.

2. Darlington, 80; Freeman, 1:282; Dorsey and Dorsey, 12, 16; Kenneth P. Bailey, 14–15, 51, 53, 61, 64, 71, 76, 162n-63n.

3. Dorsey and Dorsey, 31.

4. Orders, Dec. 28, 1755, List of Junior Officers in the Virginia Regiment, June 12, 1757, and List of Officers … Oct. 24, 1757, in *AWP*, Colonial Series, 2:240 and 4:205, 432, resp.

5. Orrill, 210.

6. *Ibid.*, 212; Harry M. Ward, *Major General Adam Stephen*, 38–39.

7. Williams, 43; Dorsey and Dorsey, 32.

8. Washington to John St. Clair, May 1 and to John Blair, May 10, 1758, in *AWP*, Colonial Series, 5:151, 157; Corkran, 149; Dorsey and Dorsey, 32.

9. Dorsey and Dorsey, 32; Orrill, 215.

10. Williams, 44.

11. Dorsey and Dorsey, 33; Corkran, 197; Robert Morgan, 62–68.

12. Dorsey and Dorsey, 33.

13. *Ibid.*; Calloway, 16; Foreman, 3; Owens, 1098–99; *Concise Dictionary of American Biography*, 936.

14. Williams, 47; Thomas D. Clark, *Frontier America*, 105; Billington and Ridge, 176.

15. Hartwell L. Quinn, 37; Hamer, 126.

16. Quote in Dorsey and Dorsey, 34.

17. Instructions to William Christian, July 27, 1776, enclosed in John Page to John Hancock, Aug. 1, 1776, in *OL*, 1:22.

18. Brown, 158.

19. Foreman, 76; Sanchez-Saavedra, *Guide to Virginia Military Organizations*, 74.

20. Patrick Henry to the General Assembly, Oct. 14, 1778 (extract), in *OL*, 1:314; Dowd, 54; Duane H. King, 120–22; Dorsey and Dorsey, 36; Calloway, 199–200.

21. Stephen Moylan to Washington, July 2, 1778, in *AWP*, 16:13.

22. General Orders, Aug. 8 and Charles Scott to Washington, Aug. 31, 1778, *AWP*, 16:267, 447–48; Simcoe, 83–85; Harry M. Ward, *Charles Scott*, 54.

23. Washington to Greene, Sept. 22, 1778, in *NG*, 2:525.

24. *AWP*, 17:29n-30n; Simcoe, 86–88.

25. Charles Scott to Washington, Sept. 12, Sept. 13, Sept. 26, and Oct 30, 1778, in *AWP*, 16:591–92, 601, 17:144–45, 650, resp.

26. Russell and Gott, 297.

27. General Orders, Sept. 11, 1779, in *FWW*, 16:262–64; Paul D. Nelson, *The Life of William Alexander*, 146.

28. Greene to Weedon, Sept. 6, 1779, in *NG*, 4:364–65n.

29. Weedon to Greene, Oct. 12, 1779, in *NG*, 4:460.

30. General Orders, April 13 and 24, 1780, Wallace, *The Orderly* Book, 132, 146; Freeman, 5:141–42; Sanchez-Saavedra, *Guide to Virginia Military Organizations*, 177–79.

31. Wright, *Continental Army*, 321.

32. *OL*, 1:181n.

33. Dorsey and Dorsey, 37.

34. *Ibid.*, 38; Harry M. Ward, *Charles Scott*, 159.

35. Dorsey and Dorsey, 38–39.

36. Kenneth P. Bailey, 171; Harry M. Ward, *Charles Scott*, 160, 193–94, 236–37n.; Williams, 53; Selby, 101–2.

7. William Grayson

1. *Virginia Herald and Fredericksburg Adviser*, March 25, 1791, in Dupriest, 116.

2. Grigsby, 1:201–2.

3. *WD*, 2:110n.; Bristow, 75–76; Harry E. Baylor, 2; Works Project Administration, 82–83; Gutzman, 9:456.

4. Harry E. Baylor, 5.

5. Bristow, 77.

6. Grayson, 197.

7. General Orders, Aug. 24, 1776, in *AWP*, 6:200–1; Heitman, 259; *OL*, 1:131n.; Kahler, 139.

8. Grayson, 200–1; Gutzman, 9:456.

9. General Orders, May 22, 1777, in *AWP*, 9:495; William Grayson to Washington, April 1, 8, and 22 and May 22, 1777, in *AWP*, 9:35–36, 86, and 237, resp.

10. General Orders, Aug. 23, Sept. 25, and Dec. 22, 1777, Feb. 8 and 25, 1778, *VFOB*, 17, 57, 162, 186, 241; Grayson, 202–3.

11. Greene to Weedon, March 7, 1778, in *NG*, 2:305–6 and n.; Grayson, 205.

12. Paul J. Sanborn, "Battle of Monmouth," 2:1083–86; Bristow, 84–86; Samuel S. Smith, *Battle of Monmouth*, 9–20; *NG*, 2:453–55n.; Trussell, 160.

13. Bristow, 88.

14. *Ibid.*; Kahler, 130; Lesser, 96, 104, 112; Wright, *Continental Army*, 322.

15. Dupriest, 6–7; Henderson, *Party Politics*, 265.

16. Dupriest, 8; "James Wilson," *EAR*, 2:1278; "Journal of Allen McLane," in Commager and Morris, eds., 2:813–14; Grigsby, 1:198.

17. Grayson to Washington, April 15, 1785, in *AWP*, Confederation Series, 2:18–19.

18. Gutzman, 456.

19. Bristow, 90; Henderson, *Party Politics*, 392–93.

20. *LD*, 23:322n.

21. Harry E. Baylor, 15.

22. Letter of James Monroe to James Madison, quoted in Bristow, 99.

23. Grigsby, 1:195.

24. *Ibid.*, 205; Harry E. Baylor, 36, 38; Nicholas

Gilman to John Sullivan, March 22, 1788, in *LD*, 25:21; Grayson, 206; Reardon, 138; Kaminski and Saladino, eds., 10:1444–45.

25. McDonald, 231; Grigsby, 230.

26. *AWP*, Presidential Series, 4:77n., 310n.

27. David Stuart to Washington, March 15, 1790, *AWP*, Presidential Series, 5:235; *JP*, 16:230n; Bristow, 114, 117.

28. Harry E. Baylor, 56.

29. Dupriest, 115–16.

8. William Heth

1. R.A. Brock, ed., "Orderly Book of Major William Heth," 11:320–21; Flickinger, 27.

2. Dunmore to Dartmouth, Dec. 24, 1774, in Thwaites and Kellogg, 383, 421.

3. R.A. Brock, ed., "Orderly Book of Major William Heth," 322n..

4. Kenneth Roberts, *March to Quebec*, 335; Flickinger, 29.

5. Kenneth Roberts, *March to Quebec*, 335.

6. Higginbotham, 36–49; Cecere, *An Officer of Very Extraordinary Merit*, 30; Morrissey, 60.

7. "Memorable Attack on Quebec: Diary of Captain Charles Porterfield" (extracts), *Magazine of American History*, 21 (1889): 319.

8. Flickinger, 30.

9. Cecere, *Porterfield*, 30; Higginbotham, 50–51.

10. Flickinger, 47.

11. *Ibid.*, 40.

12. Heitman, 287.

13. e.g., June 19, 1777, in R.A. Brock, "Orderly Book of Major William Heth 363.

14. John Chilton to Charles Chilton, Aug. 17, 1777, in Cecere, *They Behaved Like Soldiers*, 110.

15. Cecere, *They Behaved Like Soldiers*, 56; Cecere, *An Officer of Very Extraordinary Merit*, 52–53; Harry M. Ward, *General William Maxwell and the New Jersey Continentals* (Westport, CT: Greenwood Press, 1997), 68.

16. Cecere, *An Officer of Very Extraordinary Merit*, 64; Ward, *Maxwell*, 68; Russell and Gott, 204.

17. Heth to Daniel Morgan, Sept. 30, 1777, in Flickinger, 31.

18. Heth to Daniel Morgan, Oct. 24, 1777, in *ibid.*, 33.

19. Heth to Col. John Lamb, Oct. 12, 1777, in Commager and Morris, eds., 1:629–30; Russell and Gott, 219.

20. *VFOB*, Nov. 22, 1777, 137.

21. Stryker, *The Battle of Monmouth*, 288–95.

22. Russell and Gott, 283.

23. Borick, *A Gallant Defense*, 36–37; Harry M. Ward, *Charles Scott*, 73; Cecere, *Great Things Are Expected*, 156–57.

24. Ward, *Scott*, 73–77; Heitman, 287.

25. R.A. Brock, "Orderly Book of Heth," 329; Richard L. Jones, 262–63; Jeff M. O'Dell, 31, 59, 63; Heth Diary, June 13, 1788, in Kaminski and Saladino, eds., 9:1622.

26. Higginbotham, 178, 180.

27. R.A. Brock, "Orderly Book of Heth," 329.

28. *Ibid.*, 322; Flickinger, 34; John Marshall to Heth, March 1, 1783, in *MP*, 1:98–99.

29. Committee of House of Delegates to Commis-

sioners on Illinois Accounts, Dec. 31, 1787, in *MP*, 1:243–44, 247; George Mason to the Office of Illinois Accounts, Dec. 20 and John Pierce to House of Delegates, Dec. 25, 1787, in Rutland, ed., 3:1030n., 1032–36; Ferguson, 216–19; R.A. Brock, "Orderly Book of Heth," 323; Flickinger, 34.

30. Heth Diary, June 25, 1788, in Kaminski and Saladino, 9:1677.

31. Alexander McDonald to Jefferson, March 22, 1790, in *JP*, 16:263.

32. McDonald to Jefferson, April 25, 1790, in *JP*, 16:382–83.

33. Flickinger, 34.

34. R.A. Brock, ed., "Orderly Book of Heth," 329–30.

9. Josiah Parker

1. Edward C. Carter, 2:549; *RV*, 2:224n-25n.; *DAB*, 7:234.

2. "Virginia Legislative Papers, *VMHB* 19 (1910): 390n.; Rutland, ed., 1:249n., 252n.; Helen King, 572–74.

3. Woodford to President of the Convention, Dec. 4 and 12, 1775, in *RV*, 5:50, 117.

4. *Biographical Directory of the American Congress, 1774–1996*, 1628; "Orderly Book of the Company of Captain George Stubblefield," 156–57; Harry M. Ward, *Charles Scott*, 23.

5. Heitman, 426.

6. Helen King, 61; Harry M. Ward, *Charles Scott*, 24–25; *DAB*, 7:234.

7. Harry M. Ward, *Charles Scott*, 25–27.

8. Washington to John Hancock, Jan. 27, 1777, in *AWP*, 8:161, 163n.; Prince, ed., 1:385; Harry M. Ward, *Major General Adam Stephen*, 156; Russell and Gott, 158–59.

9. Letter from a General Officer, Sept. 22, 1777, in Catesby W. Stewart, 2:873; Lee, 89; Cecere, *An Officer of Very Extraordinary Merit*, 58–59.

10. General Orders, Sept. 10, 1777, in *AWP*, 11:373; Enclosure to Letter of Charles Carroll Sr. to Charles Carroll Jr., Oct. 9, 1777, in *LD*, 8:87n, 157n.

11. Josiah Parker to —, Dec. 2, 1777, in Parker, 260.

12. Heitman, 126; *DAB*, 7:234.

13. Josiah Parker to Thomas Riche, June 18, 1779, in Parker, 261.

14. *Ibid.*

15. Jefferson to Josiah Parker, Oct. 26, 1780, in *JP*, 4:71–72.

16. Steuben to Josiah Parker, Jan. 13, 1781, R. M. Hughes, ed., "Revolutionary Correspondence of Col. Josiah Parker, Isle of Wight County," *VMHB*, 22 (1914): 259–60.

17. Steuben to Josiah Parker, Jan. 13, 1781, in *ibid.*, 259–60.

18. Cecere, *Great Things are Expected*, 198–99.

19. Thomas Nelson to Josiah Parker, June 8, 1781, "Revolutionary Correspondence of Col. Josiah Parker," 260–61.

20. Norfleet, 197–98; Helen King, 63.

21. Lafayette to Josiah Parker, July 8, 1781, "Revolutionary Correspondence of Col. Josiah Parker," 262.

22. McBride, 179.

23. e.g., Josiah Parker to Speaker of the Assembly, June 9, 1781 and Josiah Parker to Gov. Nelson, June 29, 1781, in *CSP*, 2:150, 189. By July 1, 1781, Parker commanded a force of 522 men.

24. Josiah Parker to Lafayette, Aug. 19, 1781, in *LP*, 4:334.

25. Josiah Parker to William Davies, Aug. 25, 1781, in *CSP*, 2:357.

26. Hast, 112–13.

27. "Calendar of Omitted Letters," Parker to Lafayette, Aug. 25, 1781, in *LP*, 4:510.

28. Helen King, 64–65.

29. Edward C. Carter II, ed., 2:549.

30. Helen King, 41.

31. *Ibid.*, 316.

32. Eugene P. Link, *Democratic Republican Societies, 1790–1800* (New York: Columbia University Press, 1942), 155.

33. Extract of a Journal Kept by Bolling Stark, 1787, in *CSP*, 4:384–87.

34. Edward C. Carter II, ed., 2:439; Madison to Jefferson, March 29, 1789, in *MadP*, 12:37.

35. Edward C. Carter II, ed., 2:540; Grigsby, 2 279; *MP*, 3:37n.; Bernhard, 166–67.

36. William T. Parker, *Gleanings from the Parker Records* (Statesboro, GA: Bulloch-Bryan-Candler, n.d., orig. publ. 1894), 39.

37. Link, *Democratic-Republican Societies*, 99. J. James Henderson, "Quantitative Approaches to Party Formation in the United States," *WMQ*, 2d ser. 30 (1973): 319–20; Bernhard, 244.

38. Norfleet, 198; Helen King, 449.

10. Richard Parker

1. Heitman, 424–26; Gwathmey, 604.

2. Lee, 160; "The Parker Family of Essex, the Northern Neck &c," *VMHB* 6 (1999): 88; Parker, 251.

3. Woodford to the Virginia Convention, Dec. 4, 1775 and Woodford to the President of the Convention, Jan. 5, 1776, Catesby W. Stewart, 2:527, 588.

4. *RV*, 6:281–82, includes quotes.

5. Heitman, 426.

6. Parker, 251.

7. Heitman, 426.

8. General Orders, Aug. 28, 1777, in *NG*, 2:147, 148n..

9. *Ibid.*, 4:17n.; "Revolutionary Pension Declarations," *VMHB* 20 (1912): 264.

10. Weedon to John Page, Oct. 4, 1777, quoted in Harry M. Ward, *Duty, Honor or Country*, 106.

11. *VFOB*, Dec. 19, 1777, 160; "Revolutionary Army Orders," *VMHB* 13 (1906): 183 and 14:347–48; Heitman, 426.

12. Greene to Jacob Greene, July 2, 1778, in *NG*, 2:450.

13. *Ibid.*, 450–51; Stirling to William H. Drayton, Aug. 15, 1778, quote in Cecere, *Porterfield*, 104; Stryker, *Battle of Monmouth*, 210.

14. Richard Parker to Greene, May 12, 1779, in *NG*, 4:16–17n.; Young, 178; "Southern Theater, Military Operations," in *EAR*, 2:1088–89.

15. Washington Richard Parker, May 7, 1779, in *FWW*, 15:17–18; Wallace, ed., 5–6, 10–12; Cecere, *Great Things are Expected*, 152–56; "Savannah, Georgia," in *EAR*, 2:1038–40; *NG*, 4:367; Mattern, *Benjamin Lincoln*, 78.

16. Wallace, ed., 20n.

17. Harry M. Ward, *Charles Scott*, 75.

18, Borick, *A Gallant Defense*, 38–39; Wallace, ed., 20; Cecere, *Great Things are Expected*, 15.

19. Wallace, ed., 56; Harry M. Ward, *Charles Scott*, 75.

20. Borick, *A Gallant Defense*, 121.

21. Tustin, ed., 240–41; Wallace, ed., 143; Lumpkin, 46; Borick, "Expedition," 1:207.

22. Wallace, ed., 111.

23. *Ibid.*, 143–44; Borick, "Expedition," 1:207–8; Tustin, ed., 238; Mattern, *Benjamin Lincoln*, 103.

24. "General William Moultrie's Journal," April 24, 1780, in Commager and Morris, eds., 2: 1106.

11. Charles "Charley" Porterfield

1. Washington to Patrick Henry, Oct. 3, 1777, *AWP*, 11:382.

2. McIlhany, 30; Bell, 28.

3. Cecere, *An Officer of Very Extraordinary Merit*, 304; Dudley, "A Sketch of the Military Services Performed by Guilford Dudley, then of the Town of Halifax, North Carolina, during the Revolutionary War," *Southern Literary Messenger*, 11 (1845): 231.

4. Cecere, *An Officer of Very Extraordinary Merit*, 5.

5. Porterfield, 318.

6. Cecere, *An Officer of Very Extraordinary Merit*, 12–13.

7. Porterfield, 319; Daniel Morgan to Henry Lee. n.d., in Scheer and Rankin, 126; Russell and Gott, 92.

8. Waddell, ed., 144–52; see also Flickinger.

9. Higginbotham, 54; Cecere, *An Officer of Very Extraordinary Merit*, 37; "Daniel Morgan," *EAR*, 2:749.

10. Cecere, *An Officer of Very Extraordinary Merit*, 36–37, 45–47; Heitman, 401, 448.

11. Cecere, *An Officer of Very Extraordinary Merit*, 51–55.

12. Quoted in *ibid.*, 60.

13. Marshall quote, *ibid.*, 66.

14. Washington to Patrick Henry, Oct.3, 1777, in *AWP*, 11:382.

15. Russell and Gott, 221.

16. Marshall, 3:29.

17. Cecere, *An Officer of Very Extraordinary Merit*, 93.

18. *Ibid.*, 100; Samuel S. Smith, *Battle of Monmouth*, 28, 32.

19. General Orders, July 13, 1778, in *AWP*, 16:60; Cecere, *An Officer of Very Extraordinary Merit*, 106.

20. *AWP*, 11:383n.

21. Cecere, *An Officer of Very Extraordinary Merit*, 107, 110.

22. Board of War to Charles Porterfield (abstract), in *JP*, 3:337n.

23. Jefferson to Major Galvan, May 28 and to Washington, June 11, 1780, in *JP*, 3:401, 433.

24. Cecere, *An Officer of Very Extraordinary Merit*, 113–14, 122–23, 125–26.

25. Dudley, "Sketch of Military Service," 144–48, 231–35, 281–85. See Appendix. The "Sketch" is also printed

in Jim Piecuch, ed., *The Battle of Camden: A Documentary History* (Charleston, SC: The History Press, 2006) and Cecere, *An Officer of Very Extraordinary Merit*, 136–44.

26. Dudley, 146.

27. *Ibid.*, 147, 231–32.

28. *Ibid.*, 231–35.

29. Porterfield to Gates, Aug. 20, 1780, in Cecere, *An Officer of Very Extraordinary Merit*, 150.

30. *Ibid.*, 151–52.

12. Thomas Posey

1. Posey, 227; "Historical and Genealogical Notes," *WMQ*, 1st series 6 (1897): 68.

2. Posey, 6.

3. *Ibid.*, 18; Thomas A. Mason, 723; "Historical and Genealogical Notes," *WMQ*, 1st series 6(1897): 66.

4. William Claiborne to William Preston, Sept. 12, 1774, Thwaites and Kellogg, eds., 196 and n.

5. Thomas A. Mason, 723.

6. Michael Cecere, *Thomas Posey*, 75–80; Harry M. Ward, *Duty, Honor or Country*, 52–54.

7. Quote in Cecere, *Great Things are Expected*, 126; Posey, 37–39.

8. Cecere, *Thomas Posey*, 89; Posey, 39–40.

9. Cecere, *Thomas Posey*, 95–96; Posey, 41.

10. Cecere, *Thomas Posey*, 98–99; Posey, 50–51; Johnston, 69.

11. "Journal of Captain Allen McLane," in Commager and Morris, eds., 2:723; Posey, 53–59; Johnston, 81–84.

12. Christian Febiger to Col. Heth, Sept. 13, 1779, in Johnston, 189.

13. Posey, 76–78; Cecere, *Thomas Posey*, 136.

14. Posey, 82.

15. *Ibid.*, 92–96; Lee, 558–59n.; Cashin, 150–52; Nelson, *Anthony Wayne*, 175–76.

16. Heitman, 448.

17. Posey, 45, 110, 112.

18. Posey, 126, 145; Heitman, 448.

19. Posey, 150–51.

20. *Ibid.*, 165–66; Thomas A. Mason, 723.

21. Posey, 177.

22. *Ibid.*, 194–95 203; Thomas A. Mason, 723.

23. Cayton, 252; Barnhart and Riker, 417, 430; Thomas A. Mason, 723.

24. Posey to Secretary of War, Jan. 25, 1816, in Esarey, ed., 2:715; Cayton, 250, 258; Barnhart and Riker, 460–61; Posey, 246–47, 256.

25. Posey to Secretary of War, May 2, 1814, in Esarey, ed., 2:648; Posey, 212; Barnhart and Riker, 418.

26. Posey, 242–43.

27. *Ibid.*, 222, 257–58; "Historical and Genealogical Notes," *WMQ*, 1st series 6 (1897): 68.

28. Posey, 103.

13. Gustavus "Gusty" Brown Wallace

1. Russell and Gott, 287.

2. Embry, 127.

3. Mace Clements to John Cropper, Nov. 14, 1778, quoted in Russell and Gott, 287.

4. Michael Wallace to Wallace, May 14, 1775 and William Wallace to Michael Wallace, March 28, 1776, in Catesby W. Stewart, 2:373, 643; Hayden, 709–13; Heitman, 566–67.

5. Will of Michael Wallace Sr., proved and recorded June 4, 1767, Wallace Family Papers, University of Virginia; Embry, 126.

6. Gustavus Brown Wallace to James Hunter, June 23, 1773 and to Michael Wallace, Jan. 30 and June 13, 1775, Wallace Family Papers.

7. Gustavus Brown Wallace to Michael Wallace, May 15, 1775, *ibid.*

8. Embry, 126–27; Sanchez-Saavedra, ed., *A Guide to Virginia Military Organizations*, 39.

9. Russell and Gott, 113; Harry M. Ward, *Duty, Honor or Country*, 57–59.

10. Wallace to Michael Wallace, Sept. 18, 1776 in Tyler, ed., "Old Virginia Line in the Middle States," 94.

11. *Ibid.*, 94–95; Weedon to John Page, Sept. 20, 1776, quoted in Russell and Gott, 118.

12. Harry M. Ward, *Duty, Honor or Country*, 65, 67.

13. Chilton "Diary," quoted in Catesby W. Stewart, 2:817–18.

14. Dr. James Wallace to Michael Wallace, Oct. 12, 1777, in Tyler, ed., "Old Virginia Line in the Middle States," 134–35.

15. Heitman, 566.

16. Wallace to Michael Wallace, Jan. 27, Feb. 13, March 28, and May 16, 1778, Wallace Family Papers.

17. Dr. James Wallace to Michael Wallace, Sept. 15, 1778, in Catesby W. Stewart, 2:987; "Revolutionary Army Orders," *VMHB*, 15 (1908): 167; Sanchez-Saavedra, ed., *Guide Virginia Military Organizations*, 178; Heitman, 566.

18. Catesby W. Stewart, 2:993.

19. Wallace to John Cropper, May 12, 1779, in *ibid.*, 2:1026–27; Wallace to Michael Wallace, Dec. 7, 1779, Wallace Family Papers; Russell and Gott, 317.

20. Wallace to Michael Wallace, June 7, 1780, Wallace Family Papers; Catesby W. Stewart, 2:1180.

21. Embry, 127; Heitman, 566.

22. Wallace to Michael Wallace, May 30, 1782, Wallace Family Papers; Hayden, 704.

23. Wallace to Dr. James Wallace, Sept. 18, 1784, Wallace Family Papers.

24. Wallace to James Madison, March 4, 1789, in *MadP*, 12:3.

25. Gillett, 4–5.

26. Russell and Gott, 332n.; Embry, 127–28.

14. George Baylor

1. "The Will of John Baylor, New Market," *VMHB*, 24 (1916): 368–70; Catesby W. Stewart, 1:646; Johnson and Crookshanks, 64–65, 86–87; Fairfax Harrison, "The Equine FFVs," *VHMB*, 35 (1927): 356–60; *WD*, 3:141n.; Robertson, 17; Orval W. Baylor and Bedinger, 11.

2. Nelson, "George Baylor," *DVB*, 1:402; Catesby W. Stewart, 1:646.

3. Meeting of the Caroline Committee of Safety, Dec. 16, 1774, in Catesby W. Stewart, 1:341; Wingfield, 38.

4. Edmund Pendleton to Washington, July 15 and General Orders, Aug. 15, 1775, in *AWP*, 1:110, 309; *WD*, 3:141n.; Freeman, 2:4.

5. Washington to Joseph Reed, Nov. 17, 1775, in *AWP*, 2:407.

6. Washington to Charles Lee, Feb. 10, 1778, quote in Leftowitz, 28.

7. John Hancock to Washington, Jan. 9, 1777, in *AWP*, 8:24; Catesby W. Stewart, 1:735; Fischer, *Washington's Crossing*, 251; Freeman, 4:321n.; Nelson, "Christopher Gist," in *DVB*, 1:402.

8. Baylor to Washington, Feb. 7 and 26, 1777, in *AWP*, 8:268, 444, resp.; Baylor to Washington, Aug. 18, 1777, in *AWP*, 10:656; Washington to Baylor, March 28 and May 17, 1777, "Original letters," *Virginia Historical Register*, 2 (1849): 143–46; Catesby W. Stewart, 2:767.

9. General Orders, Aug. 21 and 23, 1777, in *AWP*, 11:19, 49; Catesby W. Stewart, 1:797.

10. Order of Battle, Dec. 4–5, in *AWP*, 12:534.

11. Loescher, 66–67.

12. *Ibid.*, 68; Baylor to Washington, May 4 and Washington to Stephen Moylan, May 24, 1778, in *AWP*, 15:28, 211; Baylor to Washington, 27 May, 1778, in *AWP*, 15:235.

13. Congressional Resolution, May 17, 1778, in Loescher, 148–49.

14. "Genealogy," *VMHB*, 25 (1917): 319; Baylor and Bedinger, 188.

15. Baylor to Washington, July 13, 1778, in *AWP*, 16:62; Loescher, 69.

16. Baylor to Washington, Aug. 3, 1778, in *AWP*, 16:225–26.

17. Loescher, 70, 73.

18. Baylor to Washington, Sept. 26, 1778, in *AWP*, 17:138; Leftowitz, 100–101; Burnett, 96.

19. Loescher, 75; Sanborn, "Baylor's Massacre," 104–5; "Tappan Massacre," in *EAR*, 2:1138–39.

20. Thomas Jones quote in Leftowitz, 102.

21. Baylor to Washington, Oct. 19, 1778, in *AWP*, 17:456; Demarest, 72.

22. Washington to Henry Lee, April 30 and to Board of War, June 9, 1779, in *FWW*, 14:489, 15:251; Loescher, 76, 94, 147; Berg, 30–31.

23. Loescher, 94–95.

24. *Ibid.*, 95; William Wilmot to Ichabod Burnet, Sept. 22, 1782, in *NG*, 11:693–694.

25. Noncommissioned officers of Baylor's regiment to Greene and Nelson [Benj. Harrison], June 10, 1783, in *PCC*; May 29 and 30, 1783, in Hall, ed., 3:261, 263; Greene to Gov. Harrison, May 21, 1783, in *CSP*, 3:186; Harrison to Virginia Delegates, May 31, 1783, in *MadP*, 7:96–97 and n.; Higginbotham, 175–76; Harry M. Ward, *Charles Scott*, 36; Thayer, 422–23.

26. Heitman, 92.

27. Nelson, "George Baylor," 403; Wingfield, 375.

15. Theodorick Bland, Jr.

1. Charles Campbell, ed., 1:xv.

2. *Ibid.*, xv–xix; "Some Virginians Educated in Great Britain," *VMHB*, 21 (1913): 196; Tyler, "The Medical Men of Virginia," 156–57; Chase, 5; Potts, 25, including quote.

3. Chase, 15.

4. Nagy, 8; Charles Campbell, ed., 1:xxiii–xxiv.

5. Charles Campbell, ed., 1:xxv; Chase, 15; Loescher, 4, 7; Heitman, 167.

6. Washington to Bland, Aug. 30, 1777, in Charles Campbell, ed., 1:63.

7. Washington to Bland, Aug. 30 and Sept. 11, 1777, in *ibid.*, 63; Bland to Washington, Sept. 11, 1777, in *FWW*, 11:198; *AWP*, 11:189–191n.

8. Quote in Mattern, 947.

9. Bland to Washington, June 5, 1778, and Aug. 30, 1778, in *AWP*, 15:318, 16:434; Mays, ed., 1:266n; Charles Campbell, ed., 1:xxviii–xxix.

10. Washington to Bland, Nov. 5, 8, and 25, 1778, in *FWW*, 13: 07, 208–9n., 313 resp.; Washington to Jedediah Huntington, Nov. 22, 1778, in *FWW*, 13:307; Washington to Israel Putnam, Nov. 20, in Charles Campbell, ed., 1:xxix.

11. Washington to Board of War, Nov. 18, 1778, in *FWW*, 13:274–75.

12. William M. Dabney, 53–56; Knepper, 151, 153.

13. Washington to the Board of War, Feb. 28 and to Bland, Feb. 28, 1779, in *FWW*, 14:162, 164.

14. Washington to Bland, Aug. 20, 1779, in *FWW*, 16:139; Jefferson to Bland, June 8, 1779, in Charles Campbell, ed., 1:134; Sampson, 119.

15. Harry M. Ward, *Between the Lines*, 110.

16. Jefferson to Washington, July 17, 1779, in *JP*, 3:41.

17. Washington to Bland, Oct. 13, 1779, in *FWW*, 16:463; Metzger, 264.

18. Jefferson to Samuel Huntington, Nov. 16, 1779, in *JP*, 3:191–92; Washington to Woodford, Dec. 14, 1779, in *FWW*, 17:258–59; Charles Campbell, ed., 1:xxxi; Sampson, 138; Gwathmey, 760.

19. Virginia Delegates to Harrison, June 15, 1782, in *MadP*, 4:336; *LD*, 16:xxiv, 17:xiii–xiv; Virginia Delegates to Benjamin Harrison, Feb. 4, 1783, in *LD*, 19:659.

20. Thomas Rodney's Notes, March 8, 1781, in *LD*, 17:38.

21. John Sullivan to committee, Nov. 7, 1780, in *ibid.*, 16:306; Chase, 16.

22. Bland to Washington, March 22, 1783, in *LD*, 20:70–71.

23. Bland to Jefferson, Nov. 22 and Virginia Delegates to Jefferson, Dec. 13, in *LD*, 20:374–75, 442.

24. Treat, 235.

25. Committee on the Pennsylvania Mutiny to Joseph Reed, Jan. 6–7, Jan. 10–11, in *LD*, 16:549, 554n., 587–88; Washington to Philip Schuyler, Jan. 10, 1781, in *FWW*, 21:80 and n.; *LP*, 3:248n.; Van Doren, 99–102.

26. Bland to Richard Henry Lee, Feb. 6, 1781, in *LD*, 16:681.

27. Bland to Jefferson, June 3, 1781, in *JP*, 6:73.

28. Bland to Mrs. Laurence, Aug. 29, 1781, in *LD*, 17:573.

29. Bland to St. George Tucker, Sept. 17 and Oct. 27, 1780 and Jan. 26, 1781, in *LD*, 16:77, 276, 625.

30. Chase, 16.

31. David Stuart to Washington, Nov. 8, 1786, in *AWP*, Confederation Series, 4:346; Reardon, 87.

32. James Madison to Jefferson, April 22, 1788, in *MadP*, 11:28; Grigsby, 2:365.

33. Mattern, "Theodorick Bland," 947; Chase, 16.

34. Nagy, 11; Will of Theodorick Bland, *VMHB*, 3 (1896): 315–16; Jefferson to William Carmichael, May 31, 1799, in *JP*, 16:450; Charles Campbell, ed., 1:viii; Chase, 16.

35. Charles Campbell, ed., 1:xxxi.

36. Nagy, 12.

16. William Washington

1. Haller, 1, 3; *AWP*, 11:553n.

2. Haller, 19; Fore, 1.

3. Haller, 19–20; Monroe Johnson, 112.

4. "Washington Chronology," 5; Heitman, 74.

5. Haller, 32–33.

6. *Ibid.*, 35; Fore, 5.

7. Haller, 36.

8. Fore, 7; Heitman, 74.

9. Washington to Board of War, May 22 and to William Washington, Nov. 19, 1779, in *FWW*, 15:127, 17:135; Haller, 52–53; Fore, 7–8

10. Haller, 53–54, 57.

11. *Ibid.*, 57, 65; Tarleton, 16; Fore, 9; Uhlendorf, ed., 387; Bass, 74.

12. Haller, 65.

13. Jesse Root to Oliver Ellsworth, Dec. 25, to Jonathan Trumbull, Dec. 27, and Ezekiel Cornell to William Greene, Dec. 30, 1780, in *LD*:16: 483, 507, 516; Greene to Francis Marion, Dec. 4, to Jefferson, Dec. 6, and to William Smallwood, Dec. 6, 1780, in *NG*, 6:521, 531, 539 and n.; General Orders, Jan. 6, 1781, in *FWW*, 21:64; quote from Loescher, 84.

14. Washington to Greene, Jan. 9, 1781, in *FWW*, 21:87.

15. Greene to Daniel Morgan, Dec. 16 and to William Washington, Dec. 16, 1780, in *NG*, 6:589, 590; J.D. Bailey, 45.

16. Haller, 81.

17. *EAR*, 1:481.

18. Edward Stevens to Jefferson, Jan. 24, 1781, in *JP*, 4:41; Haller, 84, 92; Loescher, 89–90; Kenneth Roberts, *The Battle of Cowpens*, 59–61.

19. Haller, 97.

20. J.D. Bailey, 50–51.

21. *Ibid.*, 54–66, quote p. 66.

22. Hatch, *The Battle of Guilford Courthouse*, 81–82; Hamilton, 70–76, 79; Thomas E. Baker, 66–76.

23. Greene to Samuel Huntington, March 16, 1781, in *NG*, 7:434–35; Thomas E. Baker, 73.

24. Haller, 115.

25. Fore, 11.

26. Lumpkin, 179–83; Loescher, 92.

27. William Washington to Greene, June 14 (abstract), Henry Lee to Greene, June 22, and William Washington to Greene, July 5, 1781, in *NG*, 8:389, 442, 449; Fore, 12; Haller, 192–93.

28. Elias Boudinot to Lewis Pintard, Oct. 3 and Abraham Clark to James Caldwell, Oct. 3, 1781, in *LD*, 8:109, 110; Lumpkin, 216; Haller, 143–46.

29. "John Chang" deposition in John C. Dann, ed., 233.

30. Haller, 149.

31. *Ibid.*, 151, 171, 174; Bailey and Cooper, 3:750.

32. *Journal of the Convention of South Carolina*, 13, 30, 42; Bailey and Cooper, 3:751; Haller, 56, 163–64, 188; Fore, 15; Harriett K. Leiding, *Charleston: Historic and Romantic* (Philadelphia: J. B. Lippincott Company, 1931), 160; Zahnhiser, 125.

33. Haller, 159–60, 162, 193; Fore, 17, 20; Bailey and Cooper, 3:780–81.

34. Haller, 158–59.

35. Bailey and Cooper, 3:751; Fore, 17.

36. Heitman, 514.

37. J.D. Bailey, 54; Haller, 177, 194.

38. Lee, 588–89.

39. *Proceedings of the Inauguration of the Monument*, 84.

17. Charles Harrison

1. Quote in Peterson, *Round Shot and Rammers*, "Preface."

2. Normal K. Risjord, "Benjamin Harrison," in *ANB*, 10:197; Morton, 21–22; "Harrison of James River," *VMHB*, 34 (1926): 384; Hege, 3–4; Teeter, 10–11.

3. "Harrison of James River," 97.

4. Huntley, *Peninsular Pilgrimage*, 356.

5. *WD*, 5:38n; McGhan, 516; "Harrison of James River," 386. Charles Harrison's eldest son, Charles, a captain in the regular army, was killed in a duel with a Lieutenant Wilson in 1796 (Torrence, 12).

6. John Page to Jefferson, July 20, 1776, in *OL*, 1:10; "Gwynn's Island," *EAR*, 1:475–76.

7. Heitman, 276.

8. *AWP*, 8:161n.; Charles Harrison to Washington, April 20, Thomas Nelson to Washington, Sept. 5, and Patrick Henry to Washington, Oct. 29, 1777, in *AWP*, 9:218–19, 11:155, 12:51, resp.; Wright, *Continental Army*, 104.

9. Washington to John Hancock, May 24, 1777, in *AWP*, 9:519 and n.; Peterson, *The Book of the Continental Soldier*, 261.

10. Washington to Henry Knox, Jan. 8 and to the Continental Congress, Jan. 29, 1778, in *AWP*, 13:182, 401, "Booker Family," *VMHB*, 7 (1899): 431; Sekel, "The Continental Artillery," 2, 3n.

11. Stryker, *The Battle of Monmouth*, 207, including quote.

12. *Ibid.*, 208.

13. Greene to Charles Harrison, Dec. 6, 1779, in *NG*, 5:149; Sekel, "Continental Artillery," 15, 81; Sekel, "The Historical Background of the Pluckemin Encampment,"11–12.

14. Wright, *Continental Army*, 336.

15. Jefferson to Muhlenberg, April 12, 1780, in *JP*, 3:352.

16. Gates to Jefferson, Aug. 30, 1780, in *JP*, 3:525.

17. Jefferson to Washington, Sept. 3 and 23, 1780, in *JP*, 3:593, 550; "Camden Campaign," *EAR*, 1:152.

18. *NG*, 7:25n.; Greene to Steuben, March 5, 1781, in *NG*, 7:397; "Harrison of James River," 385.

19. Charles Harrison to Greene, Dec. 28, 1780 and Greene to Harrison, Feb. 16, 1781, in *NG*, 7:25, 327; Steuben to Jefferson, Dec. 21, 1780, Steuben's Queries, with Jefferson's Answer, before Jan. 14, 1781, and Jefferson to Nelson, Feb. 16, 1781, in *JP*, 4:219, 357, 631, resp.

20. Jefferson to Samuel Huntington, March 21, 1781, in *JP*, 5:198; Babits, "Guilford Courthouse," 471.

21. Greene to Samuel Huntington, April 25, in Commager and Morris, eds., 2:1176; Greene to Samuel Huntington, April 27, 1781, in *NG*, 8:156–67.

22. Greene to Harrison, Aug. 10 and Aug and to Board of War and Aug. 18, 1781, in *NG*, 9:57–58 and n., 198; Harrison to Greene Aug. 20, 22, 28, 1781, in *NG*, 9:214, 225, 265 (abstract).

23. Harrison to Greene, Dec. 22, 1781, in *NG*, 10:88n. (abstract).

24. Greene to Harrison, Jan. 25, 1782 (abstract), in *NG*, 260 and n.

25. William Pierce to Harrison, April 26 (abstract) and Harrison to Greene, June 14, 1782, in *NG*, 11:125, 330.

26. At a Council of War, April 7, 1783, in *NG*, 12:586; *NG*, 13:19n.

27. Heitman, 276; "Harrison of James River," 385.

28. Harrison to Herbert Claiborne, Sept. 30, 1783, quote in *ibid*.

29. *Ibid.*, 386; Torrence, 11.

30. *WD*, 5:38n.

18. James Innes

1. Grigsby, 1:326.

2. *Ibid.*

3. Carson, *James Innes*, 12–13; Shepard, 666–67.

4. Carson, "The Fat Major of the F.H.C.," 80–81.

5. Grigsby, 1:324; "Journal of the President and Masters of William and Mary College," 134–35.

6. Catesby W. Stewart, 2:361.

7. Grigsby, 1:325.

8. Harry M. Ward, *Duty, Honor or Country*, 80n. Funeral on Jan 16, 1777.

9. Quoted in Catesby W. Stewart, 2: 873.

10. Shepard, 667.

11. Catesby W. Stewart, 2:745–46.

12. Shepard, 667.

13. Carson, *James Innes*, 106.

14. Goldenberg and Stoer, 186–87.

15. *Ibid.*, 187–88.

16. Shepard, 667.

17. Carson, *James Innes*, 114.

18. *Ibid.*, 115.

19. William Tatham to William A. Burwell, June 13, 1805, in Carson, *James Innes*, 123; Carson, "The Fat Major," 92.

20. Thomas Nelson to Jefferson, Jan. 4, and Innes to Jefferson, Feb. 21, 1781, in *JP*, 4:307, 675.

21. Jefferson to Weedon, April 23 and Jefferson to Steuben, April 24, in *JP*, 5:546, 549.

22. Carson, "Fat Major," 93–94; Carson, *James Innes*, 142 and various correspondence on pp. 145–52.

23. Carson, *James Innes*, 153; "The Cocke Family," 440.

24. Theodore Bland to St. George Tucker, June 17, 1782, in *LD*, 18:584–85n.

25. Shepard, 667; Carson, *James Innes*, 155; Leonard Baker, 157–60, quote, p. 160.

26. Kaminski and Saladino, eds., 10:1654n.

27. Martin Osten to Comte de Luzerne, June 28, 1788, in *ibid.*, 1690.

28. *Ibid.*, 1536.

29. *Ibid.*, 1739.

30. *Ibid.*, 1522.

31. *Ibid.*, 1523.

32. *Ibid.*, 1524.
33. Shepard, 667.
34. Carson, *James Innes*, 157–58.
35. Grigsby, 1:328n.
36. Carson, *James Innes,* 158–59.
37. Quote in *ibid.*, 159–60; Grigsby, 1:319n.

19. Robert Lawson

1. Walter S. Lewis Jr. to Prof. R.H. Woody, March 29, 1963, Robert Lawson Papers, Duke University Library.
2. Prince Edward County Committee — Resolution, *RV*, 4:441; Bradshaw, *History of Prince Edward County, Virginia*, 53.
3. *JCC*, Aug. 13, 1776, 5:649; *AWP*, 3: 47n.; *RV*, 6:392, 394n.; Bradshaw, *History of Prince Edward County*, 194, 197; "Virginia's Soldiers in the Revolution," *VMHB*, 20 (1912): 187.
4. "Virginia's Soldiers in the Revolution," *VMHB*, 22 (1914): 180.
5. *Ibid.*, 20 (1912): 187; *AWP*, 8:62n.; *JCC*, July 16, 1777, 8:556; Elbridge Gerry to Joseph Trumbull, Jan. 2, 1777, in *LD*, 6:19; Thomas Eliot to Washington, March 22, 1777, in *AWP*, 8:616.
6. Robert Lawson to Washington, July 10 and General Orders, Aug. 19, Sept. 1, and Sept. 7, 1777, in *AWP*, 10:244n. (abstract), 11:2, 118, 167, resp.; Heitman, 344.
7. Deposition of William Bishop, July 1, 1820, *Virginia Military Records from the VMHB, WMQ, and Tyler's Quarterly*, 724; Samuel S. Smith, *The Battle of Brandywine*, 19, 30.
8. Eight Continental Field Officers to Washington, Nov.—, 1777, in *AWP*, 12:447–49.
9. *JCC*, Dec. 17, 1777, 9:1033.
10. Bill Granting Free Pardons, April 13, 1778, in *JP*, 2:178–79.
11. *Journal of the House of Delegates*, 1778, 4–5; 1779, 4–5; 1780, 5
12. *JP*, 3:58n.
13. Lawson to Patrick Henry, May 15, 1779, in Catesby W. Stewart, 2:1029–30; Robert Forsyth to Greene, May 19, 1779, in *NG*, 4:48; Edmund Pendleton to Woodford, May 24, 1779, Mays, ed., 1:283.
14. Muhlenberg, 18–20.
15. Muhlenberg to Gen. Horatio Gates, Nov. 7, 1780, in *ibid.*, 208–12; "Steps to be Taken to Repel General Leslie's Army," Oct. 22, Jefferson to Lawson, Oct. 25, and Weedon to Jefferson, Nov. 2, 1780, in *JP*, 4:91.
16. Resolution of the House of Delegates, Oct.–, 1780, in *JP*, 6:643 (Appendix); Greene to Steuben, Nov. 20, 1780, in *NG*, 6:497, 503n.; Lawson to Jefferson, Nov. 24, 1780, in *JP*, 4:151; Resolution of the House of Delegates, Nov. 30, 1780, Robert Lawson Papers; Return of Volunteers Commanded by Brigadier General Lawson, Nov.–, 1780, Steuben Papers, microfilm edition, NYHS; Steuben to Greene, Dec. 4, 1780, in *NG*, 6:583.
17. Josiah Parker to Steuben, Jan. 20, 1781, Steuben Papers; Muhlenberg to Steuben, Jan. 31, 1781, in Muhlenberg, 381.
18. Steuben to Board of War, Jan. 29, to Muhlenberg, Jan. 31, and Lawson to Muhlenberg, Feb. 6, 1781, Steuben Papers; Muhlenberg to Lawson, Jan. 30, 1781, Robert

Lawson Papers; Lawson to Josiah Parker, Feb. 6, 1781, VHS.
19. Muhlenberg to Steuben, Jan. 31, 1781, in Muhlenberg, 381–82.
20. Steuben to Lawson, Feb. 2, Muhlenberg to Lawson, Feb. 2, Muhlenberg to Lawson, Feb. 3, and Steuben to Muhlenberg, Feb. 13, 1781, Robert Lawson Papers; Lawson to Muhlenberg, Feb. 3, 1781, Steuben Papers.
21. Lawson to Steuben, Feb. 6, 1781, Steuben Papers.
22. Greene to Lawson, Feb. 17, 1781, in *NG*, 7:301.
23. Lawson to Jefferson, Feb. 16, 1781, in *JP*, 4:630.
24. Lawson to Greene, Feb. 27, 1781 (abstract), and March 2–4, in *NG*, 7:383, 389.
25. Thomas E. Baker, 33–39, 44–45; Thayer, 326–27; Boatner, 371; Burns, 29.
26. Hatch, *Battle of Guilford Courthouse*, 57–58; Thomas E. Baker, 47, 52–57, 60–61, 73.
27. Quote from Charles Stedman, *History ... American War* (1794), in Hatch, *Battle of Guilford Courthouse*, 59.
28. Quote from Henry Lee, *ibid.*
29. Quote of Greene to Jefferson, March 16, 1781, in *ibid.*, 70.
30. Return of the Militia Killed, Wounded, and Missing ... March 17, 1781, in Tarleton, 311.
31. Greene to Jefferson, March 31 and Lawson to Jefferson, May 1, 1781, in *JP*, 5:240, 583; Lawson to Greene, April 2, 1781, in *NG*, 8:28.
32. Lawson to Greene, April 7 and Greene to Edward Stevens, April 7, 1781, in *NG*, 8:61.
33. Greene to James Read, May 9 and Lafayette to Greene, May 24, 1781, in *NG*, 8:309.
34. John Pryor to Greene, June 5 and Steuben to Greene, June 9, 1781 (abstract), in *NG*, 8:354, 373.
35. Gottschalk, 266–67; "Some Revolutionary Soldiers," *VMHB*, 35 (1937): 44.
36. Lafayette to Charles Dabney, July 7 and to Greene, July 8, 1781, in *LP*, 4:235–36 and 238.
37. House of Delegates Resolution, June 28, 1782, Lawson Papers; Edmund Randolph to James Madison, in *MadP*, 5:263, 7:122n.; Bradshaw, *Prince Edward County*, 227; R.S. Thomas, "Public Officers, 1781," *VMHB*, 5 (1897): 216.
38. Lawson to Court of Charlotte County, March 1781, in W.S. Morton, "Charlotte County Records," in *Virginia Military Records*, 125.
39. Lawson Circular Letter to Cumberland et al., counties, Aug. 3, 1781, Lawson Papers; Lafayette to Thomas Nelson, July 1 and Aug. 20, 1781, in *LP*, 4:228 and 337.
40. Edward Carrington to Greene, April 15, 1781 (abstract), in *NG*, 9:347; David A. Skaggs, "Siege of Yorktown," *EAR*, 1292, map 1294; Evans, *Thomas Nelson of Yorktown*, 118.
41. Nelson to Lawson, Oct. 20, 1781, in *OL*, 3:88.
42. Nelson to Lawson, Oct. 22, 1781, in *OL*, 3:91.
43. Carpenter, 7–65; Burke Davis, *The Campaign That Won America*, 279; Bowie, 21–22; Young, ed., 123, 188n.
44. Benjamin Lawson (brother) to Lawson, April 6, 1782, Lawson Papers; *NG*, 10:497n.
45. Petition to House of Delegates, May 16, 1782, in Bradshaw, *Prince Edward County*, 129–30; George Mason to Washington, Nov. 24, 1787, in *AWP*, Confederation Series, 5:452–53; Richard Claiborne to Jefferson, Feb. 17, 1788, in *JP*, 12:602.

46. Bradshaw, *Prince Edward County*, 140.
47. *Ibid.*, 227.
48. Lawson to Beverly Randolph, March 21, 1785, Lawson Papers; Morrison, 45–46.
49. Bradshaw, *Prince Edward County*, 239, 260.
50. "Today and Yesterday in the Heart of Virginia," *Farmville Herald* (1935): 143.
51. Resolution, 1805, Society of Cincinnati Papers, VHS.
52. Charles M. Thurston to Mayor of Winchester, Nov. 15, 1787, and William Finnie to Horatio Gates, March 24, 1788, in Kaminski and Saladino, eds., 8:165, 515; Grigsby, 2:365; Brinkley, 35; Bradshaw, *Prince Edward County*, 142–43.
53. Adam Stephen Lawson,—, 1789, Lawson Papers; Bradshaw, *Prince Edward County*, 359.
54. Jefferson to Lawson, Aug. 31, 1787, in *JP*, 29:520.
55. Sarah Meriwether Pierce Lawson to Edward Carrington, Nov. 23, 1804, VHS.
56. Jefferson to William Short, March 12, 1790, in *JP*, 16:228.
57. Walter S. Lewis to Prof. R.H. Woody, March 29, 1936, Lawson Papers; Morrison, 72–73.
58. Pulliam, 52; Tyler, *Encyclopedia of Virginia Biography*, 2:331; *National Encyclopedia of American Biography*, 1:70.
59. George Mason to Charles Cotesworth Pinckney, Dec. 21, 1787, Lawson Papers.
60. *RV*, 2:345.

20. Edward Stevens

1. Wust, 25, 833.
2. Mildred C. Jones, 67.
3. *Virginia Gazette*, Oct. 20, 1775, quoted in Michael Sanchez-Saavedra, "All Fine Fellows …" in Mary S. Jones, ed., 16. The article is also published in *Virginia Cavalcade* (summer 1974), 4–11.
4. Extract from the "Diary" of Captain Philip Slaughter, 1775 to 1849, in Slaughter, *History of St. Mark's Parish*, 107.
5. Sanchez-Saavedra, "All Fine Fellows," in Mary S. Jones, ed., 19.
6. Catesby W. Stewart, 1:482, 503–4.
7. John T. S. Kearns, "The Importance of the Battle of Great Bridge," in Mary S. Jones., ed., 23; Leonard Baker, 31–38.
8. *Virginia Gazette*, Jan. 6, 1776, quote in Catesby W. Stewart, 1:583.
9. *Ibid.*, 591.
10. Stevens to Washington, May 15, 1777, in *AWP*, 9:435, 315n.; Board of War (Virginia) Resolution, Feb. 5, 1777, in *OL*, 1:98; Sanchez-Saavedra, *Guide to Virginia Military Organizations*, 61, 88; "William Burton," *WMQ*, 1st series, 11 (1903): 213.
11. General Orders, June 17, 1777, in *AWP*, 10:58.
12. *VFOB*, Brigade Orders, Aug. 22, 1777, 16.
13. Samuel S. Smith, *The Battle of Brandywine*, 21, 30; Harry M. Ward, *Duty, Honor or Country*, 101–2; Catesby W. Stewart, 2:808.
14. Deposition, March 15, 1812, in William Sheppard, "Shepard and Other Buckingham Families," 179.
15. Stevens to Washington, Jan. 19 and Henry Lee to Washington, Jan. 20, 1778, in *AWP*, 13:285, 292.
16. Stevens to Washington, Jan. 24, 1778, in *AWP*, 13:335, 336n; Leftowitz, 153.
17. Declaration of John Harris, in "Notes and Queries," *VMHB*, 10 (1912): 205–6; Jefferson to Stevens, Aug. 4, 1780, in *JP*, 3:528–30; McCrady, 666; Landers, 10; Howard M. Wilson, 144; McBride, 149–50.
18. McBride, 151–52, including quote from "Petition of Certain Deserters," Oct. 7, 1780; McCrady, 667–70.
19. "James Hopkins," in Revolutionary Pension Declarations from Pittsylvania County," *VMHB*, 25 (1917): 154; McCrady, 672; Christopher Ward, 2:724–725; Nelson, "Major General Horatio Gates," 140–144.
20. Landers, 44–45; McBride, 150–53.
21. Stevens to Jefferson, Aug. 20, 1780, in *JP*, 3:558; Nelson, "Gates as Military Leader," 145–49; Christopher Ward, 2:302; "Jefferson after Camden," *Tyler's Quarterly*, 7 (1926): 82–83.
22. Stevens to Jefferson, Aug, 20, 1780, in *JP*, 3:589; Treacy, 26; Boatner, 369–70.
23. Gates to Jefferson, Aug. 30 and Stevens to Jefferson, Aug. 30, in *JP*, 3:574, 577.
24. McBride, 156.
25. Jefferson to County Lieutenants … Sept. 4, in *JP*, 3:603–4; Stevens to Jefferson, Oct. 24, Oct. 27, Oct. 30, and Nov. 4 and 18, 1780, in *JP*, 4:65, 76, 81, 112, 125.
26. "Hopkins," in "Revolutionary Pension Declarations from Pittsylvania County," 155.
27. Jefferson to Stevens, Oct. 22, 1780 and Stevens to Jefferson, Nov. 10, 18, and 24, 1780, in *JP*, 4:59, 112, 125–26, 153, resp.
28. Greene to Jefferson, Jan. 26 and Stevens to Jefferson, Feb. 8, 1781, in *JP*, 4:455, 562–63; Greene to Steuben, Jan. 13 and to Benjamin Harrison, Jan. 20, 1781, in *NG*, 7:110, 162.
29. Greene to Stevens, Feb. 19, 1781 (abstract), in *NG*, 6:316; Treacy, 158–59.
30. Thayer, 324–26; Hatch, *Battle of Guilford Courthouse*, 27.
31. Greene to Samuel Huntington, March 16, 1781, in *NG*, 7:434; quote from *Annual Register for 1781*, in Hatch, *Battle of Guilford Courthouse*, 57.
32. David Schenck, *North Carolina, 1780–81: Being a History of the Invasion of the Carolinas by the British Army* (Spartanburg, SC: The Reprint Company, 1967, orig. pub. 1889), 362; letter of Pendleton, March 24, 1781, in Mays, ed., 1:316; Hatch, *Battle of Guilford Courthouse*, 69.
33. Tarleton, 276.
34. "American Losses at Guilford," in Hatch, *Battle of Guilford Courthouse*, 121.
35. Quote from Stedman, *American War*, in *ibid.*, 52.
36. Greene to Samuel Huntington, March 16, 1781, in *NG*, 7:435.
37. Greene to Jefferson, March 27, 1781, in *NG*, 7:471, 472n.
38. Greene to Jefferson, March 31 and April 7, 1781, in *NG*, 7:17, 63.
39. Virginius Dabney, "Jack Jouett's Ride," 58; Page Smith, 1631–32.
40. Stevens to Gov. Thomas Nelson, July 14, 1781, in *CSP*, 2:245; "Revolutionary Pension, Declarations from Pittsylvania Count," *VMHB*, 17 (1909): 77.
41. Nelson to Stevens, Aug. 1 and Stevens to Nelson, Aug. 10, 1781, in *CSP*, 2:283 and 310.

42. Edward Carrington to Greene, Sept. 15, 1781, in *NG*, 9:347.

43. Johnston, *Yorktown Campaign*, 55, 116.

44. Harry M. Ward, *Duty, Honor or Country*, chapter 12; Evans, *Thomas Nelson*, 118.

45. Gov. Harrison to Stevens, June 25, 1782, in *OL*, 3:254.

46. Harrison to Count Rochambeau, June 26, to Washington, July 11, and to Le Chevalier de la Valette, July 12, 1781, in *OL*, 3:257, 265, 268.

47. Harrison to Stevens, Aug. 21, to Sundry County Lieutenants, Aug. 21, and to Virginia Delegates, Aug. 23, 1782, in *OL*, 3:301–304.

48. Kaminski and Saladino, eds., 8:lviii; Scheel, 360.

49. *Journal of the Senate of the Commonwealth of Virginia*, 1787: pp. 4, 9; 1788: pp. 43, 57, 89; 1790: p. 100.

50. Andrew Sheperd to James Madison, March 17, 1788, Kaminski and Saladino eds., 9:578.

51. Stevens to Jefferson, Sept. 14, 1791, in *JP*, 22:146; Edward Carrington to Alexander Hamilton, Oct. 8, 1791, "Home Manufacturers in Virginia in 1791: Letters of Gen. Edward Carrington to Alexander Hamilton," *WMQ*, 2d series, 2 (1922): 139, 147.

52. *Historic Culpeper*, 9, 12–13, 18–19, 25, 29.

53. *Ibid.*, 124; Scheel, 108.

54. *Historic Culpeper*, 134, 138; Mary S. Jones, "Stevensburg: an Ancient Town of Renown," in Jones, ed., 97.

55. Tyler, *Encyclopedia of Virginia Biography*, 2:173.

56. "List of Obituaries," *VMHB*, 20 (1912): 291; McGroarty, 159–60.

21. John "Jack" Jouett

1. Harris, 58, 355, 442; Jouett, 143.

2. Jouett, 143, 146; Heitman, 326.

3. Cornwallis to Henry Clinton, June 30, 1781 (extract), in Tarleton, 349; Merrill, 24; Maass, 153.

4. McGehee, 11, 13.

5. "Diary of Arnold's Invasion," in *JP*, 4:261; Jouett, 144; Virginius Dabney, "Jack Jouett's Ride," *Magazine of Albemarle County History*, 30 (1972): 21; Merrill, 25.

6. Dabney, "Jack Jouett's Ride," 21; Merrill, 24–25.

7. Dabney, "Jack Jouett's Ride," 23; Selby, 282; Nicholas Everleigh to Jefferson, Nov. 25, 1780, in *JP*, 4:153.

8. Christopher Hudson's Deposition, July 26, 1804, in *JP*, 4:277; Rector Hudson, ed., 99–105; Kibler, 49–57; Trist Wood, 190–91.

9. "Diary of Arnold's Invasion," in *JP*, 4:264; Jouett, 146–47.

10. Hammon, ed., 73; Bakeless, 258–59; Merrill, 26; Morgan, 320–3.

11. Maass, 154–55.

12. Quote in Jouett, 148; Dabney, "Jouett's Ride," 26.

13. Maass, 157.

14. Manahan, 93–94; Collins, 1:354, 357, 619; Jouett, 154–55; Green, *The Spanish Conspiracy*, 221.

15. Remini, 60–62; Harry M. Ward, *Charles Scott*, 104.

16. Collins, 1:578; Jouett, 155; Haley, "Epilogue," in *Jack Jouett's Ride*, n.p.

17. Collins, 1:619; Dabney, "Jouett's Ride," 27.

18. Jouett, 155.

19. Collins, 1:619.

22. Charles Dabney

1. Charles W. Dabney, "Genealogical Queries: Dabney-Brent," 163.

2. Robert B. Lancaster, *A Sketch of the Early History of Hanover County, Virginia* (Ashland: *Herald Progress*, 1957), 2:37.

3. "Virginia State Troops in the Revolution," *VMHB*, 26 (1918): 186.

4. *VMHB*, 27 (1919): 63; "Virginia Committee of Safety Minutes," in *RV*, 7, pt. 2:688.

5. *JP*, 5:196n.; "Virginia Soldiers in the Revolution," *VMHB*, 21 (1913): 341; Sanchez-Saavedra, *Guide to Virginia Military Organizations*, 113; Gwathmey, 302.

6. Charles W. Dabney, ed., *The John Blair Dabney Manuscript, 1795–1868*, 18.

7. Charles W. Dabney, "Colonel Charles Dabney of the Revolution: His Service as Soldier and Citizen," *VMHB*, 51 (1943): 187; "Virginia Revolutionary Soldiers," *VMHB*, 37, (1929): 358; Lesser, 72.

8. Dabney, ed., *John Blair Dabney Manuscript*, 12.

9. Heitman, 183.

10. Lesser, 128.

11. Johnston, 215; Cecere, *Thomas Posey*, 99–100; Dabney, ed., *John Blair Dabney Manuscript*, 13; Berg, 136.

12. Dabney, ed., *John Blair Dabney Manuscript*, 13.

13. Anthony Wayne to Washington, July 17, 1779, in Johnston, 165.

14. Dabney to Thomas Nelson, Feb. 14, 1781, in *JP*, 4:651.

15. "Return of Militia," in *JP*, 5:29.

16. Dabney to Jefferson, March 23, 1781, in *JP*, 214; Dabney to Weedon, March 23, 1781, Allyn K. Ford Collection, Minnesota Historical Society, microfilm edition.

17. Dabney to William Davies, May 30, 1781, in *CSP*, 2:129.

18. Lafayette to Dabney, July 7, 1781, in *LP*, 4:235–36.

19. Dabney to William Davies, Aug. 4, 27, and 29, in *CSP*, 2:292, 364, 368.

20. Dabney to William Davies, Oct. 10, 1781, in *CSP*, 2:540; General Orders, Oct. 6, 1781, in Johnston, 137n.

21. Quote from Dabney, ed., *John Blair Dabney Manuscript*, 15.

22. *NG*, 11:388n. Sanchez-Saavedra, *Guide to Virginia Military Organizations*, 135–36.

23. Gov. Harrison to George Rogers Clark, March 24 and to Dabney, Aug. 19, 1782, in *OL*, 3:181, 298; Dabney to Gov. Harrison, July 20, 1782, in *CSP*, 3:224; Sanchez-Saavedra, *Guide to Virginia Military Organizations*, 136.

24. Gov. Harrison to Washington, Aug. 1, 1782, in "Letters from the Governor's Letter Books," *Tyler's Quarterly*, 4 (1923): 423; Alexander Dick to the Governor, Nov. 22, 1782, in *CSP*, 3:378.

25. Sanchez-Saavedra, *Guide to Virginia Military Organizations*, 135–36.

26. Dabney, ed., *John Blair Dabney Manuscript*, 14.

27. *Ibid.*, 17; Charles W. Dabney, "Colonel Charles Dabney," 194–95.

28. Dabney, ed., *John Blair Dabney Manuscript*, 19–21.

29. *Ibid.*, 23; Gwathmey, 203.

30. Dabney, "Colonel Charles Dabney," 190.

23. Anna Maria Lane

1. Two biographical sketches contain about all that is known of Anna Maria Lane: E.M. Sanchez-Saavedra, "The Trooper was a Lady: Being Some Account of Anna Maria Lane, a Private Soldier of The Revolution," *Richmond Literature and History Quarterly*, 1 (1978), 33–37; and Sandra G. Treadway, "Anna Maria Lane: An Uncommon Common Soldier of the American Revolution," *Virginia Cavalcade*, 37 (1988): 134–43. A useful but less reliable biographical item is John A. Carter, "Richmond's Anna Maria Lane — Heroine of Germantown," *Richmond*, 14 (May 1928): 3, 6, 16, 32.

2. Charles E. Claghorn, *Women Patriots of the American Revolution* (Metuchen, NJ: Scarecrow Press, 1991), 120; Treadway, 135.

3. Mayer, 144–45; Sanchez-Saavedra, "Lane," 34–35; Nichols, 193.

4. Ray Thompson, *Washington at Germantown*, 26–27; Ray Thompson, *Washington at Whitemarsh*, 9.

5. Clyne, 135.

6. Treadway, 137; Mattern, *Benjamin Lincoln*, 78; Cecere, *Great Things are Expected*, 153.

7. Sanchez-Saavedra, "Lane," 35; Berg, 119.

8. Treadway, 137–38; Sanchez-Saavedra, "Lane," 35–36.

9. Treadway, 137, 139; Sanchez-Saavedra, "Lane," 36.

10. Mordecai, 72.

11. Dr. John Foushee to City Health Officer, Jan., 1802, in John A. Carter,v16, 32; Treadway, 140.

12. Quote from Gov. William Cabell's message of Jan. 28, 1808, in Treadway, 36–37.

13. Act of Feb. 8, 1808, *Statutes at Large of Virginia*, new series, 3 (Richmond: 1816), 432.

14. John Lane file, Feb. 21, 1816, Auditor Records, *Virginia Revolutionary War State Pensions*, 68; State Auditor's Office Accounts, *passim*, LV.

15. Sanchez-Saavedra, "Lane," 37.

16. Receipt Nov. 10, 1816, John Lane File, *Virginia Revolutionary War State Pensions*, 68.

17. Treadway, 142.

18. John Lane File, 68.

24. William Campbell

1. General Orders, Aug. 25, 1781, in *LP*, 4:359n.

2. Lyman C. Draper, 400; Summers; Harry M. Ward, "William Campbell," 304; Paul D. Nelson, "William Campbell," in *DVB*, 2:583; Malgee, 3–7.

3. "A Return of Militia from Fincastle," Sept. 7, 1774, in Thwaites and Kellogg, eds., 189.

4. Quote in Malgee, 41; Hartwell Quinn, 28–29.

5. Malgee, 43–44, 47–48.

6. Summers, 272–73.

7. Malgee, 76–78, 81–83; Ward, "Campbell," 304; Evans, "Trouble in the Backcountry," 188–89.

8. Malgee, 83.

9. Patricia G. Johnson, 223–24; Summers, 275–77; Malgee, 85; Hartwell L. Quinn, 58–59.

10. Malgee, 90.

11. *Ibid.*, 91–100, 106, 108, 113, 115–18.

12. Crowson, 26–27; Dykeman, 48; W. J. Wood, 196; Malgee, 147.

13. Statement of Israel Hayter, in Dunkerly, ed., 122; Malgee, 141–51; Dykeman, 59; Crowson, 27.

14. Edgar, 119; Crowson, 28; Malgee, 157.

15. Statement of William Moore, in Dunkerly, ed., 121.

16. W.J. Wood, 204.

17. Campbell to Jefferson, Oct. 31, 1780, in Dunkerly, ed., 28, 30; Lyman C. Draper, 352, 360.

18. Quote in Dykeman, 71.

19. *Ibid.*, 71, 74; Robert Campbell Report in Draper, 539–40.

20. *Historical Statements concerning the Battle of Kings Mountain*, 32.

21. Pancake, 178; W.J. Wood, 242–43; Konstam, 49–53; Summers, 350–51; "Wetzell's Mills," in *EAR*, 2:1263–64.

22. Burke Davis, *The Cowpens-Guilford Courthouse Campaign*, 165–66; Malgee, 215–216, 219–21; Pancake, 183, 185; Lyman C. Draper, 393.

23. Greene to Campbell, March 19, 1781, in Summers, 356–57

24. *Ibid.*, 257; Lyman C. Draper, 394.

25. Lafayette to Thomas Nelson, June 28, 1781, in *LP*, 4:218; Malgee, 227–35; Lyman C. Draper, 398.

26. Lyman C. Draper, 397; Summers, 369.

27. Lyman C. Draper, 396.

28. Crowson, 29; Malgee, 264.

29. Lyman C. Draper, 401.

30. Quote in Malgee, 249.

25. William Crawford

1. The contention that William Crawford was born in 1722, is made by several writers, most notably Grace U. Emahiser in *From River Clyde to Tymochtee and Col. William Crawford* (no pl.: priv. pr., 1969), is not supported by conclusive evidence. A contemporary account, by a fellow captive, was published in 1798: *Narrative of a Late Expedition Against the Indians with an Account of the Barbarous Execution of Col. Crawford and the Wonderful Escape from Captivity of Dr. John Knight & John Slover* (facsimile, Ann Arbor: University Microfilms, 1976) notes that William Crawford was 50 years old at the time of his death.

2. O'Donnell, "William Crawford," 710; Emahiser, 10; "William Crawford," in *EAR*, 3:541.

3. O'Donnell, "William Crawford," 710; Richards, 415.

4. "List of Junior Officers in the Virginia Regiment," June 12, 1757, Memoranda July 29-Aug. 3, 1757, and Robert Stewart to Washington, Aug. 8, 1758, in *AWP*, Colonial Series, 4:205, 340, 5:380–81, 269n.; Sadosky, 544.

5. *AWP*, Colonial Series, 8:29n.

6. James H. Anderson, 3–6; Emahiser, 106.

7. Petition to Lord Dunmore and the Virginia Council, c. Nov. 4, 1772, in *AWP*, Colonial Series, 9:118.

8. *Ibid.*, 9:382n.; Dunn, 11–13.

9. Washington to Dunmore, April 3, 1775, in *AWP*, Colonial Series, 10:321.

10. Alfred P. James, 168.

11. O'Donnell, "William Crawford," 710; Richards, 415.

12. Thwaites and Kellogg, eds., 81n.

13. *Ibid.*, 103; "Crawford," *EAR*, 1:286.

14. Thwaites and Kellogg, eds., 302n.

15. Crawford to Washington, Nov. 14, 1774, in *AWP*, Colonial Series, 10:182, 183n.

16. Dunn, 132, 135; Hassler, 13–14.

17. James H. Anderson, 9–10; "Crawford," in *EAR*, 1:286; Heitman, 177.

18. O'Donnell, "William Crawford," 710.

19. "Diary of John Chilton," Sept. 3, 1777, 289; Sipe, 867.

20. James H. Anderson, 9.

21. Hassler, 66; Sipe, 867, 873.

22. Russell and Gott, 350; James H. Anderson, 12.

23. Sipe, 627.

24. *Ibid.*, 648–56; Eckert, 252; Sipe, 659.

25. James H. Anderson, 14, including quote; Sipe, 659.

26. James H. Anderson, 20–23; "Crawford's Defeat," in *EAR*, 1:288; Sipe, 600–61.

27. The following account is from Knight, *Narrative of a Late Expedition*.

28. Quote from Eckert, 264.

29. Washington to the Board of War, May 23, 1778, in C.W. Butterfield, ed., 70.

26. James Armistead Lafayette

1. Elizabeth Kuebler-Wolf, "James Armistead Lafayette," in Gates and Higginbotham, eds., 138; Harry M. Ward and Harold E. Greer, Jr., 127. James Armistead Lafayette's petition to the Virginia legislature of 1818 states that he was 70 years old at the time.

2. *Black History Virginia Profiles*, James Lafayette, Vertical File, VHS.

3. Salmon, 81; Tucker, "Revolutionary War Spy."

4. Burke Davis, *Black Heroes of the American Revolution*, 55.

5. *Ibid.*, 55.

6. Writers Project of the WPA, *The Negro in Virginia*, 22–23.

7. Certificate by Gen. Lafayette, Nov. 21, 1784, facsimile, in James Lafayette Vertical File, VHS.

8. Journal of the House of Delegates, Dec. 4, 1784, in *LP*, 5:279n.

9. Transcript of James Armistead Lafayette's petition of Nov. 30, 1786, in James Lafayette Vertical File, VHS.

10. *LD*, 5:279n.; Kaplan, 36.

11. Kuebler-Wolf, "James Armistead Lafayette," 138.

12. Salmon, 82.

13. A transcription of James Armistead Lafayette's petition of Dec. 28, 1818, is in the James Lafayette Vertical File, VHS. James Armistead Lafayette's petitions are in different handwritings, further indication of his illiteracy. In the petitions he calls himself James Lafayette.

14. Tucker, "Revolutionary War Spy."

15. R. Lewis Wright, 105–6; quote from Callahan, ed., 402–3.

16. Kuebler-Wolf, "James Armistead Lafayette," 139; Hart, 362; Virginius Dabney, *Richmond: The Story of a City*, 29.

17. Tucker, "Revolutionary War Spy"; Salmon, 85.

27. Edward Carrington

1. Greene to Washington, April 24, 1779, in *NG*, 3:427.

2. Greene to Alexander McDougall, March 28, 1778, in *NG*, 2:326.

3. *Ibid.*, 13:463n.; Stuart Leibiger, "Edward Carrington," in *DVB*, 3:33; Konigsberg, 19–21.

4. Cumberland County Committee Resolution, Aug. 24, 1775, in *RV*, 4:51–52, 54n., 267n.

5. *AWP*, 17n, 4n.; Heitman, 133.

6. Konigsberg, 19–21.

7. *Ibid.*, 22–28; *JCC*, Aug. 19, 1777, 8:655; *LD*, 8:84n.

8. Konigsberg, 31.

9. *Ibid.*, 32–33, including quote; Rankin, 157; Russell and Gott, 279; Christopher Ward, 2:502.

10. General Orders, Sept. 10, 1779, in *FWW*, 6:259; "Edward Carrington," in *EAR*, 1:171: Konigsberg, 34.

11. Konigsberg, 55, 58.

12. Horatio Gates to Jefferson, Aug. 3, 1780, in *JP*, 3:525; "Narrative of Colonel Otho Williams, 1780," in Commager and Morris, eds., 2:1126.

13. Konigsberg, 61, 66.

14. *Ibid.*, 72; Greene to Carrington, Dec. 4, 1780, in *NG*, 7:516–17n.; Greene to Joseph Reed, Jan. 9, 1781, in Commager and Morris, eds., 2:1152; Pancake, 129.

15. Carrington to Greene, Dec. 6, 1780, in *NG*, 6:537, 514n.; Thayer, 291.

16. Carrington and Richard Claiborne, "Plan for the Quartermaster Department in Virginia," Jan. 1, 1781, in *JP*, 4:285–87.

17. Konigsberg, 81–82.

18. Lee, 250.

19. Konigsberg, 95–107.

20. *NG*, 7:426n., 445n.; Instructions to Carrington concerning an Exchange of Prisoners, March 11 and Carrington to Greene, May 8, 1781, in *NG*, 7:425, 8:221.

21. *Ibid.*, 7:440n., 441n.

22. Lumpkin, 180; Christopher Ward, 2:802–3.

23. Purcell, comp., 84.

24. Konigsberg, 114–15; Trussell, 194–208.

25. Greene to Carrington, May 18 and Carrington to Greene, July 6, 1782, in *NG*, 11:198–99, 406–8; *MadP*, 4:145n.

26. Konigsberg, 157, 176–77.

27. *Ibid.*, 162–63.

28. *Ibid.*, 158.

29. Resolution Ordering Election of Northwest Claims Commission, House of Delegates, June 1, 1784, in *MadP*, 8:51.

30. *MP*, 1:117n.; *Biographical Directory of American Congress, 1776–1996*, 786.

31. Konigsberg, 248–49.

32. Carrington to Madison, July 25, 1787, in *MadP*, 10:113–14.

33. Carrington to Gov. Edmund Randolph, Dec. 8, 1786, in *CSP*, 4:195–96.

34. Carrington to Madison, Sept. 23, 1787, in *MadP*, 10:172.

35. Reardon, 121.

36. Carrington to George Eve, Jan. 2, 1789, in *MadP*, 11:405.

37. Coutre, 510.

38. Leibiger, "Carrington," 34.

39. Carrington to Madison, Oct. 24, 1788, in *MadP*, 11:314–15.

40. Konigsberg, 420.

41. *Ibid.*, 468.

42. "Home Manufactures in Virginia in 1791: Letters to Alexander Hamilton from Edward Carrington," *WMQ*, 2d ser., 2 (1922): 139–42.

43. Leibiger, "Carrington," 35.

44. Konigsberg, 464.

45. Carrington to Greene, Feb. 27, 1785, in *NG*, 13:426.

46. Carrington to the Governor, Feb. 8, 1795, in *CSP*, 7:430–31.

47. Leibiger, "Carrington," 35.

48. *Ibid.*

49. Timothy Pickering to John Marshall, Jan. 17, 1826, in Herbert A. Johnson et al., eds., 10:265.

50. "List of Obituaries," *VMHB*, 20 (1912): 290, 368; Tyler, *Encyclopedia of Virginia History*, 2:7; Ward and Greer, *Richmond during the Revolution*, 29.

28. William Davies

1. Pilcher, *Samuel Davies: Apostle of Dissent*, 8, 35, 39; Winthrop S. Hudson, 25, 74.

2. Bill, 23; James McLachan, 1:490–91.

3. McLachan, 1:491.

4. *RV*, 5:87n.

5. *Ibid.*, 4:125n.

6. McLachan, 1:491; Berg, 123.

7. Sanchez-Saavedra, *Guide to Virginia Military Organizations*, 30; *RV*, 5:249n.

8. Lesser, 33.

9. Sanchez-Saavedra, *Guide to Virginia Military Organizations*, 29; *JCC*, Sept. 19 and Oct. 5, 1776, 5:783, 849.

10. Heitman, 187; Sanchez-Saavedra, *Guide to Virginia Military Organizations*, 51.

11. *NG*, 2:207n.; *VFOB*, Sept. 17, 1777, 53, 83; Heitman, 187.

12. *VFOB*, Dec. 20, 1777 and Jan. 17, Feb. 3, and March 9, 1778, 160, 194, 220, 251.

13. *Ibid.*, April 6 and 19, 1778, 280, 293; General Orders April 19, 1778, in *AWP*, 14:554.

14. Washington to Henry Laurens, Jan. 1, June 4, and July 22, 1778, in *AWP*, 13:104–5n., 15:308, 16:121; General Orders, June 21, 1779, in *FWW*, 15:293; Washington to Woodford, Dec. 14, 1779, in Catesby W. Stewart, 2:1133; *NG*, 4:512n.

15. Washington to Davies, Dec. 16, 1779, in *FWW*, 17:274; Washington to Woodford, Dec. 14, 1779, Woodford to Washington, March 8 and Davies to Robert Hanson Harrison, March 20, 1780, in Catesby W. Stewart, 2:1133, 1156–57, 1153.

16. Woodford to Washington, March 8 and Davies to Robert Hanson Harrison, in Catesby W. Stewart, 2:1156–57.

17. Davies to Robert Hanson Harrison, March 20, in Catesby W. Stewart, 2:1158; Washington to Davies, April 20, 1780, in *FWW*, 18:289; Jefferson to Davies, Aug. 9, Sept. 3 and 9, 1780, in *JP*, 3:536, 587–88, 619.

18. Timothy Pickering to Jefferson, Oct. 19, 1780, in *JP*, 4:48.

19. Greene to Steuben, Nov. 20, 1780, in *NG*, 6:497.

20. *Ibid.*, 6:498n.

21. Young, ed., 180; see Bettie W. Weaver, *The Continental Training Depot*.

22. Jefferson to Davies, Feb. 1 and March 13, 1781, in *JP*, 4:492–93, 5:137; *MadP*, 2:199n.

23. Steuben to Greene, Jan. 9 and 24, 1781, in *NG*, 7:77, 186, 80n.

24. Davies to Greene, April 2, 1781 (abstract), in *NG*, 8:26–27; Jefferson to Davies, March 22, 1781, in *JP*, 5:204–5 and n.; Weaver, *passim*.

25. Jefferson to Lafayette, March 24, 1781, in *LP*, 3:412–13n; *NG*, 13:413n.

26. Jefferson to Virginia Delegates, March 26, 1781, in *MadP*, 3:31–32n.

27. Davies to Lafayette, Aug. 15, 1781, in *LP*, 4:326–28n.

28. Davies to Lafayette, Sept. 7, 1781, in *LP*, 390.

29. Davies to Lafayette, in *LP*, 390. Davies to Weedon, Aug. 3, 1781, Allyn K. Ford Collection, Minnesota Historical Society, VHS microfilm; Thomas Nelson to Davies, Sept. 16 and 27, 1781, in *OL*, 3:54, 73.

30. Evans, *Thomas Nelson*, 107.

31. Davies to Steuben, April 3, 1781, Steuben Papers, NYHS; Davies to Jefferson, April 12, 1781, in *JP*, 5:418–19.

32. David Jameson to Lafayette, Aug. 31, 1781, in *LP*, 4:379; McDonnell, 460–61, 493.

33. Greene to Davies, July 17, 1781, in *NG*, 9:23–24.

34. Governor Harrison to Davies, March 26 and 30 and April 2, 1782, in *OL*, 3:182, 187, 190.

35. Harrison to Charles Cameron, Dec. 13, 1782 in *OL*, 3: 400; *MadP*, 5:320.

36. *MadP*, 12:12n; McLachan, 1:492.

37. *LD*, 25:510n.

38. Pitch, 18; Ferguson, 217, 314, 324.

39. Ferguson, 324.

40. Samuel Dexter to Madison, March 25, 1801, in *MadP*, Secretary of State Series, 1:45, and n.

41. Thomas Newton to Jefferson, Sept. 25, 1801, in *JP*, 35:348.

42. *MadP*, 3:32n.

43. McLachan, 1:492.

Bibliography

Manuscripts (chiefly microfilm collections)

Chadwyck-Healy Co., Cambridge, UK
Papers of John Paul Jones
Chicago Historical Society
George Weedon-John Page Correspondence
Duke University
Robert Lawson Papers
Library of Congress
Papers of George Washington
Library of Virginia
Auditor Office Accounts
Legislative Petitions
Virginia Revolutionary War Pension Applications
Minnesota Historical Society
Allyn K. Ford Collection
National Archives
Papers of the Continental Congress

New-York Historical Society
Friedrich Wilhelm Von Steuben Papers
University of Illinois, Urbana
Richard Clough Anderson Papers
University of Virginia
Lee Family Papers
Wallace Family Papers
Virginia Historical Society
Charles Dabney Papers
Mercer Papers
Robert Lawson to Col. Josiah Parker, Feb. 6, 1781
Sarah Meriwether Pierce Lewis to Edward Carrington, Nov. 23, 1804
Society of Cincinnati Papers
Wisconsin State Historical Society
Lynam C. Draper Collection

Primary Sources

Abbott, W. W. et al., eds. *The Papers of George Washington*, Revolutionary War Series, Colonial Series, Confederation Series, Presidential Series. Charlottesville: University Press of Virginia, 1983–present.

"Action between American and British Barges in the Chesapeake Bay, November 1782." *Maryland Historical Magazine* 4 (1909): 115–33.

Alcock, John P. *Fauquier Families, 1789–1799: Comprehensive Indexed Abstracts.* Athens, GA: Iberian Publishing Company, 1994.

"American Prisoners at Forton Prison, England, 1777–1779." *New England Genealogical and Historical Register* 33 (1879): 33–39.

"Arnold's Incursions and Capture of Richmond in January 1781." (Letter of John Page to Col. Theodorick Bland). *Virginia Historical Register* 4, no. 4 (1851): 195–99.

Barnes, John S., ed. *Fanning's Narrative: Being the Memoirs of Nathaniel Fanning of the Revolutionary Army.* New York: De Vinne Press, 1912, orig. publ. 1806.

Brock, R. A., ed. "Orderly Book of Major William Heth of the Third Virginia Regiment." In *Collections of the Virginia Historical Society*, new series, 11 (1921): 317–76.

Burns, Annie W., ed. *Revolutionary War Pensions of Soldiers Who Settled in Fayette County, Kentucky.* Salem, MA: Higginson Book Company, 1936.

Butterfield, C. W., ed. *The Washington-Crawford Letters.* Cincinnati, OH: Robert Clarke Company, 1877.

Butterfield, L. H., ed. *Diary and Autobiography of John Adams.* Vol. 1. Cambridge, MA: Harvard University Press, 1961.

Campbell, Charles, ed. *The Bland Papers: Being a Selection from the Manuscripts of Colonel Theodorick Bland, Jr.* 2 vols. Petersburg: Edmund and Julian, 1840 and 1843.

Carlyle, Thomas. *On Heroes, Hero-Worship and the*

Heroic in History. Edited by Carl Niemeyer. Lincoln, NE: University of Nebraska Press, 1966.

Carter, Edward C. II, ed. *The Virginia Journals of Benjamin Henry Latrobe*. 2 vols. New Haven, CT: Yale University Press, 1977.

"Charles Allen's Revolutionary Service." *Tyler's Quarterly Magazine* 8 (1927): 253–54.

Chastellux, Francois Jean, Marquis de. *Travels in North America in the Years 1780, 1781 and 1782*. 2 vols. Edited by Howard C. Rice. Chapel Hill: University of North Carolina Press, 1963.

Chilton, John. "The Diary of Captain John Chilton, 3d Virginia Regiment." *Tyler's Quarterly Magazine* 12 (1931): 283–89.

Clark, Thomas D., ed. *The Voice of the Frontier: John Bradford's Notes on Kentucky*. Lexington, KY: University Press of Kentucky, 1993.

Clark, William B., and William J. Morgan, eds. *Naval Documents of the American Revolution*. 7 vols. to date. Washington, DC: Naval Historical Center, 1964.

Clinton, Henry. *The American Rebellion*. Edited by William B. Willcox. Hamden, CT: Archon Books, 1971, orig. pub. 1954.

"The Cocke Family." *VMHB* 4 (1896): 431–50.

Commager, Henry S., and Richard B. Morris, eds. *The Spirit of Seventy-Six*. 2 vols. Indianapolis, IN: Bobbs-Merrill Company, 1958.

Crozier, William, ed. *Virginia County Records*. Vol. 1, *Spotsylvania County, 1721–1800*. New York: Fox, Duffield and Company, 1905.

Cutter, William B., ed. "A Yankee Privateersman in Prison in England." *New England Historical & Genealogical Register* 30–33 (July 1876-January 1897): 343–52, 18–20, 212–13, 284–88, 70–73, 165–68, 280–86, 36–40.

Dabney, Charles W., ed. *The John Blair Dabney Manuscript, 1795–1868*. Richmond, VA: n.p., 1942 (written in 1850).

Dann, John C., ed. *The Revolution Remembered: Eyewitness Accounts of the War for Independence*. Chicago: University of Chicago Press, 1980.

Darlington, William M., ed. *Christopher Gist's Journals*. Bowie, MD: Heritage Books, 2002, orig. pub. 1893.

deKoven, Mrs. Reginald. *The Life and Letters of John Paul Jones*. Vol. 1. New York: Charles Scribner's Sons, 1930.

Dick, Charles. "Manufacture of Small Arms at Fredericksburg: Letters by Charles Dick." *Sons of the Revolution in the State of Virginia Magazine* (July 1929): 3–33.

Dorman, John F., comp. *Virginia Revolutionary Pension Applications*. 50 vols. Washington, DC: J. F. Dorman, 1958.

Echeverria, Durand, and Orville T. Murphy, eds. "The American Revolutionary Army: A French estimate in 1777." In *Military Analysis of the Revolutionary War*, 201–17. Millwood, NY: KTO Press, 1977.

Elias, Robert H., and Eugene D. Finck, eds. *Letters of Thomas Attwood Digges*. Columbia, SC: University of South Carolina Press, 1982.

Esarey, Logan, ed. *Governors' Messages and Letters ... William Henry Harrison ... John Gibson ... Thomas Posey*. Vol. 2. Indianapolis, IN: Indiana Historical Commission, 1982.

Ewald, Johann. "Diary of Captain Johann Ewald." In Uhlendorf, ed., 30–102.

Fall, Ralph E., ed. *The Diary of Robert Rose*. Verona, VA: McClure Press, 1977.

Finley, Samuel. "Samuel Finley to Dr. Jacob Hall, July 2, 1781." *WMQ*, 1st ser., 23 (1915): 46–47.

Fitzpatrick, John C., ed. *The Writings of George Washington*. 39 vols. Washington, DC: Government Printing Office, 1931–44.

Flickinger, B. Floyd, ed. "Diary of Lieutenant William Heth while a Prisoner in Quebec, 1776." *Annual Papers of the Winchester Historical Society* 1 (1931): 27–118.

Ford, Worthington C., ed. *Journals of the Continental Congress*. 34 vols. Washington, DC: Government Printing Office, 1904–37.

Francisco, Peter. "Peter Francisco to the General Assembly, Nov. 11, 1820." *WMQ*, 1st ser., 13 (1905): 217–19.

"Francisco's Pension: Petition to the U.S. Congress." In "The Revolution in Virginia," *The Daily Progress*, 15 Feb. 1976, 5–7.

"Fredericksburg District Court Deed Book A." *The Virginia Genealogist*. Vol. 37.

Fries, Adelaide L., ed. *Records of the Moravians of North Carolina*. Vol. 4. Raleigh, NC: State Department of Archives and History, 1968.

Gilliam, Hubert, and Jim Glanville. "An Unexpected Enemy and the Turn of the Tides: Andrew Creswell's Kings Mountain Letter." *The Smithfield Review* 10 (2006): 5–20.

Greene, Jack P., ed. *The Diary of Colonel Landon Carter of Sabine Hall, 1752–1778*. Vol. 2. Charlottesville: University Press of Virginia, 1965.

Hall, Wilmer L., ed. *Journals of the Council of State of Virginia*. Vol. 3. Richmond: Library of Virginia, 1952.

Harwell, Richard B., ed. *The Committees of Safety of Westmoreland Fincastle: Proceedings, 174–76*. Richmond: Library of Virginia, 1956.

Henry, William W. *Patrick Henry: Life, Correspondence, and Speeches*. 3 vols. New York: Charles Scribner's Sons, 1891.

Hinrichs, Johann. "Diary of Johann Hinrichs." In Uhlendorf, ed., 103–363.

"Home Manufactures in Virginia in 1791: Letters to Alexander Hamilton from Edward Carrington." *WMQ*, 2d ser., 2 (1922): 139–45.

Hopkins, James F., ed. *The Papers of Henry Clay*. Vol.

1. Lexington, KY: University of Kentucky Press, 1959.

Hough, Franklin B., ed. *Siege of Charleston by the British Fleet and Army.* Spartanburg, SC: The Reprint Company, 1975, orig. pub. 1867.

Hoyt, William H., ed. *The Papers of Archibald D. Murphey.* Vol. 2. Raleigh, NC: E.M. Uzzell and Company, 1914.

Hudson, Rector, ed. "Statement of Christopher Hudson." *Tyler's Quarterly Historical and Genealogical Magazine* 22 (1941): 90–105.

Hutchinson, William T., et al., eds. *The Papers of James Madison.* Vols. 1–12. Chicago: University of Chicago Press and Charlottesville: University of Virginia Press, 1962–1979.

Idzerda, Stanley J., ed. *Lafayette and the Age of the American Revolution: Selected Letters and Papers, 1776–1790.* 5 vols. Ithaca, NY: Cornell University Press, 1977–1983.

Jackson, Donald, et al., eds. *The Diaries of George Washington.* 6 vols. Charlottesville: University of Virginia Press, 1976–1979.

James, James A., ed. *George Rogers Clark Papers, 1781–1784. Collections of the Illinois State Historical Society,* Virginia Series. Vol. 4. Springfield: Illinois State Historical Library, 1926.

Johnson, Herbert A., et al., eds. *The Papers of John Marshall.* Vols. 1–5 and 10. Chapel Hill: University of North Carolina Press, 1974–1987 and 2000.

Journal of the Convention of South Carolina which Ratified the Constitution of the United States, May 23, 1788. Atlanta, GA: Foote & Davies Company, 1928.

Journal of the House of Delegates, published in annual editions, 1778–1790. Richmond, VA: Thomas W. White, 1827–28.

"Journal of the President and Masters of William and Mary College." *WMQ,* 1st ser., 15 (1907): 1–14, 134–42, and 16 (1908): 75–80.

Journal of the Senate of the Commonwealth of Virginia, 1785–90. Richmond, VA: Thomas T. White, 1827–28.

Jungstedt, Mrs. Milnor. "Notes from Declarations Made by Applicants for United States Pensions." *WMQ,* 2d ser., 6 (1926): 155–62.

Kaminski, John P., and Gaspard J. Saladino, eds. *The Documentary History of the Ratification of the Constitution.* Vols. 8–10. Madison, WI: State Historical Society of Wisconsin, 1988–93.

Kilby, John. "Narrative as Seaman of the Bonhomme Richard." *Maryland Historical Magazine* 67 (1972): 24–53.

King, George H. S. "Notes from the Journal of John Mercer." *Virginia Genealogist* 4 (1960): 153.

Knight, John. *Narrative of a Late Expedition Against the Indians with an Account of the Barbarous Execution of Col. Crawford and the Wonderful Escape from Captivity of Dr. John Knight & John Slover.* New York: Garland, 1978, orig. pub. 1798.

Knopf, Richard C., ed. *Anthony Wayne: A Name in Arms—The Wayne-Knox-Pickering-McHenry Correspondence.* Pittsburgh, PA: University of Pittsburgh Press, 1960.

Lee, Henry. *Memoir of the War in the Southern Department of the United States.* New York: Arno Press, 1969, orig. pub. 1869.

"Letters from the Governor's Letter Books." *Tyler's Quarterly Magazine* 4 (1923): 415–25.

Line, Greg I., et al., eds. *Papers of John Adams.* Vol. 7. Cambridge, MA: Harvard University Press, 1989.

Lopez, Claude A., ed. *Papers of Benjamin Franklin.* Vol. 27. New Haven, CT: Yale University Press, 1988.

MacKenzie, Frederick. *Diary of Frederick MacKenzie.* 2 vols. New York: Arno Press, 1968, orig. pub. 1930.

Marshall, John. "Letters of John Marshall to His Wife." *WMQ,* 2d ser., 2 (1922): 73–90.

Mason, Frances, ed. *My Dearest Polly: Letters of Chief Justice John Marshall to His Wife.* Richmond, VA: Garrett and Massie, 1961.

Maxwell, William, ed. "Original Letters from George Washington to Colonel Baylor." *Virginia Historical Register* 2 (1849): 140–46.

Mays, David J., ed. *Letters and Papers of Edmund Pendleton.* 2 vols. Charlottesville: University Press of Virginia, 1967.

McGhan, Judith, indexer. *Virginia Vital Records.* Baltimore, MD: Genealogical Publishing Company, 1984.

McIlwaine, H. R., ed. *The Official Letters of the Governors of the State of Virginia.* 3 vols. Richmond, VA: D. Bottom, Superintendent of Public Printing, 1926–29.

Memoirs of Rear Admiral Paul Jones. 2 vols. Edinburgh: Oliver and Boyd, 1830.

Middlebrook, Louis F., ed. *The Log of the "Bonhomme Richard."* Mystic, CT: Marine Historical Association, 1936.

Palmer, W. P., et al., eds. *Calendar of Virginia State Papers.* 11 vols. Richmond, VA: James E. Goode, printer, 1875–93.

Philip, Mark, ed. *Rights of Man, Common Sense, and Other Political Writings of Thomas Paine.* New York: Oxford University Press, 1995.

"Phillips and Arnold's Incursion and Capture of Petersburg, April 1781." *Virginia Historical Record* 4, no. 4 (1851): 199–203.

Pilcher, George W., ed. *The Reverend Samuel Davies Abroad: The Diary of a Journey to England and Scotland, 1753–1758.* Urbana: University of Illinois Press, 1967.

Porterfield, Charles. "Memorable Attack on Quebec: Diary of Captain Charles Porterfield." *Magazine of American History* 21 (1889): 318–19.

Prince, Carl, ed. *Papers of William Livingston.* Vol. 1. Trenton, NJ: New Jersey Historical Commission, 1979.

"Rev. John Lyon Tried by a Court Martial in Accomack County, August 8, 1781." *WMQ*, 2d ser., 2 (1922): 285–88.

"Revolutionary Army Orders." *VMHB* 13 (1906): 337–50; 15 (1908): 165–76; 18 (1910): 170–76.

"Revolutionary Army Records." *VMHB* 14 (1906): 180–7 and 21 (1913): 24–32.

"Revolutionary Correspondence of Col. Josiah Parker, Isle of Wight County, Virginia." *VMHB* 22 (1914): 257–66.

"Revolutionary Pension Declarations from the Records of Pittsylvania County." *VMHB* 16 (1908): 174–83; 17 (1909): 73–80; 20 (1912): 259–66; 25 (1917): 149–60.

Rice, Howard C., ed. *The American Campaigns of Rochambeau's Army, 1780, 1781, 1782.* Princeton, NJ: Princeton University Press, 1972.

Roberts, John M., ed. *A Revolutionary Soldier.* New York: Arno Press, 1979, orig. pub. 1859.

Roberts, Kenneth, ed. *March to Quebec: Journals of the Members of Arnold's Expedition.* Garden City, NY: Doubleday and Company, 1947.

Rutland, Robert A., ed. *Papers of George Mason.* Vols. 2–3. Chapel Hill: University of North Carolina Press, 1970 and 1972.

Showman, Richard K., et al. *The Papers of Nathanael Greene.* 12 vols. Chapel Hill: University of North Carolina Press, 1976–2001.

Simcoe, John G. *A Journal of the Operations of the Queen's Rangers.* New York: Arno Press, 1968, orig. pub. 1844.

Slaughter, Phillip. "Extract from the Diary of Captain Philip Slaughter." In *History of St. Mark's Parish, Culpeper,* edited by Phillip Slaughter. Baltimore, MD: Innes and Company, 1877.

Smith, Paul M., ed. *Letters of Delegates to Congress, 1774–1789.* 26 vols. Washington, DC: 1976–2000.

"Some Colonial Records." *VMHB* 10 (1903): 371–82.

Spiler, Robert E., ed. *The Collected Works of Ralph Waldo Emerson.* Vol. 1. Cambridge, MA: Harvard University Press, 1971.

Syrett, Harold C., ed. *Papers of Alexander Hamilton.* Vol. 11. New York: Columbia University Press, 1966.

Tarleton, Banastre. *A History of the Campaigns of 1780*

and *1781 in the Southern Provinces of North America.* New York: Arno Press, 1968, orig. pub. 1787.

Taylor, Robert J., et al., eds. *The Papers of John Adams.* Vols. 1–10. Cambridge, MA: Harvard University Press, 1977–1996.

Thompson, George. "Diary of George Thompson of Newburyport Kept at Forton Prison, England, 1777–1781." *Essex Institute Historical Collections* 76 (1940), 221–42.

Thwaites, Reuben G., and Louise P. Kellogg, eds. *Documentary History of Dunmore's War, 1774.* Bowie MD: Heritage Books, 1989, orig. pub. 1905.

Tischendorf, Alfred, and E. Taylor Parks, eds. *The Diary and Journal of Richard Clough Anderson, Jr.* Durham, NC: Duke University Press, 1964.

Tustin, Joseph P., ed. *Diary of the American War: A Hessian Journal—Captain Johann Ewald.* New Haven, CT: Yale University Press, 1979.

Uhlendorf, Bernhard A., ed. *The Siege of Charleston.* Ann Arbor, MI: University of Michigan Press, 1938.

Valley Forge Orderly Book of General George Weedon. New York: Arno Press, 1971, orig. pub. 1902.

Van Schreevan, William J., et al., eds. *Revolutionary Virginia: The Road to Independence.* 7 vols. Charlottesville: University Press of Virginia, 1973–83.

"Virginia Legislative Papers." *VMHB* 18 (1910): 373–93.

Von Huyn. "Diary of Major General Johann Christophe von Huyn." In Uhlendorf, ed. 365–397.

Waddell, Joseph A., ed. "Diary of a Prisoner of War at Quebec" (Charles Porterfield). *VMHB* 9 (1901): 144–52.

Wallace, Lee A., ed. *Orderly Book of Captain Benjamin Taliaferro.* Richmond: Virginia State Library, 1980.

"Will of Colonel Theodorick Bland." *VMHB* 3 (1896), 315–16.

"Will of John Baylor of New Market." *VMHB* 24 (1916): 367–73.

Young, Chester R., ed. *Westward into Kentucky: The Narrative of Daniel Trabue.* Lexington, KY: University Press of Kentucky, 1981.

Secondary Sources

Abernethy, Thomas P. *Western Lands and the American Revolution.* New York: D. Appleton-Century Company, 1937.

Abodaher, David J. *Freedom Fighter: Casimir Pulaski.* New York: Julian Messner, 1969.

Alexander, John K. "Forton Prison during the American Revolution: A Case Study of British Prisoners of War Policy and the American Prisoner Response to That Policy." *Essex Institute Historical Collections* 103 (1967): 365–89.

Allard, Dean C. "The Potomac Navy of 1776." *VMHB* 84 (1976): 411–30.

"Anderson." *WMQ*, 2d ser. 10 (1930): 214.

Anderson, Edward L. *The Andersons of Gold Mine, Hanover County, Virginia.* No place or publisher, 1913.

_____. *Soldier and Pioneer: A Biographical Sketch of Lt. Col. Richard C. Anderson of the Continental Army.* New York: G.P. Putnam's Sons, 1879.

Anderson, James H. "Colonel William Crawford."

Ohio Archaeological and Historical Publications 6 (1898): 1–34.

Andrews, Wayne, ed. *Concise Dictionary of American Biography*. New York: Charles Scribner's Sons, 1962.

"Army Officer Who Refused Iraq Duty is Allowed to Resign." *New York Times*, 27 September 2009.

Ashe, S. A. "The Battle of Shallow Ford." *Tyler's Quarterly* 9 (1928): 48–51.

Ashe, Samuel A. *History of North Carolina*. Vol.1. Spartanburg, SC: The Reprint Company, 1971, orig. pub. 1925.

Babits, Lawrence E. *A Devil of a Whipping: The Battle of Cowpens*. Chapel Hill: University of North Carolina Press, 1998.

_____. "Guilford Courthouse, North Carolina." In *EAR*, vol.1, edited by H. E. Selesky, 465–74.

_____. "Hobkirk's Hill (Camden), South Carolina." In *EAR*, vol.1, edited by H. E. Selesky, 508–11.

Bailey, J. D. *Some Heroes of the American Revolution*. Spartanburg, SC: Southern Historical Press, 1976, orig. pub. 1924.

Bailey, Kenney P. *Christopher Gist*. Hamden, CT: Archon Books, 1976.

Bailey, N. Louise, and Elizabeth I. Cooper. *Biographical Directory of the South Carolina House of Representatives*. Vol. 3. Columbia, SC: University of South Carolina Press, 1981.

Bakeless, John. *Daniel Boone*. New York: William Morrow and Company, 1939.

Baker, Leonard. *John Marshall: A Life in Law*. New York: Macmillan Publishing Company, 1974.

Baker, Thomas E. *Another Such Victory: The Story of the American Defeat at Guilford Courthouse that Helped Win the War for Independence*. New York: Eastern Acorn Press, 1981.

Barnes, Alton B. *John Cropper: A Life Fully Lived*. Onley, VA: Lee Howard Company, 1989.

Barnhart, John D., and Dorothy L. Riker. *Indiana to 1816: The Colonial Period*. Indianapolis, IN: Indiana Historical Bureau and Indiana Historical Society, 1971.

Bass, Robert D. *The Green Dragoon: The Lives of Banastre Tarleton and Mary Robinson*. Columbia, SC: Sandlapper Press, 1973, orig. pub. 1957.

Baylor, Orval, and Henry Bedinger. *History of the Baylors*. LeRoy, IL: Letter Journal Printing Company, 1914.

Bell, Richard P. "The Brothers Porterfield." *Augusta County Historical Society Bulletin* 5, no. 1 (1969): 28–37.

Bellesiles, Michael. "Edward Carrington" and "James Lafayette." In *EAR*, vol. 1, edited by H. E. Selesky, 71, 597.

Belue, Ted. F. "Crawford's Sandusky Expedition, May–June 1782." In *ARE*, vol. 1, edited by R. L. Blanco, 416–20.

Bentley, Eric R. *A Century of Hero-Worship*. Philadelphia, PA: J.B. Lippincott Company, 1944.

Berg, Fred A. *Encyclopedia of Continental Army Units*. Harrisburg, PA: Stackpole Books, 1972.

Berkin, Carol. *Revolutionary Mothers: Women in the Struggle for American Independence*. New York: Alfred A. Knopf, 2005.

Bernhard, Winfred E. A. *Fisher Ames: Federalist and Statesman*. Chapel Hill: University of North Carolina Press, 1965.

Bill, Alfred H. *A House Called Morven*. Princeton, NJ: Princeton University Press, 1954.

Billias, George A. *General John Glover and His Marblehead Mariners*. New York: Henry Holt and Company, 1960.

Billington, Ray A., and Martin Ridge. *Westward Expansion*. Fifth Edition. New York: Macmillan Publishing Company, 1982.

Biographical Directory of the American Congress, 1774–1996. Alexandria, VA: CQ Staff Directory, 1997.

Biographical Directory of the United States Congress, 1774–1789. Washington, DC: Government Printing Office, 1989.

Boatner, Mark M. III. *Landmarks of the American Revolution*. Revised Edition. Harrisonburg, PA: Stackpole Books, 1992.

Bodley, Thomas. *George Rogers Clark*. Boston: Houghton Mifflin Company, 1926.

"Book Notice," *WMQ*, 1st ser., 22 (1914): 142.

Booker, Marshall. "Privateering from the Bay, including Admiralty Courts and Tory as Well as Patriot Operations." In *Chesapeake Bay in the American Revolution*, edited by E. M. Eller, 261–8.

Borick, Carol P. "Expedition against Charleston, South Carolina (1780)." In *Encyclopedia of the American Revolutionary War*, vol. 1, edited by Gregory Fremont-Barnes, and Richard A. Ryerson, 205–9. Santa Barbara: ABC-CLIO, 2006.

_____. *A Gallant Defense: The Siege of Charleston, 1780*. Columbia, SC: University of South Carolina Press, 2003.

Borthick, Ray, and Jack Britton. *Medals, Military and Civilian, of the United States*. Tulsa, OK: Military Collector's Press, 1984.

Bowie, Lucy L. *The Ancient Barracks of Fredericktown*. Frederick, MD: Maryland State School for the Deaf, 1939.

Bradshaw, Herbert C. *History of Hampden-Sydney College*. Vol. 1. Durham, NC: Fisher-Harrison Corporation, 1976.

_____. *History of Prince Edward County, Virginia*. Richmond, VA: Dietz Press, 1956.

Brinkley, John L. *On this Hill: A Narrative History of Hampden-Sydney College*. Hampden-Sydney, VA: Hampden-Sydney College, 1994.

Bristow, Weston. "William Grayson." *Richmond College Historical Papers* 2, no. 1 (1917): 74–117.

Brock, R. A., ed. "The History of the Virginia Federal Convention, 1788." *Collections of the VHS*, new series, vol. 10.

Brown, John P. *Old Frontiers: The Story of the Chero-kee Indians from Earliest Times to the Date of Their Removal to the West.* Kingsport, TN: Southern Publishers, 1938.

Bruce, Kathleen. *Virginia Iron Manufacture in the Slave Era.* New York: The Century Company, 1930.

Buchanan, John. *The Road to Guilford Courthouse: The American Revolution in the Carolinas.* New York: John Wiley and Sons, 1997.

_____. *The Road to Valley Forge: How Washington Built the Army That Won the Revolution.* New York: John Wiley and Sons, 2004.

Buck, Solon J., and Elizabeth H. Buck. *The Planting of Civilization in Western Pennsylvania.* Pittsburgh, PA: University of Pittsburgh Press, 1939.

Buell, Augustus C. *Paul Jones: Founder of the Amer-ican Navy.* New York: Charles Scribner's 1903.

Bull, Robert J., et al. *The Pluckemin Archaeological Project.* No place or date, copy from Rutgers University.

Burgess, Louis A., comp. *Virginia Soldiers of 1776.* 3 vols. Spartanburg, SC: The Reprint Company, 1973, orig. pub. 1927–29.

Burnett, Louise H. "The Baylor Massacre." *Daugh-ters of the American Revolution Magazine* 102 (1968): 58–59, 96–99, 164, 192.

Callahan, John F., ed. *The Collected Essays of Ralph Ellison.* New York: Modern Library, 1995.

Callo, Joseph. *John Paul Jones: America's First Sea Warrior.* Annapolis, MD: Naval Institute Press, 2006.

Calloway, Colin G. *The American Revolution in In-dian Country.* New York: Cambridge University Press, 1995.

"Camden Campaign, July-August 1780." In *EAR*, vol. 1, edited by H. E. Selesky, 146–54.

Campbell, T. E. *Colonial Caroline: A History of Car-oline County, Virginia.* Richmond: Dietz Press, 1954.

Carmony, Donald F. *Indiana, 1816–1850: The Pioneer Era.* Indianapolis, IN: Indiana Historical Bureau and Indiana Historical Society, 1998.

Carson, Jane. "The Fat Major of the F.H.C." In *The Old Dominion: Essays for Thomas Perkins Aber-nethy*, edited by Darrett B. Rutman. Char-lottesville: University Press of Virginia, 1964.

_____. *James Innes and His Brothers of the F.H.C.* Charlottesville: University Press of Virginia, 1965.

Carter, John A. "Richmond's Anna Maria Lane — Heroine of Germantown." *Richmond* 14 (May 1928): 3, 6, 16, 32.

Cartmell, T. K. *Shenandoah Valley Pioneers and Their Descendants.* Winchester, VA: Eddy Press Corpo-ration, 1909.

Cashin, Edward J. *The King's Ranger: Thomas Brown and the American Revolution on the Southern Fron-tier.* Athens, GA: University of Georgia Press, 1989.

Cassedy, Ben. *History of Louisville.* Louisville, KY: Hull and Brother, 1852.

Cayton, Andrew. *Frontier Indiana.* Bloomington, IN: Indiana University Press, 1996.

Cecere, Michael. *Great Things are Expected from the Virginians in the American Revolution.* Westmin-ster, MD: Heritage Books, 2008.

_____. *An Officer of Very Extraordinary Merit: Charles Porterfield and the American War for Independence.* Westminster, MD: Heritage Books, 2007.

_____. *They Behaved Like Soldiers: Captain John Chilton and the Third Virginia Regiment, 1775–1778.* Westminster, MD: Heritage Books, 2007.

_____. *Thomas Posey and the 7th Virginia Regiment.* Westminster, MD: Heritage Books, 2007.

Champagne, Roger J. *Alexander McDougall and the American Revolution.* Schenectady, NY: Union College Press, 1975.

Chase, Philander D. "Theodorick Bland." In *DVB*, vol. 2, 14–16.

"The Chenowell Affair related by Charles Anderson," Dayton, 1843. In the Draper Col., (microfilm coll.), 3CC93CC9–12. State Historical Society of Wisconsin.

Claghorn, Charles. *Naval Officers of the American Revolution: A Concise Biographical Dictionary.* Metuchen, NJ: Scarecrow Press, 1985.

Clark, Thomas D. "Christopher Gist." In *The Reader's Encyclopedia of the American West*, edited by Howard R. Lamar, 443. New York: Thomas Y. Crowell Company, 1977.

_____. *Frontier America.* New York: Charles Scrib-ner's Sons, 1959.

Clyne, Patricia E. *Patriots and Petticoats.* New York: Dodd Meade Company, 1976.

Cohen, Sheldon S. "Thomas Wren: Ministering Angel of Forton Prison." *Pennsylvania Magazine of History and Biography* 102 (1979): 279–301.

_____. *Yankee Sailors in British Gaols: Prisoners of War at Forton and Mill, 1777–1778.* Newark, NJ: University of Delaware Press, 1995.

Coleman, Elizabeth D. "Guns for Independence." *Virginia Cavalcade* 13, no. 3 (1963–4): 40–47.

Collins, Lewis. *History of Kentucky.* 2 vols. Revised by Richard H. Collins. Frankfort, KY: Kentucky Historical Society, 1966, orig. pub. 1874.

Cometti, Elizabeth. "Depredations in Virginia dur-ing the Revolution." In *The Old Dominion: Essays for Thomas Perkins Abernethy*, edited by Darrett B. Rutman, 135–51. Charlottesville: University Press of Virginia, 1964.

Corkran, David H. *The Cherokee Frontier: Conflict and Survival, 1740–62.* Norman, OK: University of Oklahoma Press, 1962.

Coulter, E. M. "Richard Clough Anderson. In *Dic-tionary of American Biography*, edited by Allen Johnson, vol. 1, 271. New York: Charles Scribner's Sons, 1957.

Coutre, Richard T. *Powhatan: A Bicentennial History.* Richmond, VA: Dietz Press, 1980.

Craven, W. Frank. "William Davies." In *Princetoni-*

ans, 1748–1768: A Biographical Directory, edited by James McLachan. Princeton: Princeton University Press, 1976.

"Crawford's Defeat." In EAR, vol. 1, edited by H. E. Selesky, 287–88.

Crocker, James F. "The Parkers of Macclesfield, Isle of Wight, Virginia." VMHB 6 (1899): 420–24.

Cross, Charles B., Jr. A Navy for Virginia: A Colony's Fleet in the Revolution. Yorktown, VA: Virginia Independence Bicentennial Commission, 1981.

Crowson, E. T. "Colonel William Campbell and the Battle of Kings Mountain." Virginia Cavalcade 30 (1980): 22–29.

Dabney, Charles W. "Colonel Charles Dabney of the Revolution: His Service as Soldier and Citizen." VMHB 51 (1943): 186–99.

_____. "Genealogical Queries: Dabney-Brent." WMQ, 2d ser., 6 (1926): 163–64.

_____. "The Origin of the Dabney Family of Virginia." VMHB 45 (1937): 121–43.

Dabney, Virginius. "Jack Jouett's Ride." American Heritage 13, no. 1 (Dec. 1961): 56–59; also published in The Magazine of Albemarle County History 30 (1972): 19–27.

_____. Richmond: The Story of a City. Garden City, NY: Doubleday and Company, 1976.

Dabney, William M. After Saratoga: The Story of the Convention Army. Albuquerque, NM: University of New Mexico Press, 1954.

Daniel, James R. V. "The Giant of Virginia: Alias the Hercules of the Revolution." Virginia Cavalcade 1 (Summer, 1951): 36–39.

Davis, Burke. Black Heroes of the American Revolution. New York, NY: Harcourt Brace Jovanovich, 1976.

_____. The Campaign That Won America: The Story of Yorktown. New York: The Dial Press, 1970.

_____. The Cowpens-Guilford Courthouse Campaign. New York: J. B. Lippincott Company, 1962.

Davis, Robert P. Where a Man Can Go: Major General William Phillips, British Royal Artillery, 1731–1781. Westport, CT: Greenwood Press, 1999.

De Vorsey, Louis, Jr. The Indian Boundary in the Southern Colonies, 1763–1775. Chapel Hill: University of North Carolina Press, 1961.

Demarest, Thomas. "The Baylor Massacre: Some Assorted Notes and Information." Bergen County History (1971 Annual): 28–93.

Dicken-Garcia, Hazel. To Western Woods: The Breckinridge Family Moves to Kentucky. Rutherford, NJ: Fairleigh Dickinson University Press, 1991.

Dorsey, Jean M., and J. Maxwell. Christopher Gist of Maryland and Some of His Descendants, 1679–1957. Chicago: John S. Swift Company, 1958.

Dowd, Gregory E. A Spirited Resistance: The North American Indian Struggle for Unity, 1715–1815. Baltimore: Johns Hopkins University Press, 1992.

Draper, Lyman C. King's Mountain and Its Heroes. Cincinnati, OH: Peter G. Thompson, 1881.

Du Bellet, Louise P. Some Prominent Virginia Families. 4 vols. Baltimore: Genealogical Publishing Company, 1976, orig. pub. 1907.

Dudley, Guilford. "A Sketch of the Military Service Performed by Guilford Dudley of Halifax, North Carolina," edited by Charles Campbell. In Southern Literary Messenger 11 (1845): 144–48, 231–35, 281–2, 370–75; also published in Jim Piecuch, The Battle of Camden: A Documentary History (Charleston, SC: The History Press, 2006); also in Michael Cecere, ed., An Officer of Very Extraordinary Merit: Charles Porterfield and the American War for Independence, 136–44.

Duke, Jane T. Kenmore and the Lewises. Garden City, NY: Doubleday Company, 1945.

Dunkerly, Robert M. The Battle of King's Mountain. Charleston, SC: The History Press, 2007.

Dunn, Walter S., Jr. Choosing Sides on the Frontier in the American Revolution. Westport, CT: Praeger, 2007.

Dupriest, James E. William Grayson: A Political Biography of Virginia's United States Senator. Manassas, VA: Prince William County Historical Commission, 1977.

Dykeman, Wilma. With Sword and Fire: The Battle of Kings Mountain. Washington, DC: Department of Interior, 1978.

Eanes, Greg. Tarleton's Southside Raid: Prelude to Yorktown. Burkeville, VA: E & H Publishing Company, 2002.

Eckert, Allan W. The Frontiersmen. Boston: Little, Brown and Company, 1967.

Edgar, Walter, Partisans and Redcoats: The Southern Conflict that Turned the Tide of the American Revolution. New York: William Morrow, 2001.

Eller, Ernest McNeill. Chesapeake Bay in the American Revolution. Centreville, MD: Tidewater Publishers, 1981.

_____. "Chesapeake Bay in the American Revolution." In Chesapeake Bay in the American Revolution, 3–54.

Emahiser, Grace. From River Clyde to Tymochtee and Colonel William Crawford. No pl., self printed, 1969.

Embry, Alvin. History of Fredericksburg. Baltimore: Genealogical Publishing Company, 1994, orig. pub. 1937.

Evans, Emory G. Thomas Nelson of Yorktown: Revolutionary Virginian. Williamsburg, VA: Colonial Williamsburg Foundation, 1975.

_____. "Trouble in the Backcountry: Disaffection in Southwest Virginia during the American Revolution." In An Uncivil War: The Southern Backcountry during the American Revolution, edited by Ronald Hoffman, et al., eds. Charlottesville: University Press of Virginia, 1985.

Ewen, Frederic. Bertolt Brecht: His Life, His Art and His Times. New York: Citadel Press, 1967.

Fallaw, Robert, and Marion W. Stoer. "The Old

Dominion under Fire: The Chesapeake Invasions, 1779–1781." In *Chesapeake Bay in the American Revolution*, edited by E. M. Eller, 432–73.

Felder, Paula. *Fielding Lewis and the Washington Family: A Chronicle of 18th Century Fredericksburg*. Fredericksburg, VA: American History Company, 1998.

Ferguson, E. James. *The Power of the Purse*. Chapel Hill: University of North Carolina Press, 1961.

Ferling, John. *Almost a Miracle: The American Victory in the War of Independence*. New York: Oxford University Press, 2007.

Fischer, David. H. *The Revolution of American Conservatism: The Federalists in the Era of Jefferson*. New York: Harper and Row, 1965.

_____. *Washington's Crossing*. New York: Oxford University Press, 2004.

Fishwick, Marshall W. *American Heroes: Myth and Reality*. Washington, DC: Public Affairs Press, 1954.

Fitzpatrick, John C. *The Spirit of the Revolution*. Boston: Houghton Mifflin Company, 1924.

Flagg, C. A. et al., eds. "Virginia Soldiers in the Revolution." *VMHB*, 21 (1913), 338–46.

Floyd, William B. "Matthew Harris Jouett." In *Dictionary of American Biography*, edited by Johnson, 12:287–88.

Footner, Hulbert, *Rivers of the Eastern Shore*. New York: Farrar and Rinehart, 1944.

Foreman, Grant. *Sequoyah*. Norman, OK: University of Oklahoma Press, 1980.

"Francisco Marries Susanna Anderson." In "The Revolution in Virginia," in *The Daily Progress* (Charlottesville), 15 Feb. 1976, 7–8.

Frantz, John B., and William Pencak. *Beyond Philadelphia: The American Revolution in the Pennsylvania Hinterland*. University Park, PA: Pennsylvania State University Press, 1998.

Fraser, Walter J., Jr. *Patriots, Pistols and Petticoats*. 2d ed. Columbia, SC: University of South Carolina Press, 1993, orig. pub. 1943.

"Fredericksburg in Revolutionary Times." *WMQ*, 1st ser., 27 (1918): 73–95, 164–75, 248–57.

Freeman, Douglas S. *George Washington*. 7 vols. New York: Charles Scribner's Sons, 1949–57.

Gaines, William H. "The Battle of the Barges." *Virginia Cavalcade*, (Autumn 1954): 33–37.

Gallatin, Gaspard, ed. *Journal of the Siege of Yorktown*. Senate Document no. 322. Washington, DC: Government Printing Office, 1931.

Garden, Alexander. *Anecdotes of the American Revolution*. Charleston: A. E. Miller, 1822.

Garnett, James. "James Mercer." *WMQ*, 1st Ser., 17 (1908): 204–22.

Garraty, John A., and Mark C. Carnes, eds. *American National Biography*. 26 vols. New York: Oxford University Press, 1999; also, two supplements 2002 and 2005.

Gates, Henry L. Jr., and Evenly B. Higginbotham, eds. *African American National Biography*. New York: Oxford University Press, 2008.

Gaynor, Frank, ed. *The New Military and Naval Dictionary*. New York: Greenwood Press, 1969, orig. pub. 1951.

"Genealogical Queries." *WMQ*, 2d ser., 6 (1926): 163–65.

"Genealogy Baylor." *VMHB* 25 (1917) 302–331.

Gerson, Mark. *A Choice of Heroes: The Changing Faces of American Manhood*. Boston: Houghton Mifflin Company, 1982.

Gillett, Mary C. *The Army Medical Department, 1775–1818*. Washington, DC: Center for Military History — U.S. Army, 1980.

Goldenberg, Joseph A., and Marion W. Stoer. "The Virginia State Navy." In *Chesapeake Bay in the American Revolution*, edited by E. M. Eller, 170–203.

Goolrick, John T. *Fredericksburg and the Cavalier Country*. Richmond: Garrett and Massie, 1935.

Gordon, John W. *South Carolina and the American Revolution*. Columbia, SC: University of South Carolina Press, 2003.

Gottschalk, Louis. *Lafayette and the Close of the American Revolution*. Chicago: University of Chicago Press, 1942.

Graham, James. *The Life of General Daniel Morgan of the Virginia Line*. New York: Derby and Jackson, 1856.

"The Grave of a Remarkable Man — Peter Francisco." *Daily Dispatch* (Richmond), 30 Oct. 1866.

Grayson, Frederick W. "The Grayson Family." *Tyler's Quarterly Historical and Genealogical Magazine* 5 (1924): 195–208.

Green, Thomas. *Historic Families of Kentucky*. Baltimore: Genealogical Publishing Company, 1982, orig. pub. 1889.

_____. *The Spanish Conspiracy*. Gloucester: Peter Smith, 1967, orig. pub. 1891.

Grigsby, Hugh B., ed. *The History of the Virginia Federal Convention of 1788*. 2 vols. Edited by R. A. Brock. Richmond: Virginia Historical Society, 1890–91.

A Guidebook to Virginia's Historical Markers. Charlottesville: University of Virginia Press, 2007.

Gutzman, K. R. C. "William Grayson." *ANB* 9: 456–57.

Gwathmey, John W. *Historical Register of Virginians in the Revolution*. Baltimore: Genealogical Publishing Company, 1871, orig. pub. 1938.

"Gwynn's Island, Virginia." In *EAR*, vol. 1, edited by H. E. Selesky, 475–76.

Haley, Gail E. *Jack Jouett's Ride*. New York: Viking Press, 1973.

Haller, Stephen F. *William Washington: Cavalryman of the Revolution*. Bowie, MD: Heritage Books, 2001.

Hamer, Philip M. "The Wataugans and the Cherokee Indians in 1776." *East Tennessee Historical Society Publications*, no. 3 (1931): 108–26.

Hamilton, Charles H. *Peter Francisco: Soldier Extraordinary.* Richmond, VA: Whittet and Shepperson, 1976.

Hammon, Neal O., ed. *My Father Daniel Boone.* Lexington, KY: University Press of Kentucky, 1999.

_____ and Richard Taylor. *Virginia's Western War, 1775–1786.* Mechanicsburg, PA: Stackpole Books, 2002.

Harris, Malcolm. *History of Louisa County, Virginia.* Richmond: Dietz Press, 1936.

Harrison, Fairfax. "The Equine FFVs." *VMHB* 35 (1927): 329–70.

Harrison, Lowell H. *Kentucky's Road to Statehood.* Lexington, KY: University Press of Kentucky, 1992.

"Harrison of James River." *VMHB* 32 (1924): 97–104 and 34 (1926): 384–86.

Harrison, Richard A. *Princetonians, 1769–1776: A Biographical Dictionary.* Princeton, NJ: Princeton University Press, 1980.

Hart, James D. *The Oxford Companion to American Literature.* 4th ed. New York: Oxford University Press, 1965.

Hassler, Edgar W. *Old Westmoreland: A History of Western Pennsylvania during the Revolution.* Pittsburgh, PA: J. R. Weldon and Company, 1900.

Hast, Adele. *Loyalism in Revolutionary Virginia: The Norfolk Area and the Eastern Shore.* Ann Arbor, MI: UMI Research Press, 1982.

Hatch, Charles E. J. Jr. "The Affair Near James Island." *VMHB* 53 (1945): 172–96.

_____. *The Battle of Guilford Courthouse.* Washington: DC: U.S. Department of Interior, 1971.

Hay, Melba P. "Richard Clough Anderson, Jr." *ANB,* 1:478–79.

Hayden, Horace. *Virginia Genealogies.* Baltimore: Genealogical Publishing Company, 1966, orig. pub. 1891.

Heitman, Francis B. *Historical Register of Officers of the Continental Army.* Baltimore: Genealogical Publishing Company, 1973, orig. pub. 1914.

Henderson, J. James. *Party Politics in the Continental Congress.* New York: McGraw Hill Book Company, 1974.

_____. "Quantitative Approaches to Party Formation in the United States." *WMQ,* 3d ser., 30 (1973): 307–23.

Herold, J. Christopher, ed. *The Mind of Napoleon.* New York: Columbia University Press, 1955.

Hervey, John. *Racing in America.* Vol. 1. New York: Charles Scribner's Sons, 1944.

Higginbotham, Don. *Daniel Morgan: Revolutionary Rifleman.* Chapel Hill: University of North Carolina Press, 1961.

"Historic Culpeper, Culpeper, Va.: Culpeper Historical Society, 1973." In "Historical and Genealogical Notes and Queries," *VMHB,* 20 (1912): 312–20.

"Historical and Genealogical Notes." *WMQ,* 1st ser. 1, 6 (1897): 57–70 and 21 (1913): 292–94.

Historical Statements Concerning the Battle of King's Mountain and the Battle of Cowpens, South Carolina. 70th Congress, 1st Session, House Document no. 328. Washington, DC: Government Printing Office, 1928.

Hocker, Edward W. *The Fighting Parson of the American Revolution: A Biography of General Peter Muhlenberg.* Philadelphia, PA: priv. pr., 1936.

Hook, Sidney. *The Hero in History.* Boston: Beacon Press, 1943.

Hudson, Winthrop S. *Religion in America.* New York: Charles Scribner's Sons, 1965.

Hume, Ivor Noél. *1775: Another Part of the Field.* New York: Alfred A. Knopf, 1966.

Huntley, Elizabeth V. *Peninsular Pilgrimage.* Richmond, VA: Whittet and Shepperson, 1941.

Hurt, Douglas H. *The Ohio Frontier: Crucible of the Old Northwest, 1721–1830.* Bloomington, IN: Indiana University Press, 1996.

Jacobs, Wilbur R. *Wilderness Politics and Indian Gifts: The Northern Colonial Frontier, 1748–1763.* Lincoln, NE: University of Nebraska Press, 1950.

James, Alfred P. *The Ohio Company: Its Inner History.* Pittsburgh, PA: University of Pittsburgh Press, 1959.

"Jefferson after Camden." *Tyler's Quarterly Historical and Genealogical Magazine* 7 (1926): 61–86.

Jobson, Robert C. *A History of Early Jeffersontown and Southern Jefferson County, Kentucky.* Baltimore: Gateway Press, 1977.

Johnson, Monroe. "James Monroe, Soldier," *WMQ,* 2d ser., 9 (1929): 110–17.

Johnson, Patricia G. *William Preston and the Allegheny Patriots.* Pulaski, VA: B. D. Smith and Brothers, 1976.

Johnson, Paul. *Heroes: From Alexander to Churchill and De Gaulle.* New York: HarperCollins Publishers, 2007.

Johnson, Virginia C., and Barbara Crookshanks. *Virginia Horse Racing: Triumph of the Turf.* Charleston, SC: The History Press, 2008.

Johnston, Henry P. *The Storming of Stony Point.* New York: Da Capo Press, 1971, orig. pub. 1909.

_____. *The Yorktown Campaign and the Surrender of Cornwallis, 1781.* New York: Harper & Bros., 1881.

Jones, Mary S., ed. *An Eighteenth Century Perspective: Culpeper County, Virginia.* Culpeper, VA: Culpeper Historical Society, 1976.

_____. "Stevensburg: An Ancient Town of Renown." In *Eighteenth Century Perspective,* edited by M. S. Jones, 97–102.

Jones, Mildred C. "General Edward Stevens." In *Eighteenth Century Perspective,* edited by M. S. Jones, 67.

Jones, Richard L. *Dinwiddie County.* Richmond, VA: Whittet and Shepperson, 1976.

Jouett, Edward S. "Jack Jouett's Ride...." *Filson Club Quarterly* 24 (1950): 142–57.

Kaminkow, Martin, and Jack Kaminkow. *Mariners*

of the American Revolution. Baltimore: Magna Carta Book Company, 1967.

Kaplan, Sidney. *The Black Presence in the Era of the American Revolution.* Washington, DC: Smithsonian Institution, 1973.

Kerns, John T. S. "The Importance of the Battle of Great Bridge." In *Eighteenth Century Perspective,* edited by M. S. Jones, 23–24.

Kelly, C. Brian. "Peter Francisco." In *ARE,* vol. 1, edited by R. L. Blanco, 583–84.

Kenton, Edna. *Simon Kenton: His Life and Period, 1755–1836.* Garden City, NY: Doubleday, Dorn and Company, 1930.

Ketcham, Richard M. *The Winter Soldiers.* Garden City, NY: Doubleday and Company, 1973.

Kibler, J. Luther. "Jack Jouett, Jr. and Christopher Hudson." *Tyler's Quarterly Historical and Genealogical Magazine* 23 (1942): 49–57.

King, Duane H. "Long Island of the Holston: Sacred Cherokee Ground." *Journal of Cherokee Studies* 1, no. 2 (Fall 1976): 113–27.

King, Helen. *Historical Notes on Isle of Wight County.* Virginia Beach, VA: Donning and Company, 1993.

Kleber, John E., ed. *The Encyclopedia of Louisville.* Lexington, KY: University Press of Kentucky, 2001.

Kolp, John G. "John Cropper," *ANB,* 1: 568–70.

Konstam, Angus. *Guilford Courthouse, 1781: Lord Cornwallis's Ruinous Victory.* Westport, CT: Praeger, 2004.

Landers, H. L. *The Battle of Camden, South Carolina.* Washington, DC: Government Printing Office, 1929.

Leftowitz, Arthur S. *George Washington's Indispensable Men: the 32 Aides-de-Camp Who Helped Win American Independence.* Mechanicsburg, PA: Stackpole Books, 2003.

Lesser, Charles. *Sinews of Independence: Monthly Strength Reports of the Continental Army.* Chicago: University of Chicago Press, 1976.

Loescher, Burt G. *Washington's Eyes: The Continental Light Dragoons.* Fort Collins, CO: The Old Army Press, 1977.

Lumpkin, Henry. *From Savannah to Yorktown: The American Revolution in the South.* New York: Paragon House, 1981

Maass, John. "To Disturb the Assembly: Tarleton's Charlottesville Raid and the British Invasion of Virginia." *Virginia Cavalcade* 49 (Autumn 2000): 149–57.

Main, Jackson T. "The One Hundred." *WMQ,* 3d ser., 11 (1954): 354–84.

Manahan, John E. "Jack Jouett's Ride." *The Huguenot,* publication no. 18 (n.d.): 90–99.

Manning, Clarence A. *Soldier of Liberty: Casimir Pulaski.* New York: Philosophical Society, 1945.

Manual of Military Decorations and Awards. Washington, DC: Department of Defense, 1996.

Mapp, Alf J. "The 'Pirate' Peer: Lord Dunmore's Op-

erations in the Chesapeake Bay." In *Chesapeake Bay in the American Revolution,* edited by E.M. Eller, 55–97.

Marine Corps Heritage Foundation: "Letter of Lt. Gen. Ron Christmas, Jan. 4, 2010." Dumfries, VA.

Marshall, John. *The Life of George Washington.* 5 vols. Fredericksburg, VA: The Citizens Guild, 1926, orig. pub. 1804–7.

Mason, Thomas A. "Thomas Posey." *ANB,* 7:723–24.

Mattern, David B. *Benjamin Lincoln and the American Revolution.* Columbia, SC: University of South Carolina Press, 1995.

_____. "Theodorick Bland." *ANB,* 2:946–47.

Mayer, Holly A. *Belonging to the Army: Camp Followers and Community during the American Revolution.* Columbia, SC: University of South Carolina Press, 1996.

McCrady, Edward. *The History of South Carolina in the Revolution, 1775–1780.* New York: Russell and Russell, 1969, orig. pub. 1901.

McCullough, Rose. C. *Yesterday When It Is Past.* Richmond, VA: William Byrd Press, 1957.

McDonald, Forest. *The Formation of the American Republic, 1776–1790.* Baltimore: Penguin Books, 1965.

McDonnell, Michael. *The Politics of War: Race, Class, and Conflict in Revolutionary Virginia.* Chapel Hill: University of North Carolina Press, 2007.

McGaw, Walter D. "Captain John Harris of the Virginia Navy: A Prisoner of War in England, 1777–1778." *VMHB* 22 (1914): 160–72.

McGehee, Minnie L. "A Revolutionary Tavern." *Louisa County Historical Magazine* 8, no 1 (1976): 11–16.

McGroarty, William B. "The Family Register of Nicholas Taliaferro, with Notes." *WMQ,* 2d ser. 1 (1921): 145–66.

McIlhany, Hugh M. *Virginia Families.* Staunton, VA: Stoneburner and Prufer Printers, 1909.

McLachan, James. *Princetonians, 1748–1768: A Biographical Directory.* Princeton, NJ: Princeton University Press, 1976.

McManemin, John A. *Captains of the Navies: American Revolution.* Spring Lake, NJ: Ho-Ho-Kus Publishing Company, 1984.

Meade, William. *Old Churches, Ministers and Families of Virginia.* Vol. 2. Philadelphia, PA: J. B. Lippincott and Company, 1857.

Merrill, Boynton, Jr. *Jefferson's Nephews: A Frontier Tragedy.* Princeton, NJ: Princeton University Press, 1976.

Metzger, Charles H. *The Prisoner in the American Revolution.* Chicago: Loyola University Press, 1971.

Middleton, Arthur P. "Ships and Shipbuilding in the Chesapeake Bay and Tributaries." In *Chesapeake Bay in the American Revolution,* edited by E. M. Eller, 98–132.

Miller, Linda. "Edward Carrington." In *Encyclopedia*

of the American Revolutionary War, vol. 1, edited by Gregory Fremont-Barnes, and Richard A. Ryerson, 196–97. Santa Barbara: ABC-CLIO, 2006.

Miller, William L. *The Business of May Next: James Madison and the Founding*. Charlottesville: University Press of Virginia, 1992.

Moon, William A. *Peter Francisco: The Portuguese Patriot*. Pfafftown, NC: Colonial Publishers, 1986.

Mordecai, Samuel. *Richmond in By-Gone Days*. Richmond: Dietz Press, 1946, from 2d edition of 1860.

"Morgan and His Riflemen." *WMQ*, 1st ser., 23 (1914): 73–105.

Morgan, Robert. *Boone: A Biography*. Chapel Hill, NC: Algonquin Books, 2007.

Morison, Samuel E. *John Paul Jones: A Sailor's Biography*. Boston: Little, Brown and Company, 1959.

Morrill, Dan L. *Southern Campaigns of the American Revolution*. Baltimore: Nautical and Aviation Publishing Company, 1993.

Morrissey, Brendon. *Quebec 1775: The American Invasion of Canada*. Oxford, UK: Osprey, 2004.

Morrison, A. J. *College of Hampden-Sydney: Dictionary of Biography, 1776–1825*. Hampden-Sydney, VA: Hampden-Sydney College, 1921.

Morton, Louis, *Robert Carter of Nomini Hall*. Charlottesville: University Press of Virginia, 1969, orig. pub. 1941.

Muhlenberg, Henry A. *The Life of Major General Peter Muhlenberg of the Revolutionary Army*. Philadelphia, PA: Cary and Hart, 1849.

Nagy, Mark R. "Portrait of a Virginia Antifederalist: Theodorick Bland." *International Social Science Review* 71 (2001): 3–13.

National Encyclopedia of American Biography. Vol. 1. New York: John T. White Company, 1892.

Nelson, Paul D. *Anthony Wayne: Soldier of the Early Republic*. Bloomington, IN: Indiana University Press, 1985.

_____. "George Baylor," *DVB*, 1:402–3.

_____. *The Life of William Alexander, Lord Stirling*. University, AL: University of Alabama Press, 1987.

_____. "Major General Horatio Gates as a Military Leader: The Southern Experience." In *The Revolutionary War in the South: Power, Conflict, and Leadership*, W. Robert Higgins, ed., 149–58. Durham, NC: Duke University Press, 1979.

_____. "William Campbell." *DVB*, 2:583–85.

"New Jersey Campaign." In *EAR*, vol. 2, edited by H. E. Selesky, 809–12.

Nichols, Joan K. *Daughters of Liberty*. Boston: Houghton Mifflin, 2005.

Norfleet, Fillmore. *Saint-Mémin in Virginia: Portraits and Biographies*. Richmond, VA: Dietz, 1942.

Norton, Bruce H. *Encyclopedia of American War Heroes*. New York: Facts of File, 2002.

"Notes and Queries." *VMHB* 20 (1912): 205–7 and 38 (1930): 167–80.

O'Dell, Jeff M. *Inventory of Early Architecture and Historic Sites*. Richmond, VA: Systems Printing, 1976.

O'Donnell, James H. III. *Southern Indians in the Revolution*. Knoxville, TN: University of Tennessee Press, 1973.

_____. "William Crawford." *ANB*, 5:710–11.

"Officers of the Mosquito." *Tyler's Quarterly Magazine* 8 (1927): 137–38.

"Officers of the State Legion." *VMHB* 29 (1921): 505.

O'Kelly, Patrick. *"Nothing but Blood and Slaughter": Military Operations and Order of Battle in the Revolutionary War in the Carolinas*. 4 vols. No pl.: Blue Horse Tavern Press, 2004.

"Orderly Book of the Company of Captain George Stubblefield, Fifth Virginia Regiment." *Virginia Historical Collections*, new series, 6 (1887): 141–91.

"Original Letters." *Virginia Historical Register* 2 (1849): 140–46.

Orrill, Lawrence A. "Christopher Gist and His Sons." *Western Pennsylvania Historical Magazine* 15 (1932): 191–218.

Otis, James. *The Life of John Paul Jones*. New York: A. L. Burt Company, 100.

Owens, Kenneth N. "Sequoyah." In *The Reader's Encyclopedia of the American West*, edited by R. Howard Lamar, 1098–99. New York: Thomas Y. Crowell Company, 1977.

Oxford English Dictionary word "Sawney." Vol. 14. Oxford: Oxford University Press, 538.

Palmer, John M. *General Von Steuben*. Port Washington, NY: Kennikat Press, 1966, orig. pub. 1937.

Pancake, John S. *This Destructive War: The British Campaign in the Carolinas, 1780–1782*. University, AL: University of Alabama Press, 1985.

Pap, Leo. *The Portuguese Americans*. Boston: Twayne Publishers, 1981.

Parker, Augusta G. *Parker in America*. Buffalo, NY: Niagara Frontier Publishing Company, 1911.

"The Parker Family of Essex, the Northern Neck &c." *VMHB* 6 (1999): 86–88, 301–5.

"The Parkers of Virginia." *VMHB* 5 (1897–98): 444–47.

Parramore, Thomas C. "The Great Escape from Forton Gaol: An Incident of the Revolution." *North Carolina Historical Review* 45 (1968): 348–56.

Paullin, Charles O. *The Navy in the American Revolution*. New York: Haskell House Publishers, 1971.

"Peter Francisco." In *EAR*, vol. 1, edited by H. E. Selesky, 385–86.

Peterson, Harold L. *The Book of the Continental Soldier*. Harrisburg, PA: The Stackpole Company, 1968.

_____. *Round Shot and Rammers*. Harrisburg, PA: Stackpole Books.

Pieper, Thomas J., and James B. Gidway. *Fort Laurens, 1778–1779: The Revolutionary War in Ohio*. Kent, OH: Kent State University Press, 1976.

Pilcher, George W. *Samuel Davies: Apostle of Dissent in Colonial Virginia*. Knoxville, TN: University of Tennessee Press, 1971.

Pitch, Anthony. *The Burning of Washington: The*

British Invasion of 1814. Annapolis, MD: Naval Institute Press, 1998.

Porter, Nannie F. and Catherine F. Albertson. *The Romantic Record of Peter Francisco*. Staunton, VA: The McClure Company, 1929.

Posey, John T. *General Thomas Posey: Son of the American Revolution*. East Lansing, MI: Michigan State University Press, 1992.

Potts, Louis W. *Arthur Lee: A Virtuous Revolutionary*. Baton Rouge, LA: Louisiana State University Press, 1981.

Prelinger, Catherine M. "Benjamin Franklin and the American Prisoners of War during the American Revolution." *WMQ*, 3d Ser., 32 (1974): 261–94.

Proceedings of the Inauguration of the Monument Erected by the Washington Light Infantry to the Memory of Col. William Washington. Charleston: Walker, Evans, and Company, 1858.

Pulliam, David L. *The Constitutional Conventions of Virginia*. Richmond, VA: John T. West, 1901.

Purcell, L. Edward, comp. *Who Was Who in the American Revolution*. New York: Facts on File, 1993.

Quarles, Benjamin. *The Negro in the American Revolution*. Chapel Hill: University of North Carolina Press, 1996, orig. pub. 1961.

Quinn, Hartwell L. *Arthur Campbell: Pioneer and Patriot of the "Old Southwest."* Jefferson, NC: McFarland and company, 1990.

Quinn, S. J. *History of Fredericksburg, Virginia*. Richmond, VA: The Heritage Press, 1908.

Rankin, Hugh F. *The North Carolina Continentals*. Chapel Hill: University of North Carolina Press, 1971.

Ravenel, Mrs. St. Julien. *Charleston: The Place and the People*. New York: The Macmillan Company, 1931.

Reardon, John J. *Edmund Randolph: A Biography*. New York: Macmillan Publishing Company, 1974.

Remini, Robert V. *Andrew Jackson and the Course of American Empire*. New York: Harper and Row, 1977.

"The Revolution in Virginia — Peter Francisco." *The Daily Progress* (Charlottesville) 1–13, 15 Feb. 1976.

Rhinesmith, Donald. "October 1781: The Southern Campaign Ends at Yorktown." *Virginia Cavalcade*, (Autumn 1981): 53–77.

Richards, Miles S. "William Crawford." In *ARE*, vol. 1, edited by R. L. Blanco, 415–16.

Richardson, Edward. *Standards and Colors of the American Revolution*. Philadelphia, PA: University of Pennsylvania Press, 1982.

Riley, Jonathan. *Napoleon as a General*. New York: Hambleton Continuum, 2007.

Risch, Erna. *Supplying Washington's Army*. Washington, DC: Center of Military History-U.S. Army, 1981.

Roberts, Kenneth. *The Battle of Cowpens: The Great Morale Builder*. Garden City, NY: Doubleday and Company, 1958.

Robertson, William H. P. *The History of Thoroughbred Racing in America*. Englewood Cliffs, NJ: Prentice-Hall, 1964.

Russell, Charles H. "Inscriptions on Tombs at Bowman's Folly, Accomac." *WMQ*, 2d ser., 5 (1925): 272–75.

Russell, T. Triplett, and John K. Gott. *Fauquier County in the Revolution*. Warrenton, VA: Fauquier County American Bicentennial Commission, 1976.

Sadosky, Leonard. "William Crawford." *DVB*, 3:544–46.

Salmon, John. "A Mission of the Most Secret and Important Kind: James Lafayette and American Espionage in 1781." *Virginia Cavalcade* 31 (Autumn 1981): 78–85.

Sampson, Richard. *Escape in America: The British Convention Prisoners, 1777–1785*. Wiltshire, UK: Picton Publishing, 1995.

Sanborn, Paul. J. "Battle of Monmouth." In *ARE*, vol. 2, edited by R. L. Blanco, 1080–88.

_____. "Baylor's Massacre." In *ARE*, vol. 1, edited by R. L. Blanco, 103–5.

Sanchez-Saavedra, E. M. "All Fine Fellows and Well-Armed: The Culpeper Minute Battalion." *Virginia Cavalcade*, (Summer 1974): 4–11. Also in *Eighteenth Century Perspective*, edited by M. S. Jones, 15–21.

_____, comp. *A Guide to Virginia Military Organizations in the American Revolution, 1774–1787*. Richmond: Virginia State Library, 1978.

_____. "The Trooper was a Lady: Being some Account of Anna Maria Lane, a Private Soldier of the Revolution." *Richmond Literature and History Quarterly* 1 (1978): 33–37.

Scheel, Eugene M. *Culpeper: A Virginia County's History Through 1920*. Culpeper, VA: Culpeper Historical Society, 1982.

Scheer, George F. "Henry Lee on the Southern Campaign." *VMHB* 51 (1943): 141–50.

_____, and Hugh F. Rankin. *Rebels and Redcoats*. Cleveland, OH: World Publishing Company, 1957.

Schenck, David. *North Carolina, 1780–81: Being a History of the Invasion of the Carolinas by the British Army under Lord Cornwallis in 1780–81*. Spartanburg, SC: The Reprint Company, 1967, orig. pub. 1889.

Sekel, Clifford. "The Historical Background of the Pluckemin Encampment." In *The Pluckemin Archaeological Project*, edited by Rotch Bull, et al. Madison, NJ: Drew University Institute for Archaeological Research; Far Hills, NJ: Upper Raritan Watershed Association, 1979.

Selby, John E. *The Revolution in Virginia, 1775–1783*. Williamsburg, VA: Colonial Williamsburg Foundation, 1988.

Selesky, Harold E. "Savannah, Georgia." In *EAR*, vol. 2, edited by H. E. Selesky, 1036–40.

Shepard, E. Lee. "James Innes." *ANB*, 11:666–67.

Shepard, William. "Shepard and Other Buckingham Families." Part 2. *WMQ*, 7th ser., 7 (1927): 174–80.

Sipe, C. Hale. *The Indian Wars of Pennsylvania*. Harrisburg, PA: The Telegraph Press, 1931.

Skaggs, David A. "Yorktown siege," in *EAR*, vol. 2, edited by H. E. Selesky, 1291–99.

Slater, Joseph, ed. *The Collected Works of Ralph Waldo Emerson*. Vol. 2 Cambridge, MA: Harvard University Press, 1979.

Smith, Charles R. *Marines in the Revolution: A History of the Continental Marines in the American Revolution, 1775–1783*. Washington, DC: Headquarters, U.S. Marine Corps, 1975.

Smith, Glenn C. "Charlottesville, Virginia and the American Revolution, 1775–1783." *Tyler's Quarterly Historical and Genealogical Magazine* 24 (1943): 172–86.

Smith, Justin H. *Our Struggle for the Fourteenth State*. 2 vols. New York: G. P. Putnam's Sons, 1907.

Smith, Page. *A New Age Now Begins: A People's History of the American Revolution*. 2 vols. New York: Penguin Books, 1976.

Smith, Samuel S. *The Battle of Brandywine*. Monmouth Beach, NJ: Phillip Freneau Press, 1976.

_____. *The Battle of Monmouth*. Monmouth Beach, NJ: Philip Freneau Press, 1964.

_____. *The Battle of Princeton*. Monmouth Beach, NJ: Philip Freneau, 1967.

"Some Virginians Educated in Great Britain." *VMHB* 21 (1912): 196–98.

Sosin, Jack M. *The Revolutionary Frontier, 1763–1783*. New York: Holt, Rineheart and Winston, 1967.

"The State Regiments of the American Revolution." *Tyler's Quarterly Magazine* 8 (1927): 247–52.

Stewart, Catesby W. *The Life of Brigadier General William Woodford of the American Revolution*. 2 vols. Richmond, VA: Whittet and Shepperson, 1973.

Stewart, Robert A. *The History of the Virginia Navy of the Revolution*. Richmond, VA: Mitchell and Hotchkiss, 1933.

_____. *Index to Printed Virginia Genealogies*. Baltimore: Genealogical Publishing Company, 1970, orig. pub. 1930.

The Story of the Campaign and Siege of Yorktown. Senate Document no. 318. Washington, DC: Government Printing Office, 1931.

Stryker, William S. *The Battle of Monmouth*. Princeton, NJ: Princeton University Press, 1927.

_____. *The Battles of Trenton and Princeton*. Boston: Houghton Mifflin and Company, 1898.

Summers, Lewis P. *History of Southwest Virginia, 1746–1787: Washington County, 1777–1870*. Baltimore: Genealogical Publishing Company, 1966, orig. pub. 1903.

Sutherland, Daniel D. *Seasons of War: The Ordeal of a Confederate Community, 1861–65*. New York: The Free Press, 1995.

Taaffe, Stephen R. *The Philadelphia Campaign, 1777–1778*. Lawrence, KS: University Press of Kansas, 2003.

Talbert, Charles G. *Benjamin Logan: Kentucky Frontiersman*. Lexington, KY: University of Kentucky Press, 1962.

Taliaferro, Henry G. *The Descendants of John Taliaferro*. *Virginia Genealogy* 48 (2004): 207–27.

Thayer, Theodore. *Nathanael Greene: Strategist of the American Revolution*. New York: Twayne Publishers, 1960.

Thomas, Evan. *John Paul Jones: Sailor, Hero, Father of the American Navy*. New York: Simon and Shuster, 2003.

Thomas, R. S. "Public Officers, 1781." *VMHB* 5 (1899): 216–18.

Thompson, Ray. *Washington at Germantown*. Fort Washington, PA: The Bicentennial Press, 1971.

_____. *Washington at White Marsh*. 2d ed. Fort Washington, PA: The Bicentennial Press, 1974.

Titus, James. *The Old Dominion at War: Society, Politics and Warfare in Late Colonial Virginia*. Columbia, SC: University of South Carolina Press, 1991.

"Today and Yesterday in the Heart of Virginia." *Farmville (Virginia) Herald*, 1935.

Torrence, Clayton, ed. "The Petersons, Claibornes, and Harrisons and Some of Their Connections." *WMQ*, 2d Ser., 2 (1922): 1–19.

Treacy, M. F. *Prelude to Yorktown: The Southern Campaign of Nathanael Greene*. Chapel Hill: University of North Carolina Press, 1963.

Treadway, Sandra G. "Anna Maria Lane: An Uncommon Common Soldier of the American Revolution." *Virginia Cavalcade* 37 (1988): 134–43.

Treat, Payson, J. *The National Land System, 1785–1820*. New York: E. B. Treat and Company, 1910.

Trible, David B. "Christopher Gist and Settlement on the Monongahela, 1752–1754." *VMHB* 63 (1985): 15–27.

Trussell, John B. B., Jr. *The Pennsylvania Line: Regimental Organization and Operations, 1776–1783*. Harrisburg, PA: Pennsylvania Historical and Museum Commission, 1977.

Tucker, George. "Revolutionary War Spy: The Slave Who Served as a Double Agent." *The Virginian Pilot-Ledger-Star*, 16 Oct. 1988.

Tyler, Lyon G. *Encyclopedia of Virginia Biography*. Vols. 1 and 2. New York: Lewis Historical Publishing Company, 1915.

_____. "Fredericksburg in Revolutionary Days." *WMQ*, 1st ser., 27 (1918): 73–95, 164–75, 248–58.

_____. "The Medical Men of Virginia." *WMQ*, 1st ser., 19 (1910): 145–61.

_____, ed. "The Old Virginia Line in the Middle States." *Tyler's Historical and Genealogical Magazine* 12 (1931): 1–42, 90–141, 198–203, 283–89.

Tyson, Carolyn A., and Rowland Gill. *An Annotated*

Bibliography of Marines in the American Revolution. Washington, DC: Headquarters, U.S. Marines, 1972.

Van Atta, John R. "Conscription in Revolutionary Virginia: The Case of Culpeper County, 1780–1781." *VMHB* 92 (1984): 163–81.

Van Doren, Carl. *Mutiny in January.* New York: Viking Press, 1943.

Virginia Biographical Dictionary. New York: Somerset Publishers, 1999.

"Virginia Legislative Papers." *VMHB* 14 (1907): 246–59.

"Virginia Legislative Petitions." *VMHB* 18 (1910): 373–93

Virginia Military Records from the VMHB, WMQ and Tyler's Quarterly. Baltimore: Genealogical Publishing Company, 1983.

"Virginia Revolutionary Soldiers." *VMHB* 27 (1929): 358–60.

Virginia Revolutionary War State Pensions. Richmond: Virginia Genealogical Society, 1980.

"Virginia Soldiers in the Revolution." *VMHB* 19 (1911): 402–14; 20 (1912): 181–94, 267–81; 21 (1913): 337–46.

"Virginia State Troops in the Revolution." *VMHB* 26 (1918): 182–89; 27 (1919): 62–67.

"The Wallace Family." *WMQ*, 1st ser., 13 (1905): 179–82.

Ward, Christopher. *The War of the Revolution.* 2 vols. New York: Macmillan Company, 1952.

Ward, Harry. M. *Between the Lines: Banditti of the American Revolution.* Westport, CT: Praeger, 2002.

_____. *Charles Scott and the "Spirit of '76."* Charlottesville: University Press of Virginia, 1988.

_____. *Duty, Honor or Country: General George Weedon and the American Revolution.* Philadelphia, PA: American Philosophical Society, 1979.

_____. *Invasion: Military Operations near Richmond, 1781.* Richmond, VA: Richmond Bicentennial Commission, 1978.

_____. *Major General Adam Stephen and the Cause of American Liberty.* Charlottesville: University Press of Virginia, 1989.

_____. "William Campbell," *ANB*, 4:304–5.

_____, and Harold E. Greer Jr. *Richmond During the Revolution, 1775–83.* Charlottesville: University Press of Virginia, 1977.

Ware, Susan. *Forgotten Heroes: Inspiring American Portraits from Our Leading Historians.* New York: The Free Press, 1998.

Warren, Mrs. J. E. "Tompkins Family." *WMQ*, 2d ser., 10 (1930): 221–38.

"William Crawford." In *EAR*, vol. 1, edited by H. E. Selesky, 286–87.

"William Washington of Stafford County, Virginia." *WMQ*, 1st ser., 15 (1907): 132–34.

Watlington, Patricia. *The Partisan Spirit: Kentucky Politics, 1779–1792.* New York: Atheneum, 1972.

Weaver, Bettie W. *The Continental Training Depot and General Rendez-vous at Chesterfield Courthouse, Virginia, 1780–1781.* Midlothian, VA: privately printed, 1976.

Wecter, Dixon. *The Hero in America.* Ann Arbor, MI: University of Michigan Press, 1941.

"Wetzell's Mills, North Carolina." In *EAR*, vol. 2, edited by H. E. Selesky, 1263–64.

White, Virgil. *Genealogical Abstracts of Revolutionary War Pension Files.* Vol. 1. Waynesboro, TN: National Historical Publishing Company, 1990.

Whiteslaw, Ralph T. *Virginia's Eastern Shore: A History of Northampton and Accomack Counties.* 2 vols. Richmond: Virginia Historical Society, 1951.

"William Burton." *WMQ*, 1st ser., 11 (1903): 2–3–14.

Williams, Samuel C. "Nathaniel Gist: Father of Sequoyah." *East Tennessee Historical Society Publication*, no. 5 (1933): 39–54.

Wilson, Howard N. *Great Valley Patriots: Western Virginians in the Struggle for Liberty.* Verona, VA: McClure Printing Company, 1976.

Wingfield, Marshal. *A History of Caroline County.* Baltimore: Regional Publishing Company, 1975, orig. pub. 1924.

Wise, Bartolt. "Memoir of General John Cropper of Accomack." *Collections of the VHS*, new series, 11 (1892): 273–315.

Wood, Trist. "John Jouett and Christopher Hudson." *Tyler's Quarterly and Genealogical Magazine* 24 (1943): 190–91.

Wood, W. J. *Battles of the Revolutionary War, 1775–1781.* Chapel Hill, NC: Algonquin Books, 1990.

Works Projects Administration. *Prince William: The Story of Its People and Its Places.* Richmond, VA: Whittet and Shepperson, 1941.

Wright, R. Lewis. *Artists in Virginia before 1900: An Annotated Checklist.* Charlottesville: University Press of Virginia, 1983.

Wright, Robert I., Jr. *The Continental Army.* Washington, DC: Center of Military History–U.S. Army, 1983.

_____. "Virginia Line." In *EAR*, vol. 2, edited by H. E. Selesky, 1216–17.

Writers Project of the WPA. *The Negro in Virginia.* New York: Hastings House, 1948.

Wust, Klaus. *The Virginia Germans* Charlottesville: University Press of Virginia, 1969.

Wyllie, Robert E. *Orders, Decorations and Insignia, Military and Civil.* New York: G. P. Putnam's Sons, 1921.

Zahnhiser, Marvin R. *Charles Cotesworth Pinckney: Founding Father.* Chapel Hill: University of North Carolina Press, 1967.

Zeleny, Jeff. "Medal of Honor Is Given to Hero of Afghan Battle." *New York Times*, 18 Sept. 2009.

Zlatich, Mark. "Uniforms of the 1st Regiment of Continental Light Dragoons." *Military Collector & Historian*, (Summer 1968): 36–39.

Typescripts

Bailey, James H. "Peter Francisco: Washington's One Man Regiment." Typescript, Virginia Historical Society, 1940.

Barr, Lawrence L. "A New Look at the History of Soldiers Retreat." Copy LC, 1940.

Baylor, Harry E. "The Political Career of Colonel William Grayson." MA Thesis, University of Virginia, 1933.

Black History Virginia Profiles — James Lafayette. Virginia Historical Society.

Carpenter, James L. "The Yorktown Prisoners: A Narrative Account of the Disposition of the British Army which was Captured at Yorktown, October 19, 1781." MA Thesis, College of William and Mary, 1950.

Fore, Samuel K. "William Washington — Chronology." 1997. Sent to the author.

Goodwin, Fannie B. F. "Sketches from the Life of a Favorite Soldier of 1776." Virginia Historical Society, Aug. 22, 1910.

Hege, Elma J. "Benjamin Harrison and the American Revolution." MA thesis, University of Virginia, 1939.

Hutchinson, William. "Bounty Lands of the American Revolution." Ph.D. diss., University of Chicago, 1927.

Kahler, Gerald E. "Gentlemen of the Family: General George Washington's Aides-de-Camp and Military Secretaries." MA Thesis, University of Richmond, 1997.

Knepper, George W. "The Convention Army, 1777–1783." Ph.D. diss., University of Michigan, 1954.

Konigsberg, Charles. "Edward Carrington, 1748–1810: Child of the Revolution." Ph.D. diss., Princeton University, 1966.

Malgee, David G. "A Frontier Biography: William Campbell of Kings Mountain." MA Thesis, University of Richmond, 1983.

McBride, John D. "The Virginia War Effort, 1775–1783: Manpower Policies and Practices." Ph.D. diss., University of Virginia, 1977.

Rubenstein, Asa L. "Richard Clough Anderson, Nathaniel Mason, and the Impact of Government on Western Land Speculation and Settlement, 1774–1830." Ph.D. diss., University of Illinois-Urbana-Champagne, 1986.

Sekel, Clifford, Jr. "The Continental Artillery in Winter Encampment at Pluckemin, New Jersey," MA Thesis, Wagner College, 1972.

Siener, William R. "Economic Development in Revolutionary Virginia: Fredericksburg, 1750–1810." Ph.D. diss., College of William and Mary, 1982.

Teeter, Sara E. "Benjamin Harrison: Governor of Virginia, 1781–1784." MA Thesis, University of Richmond, 1965.

Wilson, Ellen S. "Speculators and Land Development in the Virginia Military Tract: The Territorial Period." Ph.D. diss., Miami University (Oxford, Ohio), 1982.

Index

213

215